SIPRI
Stockholm International Peace Research Institute

SIPRI is an independent institute for research into problems of peace and conflict, with particular attention to disarmament and arms regulation. It was established in 1966 to commemorate Sweden's 150 years of unbroken peace.

The Institute is financed by the Swedish Parliament. The staff, the Governing Board and the Scientific Council are international. As a consultative body, the Scientific Council is not responsible for the views expressed in the publications of the Institute.

Governing board

Governor Rolf Edberg, Chairman (Sweden)
Professor Robert Neild, Vice Chairman (United Kingdom)
Mr Tim Greve (Norway)
Academician Ivan Málek (Czechoslovakia)
Professor Leo Mates (Yugoslavia)
Professor Gunnar Myrdal (Sweden)
Professor Bert Röling (Netherlands)
The Director

Director

Dr Frank Barnaby (United Kingdom)

SIPRI
Stockholm International Peace Research Institute

Sveavägen 166, S-113 46 Stockholm, Sweden
Cable: Peaceresearch, Stockholm   Telephone: 08-15 09 40

Arms Control: A Survey and Appraisal of Multilateral Agreements

sipri

Stockholm International Peace Research Institute

Taylor & Francis Ltd
London
1978

Crane, Russak & Company, Inc.
New York

First published 1978 by Taylor & Francis Ltd., London
and Crane, Russak & Company, Inc., New York

Copyright © 1978 by SIPRI
Sveavägen 166, S-113 46 Stockholm

All rights reserved. No part of this publication may be
reproduced, stored in a retrieval system or transmitted,
in any form or by any means, electronic,
mechanical, photocopying, recording or otherwise,
without the prior permission of the copyright owner.

ISBN 0 8448 1358 3

Library of Congress Catalog Card Number 78 54614

Printed in Sweden by
Almqvist & Wiksell, Uppsala 1978

PREFACE

This book is published on the occasion of the 1978 UN General Assembly special session devoted to disarmament.

It contains an analysis of the multilateral arms control agreements and comprehensive up-to-date reference material not readily available from other sources. The intention is to facilitate the important work of those dealing with arms control and disarmament problems.

The book was written by Jozef Goldblat, senior researcher at SIPRI.

Acknowledgements: A special effort was made to ensure the accuracy of the data in this book. Acknowledgement is therefore given to Ragnhild Ferm for assistance in compiling the material, and to Connie Wall and Felicity Roos for providing the editorial assistance.

April 1978

Frank Barnaby
Director

CONTENTS

Introduction 1

Chapter 1. A critical review of the multilateral arms control agreements . . . 4
   I. *Scope of the obligations* 4
      The agreements of 1959–70 – The agreements of the Disarmament Decade, the 1970s – The humanitarian laws of war
   II. *Verification and enforcement* 26
      Acquisition of information – Non-compliance and sanctions – Verification institutions
   III. *The final clauses* 35
      Parties – Depositaries – Succession – Entry into force – Amendments and reservations
   IV. *The negotiating machinery* 43
      The United Nations – The CCD
   V. *Conclusions* 49
      References 51

Chapter 2. Multilateral arms control agreements 53
   I. *Selected pre-World War II agreements* 53
      Declaration of St. Petersburg, 1868 53
      Hague Declaration (IV,2) concerning asphyxiating gases, 1899 54
      Hague Declaration (IV,3) concerning expanding bullets, 1899 54
      Hague Convention (IV) respecting the laws and customs of war on land, 1907 55
      Hague Convention (VIII) relative to the laying of automatic submarine contact mines, 1907 57
      Hague Convention (IX) concerning bombardment by naval forces in time of war, 1907 58
      Hague Declaration (XIV) prohibiting the discharge of projectiles and explosives from balloons, 1907 60
      Convenant of the League of Nations, 1919 60
      Treaty regulating the status of Spitsbergen and conferring the sovereignty of Norway, 1920 61
      Geneva Protocol for the prohibition of the use in war of asphyxiating, poisonous or other gases, and of bacteriological methods of warfare, 1925 64
   II. *The post-World War II agreements* 66
      Charter of the United Nations, 1945 66
      Convention on the prevention and punishment of the crime of genocide, 1948 66

Geneva Convention IV) relative to the protection of civilian persons in
  time of war, 1949 68
Statute of the International Atomic Energy Agency, 1956 71
Antarctic Treaty, 1959 72
US-Soviet joint statement of agreed principles for disarmament negotia-
  tions, 1961 75
Treaty banning nuclear weapon tests in the atmosphere, in outer space and
  under water, 1963 77
Treaty on principles governing the activities of states in the exploration
  and use of outer space, including the moon and other celestial bodies,
  1967 78
Treaty for the prohibition of nuclear weapons in Latin America, 1967 ... 80
Security Council resolution on security assurances to non-nuclear weapon
  states, 1968 87
Treaty on the non-proliferation of nuclear weapons, 1968 88
Treaty on the prohibition of the emplacement of nuclear weapons and other
  weapons of mass destruction on the seabed and the ocean floor and in the
  subsoil thereof, 1971 90
The structure and content of agreements between the International Atomic
  Energy Agency and states required in connection with the Treaty on the
  non-proliferation of nuclear weapons, 1971 92
Convention on the prohibition of the development, production and stockpiling of bacteriological (biological) and toxin weapons and on their
  destruction, 1972 103
Agreement between Belgium, Denmark, the Federal Republic of Germany,
  Ireland, Italy, Luxembourg, the Netherlands, the European Atomic
  Energy Community and the International Atomic Energy Agency in
  implementation of Article III, (1) and (4) of the Treaty on the non-
  proliferation of nuclear weapons, 1973 105
  Protocol 119
Declaration of Ayacucho, 1974 121
Document on confidence-building measures and certain aspects of security
  and disarmament, included in the Final Act of the Conference of Security and Co-operation in Europe, 1975 121
Convention on the prohibition of military or any other hostile use of
  environmental modification techniques, 1977 123
  Understandings relating to the Convention on the prohibition of military
  or any other hostile use of environmental modification techniques,
  worked out at the Conference of the Committee on Disarmament ... 125
Geneva Protocol additional to the Geneva Conventions of 12 August 1949,
  and relating to the protection of victims of international armed conflicts
  (Protocol 1), 1977 125
Resolution 22 of the Diplomatic Conference on the reaffirmation and
  development of international humanitarian law applicable in armed
  conflicts; Follow-up regarding prohibition or restriction of use of certain
  conventional weapons, 1977 137
Guidelines for nuclear transfers, 1977 138

**Chapter 3. Status of the implementation of multilateral arms control agreements,
as of 31 December 1977** 145

  I. *The 1925 Geneva Protocol* 145

II. *Major post-World War II agreements* 151
        Antarctic Treaty – Partial Test Ban Treaty – Outer Space Treaty – Treaty of Tlatelolco – Non-Proliferation Treaty – Sea-Bed Treaty – BW Convention – ENMOD Convention

Appendix A. Member states of the United Nations and other states party to the major arms control agreements 195
        State – Year of UN admission – Area – Population – Per capita GNP – Per capita military expenditure

Appendix B. Major UN General Assembly arms control resolutions adopted in the Disarmament Decade of the 1970s, and the record of voting 200

    Disarmament Decade 200
    Strategic arms limitation 201
    Nuclear weapon tests 202
    Non-proliferation of nuclear weapons 203
    Outer space 205
    Sea-bed 206
    Nuclear weapon-free zone in Africa 207
    Nuclear weapon-free zone in the Middle East 207
    Nuclear weapon-free zone in South Asia 208
    Nuclear weapon-free zone in the South Pacific 209
    Nuclear weapon-free zone in Latin America 209
    Definition of a nuclear weapon-free zone and obligations of nuclear powers 210
    Indian Ocean as a zone of peace 210
    Security of non-nuclear weapon states 212
    Renunciation of the use of force and prohibition of the use of nuclear weapons 213
    Chemical and biological weapons 214
    Environmental warfare 215
    Napalm and other incendiary weapons 215
    New weapons of mass destruction 215
    Human rights in armed conflicts 216
    Reduction of military budgets 217
    Disarmament and development 218
    Disarmament and international security 219
    Disarmament and détente 220
    Regional disarmament 220
    General and complete disarmament 220
    UN role in disarmament 221
    World Disarmament Conference 222
    UN General Assembly special session on disarmament 222

Appendix C. Notifications of military manoeuvres in compliance with the Final Act of the Conference on Security and Co-operation in Europe 223
        State giving notification – Date of notification – Duration of manoeuvre – Designation of manoeuvre – Number of troops involved – Area of manoeuvre

Appendix D. Nuclear explosions, 1945–77 228
  I. *16 July 1945 – 5 August 1963*
 II. *5 August 1963 – 31 December 1977*
III. *16 July 1945 – 31 December 1977*

Appendix E. Summaries of bilateral arms control agreements, 1963–77 229

    US-Soviet Memorandum of understanding regarding the establishment of a direct communications link, 1963 229
    Statements by the USA and the USSR on the reduction of fissionable materials production, 1964 229
    British-Soviet Agreement on the establishment of a direct communications line, 1967 230
    Agreement on measures to improve the USA-USSR direct communications link, 1971 230
    Agreement on measures to reduce the risk of outbreak of nuclear war between the USA and the USSR, 1971 230
    US-Soviet Agreement on the prevention of incidents on and over the high seas, 1972 231
    US-Soviet Treaty on the limitation of anti-ballistic missile systems, 1972 . 231
    US-Soviet Interim Agreement on certain measures with respect to the limitation of strategic offensive arms, 1972 231
    Agreement on basic principles of relations between the USA and the USSR, 1972 232
    US-Soviet Memorandum of understanding regarding the establishment of a Standing Consultative Commission, 1972 233
    Protocol to the US-Soviet Agreement on the prevention of incidents on and over the high seas, 1973 233
    Protocol with regulations regarding the US-Soviet Standing Consultative Commission, 1973 233
    US-Soviet Agreement on basic principles of negotiations on the further limitation of strategic offensive arms, 1973 233
    US-Soviet Agreement on the prevention of nuclear war, 1973 234
    Protocol to the US-Soviet Treaty on the limitation of anti-ballistic missile systems, 1974 234
    US-Soviet Treaty on the limitation of underground nuclear weapon tests, 1974 235
    Joint US-Soviet Statement on the question of further limitations of strategic offensive arms, 1974 235
    Joint British-Soviet Declaration on the non-proliferation of nuclear weapons, 1975 236
    US-Soviet Treaty on underground nuclear explosions for peaceful purposes, 1976 236
    French-Soviet Agreement on the prevention of the accidental or unauthorized use of nuclear weapons, 1976 237
    French-Soviet Declaration on the non-proliferation of nuclear weapons, 1977 237
    British-Soviet Agreement on the prevention of an accidental outbreak of nuclear war, 1977 238

Introduction

Square-bracketed numbers, thus [1], refer to the list of references on page 51.

The practice of negotiating disarmament in an international forum with a view to making the measures adopted applicable to many nations is relatively recent.[1] Apart from the 1899 and 1907 Hague Conferences, which made an attempt to codify the laws of war, only one conference was held prior to World War II to discuss the universal reduction and limitation of armaments: the world conference convened on 2 February 1932, under the auspices of the League of Nations, and attended by representatives from more than 60 states. After several years of work, general agreement seemed to exist on the following principles: (*a*) prohibition of certain methods of war; (*b*) qualitative and quantitative limitation of armaments; (*c*) supervision of the manufacture of and trade in arms; (*d*) publicity of national defence expenditure; (*e*) supervision of the implementation of the obligations; and (*f*) guarantees of the implementation. However, agreement could not be reached as regards the application of these principles, and on 22 January 1936 the Council of the League of Nations decided to postpone the work of the conference.

The League conference never reconvened. International efforts to regulate armaments on a world-wide scale resumed only after World War II, within the framework of the United Nations Organization which was created "to save succeeding generations from the scourge of war". But unlike the Covenant of the League of Nations, which had put considerable emphasis on disarmament and had clearly defined the obligations of the League and of its members with regard to the reduction and limitation of armaments (see page 60), the Charter of the United Nations attached primary importance to collective security and made only passing reference to disarmament. Principles "governing disarmament and the regulation of armaments" have been included among the general principles of co-operation in the maintenance of international peace and security, to be considered by the UN General Assembly (see page 66. One reason for this difference lies in the fact that when the League Covenant was written many believed that World War I was caused by the arms race prior to that war, whereas a few decades later the prevalent feeling was that World War II could have been avoided if the great powers had maintained an adequate military potential as

---

[1] As distinct from demilitarization arrangements regarding particular geographic areas in one or two countries as, for example, in the US-British agreement of 1817, the so-called Rush-Bagot Agreement, which reduced, limited and equalized the two sides' naval forces on the Great Lakes.

Introduction

well as a readiness to use it. Moreover, unlike the League Covenant, the UN Charter was drafted when the war was still in full progress, and when planning a system of disarmament might have seemed ill-timed.

Nevertheless, the United Nations very early became involved in the matter of disarmament. This had been prompted chiefly by the use of atomic bombs shortly after the signing of the UN Charter, and the fear that this new weapon of unprecedented destructiveness might be used again. Indeed, the very first UN General Assembly resolution, of 24 January 1946, established a commission to deal with the problems raised by the discovery of atomic energy and to make specific proposals for the elimination from national armaments of atomic weapons and of all other major weapons of mass destruction.[2] On 14 December of the same year, the United Nations formally recognized that the problem of security was closely connected with that of disarmament and recommended a general progressive and balanced reduction of national armed forces [2]. Since then, disarmament has been regarded as one of the most important items on the international agenda.

Measures for disarmament can take many forms. Arms restraints can be assumed by states on a voluntary basis, without reciprocity. They can be part of agreed armistice arrangements following unresolved armed conflicts. They can also be imposed by victors upon defeated countries, as in the case of Germany after both World Wars. This book, however, is concerned only with agreements freely arrived at in time of peace among sovereign states, through a process of formal intergovernmental negotiation, and providing for mutual rights and obligations.

A multitude of proposals related to international disarmament, including proposals for a complete elimination of armed forces and armaments, have been made in various forums, both within and outside the framework of the United Nations. But so far, only a few so-called arms control measures have been agreed upon, imposing certain, not particularly burdensome, restrictions on the armament policies of states. Originally, the term "arms control", coined in the USA, was meant to denote measures regulating the arms race rather than stopping it; it had a connotation clearly distinct from that of the reduction of armaments or disarmament. Subsequently, however, diverse measures intended to freeze, limit or abolish certain categories of weapons; to prevent certain military activities; to regulate the deployment of forces; to proscribe transfers of certain militarily important items; to reduce the risk of an accidental war; to constrain or prohibit the use of certain arms in war; or to build up international confidence through greater

---

[2] In 1948 the UN Commission for Conventional Armaments, wishing to distinguish its terms of reference from those of the UN Atomic Energy Commission, defined weapons of mass destruction as "atomic explosive weapons, radioactive material weapons, lethal chemical and biological weapons, and any weapons developed in the future which have characteristics comparable in destructive effect to those of the atomic bomb or other weapons mentioned above" [1].

openness in the military field, have come to be included under the rubric of arms control.[3] It is in this broad sense that the term "arms control" will be used in the book.

The arms control agreements hitherto concluded are either bilateral or multilateral. In the latter category, some are of a regional nature, in the sense that they are valid only for nations of a given geographical zone or continent. The format of the agreements varies from treaties, conventions or protocols, to statutes, charters or special decisions of international organizations, to joint or simultaneous statements or declarations by governments, to exchanges of letters among the states concerned.

This publication deals primarily with the multilateral arms control agreements reached since World War II.[4] Chapter 1 is a review and assessment of the essential features of the agreements. Chapter 2 contains the texts of the relevant documents, as well as such pre-World War II treaties or declarations which relate to the topics discussed. Chapter 3 contains a tabular presentation of the status of the implementation of the most important multilateral agreements analysed and reprinted in Chapters 1 and 2. And finally, the bilateral arms control agreements are summarized in Appendix E.

---

[3] Alva Myrdal, former Swedish Minister for Disarmament, regrets that the term "arms control" has come into usage, and suggests that "control" should apply only to verification.
[4] Armaments limitations of the members of the Western European Union (Belgium, France, the Federal Republic of Germany, Italy, Luxembourg, the Netherlands, and the United Kingdom) are not included because of the special circumstances under which they were agreed to in 1955: the Union was conceived as a means of making the rearmament of FR Germany acceptable to those in Western Europe who feared German remilitarization and, thereby, to remove the political obstacles to a West German contribution to NATO.

1. A critical review of the multilateral arms control agreements

Square-bracketed numbers, thus [1], refer to the list of references on page 51.

This chapter consists of five sections. The first section explains, in brief, the scope of the obligations undertaken by the parties to arms control agreements, and attempts to estimate whether, and to what extent, each agreement has affected the arms race, reduced the likelihood of war, or contributed to the overall goal of disarmament. The second section deals with verification of compliance and discusses the inconsistencies of the existing arrangements. The third section reviews the so-called final clauses of the agreements, emphasizing the problems of universality, succession, reservations and amendment procedures. The fourth section describes the present negotiating machinery and its deficiencies, and suggests certain improvements. The fifth and concluding section makes a plea for an integrated, as opposed to piecemeal, approach to disarmament.

In this chapter, the agreements printed in italics are those reproduced in Chapter 2.

1. *Scope of the obligations*

The main undertakings assumed in the multilateral arms control agreements already in force, or about to enter into force, include:

(*a*) prevention of militarization or of military nuclearization of certain areas or environments;
(*b*) restrictions on weapon tests;
(*c*) prevention of the spread among nations of specified weapons;
(*d*) prohibition of production as well as elimination of stocks of certain types of weapons;
(*e*) prohibition of the use of certain methods of warfare;
(*f*) observance of the rules of conduct in war;
(*g*) notification of certain military activities; and
(*h*) verification of obligations contracted under previously signed treaties.

These types of undertakings might form convenient categories for classifying arms control agreements, were it not for the fact that the commitments undertaken are in fact often similar in nature and interrelated. The agreements are therefore reviewed rather in chronological order, by date on which they were opened for signature, with the exception of the rules of conduct in war (the so-called humanitarian laws of war), which are grouped under one heading.

Scope of the obligations

The agreements of 1959–70

The 1959 Antarctic Treaty (for the text and parties, see pages 72 and 152) declared that the area south of 60° South Latitude shall be used exclusively for peaceful purposes. The Treaty prohibits any measures of a military nature, such as the establishment of military bases or fortifications, the carrying out of military manoeuvres or the testing of any type of weapons. There is also a ban on nuclear explosions in the Antarctic, whatever their nature, as well as on the disposal of radioactive waste material, subject to possible future international agreements on these subjects.

The Antarctic Treaty is an important preventive measure, the first of its kind to be concluded after World War II.[1] Its denuclearization clause, which has helped to prevent the use of the empty expanses of the Antarctic as a nuclear testing ground or a nuclear weapon base, is particularly significant.

The arms control purpose of the Antarctic Treaty was closely linked with three other objectives: to establish a foundation for international co-operation in scientific investigation in Antarctica, successfully initiated during the 1957–58 International Geophysical Year; to protect the unique Antarctic environment; and to avert discord over territorial claims.

Co-operative exploration of the Antarctic continent has been ensured by the undertaking of the parties to exchange scientific personnel and information. Preservation and conservation of living resources in Antarctica have been included in the list of the topics to be regularly reviewed by consultative meetings, and have figured prominently on the agenda of these meetings. As regards the politically sensitive question of territorial claims, the Treaty introduced a moratorium, implying neither renunciation nor recognition of "previously asserted rights of or claims to" territorial sovereignty in Antarctica, and prohibiting the making of new claims or the extension of existing ones. By the 1950s, seven states—Argentina, Australia, Chile, France, New Zealand, Norway and the UK—had claimed sovereignty over areas of Antarctica on the basis of discovery, exploration, geographic proximity or territorial continuity; in the case of Argentina, Chile and the UK, the claims overlap. Only some 15 per cent of the Antarctic land mass remains unclaimed. The moratorium established by the Antarctic Treaty can be terminated 30 years from the date of entry into force of the Treaty, that is, after 1991, at which time any party may request the convening of a conference to review its operation.

The scarcity of world food, mineral and hydrocarbon resources will continue to turn mankind's attention towards the potential of areas as yet untapped, and it has been known for some time that there are deposits of

---

[1] An outstanding example of a similar pre-World War II agreement is the 1920 *Treaty regulating the status of Spitsbergen and conferring the sovereignty of Norway* (for the text and parties, see page 61), which prohibits the establishment of any naval base or the construction of any fortification in Spitsbergen (Svalbard), a group of islands lying north of Scandinavia and with no aboriginal population.

precious minerals on the Antarctic continent and that the waters in that part of the world are rich in living resources. The special interest of the past few years in Antarctica is related to indications that its continental shelf may contain oil and gas.

Economic activity in Antarctica has been neither expressly permitted nor prohibited by the Antarctic Treaty, but it is not considered contrary to its principles or its purposes. In fact, exploitation of the living marine resources of the area has already begun and a régime to control fishing there is being negotiated. However, if and when exploitation of the Antarctic mineral resources becomes a practical proposition,[2] a struggle might erupt for national rights to territorial possessions containing these resources. This could be a struggle among the original claimants, especially where claims overlap, or between them and non-claimants active in Antarctica or also with "third states", that is, new claimants demanding a share. (It should be noted that the USA and USSR have neither made nor recognized territorial claims, but have established their *de facto* presence all over the continent through scientific stations and resource-oriented geological and other research programmes.) It is conceivable that a nation may resort to the use of force to assert its rights over other contenders, or to guard against infringements on its economic activities. Such action would bring about a collapse of the legal order currently prevailing under the Treaty: Antarctica would cease to be a non-militarized zone and would become a danger zone instead.

Representatives at the Ninth Antarctic Treaty Consultative Meeting, held in London from 19 September to 7 October 1977, recommended that intensive studies be carried out on the environmental implication of mineral resource activities in Antarctica and that an internationally agreed approach to other aspects of these activities be worked out [4]. But, to forestall developments dangerous to the environment and ecology, to preserve Antarctica as an area of unprecedented international scientific co-operation and to secure peace, it would be best to impose a total ban on hydrocarbon and other mineral exploitation. Failing such a ban, Antarctica, which has no permanent population and has never been effectively occupied or under the control of any state, should be formally recognized as a common heritage of mankind and its resources exploited in the interest of all nations, just as the sea-bed beyond the limits of national jurisdiction is planned to be used. These areas, as well as outer space, which has already been declared the province of all mankind, have, from the legal point of view, similar characteristics. Internationalization would be a fair solution from the economic point of view. It would also remove the sources of inter-state friction and conflict, and would reinforce the demilitarized status of the Antarctic.

---

[2] The possibility of exploiting the mineral resources of Antarctica is some 15 years away, and probably more [3].

Scope of the obligations

The 1963 Partial Test Ban Treaty (for the text and parties, see pages 77 and 152) prohibits any nuclear explosions (that is, also those which are intended for peaceful purposes) in the atmosphere, outer space or under water, or in any other environment if the explosion would cause radioactive debris to be present outside the territorial limits of the country conducting it. In agreeing to this limitation, the original parties—the UK, the USA and the USSR—stated that they were seeking to put an end to the contamination by radioactive substances of man's environment, slow down the nuclear arms race, check the spread of nuclear weapons to other nations and facilitate progress towards disarmament.

The PTBT has helped to curb the radioactive pollution caused by nuclear explosions, but it could not stop it altogether: non-party nuclear powers (France and China) continued testing in the atmosphere, and underground explosions, permitted under the Treaty, often also release radioactive products into the air.[3] Moreover, the arms control objectives of the Treaty have not been even partially achieved.

By the time the PTBT was concluded, the two main testing states, the USA and the USSR, had already carried out extensive series of explosions in the atmosphere and knew that this activity could be continued underground. In fact, since 1963 they have carried out more nuclear explosions than during the period preceding the signing of the PTBT (see Appendix D). This has enabled them to develop new generations of nuclear warheads and of related delivery vehicles. In other words, the nuclear arms race has been allowed to continue unhampered.

The PTBT did not prevent China, a non-party, from joining the "nuclear club" one year after the Treaty's entry into force. There is not even an indication that the Treaty has played a role in inhibiting the proliferation of nuclear weapons among the states which have subscribed to it. While it may be less convenient for an incipient nuclear weapon state to conduct tests in the underground environment than in the atmosphere, a country determined to acquire a nuclear weapon capability would not be deterred by such technical difficulties. Thus, India, a party to the PTBT, managed to explode a nuclear device underground without exposing itself to a charge of violation of the Treaty.[4]

It is generally recognized that the ban on atmospheric tests helped to improve US-Soviet relations, which were strained by the 1962 Cuban missile crisis. But, apart from the establishment of a direct communications link ("the hot line") between the US and Soviet governments for use in time of

---

[3] There have even been radioactive leakages spreading outside the territory of the testing states party to the PTBT, and some governments have taken exception to these occurrences. Indeed, it is safe to state that radioactive material venting from an underground test to the surface cannot be entirely contained within the boundaries of the testing state.
[4] A complaint by Pakistan about the radioactive contamination of its territory from the Indian underground explosion was rejected by India, and the matter has not been pursued.

emergency (see Appendix E, page 229), the improved political climate did not contribute in any appreciable way to the promotion of disarmament. The pledge given by the UK, the USA and the USSR in the preamble and Article I of the PTBT—to achieve the discontinuance of all nuclear weapon test explosions for all time—has not as yet been fulfilled.

Limitations on the *size* of nuclear explosions, which were included in the 1974 US-Soviet Threshold Test Ban Treaty (TTBT), may constrain the development and testing of high-yield warheads and bombs (see Appendix E, page 235). But the yield threshold, 150 kilotons, is so high (10 times higher than the yield of the bomb dropped on Hiroshima in 1945) that the parties cannot be experiencing onerous restraint in continuing their nuclear weapon programmes. The USA and the USSR have even agreed, in an unpublished addendum to the TTBT [5], that one or two "slight" breaches per year would not be considered a violation of the Treaty.[5] Neither has the TTBT imposed any specific restrictions on the number of tests.[6] In any event, limitation, or even an agreed temporary cessation of nuclear weapon tests, is no substitute for a comprehensive test ban treaty of unlimited duration, to which the UK, the USA and the USSR are formally committed.

Although the discontinuation of test explosions could not stop all development of nuclear warheads, since certain improvements in nuclear weapons do not require tests involving nuclear reactions, and since important improvements in nuclear capabilities can also result from the modernization of the delivery vehicles, a permanent ban on all nuclear tests would decelerate the qualitative arms race: it would narrow one channel of competition among the great powers. It would also reinforce the Treaty on the non-proliferation of nuclear weapons (see below, page 13).

The 1967 Outer Space Treaty (for the text and parties, see pages 78 and 152) lays down principles governing peaceful activities of states in outer space. The follow-up agreements—namely, the Agreement on the rescue of astronauts, the return of astronauts and the return of objects launched into outer space; the Convention on international liability for damage caused by space objects; and the Convention on registration of objects launched into outer space—address themselves to technical and legal aspects of international co-operation in the exploration and use of outer space for peaceful

---

[5] The reason given for adopting this escape clause was that it might be difficult precisely to predict the explosive force of underground blasts. This is true, but an allowance for accidental "technical" breaches could easily fall into a pattern of planned breaches.

[6] Under Article I of the Threshold Test Ban Treaty, the parties committed themselves to restrict the number of tests to a minimum. The meaning of the term "minimum" was explained by a representative of the US Energy Research and Development Administration (ERDA) and the director of the US Arms Control and Disarmament Agency (ACDA), at a press conference held on 28 May 1976 in Washington. It was then stated that the concept of minimum testing does not imply a reduction of the amount of testing, and that the relevant treaty provision reflects an intention to keep the test programme "to the minimum national security needs on both sides".

purposes. Only one clause of the Outer Space Treaty itself (Article IV) is directly related to arms control: it elaborates on a UN General Assembly resolution, unanimously adopted in 1963 [6], and prohibits the placing in orbit around the Earth of any objects carrying nuclear weapons or any other kinds of weapons of mass destruction, the installation of such weapons on celestial bodies, or the stationing of them in outer space in any other manner.[7] The establishment of military bases, installations and fortifications, the testing of any type of weapons and the conduct of military manoeuvres on celestial bodies are also forbidden.

In considering the potential of weapons placed in orbit around the Earth, the following drawbacks from the technological point of view must be taken into account.

Hitting a predetermined target on the Earth's surface, which lies on the path defined by the orbit, would be feasible only at certain hours or on certain days. A malfunction of the orbiting weapon could cause unintentional destruction on the territory of the enemy or even a third state, as well as of the launching state itself. There would also be problems of maintenance, as well as of command and control. The weapon could be relatively easily intercepted or rendered inoperative. Placing nuclear weapons on manned orbiting stations would remove only some of these operational inconveniences. On balance, the disadvantages of placing nuclear weapons in outer space seemed to so outweigh their military usefulness that the USA and the USSR had little difficulty in agreeing to ban them. Both powers have continued to rely on ground-based and sea-based nuclear weapons which can both be better maintained and controlled, and also launched with greater accuracy.

However, the outer space environment has not been denuclearized. The flight through outer space of ballistic missiles carying nuclear weapons from one point to another on the Earth's surface has not been forbidden. Even nuclear weapons placed in orbit but flying less than one full revolution round the Earth, the so-called fractional orbital bombardment systems (FOBS), seem to have escaped proscription. Moreover, the deployment in outer space of weapons not capable of mass destruction is subject to no restriction whatever. This has left a wide margin for permitted military activities, an opportunity which is being taken advantage of by the USA and the USSR and perhaps other states. In addition to space-based anti-missile defences not prohibited by the 1972 US-Soviet ABM Treaty, both sides are engaged in developing devices capable of intercepting, destroying or disabling satellites in orbit, adding a new dimension to the arms race.

Since the danger of a war conducted from a planet against a state on Earth is an unrealistic prospect, the arms control effect of the undertaking to use

---

[7] "Weapons of mass destruction" are not defined in the Treaty, but the general understanding is that, in addition to nuclear, they include at least chemical and biological weapons as well.

celestial bodies exclusively for peaceful purposes is even scantier than that of banning orbiting weapons.

Complete demilitarization of outer space is probably unattainable as long as ballistic missiles exist in weapon arsenals. But, given this situation, an agreement safeguarding satellites would be necessary to avoid war in space, to preserve strategic stability and to ensure that arms control treaties verified from space are being complied with.

The 1967 Treaty of Tlatelolco (for the text and parties, see pages 80 and 152) prohibits the testing, use, manufacture, production or acquisition by any means, as well as the receipt, storage, installation, deployment and any form of possession of nuclear weapons in Latin America.[8] The extra-continental or continental states which are internationally responsible for territories lying within the limits of the geographical zone established by the Treaty (that is, France, the Netherlands, the UK and the USA) undertake to apply the statute of military denuclearization to these territories by adhering to *Additional Protocol I* annexed to the Treaty (for the text and parties, see pages 86 and 152). Under *Additional Protocol II* (for the text and parties, see pages 86 and 152), the nuclear weapon states undertake to respect the statute of military denuclearization of Latin America, and not to contribute to acts involving a violation of the Treaty, nor to use or threaten to use nuclear weapons against the parties to the Treaty.

The Treaty of Tlatelolco is now in force for an area of more than 8 million square kilometres and inhabited by some 150 million people, the ultimate goal being to cover an area of 20 million square kilometres with a population of around 280 million. The importance of this nuclear weapon-free zone in a populous region of the world is undeniable. Nevertheless, the Treaty contains ambiguous points which may weaken its "non-armament" impact. One of them is related to so-called peaceful nuclear explosions.

Explosions of nuclear devices for peaceful purposes are allowed under the Treaty and procedures for carrying them out are stipulated (Article 18). A proviso is made that such activities must be in accordance with Article 1, which prohibits the testing, use, manufacture, production or acquisition of nuclear weapons, as well as with Article 5, which defines a nuclear weapon as "any device which is capable of releasing nuclear energy in an uncontrolled manner, and which has a group of characteristics that are appropriate for use for warlike purposes". Some countries interpret these provisions as prohibiting the manufacture of nuclear explosive devices for peaceful purposes unless or until nuclear devices are developed which cannot be used as weapons. So formulated, the condition can hardly be fulfilled because nuclear explosives, irrespective of the objective pursued, contain identical nuclear components, and their production requires essentially the

---

[8] Exact limits of the zone of application of the Treaty of Tlatelolco are specified in Article 4.

Scope of the obligations

same technology. Other countries consider that the Treaty has sanctioned peaceful explosions involving devices used in nuclear weapons. Thus, the important problem of compatibility of an indigenous development of nuclear explosive devices for peaceful purposes with participation in this nuclear weapon-free zone agreement has remained unresolved.

Another controversial point is the geographical extent of the Latin American nuclear weapon-free area. The zone of application of the Treaty embraces the territory, territorial sea, air space and any other space over which the zonal state exercises sovereignty in accordance with "its own legislation". But such legislation varies from state to state, and is not always recognized by others to be in accord with international law.[9] Moreover, upon fulfilment of the requirements specified in Article 28, paragraph 1,[10] large areas of the high seas in the Atlantic and Pacific Oceans, hundreds of kilometres off the coasts of signatory states and over which no state has claimed jurisdiction, are to be included in the nuclear weapon-free zone. To what extent this latter provision of the Tlatelolco Treaty is concordant with the freedom of navigation in international waters is a moot question. In any event, the broad definition of the zone, as contained in the Treaty, is not acceptable to all the nuclear weapon powers called upon to respect its denuclearized status.

And, finally, since neither transport nor transit of nuclear weapons has been explicitly prohibited by the Treaty, the question has arisen whether these activities are actually permitted. According to the interpretation given in 1967 by the Preparatory Commission for the Denuclearization of Latin America (COPREDAL), it was, for the following reasons, not necessary to include the term "transport" in the article dealing with the obligations of the parties. If the carrier state were one of the zonal states, transport would be covered by the prohibition on any form of possession of nuclear weapons, "directly or indirectly, by the Parties themselves, by anyone on their behalf or in any other way" (Article I). If the carrier were a state not party to the Treaty, transport would be considered identical with "transit". In this case, as the Preparatory Commission argued, the principles and rules of international law must apply, according to which it is the prerogative of the territorial state, in the exercise of its sovereignty, to grant or deny permission for transit.[11] But the explanation is not convincing. Once nuclear

---

[9] In signing Additional Protocol II of the Treaty of Tlatelolco, France, the UK and the USA stated that they would not recognize any legislation which did not, in their view, comply with the relevant rules of international law, that is, the law of the sea.

[10] These requirements are as follows: adherence to the Treaty of Tlatelolco by all states in the region which were in existence when the Treaty was opened for signature; adherence to Additional Protocols I and II of the Treaty by all states to which they are open for signature; and the conclusion of safeguards agreements with the IAEA.

[11] The USA and France also hold the view that each party to a nuclear weapon-free zone agreement should retain exclusive legal competence to grant or deny non-parties transit privileges. Both countries made a statement to this effect upon signing Additional Protocol II of the Treaty of Tlatelolco.

weapons are allowed to be in transit in Latin America, even if such transit is limited to port visits or overflights, it will be impossible to maintain that the zone has been totally and effectively denuclearized. On the other hand, it is reasonable to expect that the nuclear weapon states which have formally undertaken to observe the statute of military denuclearization of Latin America, will refrain from introducing nuclear weapons there, even if only for a short time.

The Treaty of Tlatelolco is significant as the first agreement restricting the use of nuclear weapons. But not all assurances of non-use, so far obtained, have been unconditional. The USA and the UK have reserved the right to reconsider their obligations with regard to a state in the nuclear weapon-free zone in the event of any act of aggression or armed attack by that state, carried out with the support or assistance of a nuclear weapon power. Whether or not such a hedged guarantee conforms to the spirit of Additional Protocol II is open to question.

Similar and perhaps even more complicated problems would have to be dealt with if a denuclearized régime were to be established in other parts of the world. The areas where it is most needed are conflict areas, in which hostility and mistrust prevail, while the conclusion of regional agreements presupposes at least a modicum of good neighbourly relations. It is noteworthy that a comprehensive study of the question of nuclear weapon-free zones, prepared in 1975 by governmental experts [7], failed to reconcile the contradictory views on several matters most essential for the realization of the nuclear weapon-free zone concept.

The Treaty of Tlatelolco was specifically intended to preclude the emergence of nuclear weapon powers in Latin America. This goal has not been achieved, in spite of the fact that the Treaty is in force for the overwhelming majority of the states in the region. In 1977, 10 years after the signing of the Treaty, several countries of Latin America were still not bound by its provisions.

Cuba, which in 1962 allowed Soviet nuclear weapons to be stationed on its territory, has refused to join the Treaty. Argentina has so far only signed the Treaty,[12] while Brazil has signed and ratified it but, unlike most other parties, has not waived the requirements that are to be met before the Treaty enters into force for any given country.[10] However, even if the latter two countries became party to the Treaty of Tlatelolco, they might still insist, as they have repeatedly done in the past, that they had the right to carry out their own nuclear explosions for peaceful purposes.[13] And since

---

[12] In a joint US-Argentinian communiqué issued on 21 November 1977, Argentina announced its intention to ratify the Treaty of Tlatelolco.
[13] On signing the Treaty of Tlatelolco, Argentina and Brazil each stated that, according to their interpretation, the Treaty gives the parties the right to carry out, by their own means or in association with third parties, nuclear explosions for peaceful purposes, including explosions which involve devices similar to those used in nuclear weapons.

peaceful explosions are essentially indistinguishable from military tests, any of these countries exploding a nuclear device would become, *de facto,* a nuclear power, which would defeat the purpose of the Treaty. The attitudes of Argentina and Brazil, the two largest countries in Latin America, and practically the only ones in the area with any nuclear weapon potential or aspiration, will mainly determine the success or failure of this regional denuclearization experiment. Moreover, the durability of the Treaty will depend on whether all nuclear weapon powers undertake to respect the nuclear weapon-free régime of Latin America, and whether all zonal states will effectively bar the presence of foreign nuclear forces on their territories.

It is of interest to note that there have also been attempts to limit conventional armaments in Latin America. In the 1974 *Declaration of Ayacucho* (for relevant extracts, see page 121), the six members of the so-called Andean Group (Bolivia, Chile, Colombia, Ecuador, Peru and Venezuela) plus two non-members (Argentina and Panama) undertook to create conditions permitting an effective limitation of armaments and putting an end to their acquisition for offensive purposes. The stated aim of these measures was to devote all possible resources to the economic and social development of the countries in Latin America.[14] Several meetings have taken place since the signing of the Declaration with a view to translating its provisions into an internationally binding instrument.

An agreement on conventional weapon restraints in Latin America could have a positive impact on peace and security in the area. However, the prospects for such an agreement are not bright due to the following circumstances: political as well as territorial disputes continue to exist in Latin America; the chronic instability of régimes in many Latin American countries creates a constant demand for arms for internal purposes; the major arms exporting countries do not seem to be willing to forego whatever advantages they may draw, political or economic, from continued weapon supplies to Latin America; and, in addition, the agreement envisaged by the Andean states falls short of the requirement that, to be effective, regional arms limitation must apply to all militarily significant countries of the region.

The 1968 Non-Proliferation Treaty (for the text and parties, see pages 88 and 152) prohibits the transfer by nuclear weapon states to any recipient whatsoever of nuclear weapons or other nuclear explosive devices or of control over them. The NPT also prohibits the receipt by non-nuclear weapon states from any transferor whatsoever, as well as the manufacture or other acquisition by those states, of nuclear weapons or other nuclear explosive devices. (Unlike the Treaty of Tlatelolco, the NPT has not defined a nuclear weapon or a nuclear explosive device.) In addition, the

---

[14] The Andean Group was created in 1969 for the purpose of subregional economic integration.

nuclear weapon states are not allowed to assist, encourage, or induce any non-nuclear weapon state to manufacture or acquire the devices in question. There is no express prohibition for non-nuclear weapon states party to the NPT to provide such assistance, encouragement or inducement to other non-nuclear weapon states which are not party to the NPT. But the USA and the USSR, the powers that were responsible for the formulation of the relevant provisions, have made it clear that such a case would be regarded as a violation of the Treaty.

The need to halt a wider spread of nuclear weapons grew out of the realization that the possession of these weapons by many countries would increase the threat to world security. But the concept of a treaty prohibiting the acquistion of weapons by an overwhelming majority of states, while tolerating the retention of the same weapons by a few, has given rise to controversies relating to the balance of rights and obligations of parties under international agreements. Indeed, in renouncing the nuclear weapon option under the NPT, the non-nuclear weapon states have assumed the main burden of obligation, while the nuclear weapon states, in undertaking not to disseminate the weapons, have sacrificed little if anything. In addition to retaining their nuclear arsenals, the latter powers are free to assist each other in developing nuclear warheads and in testing them; they have the right to receive from any state the material necessary to pursue their nuclear weapon programmes; they may deploy nuclear weapons on the territories of other states; and, unlike non-nuclear weapon countries, they are not obligated to subject their peaceful nuclear activities to international safeguards.

To attenuate the asymmetries inherent in the NPT, the nuclear weapon powers have undertaken to facilitate the exchange of equipment, materials and scientific and technological information for the peaceful uses of nuclear energy, with due consideration for the needs of the developing areas of the world (Article IV); to make available their services, at low cost, for peaceful applications of nuclear explosions (Article V); to pursue negotiations on measures relating to the cessation of the nuclear arms race and to nuclear disarmament, and on a treaty on general and complete disarmament (Article VI); and, under a separate arrangement, to provide security guarantees to non-nuclear weapon states. But all these "compensatory" provisions have proved to be of little consequence.

Assistance in the development of nuclear energy for peaceful purposes could have been a powerful inducement to join the NPT if it had been reserved only for the parties. But nuclear transactions have continued to be conducted according to the rules and customs of commercial competition and in keeping with the political interests of the supplier states rather than in conformity with the international non-proliferation strategy. Non-parties have not been excluded from participation in international co-operation in the nuclear field. In some instances they have even managed to secure more material supplies and technical aid than have the parties. The most striking case is that of India, which, notwithstanding its official statements that it would not subscribe to the NPT and that it was preparing a nuclear explosion, received nuclear material and associated equipment. Another example is the case of Brazil, a country which has also refused to join the NPT or to be bound by the treaty prohibiting nuclear weapons in Latin America (see above), and which nevertheless will be able to acquire a complete nuclear fuel cycle under an agreement signed in 1975 with the Federal Republic of Germany, a party to the NPT. Never before has such a comprehensive nuclear transaction been concluded. Moreover, and paradoxically enough, non-parties have been subject to less stringent control over their nuclear activities than have the parties to the NPT. *The Guidelines for Nuclear Transfers* (for the text, see page 138), worked out in 1977 by a group of nuclear supplier states (the so-called London Club), have tightened the terms of such transfers and have reduced the advantages that non-parties may derive from remaining outside the NPT. But these guidelines are still insufficient to guarantee that no further nuclear weapon proliferation will result from nuclear supplies to non-parties that are unfettered by a political commitment not to manufacture nuclear weapons. New power-generating and other technologies may drastically shorten the time needed to obtain weapon-grade nuclear material, and there is nothing in the existing agreements on nuclear transfers to prevent national efforts, not involving the materials supplied, to design weapons or to develop non-nuclear components of nuclear weapons.

A number of states party to the NPT have held high hopes that peaceful applications of nuclear explosions will help to solve some of their acute economic problems. The text of the NPT is unclear as to whether non-parties are also entitled to receive nuclear explosion services, but the conference which reviewed the Treaty in 1975 decided that they are, and thereby removed yet another incentive for states to join the NPT [8]. It should be noted that in referring to benefits derived from peaceful explosions, the Treaty employed the term "potential", which implied that the advantages remained to be demonstrated. However, in recent years growing scepticism has been expressed about the usefulness and feasibility of such explosions. Some nations favour the idea of giving them up altogether, especially since they seem to be incompatible with the envisaged comprehensive nuclear test ban treaty.

The NPT provision dealing with disarmament was included at the insistence of non-nuclear weapon states, with a view to matching the cessation of "horizontal" proliferation with the cessation of "vertical" proliferation. The idea was that the NPT should become a transitional stage in a process of nuclear disarmament. But it soon became clear that the nuclear weapon powers considered it an end in itself. In fact, the obligation undertaken was not to disarm, but to negotiate. Moreover, the term "cessation", as applied to the nuclear arms race, does not convey the same meaning for all states. For example, the US-Soviet Interim Agreement of 1972, which allowed an unlimited multiplication of nuclear warheads, and which placed no restrictions on the qualitative improvement of weapons, has often been described by the two sides as a measure meeting the requirements of the NPT, while others have seen in it an encouragement to further competition in arms.[15]

Under a 1968 *UN Security Council resolution* (for the text and record of voting, see page 87) the states foregoing the acquisition of nuclear weapons under the NPT received a pledge of immediate assistance, in accordance with the UN Charter, in the event they became "a victim of a act or an object of a threat of aggression in which nuclear weapons are used" [10]. But the value of this pledge is questionable. The resolution and the associated declarations by the UK, the USA and the USSR [11] merely reaffirm the existing UN Charter obligation to provide assistance to a country attacked, irrespective of the type of weapon employed. Since all the nuclear weapon powers are now also permanent members of the Security Council, a decision concerning military or non-military measures against a delinquent state could not be taken if any one of them cast a negative vote, inasmuch as it is inconceivable that a nation which had used nuclear weapons would consent to a collective action being taken against itself. Moreover, immediate active intervention, as envisaged by the resolution, is deemed unacceptable by some nonaligned and neutral states, unless assistance has been specifically requested by them. However, the most serious deficiency of the resolution resides in the fact that it provides for action only when a threat of nuclear attack has been made or an attack has already occurred. It does not offer assurance for the prevention of the use or threat of use of nuclear weapons. In other words, states which have decided not to acquire nuclear weapons have received no guarantee that nuclear weapons possessed by others would not be used against them.

The agreements of the Disarmament Decade, the 1970s

The 1971 Sea-Bed Treaty (for the text and parties, see pages 90 and 152) prohibits emplanting or emplacing on the sea-bed and the ocean floor and in the subsoil thereof beyond the outer limit of a sea-bed zone (coterminous with the 12-mile outer limit of the zone referred to in the 1958 Geneva Convention on the Territorial Sea and the Contiguous Zone) any nuclear weapons or any other types of weapons of mass destruction as well as structures, launching installations or any other facilities specifically designed for storing, testing or using such weapons.

Arms control with respect to the sea-bed first began to receive attention in the 1960s. At this time, advances in the technology of oceanography were

---

[15] From 1972 to 1977, the combined number of nuclear warheads on US and Soviet strategic missiles and bombers is estimated to have increased by more than 50 per cent [9].

feared to lead to the use of the sea-bed for warlike purposes. The original idea was to reserve the sea-bed beyond the limits of national jurisdiction for peaceful undertakings alone, which for many nations was tantamount to a prohibition on all military activities. But the Sea-Bed Treaty has failed to bring about the demilitarization of the area in question.

Even the denuclearization undertaking is only partial: the portion of the sea-bed which is adjacent to the coast of nuclear weapon states, and which is therefore more suitable for the emplacement of nuclear weapons than are outlying areas, has been excluded from the prohibition. Neither does the Treaty prevent the great powers from installing nuclear weapons beneath the territorial waters of other states, if those states authorize such installation, and if the operation is carried out within the 12-mile sea-bed zone. The USA, which together with the USSR sponsored the Treaty, also explained that submersible vehicles carrying nuclear weapons on board, and able to navigate in the water above the sea-bed, would be viewed as any other ship and not as violating the Treaty when they are anchored to, or resting on, the ocean bottom.

Only fixed nuclear installations or bottom-crawling vehicles which can navigate exclusively when in contact with the sea-bed, and which, moreover, are specifically designed to use nuclear weapons, have been banned. But such devices, being very vulnerable, appear not to be militarily attractive. Thus the Treaty has prohibited something which was in any case not likely to be developed. And since it permits the use of the sea-bed for facilities which service free-swimming nuclear weapon systems, it presents no obstacle to a nuclear arms race in the whole of the sea environment. Nevertheless, in joining the Treaty, some states have reserved the right to remove any weapon, installation, facility or device emplaced by other countries on their continental shelves beyond the outer limit of the sea-bed zone referred to and defined in the Treaty.

The Treaty was presented to the international community as a step towards excluding the sea-bed area from the domain of the arms race. The parties undertook to conduct negotiations in good faith concerning measures in the field of disarmament which would lead to this goal, but, so far, no such negotiations have been held. A conference of the parties, convened five years after the entry into force of the Sea-Bed Treaty to review its operation, has done little more than to ask the Conference of the Committee on Disarmament to proceed with the consideration of relevant measures.

The 1972 Biological Weapons Convention (for the text and parties, see pages 103 and 152) prohibits the development, production, stockpiling, or acquisition by other means, or retention of biological agents or toxins, of types and in quantities that have no justification for peaceful purposes, as well as weapons, equipment or means of delivery designed to use such agents or toxins for hostile purposes or in armed conflict.

Because of their uncontrollability and unpredictability, biological weapons have always been considered of little utility. But, in prohibiting the further development of biological weapons, the BW Convention has aimed at eliminating the possibility that scientific advances modifying the conditions of production, stockpiling and use of these weapons could make them militarily more attractive. The Convention is also meant to prevent the spread of biological and toxin weapons to countries which do not possess them. However, its most remarkable feature consists in the requirement to destroy the agents and toxins, as well as related weapons, equipment and means of delivery which are in the possession of the parties, or to divert them to peaceful purposes. This is the first international agreement since World War II which, by abolishing an entire class of weapons, involves some measure of "sacrifice". Indeed, after the entry into force of the Convention, the USA stated that its entire stockpile of biological and toxin agents and weapons had been destroyed and that its former biological warfare facilities had been converted to peaceful uses [12]; the UK said that it had no stocks of biological weapons [13]; and the USSR announced that it did not possess any bacteriological (biological) agents or toxins, weapons, equipment or means of delivery, as prohibited in the Convention [14].

It is regrettable that chemical weapons were not prohibited at the same time. Since 1925 these weapons had been considered together with biological weapons, and have been associated with them in the public mind. Indeed, chemical weapons may be potentially more attractive to the military than biological weapons: they are more predictable and can produce immediate effects, which are important qualities in actual combat; and they are maintained in the arsenals of certain states and have already been used on a large scale in war with disastrous consequences to the attacked nations. For these reasons, the parties to the BW Convention had to recognize that the Convention was only a step towards an agreement effectively prohibiting also the development, production and stockpiling of chemical weapons, and providing for their destruction. They have undertaken to continue negotiations with a view to reaching such an agreement.

The BW Convention does not explicitly prohibit the use of biological and toxin weapons, the general understanding being that the non-use obligation has already been included in the 1925 Geneva Protocol dealing with asphyxiating, poisonous or other gases and with bacteriological methods of warfare, and no one has contested that toxins are also covered by the Protocol. The dilemma is that, in ratifying the Geneva Protocol, many countries reserved the right to use the banned weapons against non-parties or in retaliation. These reservations are now incompatible with the BW Convention, which excludes the possibility of biological agents being used as weapons under any circumstances. The reservations should, therefore, be withdrawn, and a few states have already done so (see Chapter 3).

Scope of the obligations

The 1975 Final Act of the Conference on Security and Co-operation in Europe contains a *Document on confidence-building measures and certain aspects of security and disarmament* (for the text and signatories, see page 121). The rationale for adopting the document was formulated as follows: "to contribute to reducing the dangers of armed conflict and of misunderstanding or miscalculation of military activities which could give rise to apprehension, particularly in a situation when the participating states lack clear and timely information about the nature of such activities". However, most provisions of the document are vague or non-committal, or simply confirm a practice already existing among nations maintaining normal relations. The only provision stated in concrete terms concerns the notification of major military manoeuvres in Europe, to be given at least 21 days in advance or, in the case of a manoeuvre arranged at shorter notice, at the earliest possible opportunity prior to its starting date. The term "major" means that at least 25 000 troops are involved. Manoeuvres with fewer troops can also be considered as major if they involve "significant numbers" of troops especially trained for invasion purposes (amphibious or airborne). Manoeuvres of naval and air forces, conducted independently or jointly, are not covered by the notification requirement. The following information is to be provided for each major manoeuvre: its designation (code-name), if any; its general purpose; the states involved; the types and numerical strength of the forces engaged; and the area and estimated time-frame of its conduct. States may give additional information, particularly that related to the components of the forces engaged and the period of involvement of the troops, and may invite observers to attend the manoeuvres.

The preamble of the document states that the notification of manoeuvres "rests upon a voluntary basis"; it is, therefore, not a legally binding commitment. Nonetheless, it is a declaration of intent solemnly adopted by the representatives of the participating states at the highest possible level. And since the parties expressed their conviction of the political importance of prior notification of major military manoeuvres for "the promotion of mutual understanding and the strengthening of confidence, stability and security", and accepted the "responsibility of each of them" to implement this measure, the document carries a potential for exerting pressure on non-observing states.

The concept of advance notification of manoeuvres was introduced into the international debate at the beginning of the 1960s as part of a programme to reduce the risk of war by accident, miscalculation, failure of communications or surprise attack. It was then discussed along with the proposed establishment of observation posts, mobile observation teams and exchange of military missions, or in conjunction with a proposed prohibition on certain types of military exercises [15]. Isolated from the above-mentioned measures, notification can hardly fulfil the original role allotted to it, namely that of a warning signal for the two major military blocs, especially at a time when the means of satellite surveillance are considered sufficiently reliable to monitor significant military activities in any part of the world. Notification could, perhaps, contribute to minimizing the danger that detection of such activities might give rise to misunderstandings and provoke a rapid, possibly disproportionate military response, initiating unpremeditated hostilities. But it would then have to apply even to military manoeuvres of fewer than 25 000 troops. It would also have to cover, on an obligatory basis, military movements other than manoeuvres, since transfers of combat-ready army, naval and air force units outside their permanent garrison or base areas, especially over long distances and close to the borders of other states, may cause even greater concern than manoeuvres. Furthermore, the role of invited foreign observers would have to be clearly defined. Hitherto, it has been left entirely to the host country to determine whether the attendance of observers at the manoeuvres was to be a meaningful or simply a ceremonial act.

In spite of these deficiencies, the undertaking to notify signifies a step, though a modest one, towards openness in military affairs. Moreover, the document contains a promise that consideration will be given to the question of notification of major military movements, "bearing in mind, in particular, the experience gained by the implementation of the measures which are set forth in this document". (Notifications of manoeuvres received during 1975–78 are listed in Appendix C.)

It must be borne in mind that notification does not imply restriction. To qualify as a real arms control measure, the obligation to notify would have to be supplemented by an obligation to limit, to an agreed low level, the size and frequency of the relevant military activities as well as the area of their conduct.

The *Environmental Modification Convention,* opened for signature in 1977 (for the text and signatories, see pages 123 and 152), prohibits military or any other hostile use of environmental modification techniques.

The negotiations on the ENMOD Convention were motivated, *inter alia,* by concern that environmental forces could be used for military ends, and that environmental manipulation could have serious consequences for human welfare. But the resulting agreement has not entirely allayed this concern since it has not banned *all* environmental modification techniques for hostile purposes. Only the use of those techniques which have widespread, long-lasting or severe effects as the means of destruction, damage or injury to states party to the Convention has been prohibited.

According to an understanding reached during the negotiations (but not written into the Convention), the term "widespread" means encompassing an area on the scale of several hundred square kilometres; "long-lasting" refers to a period of months, or approximately a season; while "severe" is to be interpreted as involving serious or significant disruption or harm to human life, natural and economic resources or other assets. Exempted from the prohibition are non-hostile uses of modification techniques, even if they produce destructive effects above the threshold described above. Equally permissible are hostile uses which produce destructive effects below the threshold.

According to another understanding, the hostile use of techniques which produce earthquakes, tsunamis, an upset in the ecological balance of a region, changes in weather patterns (clouds, precipitation, cyclones of various types and tornadic storms), changes in climate patterns, changes in ocean currents, changes in the state of the ozone layer, and changes in the state of the ionosphere, is unconditionally prohibited. However, none of these phenomena seems likely to be caused through deliberate action for rational warlike purposes, that is, in such a way that the effects would be felt only, or primarily, by the enemy. Techniques that can produce more limited effects—such as precipitation modification (short of changing the weather patterns), or formation or dissipation of fog—and are likely to be used to influence the environment with hostile intent in a selected area, especially in tactical military operations (facilitating the effectiveness of other weapons) have escaped proscription. And it is precisely such techniques that may enter the sphere of military competition. As distinct from other partial treaties, which provide for further measures to be negotiated in a given field, there is no commitment to make the ENMOD Convention comprehensive by removing the established threshold in a follow-up agreement. Nor have restrictions been imposed on the development of environmental modification techniques for warlike purposes. The significance of the ENMOD Convention is therefore very limited.

The humanitarian laws of war

Efforts to reduce brutality in war have a long history. They have been motivated by ethical and religious as well as practical considerations. Of special significance was the *Declaration of St. Petersburg* of 1868 (for the text and signatories, see page 53). It proclaimed that the only legitimate objective which states should endeavour to accomplish during war is to weaken the military forces of the enemy, and that the employment of arms which uselessly aggravate the suffering of disabled men, or render their death inevitable, would be contrary to the laws of humanity.

Following the spirit of the St. Petersburg Declaration, *Declaration IV, 3* of the Hague Conference, held in 1899, prohibited the use of so-called dum-dum bullets, which expanded or flattened easily in the human body and caused more serious wounds than other bullets. (For the text and parties, see page 54.)

The Second Hague Conference, held in 1907, adopted a convention on laws and customs of land warfare, *Convention IV* (for the text and parties, see page 55), which confirmed the principles of the St. Petersburg Declaration. It stated that the right of belligerents to adopt means of injuring the enemy is not unlimited, and it prohibited the employment of arms, projectiles, or material calculated to cause unnecessary suffering. In particular, the Convention prohibited the use of poison or poisoned weapons, the treacherous killing or wounding of individuals belonging to the hostile nation or army, or the killing or wounding of an enemy who had laid down his arms or surrendered. The same conference restricted and regulated, in *Convention VIII* (for the text and parties, see page 57), the use of automatic submarine contact mines; prohibited, in *Convention IX* (for the text and parties, see page 58), the bombardment by naval forces of ports, cities, villages, habitations or buildings which were not defended; and proclaimed, in *Declaration XIV* (for the text and parties, see page 60), a prohibition on the discharge of projectiles and explosives from balloons or by other methods of a similar nature.

In addition to attempting to codify the laws of war on a world-wide scale, the two Hague Conferences brought advances in establishing institutions and procedures for settling international disputes. Plans for a third conference had to be abandoned in view of the intensified inter-state antagonisms that preceded World War I.

After the war, on 17 June 1925, the *Geneva Protocol* (for the text and parties, see pages 64 and 146) was signed, prohibiting the use of asphyxiating, poisonous or other gases, and of all analogous liquids, materials or devices, as well as the use of bacteriological methods of warfare. In the part dealing with gases, the Protocol actually ratified a prohibition previously declared in international documents. These included the *1899 Hague Declaration IV, 2* (for the text and parties, see page 54), under which the contracting powers had agreed to abstain from the use of projectiles for the diffusion of asphyxiating or deleterious gases, as well as the *1907 Hague Convention IV*, mentioned above. The need to restate the prohibition of acts already held in abhorrence and condemned by world opinion was prompted by the experience of World War I, during which the extensive use of poisonous gas resulted in as many as 1 300 000 casualties. (Of the direct antecedents of the Geneva Protocol, as far as the prohibition of chemical weapons is concerned, the 1919 Treaty of Versailles and the other peace treaties of 1919–20 were applicable only to the vanquished countries (Germany, Austria, Bulgaria and Hungary), while the 1922 Treaty of Washington, relating to the use of submarines and noxious gases in wartime, never entered into force.)

The interpretation of the scope of the Geneva Protocol has for many years been a matter of dispute. In 1969 a majority UN resolution expressed the view that the Protocol embodied the generally recognized rules of international law prohibiting the use in international armed conflicts of *all* biological and chemical methods of warfare, regardless of any technical developments, and declared as contrary to those rules the use in international armed conflicts of: (*a*) any chemical agents of warfare—chemical substances, whether gaseous, liquid or solid—which might be employed because of their direct toxic effects on man, animals or plants; and (*b*) any biological agents of warfare—living organisms, whatever their nature, or infective material derived from them—which are intended to cause disease or death in man, animals or plants, and which depend for their effects on their ability to multiply in the person, animal or plant attacked [16].

The United States had been in the forefront of states which gave the Geneva Protocol a narrow interpretation and which contended, in particular, that the use of irritants and antiplant chemicals was not covered by the Protocol. In 1975 the USA decided to renounce, as a matter of national policy, both the first use of herbicides in war except for control of vegetation within US bases and installations or around their immediate defensive perimeters, and the first use of riot control agents in war, except in such defensive military modes to save lives as: (*a*) to control rioting prisoners of war in areas under US military control; (*b*) to reduce or avoid civilian casualties when civilians are used to mask or screen attacks; (*c*) to recover downed aircrews and passengers, and escaping prisoners, in rescue missions in remotely isolated areas; or (*d*) to protect convoys outside the combat zone from civil disturbances, terrorists and paramilitary organizations [17]. This interpretation is certainly more liberal than the one previously advocated: some of the permitted uses relate to non-combatant situations or are similar to domestic police uses. Nevertheless, the US interpretation falls short of the understanding of the scope of the Geneva Protocol, as formulated in the above-mentioned UN resolution.

As a legal constraint, the Geneva Protocol has been weakened by the reservations made by a number of states which limit its applicability to nations party to it, and to first use only. The danger that the weapons prohibited by the Protocol may, under certain circumstances, be resorted to (as has occurred on several occasions since its adoption) will remain as long as these weapons are retained in the military arsenals of states.

When World War II broke out, the following agreements for the protection of war victims were in force: the Convention for the amelioration of the condition of the wounded and sick in armies in the field (which replaced the Red Cross Conventions of 22 August 1864 and 6 July 1906) and the Convention relative to the treatment of prisoners of war, both of which were signed on 27 July 1929. But none of the existing international instruments proved sufficient in providing humanitarian safeguards during World War II. Indeed, the shock of the discovery of mass crimes committed during that war led to the 1948 *Convention on the prevention and punishment of the crime of genocide*—the so-called Genocide Convention (for the text and parties, see page 70). This Convention declares genocide, defined as the commission of acts intended to destroy, in whole or in part, a national, ethnical, racial or religious group, as such, to be a crime to be prevented and punished. Further rules were worked out at a conference held in Geneva in 1949, and were included in the following four conventions: Convention (I) for the amelioration of the condition of the wounded and sick in armed forces in the field; Convention (II) for the amelioration of the condition of the wounded, sick and shipwrecked members of armed forces at sea; Convention (III) relative to the treatment of prisoners of war; and Convention (IV) relative to the protection of civilian persons in time of war. (For extracts from *Convention IV* and the parties, see page 66.)

The Geneva Conventions of 1949 were conceived primarily as a code of behaviour in wars of the traditional type, conducted between states and between regular armies. However, since World War II, most armed conflicts have been civil wars. Guerrilla warfare has been the prevalent type of such conflicts and has complicated the application of the principle that a distinction must be observed between the civilian and the military. As a result, the protection of civilians has weakened considerably. Furthermore, the laws of war which relate directly to the conduct of hostilities by banning or restricting the use of a specific weapon or type of weapon, as distinct from rules designed to accord protection to certain persons, places or objects in armed conflicts, had not developed since the 1907 Hague Conventions, with the sole exception of the above-mentioned 1925 Geneva Protocol. In particular, air warfare had remained to a great extent uncodified; area bombardment, which caused the destruction of many cities in World War II, was not expressly forbidden; and weapons which had come into existence during the past decades and which were of an especially cruel or inhumane nature had not been specifically prohibited.

To deal with all these matters, a Diplomatic Conference on the reaffirmation and development of international law applicable in armed conflicts was convened in Geneva in 1974. In 1977, at the end of the fourth session of the Conference, two protocols were adopted: Protocol I, relating to the protection of victims of international armed conflicts; and Protocol II, relating to the protection of victims of non-international armed conflicts. Both were signed on 12 December 1977.

Protocol I (for the text and signatories, see page 125) reiterates and expands the traditional rules regarding the protection of the civilian population. The prohibition against indiscriminate attacks now covers attacks by bombardment by any methods or means which treat as a single military objective a number of distinct objectives located in a city, town, village or other area containing a similar concentration of civilians or civilian objects; as well as attacks expected to cause incidental losses or injuries to civilians, which would be excessive in relation to the direct military advantage anticipated (Article 51, paragraph 5). Reprisals against the civilian population are forbidden (Article 51, paragraph 6). It is furthermore prohibited to destroy foodstuffs, agricultural areas for the production of foodstuffs, crops, livestock, drinking water installations and supplies and irrigation works, for the specific purpose of denying the civilian population those objects which are indispensable for its survival (Article 54). Dams, dykes and nuclear electric power generating stations have been placed under special protection, and shall not be attacked, if an attack on them may cause severe losses among civilians (Article 56). (This protection will, however, cease if the installations in question are used in significant and direct support of military operations and if an attack on them is the only feasible way to terminate such support). The prohibition also applies to the attack, by any means, of non-defended localities, declared as such by the appropriate authorities of a party (Article 59), or to the extension of military operations to zones on which the parties have conferred by agreement the status of demilitarized zone (Article 60).

A special provision is devoted to the protection of the natural environment against widespread, long-term and severe damage. It includes a prohibition on the use of methods and means of warfare that are intended or may be expected to cause such damage to the natural environment and thereby to prejudice the health or survival of the population (Article 55).[16]

Protocol I is applicable not only to inter-state armed conflicts, but also to conflicts in which peoples are fighting against colonial domination and alien occupation and against racist régimes in the exercise of their right to self-determination (Article 1). In this way, guerrilla fighters have been covered by international protection. In particular, they have been given the right to prisoner-of-war status if they belong to organized units under a command responsible to the party concerned, and if they carry their arms openly during each military engagement, and during such time as they are visible to the adversary before launching an attack (Articles 43 and 44). On the other hand, mercenaries, as defined in the Protocol, have no right to combatant or prisoner-of-war status (Article 47).

Several articles dealing with relief actions in favour of the civilian population have strengthened the corresponding clauses of the 1949 Geneva Convention IV. The duties of the occupying power include the provision, to the fullest extent of the means available, of supplies essential to the survival of the civilian population of the occupied territory (Article 69).

Protocol II develops and supplements Article 3, which appears in all the four Geneva Conventions of 1949, and which deals with armed conflicts not of an international character. It prescribes humane treatment of all the persons involved in such conflicts, care for the wounded, sick and shipwrecked, as well as protection of civilians against the dangers arising from

---

[16] This formulation is more restricted than that included in the Environmental Modification Convention (see page 123) because it requires the presence of all the three effects—widespread, long-term and severe—for the method and means of warfare to be prohibited.

military operations. It does not apply to internal disturbances, such as riots, sporadic acts of violence and similar acts.

The two protocols of 1977 constitute a step forward in the development of the humanitarian laws of war, even though some of their provisions lack clarity and certain definitions are imprecise. Their greatest shortcoming, however, is that they have not forbidden any specific weapon which is excessively injurious or has indiscriminate effects. Nuclear or other weapons of mass destruction, which clearly fall under this category, were not even considered at the Geneva Diplomatic Conference. The question of conventional weapons of a particularly cruel nature was discussed, in considerable detail, in an *ad hoc* committee of the Conference and at two meetings of government experts [18], but has not been resolved. In *Resolution 22* (for the text, see page 137) the Diplomatic Conference decided that a special conference should be convened, not later than 1979, with a view to reaching agreements on prohibitions or restrictions on the use of certain conventional weapons. The weapons most often mentioned in this context are incendiaries, including napalm, small-calibre high-velocity projectiles, certain blast and fragmentation weapons, including weapons the primary effect of which is to injure by fragments not detectable by X-ray, as well as mines and booby-traps.

II. *Verification and enforcement*

The problem of possible breaches of obligation has been an important issue in all arms control negotiations, due to the fact that states are generally reluctant to depend solely on good faith when matters of national security are involved.

There is, of course, no way of preventing sovereign governments from violating international commitments, openly or secretly, if they choose to disregard the potential consequences of their actions. They may, however, be deterred from doing so if they fear losing the advantages they have originally gained from the treaty; if they dread an expected or unpredictable response from the injured states; or if they are sufficiently sensitive to public disapproval to apprehend an unfavourable reaction in their own or in other countries. Deterrence of secret violations presupposes the ability to detect them. And timely detection is of essence, particularly in cases constituting an immediate military threat, because it might enable the injured party to redress the situation. This deterrence function is the main purpose of verification clauses in arms control treaties. In addition, by confirming that activities prohibited by agreements are not taking place, and that the parties are fulfilling their obligations, verification helps to generate a climate of international confidence which is indispensable for progress in arms control.

Insistence on verification measures obviously unacceptable to another party has often been used as a convenient excuse for blocking agreement when the real reason for resistance was inconvenient to admit. Normally, however, verification should include procedures for: (*a*) acquiring information about the parties' performance with respect to their undertakings; (*b*) instituting an inquiry in cases requiring clarification; and (*c*) dealing with complaints of violations. These requirements have been met in arms control agreements in a variety of ways.

Acquisition of information

As regards acquisition of information, the best developed system is found in the Antarctic Treaty. Each party to this Treaty is obliged to inform the other parties: of all expeditions to and within Antarctica; of all stations occupied there by its nationals; and of any military personnel or equipment intended to be introduced into Antarctica for scientific research or other peaceful purposes. The Treaty provides for complete freedom of access by the parties, at any time, to any area of Antarctica. All areas, including stations, installations and equipment within these areas, and all ships and aircraft at points of discharging or embarking cargoes or personnel are to be open at all times to inspection. Aerial observation is allowed. In addition, scientific personnel may be exchanged between expeditions and stations. However, only the original parties are entitled to designate observers to carry out inspection or aerial observation. Acceding states may participate in these activities if they conduct "substantial" scientific research in Antarctica.

The verification principles embodied in the Antarctic Treaty have been applied, in certain respects, in the Outer Space Treaty. The parties have agreed to inform the UN Secretary-General, as well as the public and the international scientific community, "to the greatest extent feasible and practicable", of the nature, conduct, locations and results of their activities in outer space. All stations, installations, equipment and space vehicles on the Moon and other celestial bodies are to be open to representatives of other states party to the Treaty on a basis of reciprocity. However, there is no provision for verifying the ban on placing weapons of mass destruction in orbit around the Earth; earlier proposals for inspecting space vehicles on their launch pads were abandoned.

Under the Treaty prohibiting nuclear weapons in Latin America (Treaty of Tlatelolco), each party must apply the International Atomic Energy Agency (IAEA) safeguards to its nuclear activities. It must also submit periodic reports stating that no activity prohibited under the Treaty has occurred on its territory. Supplementary information regarding any event or circumstance connected with compliance with the Treaty may be requested by the General Secretary of the Agency for the Prohibition of Nuclear Weapons in Latin America, established by the parties. Special inspections can be carried out either in accordance with the agreements concluded with the IAEA, or when a party suspects that some activity prohibited by the Treaty has been carried out or is about to be carried out on the territory of another party, or following a request by a party suspected of or charged with having violated the Treaty. Those carrying out special inspections must be granted full and free access to all places and to all information which may be necessary for the performance of their duties and which are directly connected with the suspicion of violation of the Treaty.

Under the terms of the Treaty on the non-proliferation of nuclear weapons, non-nuclear weapon parties must accept IAEA safeguards for the purpose of verification of the fulfilment of their obligations assumed under the Treaty. The safeguards are to be applied to all source or special fissionable material in all peaceful nuclear activities within the territories of such states, under their jurisdiction, or carried out under their control anywhere. *The Structure and Content of Agreements between the Agency and states required in connection with the Treaty on the Non-Proliferation of Nuclear Weapons* (as distinct from safeguards which had been in existence prior to the NPT) were agreed to in 1971 (for the text, see page 92). The NPT provides that these agreements may be concluded either by individual states or by groups of states. The latter provision was included to meet the request by the European Atomic Energy Community (Euratom) which had its own system of control. Accordingly, on 5 April 1973 an *Agreement* (for the text, see page 105) was signed between Belgium, Denmark, the Federal Republic of Germany, Ireland, Italy, Luxembourg, the Netherlands, Euratom and the IAEA. This agreement, which entered into force on 21 February 1977, provides for co-operative arrangements whereby Euratom is to act partly as an agent of its member states, partly as an instrument of the IAEA, partly as an independent unit carrying out its own statutory responsibilities, and in most respects as a buffer between the IAEA and the Euratom states.[17] There is no provision in the NPT for controlling compliance with the obligation not to transfer nuclear weapons or other nuclear explosive devices.

Parties to the Sea-Bed Treaty have the right to verify through observation the activities of other states on the sea-bed and the ocean floor and in the subsoil thereof beyond the zone defined in the Treaty, provided that observation does not interfere with such activities. The possibility of "appropriate" inspection of objects, structures, installations or other facilities, that reasonably may be expected to be of a kind prohibited in the Treaty, is also envisaged.

It is noteworthy that none of the multilateral agreements presently in

---

[17] It will be noted that the development of plutonium-fueled reactors, as distinct from the uranium-fueled reactors currently in use, may erode the safeguards system. Such a development renders practically impossible the timely detection of the diversion of nuclear material to military purposes.

Verification and enforcement

force provides for access to the territories of the great powers for the purpose of verification of arms control obligations. The offers made by the UK and the USA to submit their civilian nuclear installations to safeguards under IAEA supervision have no arms control significance, because both powers remain unrestricted in their military nuclear programmes; they should be seen rather as a demonstration to non-nuclear weapon states that the latter would not be placed at a commercial disadvantage by applying safeguards pursuant to the NPT. A breakthrough occurred in the bilateral US-Soviet Peaceful Nuclear Explosions Treaty (PNET), signed on 26 May 1976. Under this treaty the parties accepted (in addition to the exchange of specified technical data) on-site observation of certain explosions conducted for peaceful purposes to ensure that no weapon-related benefits precluded by the 1974 Threshold Test Ban Treaty were derived through such explosions.

Neither the Partial Test Ban Treaty nor the Biological Weapons Convention contains verification provisions. Implicitly, knowledge about compliance is to be gathered by national means, which do not require agreed access to the territory being monitored. (This is also the case with bilateral US-Soviet agreements on the limitation of strategic nuclear arms, which, in addition to an explicit provision for verification by national "technical" means, contain a ban on interference with the operation of such means.)

Most arms control agreements provide for consultations between the states directly concerned, or for consultations conducted through international procedures, to clarify problems which may arise in relation to the objective of, or in the application of the provisions of, these agreements.

As regards charges of violation of multilateral arms control agreements, complaints can be lodged with the UN Security Council. The Council may carry out investigations on the basis of the complaint received and decide whether a violation has occurred. Under the Antarctic Treaty and the Treaty of Tlatelolco, disputes may be referred to the International Court of Justice for settlement.

In spite of elaborate provisions, the verification procedures, as embodied in most existing treaties, suffer from lack of internal consistency. Checking compliance with arms control obligations often requires the use of sophisticated equipment—reconnaissance satellites,[18] electronic devices, and so on—in addition to the more traditional methods of collecting intelligence information. The few nations possessing such resources can, to a great extent, rely on their own national means of verification. For nations lacking the means, the mere right to verify is, to a large extent, meaningless: they are hardly in a position to ascertain whether the commitments of other parties are being observed. Some improvements in this respect have been

---

[18] In the debate on the Outer Space Treaty, it was assumed that satellite reconnaissance, like any other form of observation of a state from outside its territorial limits, violated no provision of international law.

made in the Sea-Bed Treaty, under which verification may be undertaken by any party using its own means, or with the full or partial assistance of any other party, or through international procedures. However, many states may be reluctant to resort to the aid of the technologically advanced states, and to rely for their security on such uncertain factors as the good-will of the great powers. Nonaligned or neutral states seeking direct assistance from one or another power would run the risk of compromising their status. On the other hand, the possibility of using international procedures to verify suspected Sea-Bed Treaty violations has not been specified.

Consultation relating to the implementation of arms control treaties could be of importance to states capable of monitoring compliance. For those deprived of knowledge about the behaviour of others, there may be no opportunity for consultation. Moreover, direct contacts among countries may not always be feasible. As regards indirect, international consultation, most arms control treaties use vague language to cover such an eventuality: the procedure must be "appropriate" and placed within the framework of the United Nations in accordance with its Charter. If this implies the right to approach the United Nations through the usual channels, then the clause is redundant.

Non-compliance and sanctions

Under the Treaty of Tlatelolco, the General Conference of the Agency for the Prohibition of Nuclear Weapons in Latin America takes note of cases in which, in its opinion, a party is not complying with its obligations, and makes such recommendations as it deems appropriate. In the event that non-compliance constitutes a violation which might endanger peace and security, the General Conference reports simultaneously to the UN Security Council and the General Assembly, and to the Council of the Organization of American States; it reports to the IAEA for such purposes as are relevant in accordance with its Statute. Cases of non-compliance with the nuclear safeguards are to be reported by the IAEA Director General to the Board of Governors which, in turn, reports these cases to the IAEA member states, as well as to the UN Security Council and General Assembly. Normally, however, complaints of breaches can be lodged directly with the UN Security Council, but they must contain evidence "confirming" their validity. A state lacking sufficiently reliable information and therefore not possessing such evidence may have its request for consideration rejected by the Council. And even if the Council agrees to discuss a charge which does not entirely satisfy the above requirement, there is always a danger that the case will not be given proper examination and will remain unresolved. The great-power veto has been used to block not only substantive decisions, but even proposals for investigation or observation, when the interests of the permanent members of the Council, or their allies, were involved.

Verification and enforcement

Moreover, a complainant may find himself in an awkward position if Council members, not party to a given treaty, are called upon to judge the conduct of the parties.[19]

In view of the above uncertainties, countries may hesitate to embark on a procedure which extends the inequality of states under the UN Charter to relations regulated by arms control agreements. The legitimate option left open is to withdraw, if there is an appropriate clause in the treaty, or to suspend the operation of the treaty with the defaulting state, according to general principles of international law. Actually, apart from obtaining an internationally recognized justification for abrogation, an injured country could not expect much from the United Nations, even if an offender has been condemned by the Security Council. In the prevailing political circumstances, a collective punitive action against a transgressor of an arms control treaty is unthinkable. And since international opprobrium, by itself, is a sanction of dubious efficacy, the threat of abrogation is the primary means of enforcing a treaty.

Other sanctions, if found politically feasible, do not necessarily need the approval of the UN Security Council to become effective. Thus, for example, the IAEA Board of Governors may, in the event of non-compliance with the safeguards agreements, direct curtailment or suspension of assistance being provided by the IAEA or by a member, and call for the return of materials and equipment made available to the recipient member or group of members. The IAEA may also, upon recommendation by its Board of Governors, suspend any non-complying member from the exercise of the privileges and rights of membership (Article XII of the IAEA Statute).[20] Similarly, the nuclear supplier states, members of the London Club, have decided that, in the event one or more of them believe that there has been a violation of supplier/recipient understandings resulting from the Guidelines for Nuclear Transfers, particularly in the case of an explosion of a nuclear device, or illegal termination or violation of IAEA safeguards by a recipient, suppliers should promptly consult through diplomatic channels in order to determine and assess the reality and extent of the alleged violation. Upon the findings of such consultations, the suppliers, bearing in mind the relevant provisions of the IAEA Statute (see above), should agree on an appropriate response and possible action which could include the termination of nuclear transfers to that recipient.

---

[19] The threat of a Chinese veto has made it impossible for the Security Council formally to assume the functions assigned to it by the BW Convention and to agree, through a special resolution, to receive, consider and act upon complaints about alleged breaches of the Convention.

[20] Somewhat more elaborate measures are provided for against violators of the control provisions under the Treaty which established the European Atomic Energy Community (Euratom). The sanctions to be imposed by the Commission of Euratom depend on the gravity of the offense, and range from a warning to the withdrawal of financial or technical assistance, to the placing of the respective enterprise under the administration—for a period not exceeding four months—of an appointed person or board, to the partial or total withdrawal of source or special fissionable materials.

A critical review of the agreements

The withdrawal or denunciation clauses in arms control agreements are not keyed specifically to violations, but to events related to the subject matter of the treaty which have jeopardized the "supreme interests" of the party in question. Under some recent agreements, notice of withdrawal must be given both to other parties and to the UN Security Council, with a statement on the events which the withdrawing party regards as having jeopardized its interests. Although this requirement has narrowed the margin for possible arbitrary action, the ultimate judge of such extraordinary events remains the government of the country considering abrogation. Nevertheless, in the absence of a formal UN verdict that a violation has been committed, a unilateral decision to withdraw from, or denounce, or suspend the operation of the treaty could be politically costly and hazardous, both domestically and internationally. To be on the safe side, a state planning abrogation but unwilling to depend on the uncertain outcome of the UN Security Council procedures would need to be in possession of convincing evidence of misdemeanour. To impress world opinion, the proof would have to be authoritatively confirmed by an impartial expert inquiry.

First steps towards separating international fact-finding from UN political judgement have been made in the Convention prohibiting the use of environmental modification techniques for hostile purposes. The ENMOD Convention stipulates that consultations to clarify problems relating to its objectives and to its application may include the services of a consultative committee of experts, to be convened upon request. The role of the committee is to establish facts and to provide expert views on issues raised by the party requesting its services. Voting on matters of substance is not allowed, but the right to decide, by majority vote, procedural questions relative to the organization of its work may enable the committee to order an inquiry. And since a summary of the findings, incorporating all views and information presented to the committee during its proceedings, is to be distributed to the parties, the prevailing range of opinions on matters of substance can be made discernible without recourse to voting. The essential point here is that experts will be given an opportunity to examine the particulars of each case and make their views widely known, irrespective of whether the case will eventually be considered by the Security Council. It would be left to the complaining country to draw its own conclusions from the information received and to decide upon further action. (Since the problem of response to violations is principally political and calls for discretion, denunciation or withdrawal may not always be resorted to, even should the other party's guilt be manifest.) The procedure described above is an improvement over previous practice, especially when compared to other agreements on the non-use of specific weapons, such as the 1925 Geneva Protocol dealing with chemical and bacteriological methods of warfare, where no mechanism has been provided to verify allegations of breaches.

The 1977 Protocol additional to the 1949 Geneva Conventions and relating

Verification and enforcement

to the protection of victims of international armed conflicts (Protocol I) also provides for the establishment of an international fact-finding commission to enquire into any facts alleged to be a "grave" breach, and to facilitate, through its good offices, the restoration of an attitude of respect for the Conventions and the Protocol.

However, the main dilemma is how the parties to multilateral arms control agreements—in particular those agreements which limit or prohibit the possession of certain weapons, and prescribe their elimination—would acquire information to justify setting in motion the consultative and investigative machineries. With the exception of nuclear non-proliferation obligations, which are checked on a continuous basis through a system of safeguards operated internationally, means of verifying compliance have been a virtual monopoly of the great powers. Because of the small disarmament value of the treaties concluded hitherto, the problem has not yet become acute. Apart from a few "technical" breaches of the Partial Test Ban Treaty, not considered fundamentally in violation of its purposes, no formal complaints have been made about compliance with the multilateral arms control agreements.[21]

Violations of the arms control agreements now in force would seem to have little impact on the security of states. If disclosed, their effect would be political rather than military and the disadvantage would be primarily for the violator rather than for the injured party. But for the more substantial treaties which may be reached in the future, procedures would have to be devised which guaranteed equal rights for all parties to ensure that the agreements function properly and that the obligations are being complied with. If a few powers continued to monopolize the means of verification, there would always be a danger that, for political or other reasons (for example, unwillingness to disclose the nature or the source of the evidence), they may deliberately overlook transgressions committed by some states to the detriment of others. It is clear that international specialized expert bodies, using modern technical means, are needed to apply control methods adapted to the type of activity prohibited.

---

[21] Since 1974, several allegations have been made of non-compliance by the parties with the 1972 bilateral US-Soviet treaties on strategic arms limitations (the ABM Treaty and the Interim Agreement). Only in one case has there been an admission of guilt: when the Soviet Union failed to meet the stipulated time-limits for dismantling the ICBM launchers of older types being replaced by new submarine-launched ballistic missile (SLBM) launchers on modern submarines. In other cases, the allegations appeared to have arisen from misunderstandings, or excessive reliance on statements which were made during the negotiations by one side, but were not accepted by the other side. A question was also raised, mainly in the Soviet and US press, as to whether the development of anti-satellite weapons was contrary to the existing arms control agreements [19]. It seems, however, that as long as nuclear weapons are not placed in orbit, the testing of "satellite killers" does not violate the letter of the Outer Space Treaty, and as long as there is no actual interference with reconnaissance satellites, the arms control treaties relying on verification from space cannot be considered to have been violated.

A critical review of the agreements

Verification institutions

Institutions dealing with the verification of arms control agreements could be either autonomous or form part of existing international agencies. Checking the implementation of the NPT by the IAEA, whose main task is to promote peaceful uses of nuclear energy, is an example of the latter approach. Comprehensive and general disarmament may require a comprehensive treatment of verification, on a global scale, to guard against risks to the vital security interests of states. This was recognized, as early as 1961, in the *Joint Statement of agreed principles for disarmament negotiations,* made by the USA and the USSR (the so-called McCloy-Zorin statement; for the text, see page 75) and approved by the UN General Assembly. One of the agreed principles stipulated that during and after the implementation of general and complete disarmament, the most thorough control should be exercised and that, to implement control over and inspection of disarmament, an International Disarmament Organization should be created within the framework of the United Nations. Accordingly, the Soviet draft treaty on general and complete disarmament, of 19 March 1962, provided that an organization of the parties to the Treaty would begin operating as soon as disarmament measures were initiated [20]. The organization would receive information about the armed forces, armaments, military production and military appropriations, supplied by the parties. It would have its own internationally recruited staff to exercise control, on a temporary or permanent basis, depending on the nature of the measure being carried out. The USA, in its proposal of 18 April 1962, envisaged the establishment of an international organization with the purpose of ensuring that all obligations were honoured and observed during and after disarmament, and requested that inspectors from the organization should have unrestricted access to all places necessary for the purpose of effective verification [21]. However, as long as arms control agreements deal with partial measures, the establishment of an overall, world-wide verification organization seems to be premature.[22]

Arms control treaties depend for their viability on the degree of openness among nations with regard to weapon production and deployment, arms transfers and military expenditures. An international organizational framework for the collection of such information exists within the United Nations, and the UN Secretariat has been given the specific task of improving the facilities for its dissemination [22]. But as long as governments cling

---

[22] In US-Soviet relations, a Standing Consultative Commission has been created to consider questions of compliance, to organize the exchange of information and to discuss proposals for increasing the viability of the bilateral arms control treaties (see Appendix E). There is no indication that in future agreements the two powers would be willing to resort to a larger forum and relegate their bilateral problems to some third-party consideration.

to a conservative view on national security, they will be reluctant to provide relevant data to an intergovernmental body, and this, in turn, will hinder progress towards genuine disarmament.

III. *The final clauses*

The language of the so-called final clauses of the multilateral arms control agreements concluded after World War II has undergone considerable change over the years. This change reflects a trend towards democratization of international affairs, in keeping with the increasing role of the small and medium-sized nations.

Parties

The 1959 Antarctic Treaty recognizes two categories of parties. The 12 signatories enjoy full rights: they are entitled to participate in consultative meetings; they have the right to carry out inspections; they may modify or amend the Treaty at any time through an agreement among themselves; they are empowered to decide whether or not non-UN members should be allowed to accede;[23] and only they may call a conference to review the operation of the Treaty. States which *accede* to the Treaty, do not have these rights, unless they conduct "substantial" scientific research activity in the Antarctic, such as the establishment of a scientific station or the dispatch of a scientific expedition. On the other hand, the original parties would maintain their privileged position even if they ceased to be actively engaged in Antarctic research. This exclusive character of the Antarctic Treaty—an unusual feature in a multilateral agreement of general import—may be one reason why relatively few states have acceded to it (see Chapter 3, section II). This may also, in the long run, affect the durability of the legal régime in Antarctica, because treaties cannot be binding on states which are not party to them, at least not until they are regarded as stating general international law, which apparently is not the case with the Antarctic Treaty.

However, since 1963, beginning with the Partial Test Ban Treaty, multilateral arms control agreements (with the exception of regional agreements) have been open for signature by all states, without qualification. Any state which has not signed an agreement before its entry into force, or during a prescribed period, may still subsequently accede to it and enjoy the same rights as the signatories. This is a recognition of the principle that, by their very nature, arms control treaties ought to have universal application.

---

[23] Romania and the German Democratic Republic have protested against this restriction, stating that it is contrary to the principle according to which multilateral treaties which affect the interests of the whole international community should be open for universal participation.

In this context the question has arisen as to whether, by subscribing to a treaty, an entity or a régime can gain recognition as a state or a government by parties which do not formally recognize it. To guard against such implications, certain countries have found it expedient to issue special declarations. Most of these declarations concern the non-recognition of the German Democratic Republic, Israel or Taiwan. The United Kingdom has formally stated and on several occasions repeated the view that if a régime is not recognized as the government of a state, neither signature nor the deposit of any instrument by it nor notification of any of those acts will bring about recognition of that régime by any other state. States could even have dealings with a non-recognized régime within the framework of multilateral treaties open for general adherence without thereby recognizing it. In fact, recognition can never be gained automatically and is primarily a matter of the intent of each recognizing state.

Depositaries

The above principle also applies to relations between a government acting as a depositary of a multilateral treaty and other governments wishing to take action in respect of the treaty, in that normally it is possible to make arrangements for such actions to be taken even if there are no diplomatic relations between these governments. However, if the depositary government denies the very right of another entity to exist or the legitimacy of its government (for example, the USA *vis-à-vis* the German Democratic Republic prior to 1973, or the USSR *vis-à-vis* the Republic of China since 1949), then such arrangements may not be feasible. The increasingly frequent solution resorted to, to have some intergovernmental organ act as depositary, may not be possible either, if the membership of the organization concerned is too divided on the acceptability of a particular entity or government. It was for such political reasons, related to the cold-war controversies rather than to the contents of the treaties, that in the early 1960s a novel device was developed: as distinct from previous treaties, which provided for a single depositary, the Partial Test Ban Treaty, the Outer Space Treaty, the Non-Proliferation Treaty, the Sea-Bed Treaty and the Biological Weapons Convention have designated three depositaries—the governments of the UK, the USA and the USSR. This device has helped to relieve the depositaries from the international obligation to act impartially in the performance of their functions under all circumstances.

A host of complications grew from this decision. The duties of treaty depositaries include accepting signatures; receiving instruments of ratification and accession; informing signatory and acceding states of the date of each signature, the date of deposit of each instrument of ratification or of accession, and the date of entry into force of the treaty; as well as receiving and circulating other notices, which may include proposals for amendment.

The final clauses

The language of the relevant paragraphs of the arms control agreements was not entirely clear on several points: whether, to be valid, the signature and the instrument of ratification or accession had to be deposited with more than one depositary; what was the official date of entry into force of the treaty for a party which had deposited its instrument of ratification or accession with the depositary governments at different dates; whether each depositary government had the duty to inform each signatory and acceding state of each signature and deposit of instrument of ratification or accession; and whether the depositary governments were under obligation to accept any such notifications. In practice, it has proved to be sufficient for a state to sign a treaty or to deposit its instrument of ratification or accession in one of the three capitals—London, Moscow or Washington—to become formally committed. This has facilitated wider adherence to agreements without embarrassing any depositary or potential party. In case of an action taken in different capitals on different dates, a frequent occurrence, it is presumed that the earliest date is the effective one.[24]

The depositaries do not feel obliged to accept a signature or a communication from an authority they do not recognize. For example, the USA had refused for a long time to accept the notification of signature and deposit of ratification in Moscow by the government of the German Democratic Republic, and considered itself exempt from the duty of transmitting to this government the information required by the treaties, without denying that the GDR was bound by the arms control agreements ratified by it. The USA also regards the signatures and ratifications by Byelorussia and Ukraine, which have joined the major multilateral arms control agreements with the exception of the NPT,[25] as included under the signature and ratification of the USSR. On the other hand, the USSR considers the deposit of the instrument of ratification by Taiwan in Washington as illegal, because it recognizes only the government of the Chinese People's Republic as the representative of China. Consequently, the official records of signatories and parties which are kept by the depositary governments differ. So far, this has not caused serious inconveniences, due to the fact that the number of countries which are not universally recognized is rather small. Be that as it may, in the present political situation the cumbersome procedure of dealing

---

[24] This is, *inter alia,* the approach taken by the US Arms Control and Disarmament Agency [23].
[25] The adherence of Byelorussia and Ukraine to the NPT would have posed inextricable problems. The two Soviet republics could not sign as nuclear weapon states, because it was generally agreed that there were only five such states in existence at the time the treaty was concluded—the USA, the USSR, the UK, France and China. Should they have adhered to the NPT as non-nuclear weapon states, they would have had to undertake not to receive the transfer of nuclear weapons, directly or indirectly, and not to manufacture or otherwise acquire these weapons. However, such undertakings on the part of Byelorussia and Ukraine are inconceivable: according to the Constitution of the USSR (Article 73, paragraph 8) the all-Union government has competence in matters of defence, while the constituent republics have not.

with three depositaries has no *raison d'être*. The countries which were most controversial in the past, the People's Republic of China and the German Democratic Republic, have already gained world-wide recognition and are members of the United Nations. Viet Nam has become a UN member as a single state, and there is a growing tendency towards recognition of both parts of divided Korea.

The more simple procedure, that of designating one depositary, has recently been restored in the agreement prohibiting environmental modification for hostile purposes (the ENMOD Convention). The task of depositary has now been given to the UN Secretary-General who, in addition, will play a role in implementing compliance procedures. The abolition of the institution of joint Soviet-British-US depositaries may facilitate the joining of arms control treaties by China and France, which as permanent members of the UN Security Council refuse to accept a status inferior to that of the other great powers.

Succession

The problem of succession to arms control agreements has not been uniformly resolved.[26] Some states, former non-self-governing territories, have officially informed the depositaries of arms control agreements that they consider themselves bound by these agreements by virtue of ratification by the power formerly responsible for their administration. Other such states have acceded to the arms control treaties without referring to the obligations previously undertaken on their behalf by the colonial power. The situation is less clear as regards states which, upon attaining independence, have made general statements of continuity to all treaties concluded by the power formerly responsible for their administration, but which have not notified the depositaries of the arms control agreements that their statements specifically apply to these agreements. In the opinion of some governments, a general statement of continuity made by a country attaining independence does not entitle the government with which an international convention has been deposited to consider that country as bound by the said convention.[27] In fact, newly independent states may not be entirely familiar with the obligations which have been contracted on their behalf. Irrespective of a general statement of continuity, they usually engage in examination of the individual treaties in order to determine whether they should formally succeed to them.

---

[26] The general question of succession of states to treaties has for years been under study in the International Law Commission, and is now the subject of a special conference convened by the UN General Assembly.
[27] This is, for example, the view of the French government, the depositary of the 1925 Geneva Protocol.

The two German states have followed the practice of officially informing the depositaries of their decisions concerning the applicability of each treaty concluded before World War II by the German Reich.

Viet Nam and Taiwan constitute special cases. The Republic of Viet Nam (South) signed the Partial Test Ban Treaty, the Outer Space Treaty, the Non-Proliferation Treaty, the Sea-Bed Treaty and the Biological Weapons Convention; it acceded to the 1949 Geneva Conventions for the protection of war victims, ratified the Non-Proliferation Treaty, and concluded a safeguards agreement with the IAEA under the NPT. The Democratic Republic of Viet Nam (North) and the Provisional Revolutionary Government of the Republic of South Viet Nam joined only the 1949 Geneva Conventions. In 1975, the Republic of Viet Nam (South) ceased to exist as a separate political entity. From 2 July 1976, North and South Viet Nam constitute a single state (the Socialist Republic of Viet Nam), and it is now up to the government of this unified country to decide whether it will abide by the international commitments undertaken by the former régimes.

Taiwan (the Republic of China) is party to the Partial Test Ban Treaty, the Outer Space Treaty, the Non-Proliferation Treaty, the Sea-Bed Treaty and the Biological Weapons Convention. It occupied the seat of China at the United Nations until 25 October 1971, on which date the UN General Assembly conferred the right of representation on the People's Republic of China and recognized the representatives of the PRC government as the only legitimate representatives of China to the United Nations. Since then, Taiwan has been excluded from all UN bodies. Most governments do not consider Taiwan as a legal entity separate from China.

A problem may arise over possible succession to the Non-Proliferation Treaty by a federation of West European states, should such a federation be created according to the existing proposals. For the purposes of the NPT, only a country which has manufactured and exploded a nuclear weapon or other nuclear explosive device prior to 1 January 1967 is to be considered a nuclear weapon state (Article IX). Since a European federated state would be established after this cut-off date, it would have to be regarded as a non-nuclear weapon power. On the other hand, the new state could succeed to the nuclear status of those component nations that were nuclear weapon powers prior to 1 January 1967 (France and the UK). The nuclear distinction is very important, because the NPT provides for different rights and obligations for the two categories of nations.

Entry into force

Having signed but not ratified a treaty subject to ratification, a state is generally considered obligated to refrain from acts which would defeat the object and purpose of the treaty, until such times as it has made its intention clear not to become party to it.[28] The number of ratifications necessary for an arms control treaty to enter into force is usually related to the nature of the prohibition, or the limitation, it contains. Thus, the Antarctic Treaty, which was negotiated among and signed by 12 countries, all active in Antarctica, required the deposit of instruments of ratification by all these countries. The Partial Test Ban Treaty became effective upon its ratification by the original parties—the UK, the USA and the USSR—three of the four powers which were at that time engaged in nuclear weapon testing. (France, another nuclear weapon state, refused to negotiate, and China exploded its first nuclear device only a year later.) For the Outer Space Treaty, ratification by five governments was needed. These had to include the governments of the USA, the USSR and the UK, even though only the first two powers were conducting significant activities in outer space at the time the Treaty was signed.

Under the Treaty prohibiting nuclear weapons in Latin America (Treaty of Tlatelolco), the following requirements must be met for its entry into force among the states that have ratified it: (*a*) deposit of the instruments of ratification by the governments of all the Latin American republics and all other sovereign states situated in their entirety south of latitude 35° north in the western hemisphere, which were in existence on the date when the Treaty was opened for signature; (*b*) signature and ratification of Additional Protocol I, annexed to the Treaty, by all extra-continental or continental states having *de jure* or *de facto* international responsibility for territories situated in the zone of application of the Treaty; (*c*) signature and ratification of Additional Protocol II, annexed to the Treaty, by all powers possessing nuclear weapons; and (*d*) conclusion of bilateral or multilateral agreements on the application of the safeguards system of the International Atomic Energy Agency. But all signatory states have the right to waive, wholly or in part, the above requirements. They may do so by means of a declaration annexed to the instrument of ratification or made subsequently. For those states which exercise this right, the Treaty enters into force upon deposit of the declaration, or as soon as the requirements which have not been expressly waived have been met. As a consequence of this provision, the Treaty entered into force as soon as two countries (Mexico and El Salvador) ratified it, waiving wholly the specified requirements. By 1977, 20 additional countries have made use of the waiver. Only Brazil and Chile, which ratified the Treaty in 1968 and 1974, respectively, have so far refused to do so and are, therefore, still not bound by its provisions.

The Treaty of Tlatelolco stipulates that after its entry into force for all the countries of the zone, the rise of a new power "possessing" nuclear

---

[28] Compare Article 18 of the 1969 Vienna Convention on the Law of Treaties. (The Convention will enter into force upon ratification or accession by 35 states. By September 1977, 31 states had become parties.)

weapons shall have the effect of suspending the execution of the Treaty for those countries which have ratified it without waiving the requirement that Additional Protocol II annexed to the Treaty should be signed and ratified by all powers possessing nuclear weapons, and which request such suspension. The Treaty would remain suspended until the new power ratified Protocol II. It was probably with a view to preventing such an occurrence that, after the 1974 Indian nuclear explosion, the General Secretary of the Agency for the Prohibition of Nuclear Weapons in Latin America indicated that he was expecting India to join the Protocol [24]. However, India denied that it possessed a nuclear weapon, asserting that the nuclear explosion it had conducted was intended for peaceful purposes.

The Protocols additional to the Treaty of Tlatelolco have a simple procedure: they enter into force upon deposit of the respective instruments of ratification.

The Non-Proliferation Treaty, which imposed obligations mainly on non-nuclear weapon states, required ratification by 40 states, in addition to the three nuclear weapon powers that are depositaries of the Treaty.

The Sea-Bed Treaty and the Biological Weapons Convention entered into force after the deposit of the instruments of ratification by 22 governments, which number again had to include the UK, the USA and the USSR. The Environmental Modification Convention, signed in 1977, will become effective upon ratification by 20 governments, but does not require that this number include any particular nation. However, it is obvious that without the participation of the technically most advanced states, this convention, as well as any other agreement dealing with sophisticated types of weapons, would not be meaningful. Conventions of a humanitarian nature do not need to follow the same pattern. The 1925 Geneva Protocol prohibiting the use of chemical and bacteriological methods of warfare entered into force upon the deposit of two instruments of ratification. This was also the case with the 1949 Geneva Conventions for the protection of war victims, and a similar procedure will apply to Protocols I and II to these Conventions, which were signed in December 1977.[29]

Amendments and reservations

The arms control treaties now in force may be modified by a number of different procedures. The Antarctic Treaty may be amended at any time by unanimous agreement of the parties, excluding those which have acceded to the Treaty but do not conduct substantial scientific research in Antarctica. The Partial Test Ban Treaty provides for a two-stage amending process. At the first stage, the amendment must be approved by a majority, including all

---

[29] The 1948 Genocide Convention is, in this respect, an exception. It came into force on the ninetieth day following the date of deposit of the twentieth instrument of ratification or accession.

the original parties, that is, the UK, the USA and the USSR.[30] At the second stage, when the instruments of ratification of the amendment have been deposited by a majority, including the original parties, the amendment enters into force for all parties, that is, even for those who oppose it. In other words, an amendment adopted by a majority can be automatically imposed upon a dissenting minority, though the latter could never include an original party. Thus the three nuclear powers have reserved the right of veto on any changes.

Such patently discriminatory amendment clauses have not appeared in subsequent arms control agreements. The NPT, concluded five years after the Partial Test Ban Treaty, has weakened the privileges of the great powers by requiring that a majority approving an amendment should include not only the votes of nuclear weapon states party to the Treaty, but also those of other parties which are members of the Board of Governors of the International Atomic Energy Agency. One could question the wisdom of extending the veto power over amendments to those nations that happen to be members of the IAEA Board of Governors at the time the amendment is to be approved (a power they do not enjoy in the IAEA itself); nevertheless, the curtailment of the exclusive rights of the nuclear powers has been a progressive step. Under the NPT, an amendment enters into force upon ratification by a majority including the above-mentioned states, but cannot be imposed on others. For each party it becomes effective only upon the deposit of its instrument of ratification of the amendment—an important provision in an agreement dealing with national security matters.

As a result of pressure exercised by smaller nations, the nuclear weapon powers' prerogatives concerning possible modifications of treaty provisions have been abolished altogether in recent arms control agreements: amendments enter into force for each party accepting the amendments upon their acceptance by a majority of the parties (without qualification) and thereafter for each remaining party only on the date of acceptance by it.[31]

Many arms control treaties provide for review conferences to assure that their purposes and provisions are being realized. Two such conferences have already been held: one in 1975 concerning the NPT, and another in 1977 concerning the Sea-Bed Treaty. They offer an opportunity for the parties to urge improvements in the operation of the agreements and the fulfilment of the non-implemented provisions. They have also stimulated,

---

[30] In this respect, the rights of the great powers exceed even those provided for in the amendment process of the UN Charter (Article 108). The permanent members of the Security Council do not have a veto in the first stage of this process, when the Charter amendment has to be adopted by vote of two-thirds of the members of the General Assembly. They can prevent the coming into force of an amendment only at the ratification stage, namely by refraining from ratifying.
[31] See Article XV of the Outer Space Treaty, Article VI of the Sea-Bed Treaty, Article XI of the Biological Weapons Convention, and Article VI of the Environmental Modification Convention.

especially in the case of the NPT, wider adherence to the treaties in question.[32]

The multilateral arms control treaties hitherto concluded are to remain in force indefinitely. The exceptions include the Antarctic Treaty, which has a duration of at least 30 years, and the NPT, which 25 years after its entry into force may be extended for an indefinite period or for an additional fixed period.

According to the existing practice, a state may, when signing, ratifying or acceding to a multilateral treaty, formulate a reservation, unless the reservation is prohibited by the treaty, or the treaty provides that only specified reservations, which do not include the reservation in question, may be made, or the reservation is incompatible with the object and purpose of the treaty. Many states have made reservations with regard to the 1925 Geneva Protocol, the 1948 Genocide Convention, or the 1949 Geneva Conventions. Some of these reservations have been objected to.[33] Relatively few reservations have been made with respect to arms control agreements concluded in recent years. But in statements of understanding or interpretation attached to the signatures or ratifications, some states have reserved their positions on a number of important issues. This was the case even under the Treaty of Tlatelolco which has explicitly ruled out reservations. (For the status of the implementation of multilateral arms control agreements and for reservations and statements of understanding or interpretation of these agreements, see Chapter 3.)

IV. *The negotiating machinery*

Progress, or lack of progress, in the field of arms control is determined mainly by national interests. Policy decisions are a function of interaction among various sectors of each government, and in the course of arms control negotiations each side tries, in the first place, to enlist the support of its own (as well as of its allies') political and military establishments. The outcome depends to a great extent on the general political climate in the world. Procedures for conducting negotiations are less important in this context, but adequate institutional mechanisms may further the pursued cause.

---

[32] The US-Soviet ABM Treaty also requires that a periodic review should be conducted by the parties. The first such review took place in November 1977.
[33] In 1951, the International Court of Justice was asked by the UN General Assembly for an advisory opinion on the legal effect of reservations to the Genocide Convention. The opinion issued was that a state which has made and maintained a reservation which has been objected to by one or more of the parties to the Convention, but not by others, can be regarded as being a party to the Convention if the reservation is compatible with the object and purpose of the Convention. The Court further stated that if a party to the Convention objects to a reservation which it considers to be incompatible with the object and purpose of the Convention, it can in fact consider that the reserving state is not a party to the Convention [25].

A critical review of the agreements

The United Nations

Since the creation of the United Nations in 1945, the UN General Assembly—the most widely representative of the UN organs—has been the principal forum for international policy debate. The subjects of these debates invariably include arms control and disarmament issues, which are dealt with primarily in the First (Political) Committee but also in other main General Assembly committees or directly in the plenary sessions without recourse to subsidiary bodies.

The UN General Assembly serves as a sounding-board for new ideas and proposals, which are usually incorporated in draft General Assembly resolutions requiring for their adoption a two-thirds majority of the members present and voting. The General Assembly also receives reports about ongoing multilateral negotiations and attempts to influence the talks by making specific recommendations. These recommendations have no mandatory character, but do carry some political and moral weight, especially when made unanimously. (A summary of the major resolutions adopted in the Disarmament Decade of the 1970s and the voting record are presented in Appendix B.) Essentially, however, the UN General Assembly is a deliberative body which provides a forum for official statements as well as for informal discussions.

The UN Security Council has as one of its statutory responsibilities the formulation of plans for the establishment of a system for the regulation of armaments. It is to be assisted in this work by the Military Staff Committee, consisting of the chiefs of staff of the permanent members of the Council or their representatives (Articles 26 and 47 of the UN Charter). In the early post-war period the Security Council was actively engaged in arms control discussions, but since the 1950s its role in this field has diminished. It has never requested assistance from the Military Staff Committee. Nevertheless, in the context of its responsibility for the maintenance of international peace and security, the UN Security Council has been assigned a role in several arms control agreements, mainly in dealing with complaints about breaches of obligations contracted under these agreements.

During the past 30 years a number of other UN bodies have been established to deal with disarmament issues. Some of them ceased to function upon completion of their tasks, while ohers adjourned *sine die* or were simply dissolved. By the end of 1977, a few such bodies were still in existence.

The UN Disarmament Commission, set up by the General Assembly in 1952 with a limited membership [26], and expanded in 1959 to include all UN members [27], was originally entrusted with the task of preparing proposals for the regulation, limitation and reduction of armed forces and armaments, and for the elimination of weapons of mass destruction. Subsequently, however, the Commission became a multilateral forum for discussion rather than negotiation. It has not met since 1965.

For more than 22 years, the UN Scientific Committee on the Effects of Atomic Radiation (UNSCEAR) has been dealing with a question closely related to the cessation of nuclear weapon tests. The specific task of this committee is to assemble, study and disseminate information on observed levels of ionizing radiation and radioactivity in the environment and on the effects of such radiation upon man and his environment. The composition of UNSCEAR is as follows: Argentina, Australia, Belgium, Brazil, Canada, Czechoslovakia, Egypt, France, the Federal Republic of Germany, India, Indonesia, Japan, Mexico, Peru, Poland, Sudan, Sweden, the United Kingdom, the USA, and the USSR.

A few UN bodies have been established *ad hoc* for specific issues related to arms control. One *ad hoc* committee is studying the implications of the 1971 General Assembly resolution which declared the Indian Ocean a zone of peace. Its membership includes Australia, Bangladesh, China, Democratic Yemen, Ethiopia, Greece, India, Indonesia, Iran, Iraq, Japan, Kenya, Madagascar, Malaysia, Mauritius, Mozambique, Oman, Pakistan, Somalia, Sri Lanka, the United Republic of Tanzania, Yemen, and Zambia. Another *ad hoc* committee is examining the views and suggestions expressed by governments on the convening of a World Disarmament Conference. This committee consists of Algeria, Argentina, Austria, Belgium, Brazil, Bulgaria, Burundi, Canada, Chile, Colombia, Czechoslovakia, Egypt, Ethiopia, Hungary, India, Indonesia, Iran, Italy, Japan, Lebanon, Liberia, Mexico, Mongolia, Morocco, the Netherlands, Nigeria, Pakistan, Peru, the Philippines, Poland, Romania, Spain, Sri Lanka, Sweden, Tunisia, Turkey, Venezuela, Yugoslavia, Zaire, and Zambia. States possessing nuclear weapons have been invited to co-operate or maintain contact with this committee.

There are also disarmament forums outside the UN framework, both bilateral (US-Soviet) and multilateral. In the latter category, a conference to negotiate the "mutual reduction of forces and armaments and associated measures in Central Europe" has been meeting since 1973. Eleven states, with indigenous or stationed forces in Central Europe, are full participants in the conference—the USA, Canada, the UK, the Federal Republic of Germany, Belgium, the Netherlands and Luxembourg, on the NATO side; and the USSR, the German Democratic Republic, Czechoslovakia and Poland, on the WTO (Warsaw Treaty Organization) side. Eight additional countries have special observer status—Denmark, Greece, Italy, Norway, Turkey, Bulgaria, Romania and Hungary. A second forum devoted to European matters, the Conference on Security and Co-operation in Europe (33 European states plus Canada and the USA), deals with confidence-building measures and questions related to disarmament, in accordance with the Final Act of the Conference, of 1 August 1975.

A critical review of the agreements

Another regional body, the Agency for the Prohibition of Nuclear Weapons in Latin America, was created by the parties to the 1967 Treaty of Tlatelolco. It holds consultations among member states on matters relating to the purposes, measures and procedures set forth in the Treaty and is responsible for supervision of compliance with obligations arising therefrom.

The CCD

The central institution dealing with multilateral arms control is at present the Conference of the Committee on Disarmament (CCD), which holds its sessions in Geneva. Set up as the Eighteen Nation Disarmament Committee (ENDC) in 1961, it was subsequently enlarged and re-named in 1969. Unlike their predecessor, the Ten-Nation Disarmament Committee (which had been established by a decision of the foreign ministers of France, the UK, the USA and the USSR in 1959, and met from March to June 1960), the ENDC and later the CCD included not only NATO and WTO countries, but also non-aligned states. In 1977, the membership of the CCD included Argentina, Brazil, Bulgaria, Burma, Canada, Czechoslovakia, Egypt, Ethiopia, the German Democratic Republic, the Federal Republic of Germany, Hungary, India, Iran, Italy, Japan, Mexico, Mongolia, Morocco, the Netherlands, Nigeria, Pakistan, Peru, Poland, Romania, Sweden, the USSR, the UK, the USA, Yugoslavia, and Zaire. France is also a member of the Committee, but has so far not participated in its work.

Technically, the CCD is not a UN body; the General Assembly has merely endorsed a US-Soviet agreement concerning its creation [28]. Nevertheless, it is serviced by the UN Secretariat and submits reports to the General Assembly which, in turn, requests the negotiators to take up or devote special attention to certain issues.

The CCD was established to discuss primarily general and complete disarmament [29]. Fairly soon, however, its interest shifted to partial, so-called collateral measures. Several multilateral arms control agreements have been negotiated there, namely: the Non-Proliferation Treaty, the Sea-Bed Treaty, the Biological Weapons Convention, and the Environmental Modification Convention. The Partial Test Ban Treaty, which resulted from trilateral talks held in 1963 among the UK, the USA and the USSR, had been preceded by intensive multilateral negotiations in the CCD. The CCD agenda adopted in 1968 includes the following items [30]: (*a*) further effective measures relating to the cessation of the nuclear arms race at an early date and nuclear disarmament; (*b*) non-nuclear measures; (*c*) other collateral measures; and (*d*) general and complete disarmament under strict and effective international control.

Under the first item, the CCD may discuss measures dealing with the cessation of testing, the non-use of nuclear weapons, the cessation of manufacture of weapons, the reduction and subsequent elimination of nuclear stockpiles, nuclear-free zones, and so on; under the second heading—chemical and biological warfare, regional arms limitations, and so on; under the third heading—prevention of an arms race on the sea-bed, and so on. The agenda of the CCD is open-ended, giving delegations the right to raise and discuss any disarmament subject.

Negotiations in the CCD take place at formal or informal plenary meetings, or in *ad hoc* working groups, all closed to the public and the press. To clarify technical problems, meetings of experts are arranged, sometimes with the participation of scientists from non-CCD member states. There is no voting in the CCD. While decisions, both procedural and substantive, are adopted by consensus, dissenting opinions may be written into the annual report. Once the text of a treaty has been worked out by the CCD, it is transmitted to the UN General Assembly, often with a request to have it recommended for signature and ratification by the UN member states.

The all-embracing character of its agenda and the flexibility of its procedures have contributed little to the efficacy of the CCD. Since the USA and the USSR bilaterally discuss strategic nuclear arms limitation and related issues, and even such non-nuclear matters as limitations of conventional arms transfers, the range of measures to be negotiated multilaterally has shrunk considerably. Moreover, as a body, the CCD does not initiate discussions of specific measures. Rather, the USA and the USSR usually decide which items should become the subject of regular multilateral talks. Only after these two powers have reached agreement on the basic provisions of a treaty to be concluded may the Conference negotiate the details. Proposals for substantive changes in the bilaterally agreed clauses are, as a rule, jointly resisted by the USA and the USSR.

In recent years, attempts have been made to improve the work of the existing deliberative bodies, by making it less diffuse and more goal-oriented. These attempts are reflected in proposals for streamlining the proceedings of the regular General Assembly sessions and, particularly, in the decision to convene, in 1978, a UN General Assembly special session devoted to disarmament, with a prospect of having such sessions, or world disarmament conferences, convened also in the future. The envisaged function of these large meetings is to formulate principles governing disarmament negotiations, to establish a programme of action and to assess its implementation. Of primary importance, however, is the operation of the machinery for negotiating specific agreements. Since 1976, there have been a few positive developments in this respect. The CCD has introduced improvements of a procedural character, relating to the schedule of its sessions, preparation of reports, contents of its communiqués and distribution of documents. It has also established rules for *ad hoc* groups working out draft treaties or other texts. But the necessary structural modifications have not, as yet, taken place. The existent negotiating machinery still suffers from a number of shortcomings.

A critical review of the agreements

The link with the United Nations

The loose relationship of the CCD with the United Nations is considered by most countries as objectionable. Since one of the main purposes of the United Nations is to prevent and remove threats to the peace, there is no justification for restricting its functions to exhortations or recommendations where arms control and disarmament are concerned. The UN is expected to carry the responsibility for, and be directly involved in, all multilateral arms control negotiations which concern the community of nations as a whole. Neither should the UN be excluded from talks in more restricted forums, in so far as their outcome may affect other nations as well. In other words, there is good reason for strengthening the role of the United Nations in the field of disarmament.

Though desirable in many respects, a close link between a multilateral disarmament body and the UN should not necessarily mean that all UN rules of procedure, including voting, are automatically to be applied. In matters of security, attempts at imposing the will of the majority on a dissenting minority, through procedural devices, are usually fruitless, and may even be counter-productive. It would, therefore, seem preferable to maintain the requirement of consensus among negotiators.

Structure of the negotiating body

It is generally considered that, to function effectively, a body which works out treaty texts should not be too large. It is difficult, however, to determine where the borderline for the number of participants actually lies. Experience has shown that the present size of the CCD, that is, approximately 30 members, is adequate, although a slight expansion of the membership would appear to be tolerable. The problem with such a limitation is that non-members are prevented from making contributions or having a say on matters which may involve their national interests. In fact, treaties agreed to in the CCD have often been submitted to the remaining members of the UN for approval, practically on a take-it-or-leave-it basis. This shortcoming could perhaps be remedied by adopting certain procedures—either individually or jointly. For example, the membership of the negotiating committee could comprise permanent participants, which would include the militarily most significant states, as well as non-permanent participants, subject to rotation with other states, with the understanding that, in view of the amount of expertise necessary to negotiate arms control measures, the rotation would not take place too often. Another possibility would be to keep all UN members informed, currently and in detail, about the ongoing talks, and invite them to present their views or proposals, either in writing or orally. But to avoid diluting the singular character of the negotiating body, the rights of non-members would have clearly to be circumscribed.

Yet another possibility would be to revitalize the UN Disarmament Commission and entrust it with the task of examining and possibly amending the drafts agreed to in the negotiating body, before the final texts are submitted to the General Assembly for approval.

Chairmanship

The chairmanship of the CCD is now assumed jointly, and on a permanent basis, by the USA and the USSR. [31]. (At individual meetings, the chair is rotated in alphabetical order among all CCD members, but the role of the chairman of the day has been reduced to recognizing the speakers and reading out the communiqués.) The co-chairmanship was established in the early 1960s, in recognition of the special position of the two most powerful nations in the field of armaments, and as a realization of the fact that their consent was indispensable in reaching agreement on meaningful arms control measures.

At the initial stage, the institution of US-Soviet co-chairmanship was helpful in smoothing out the conduct of business and in facilitating informal work at the CCD, but its usefulness has diminished and is no longer well suited to current political circumstances. Indeed, it is now deemed to be an obstacle in drawing China and France into the negotiating process. The question of chairmanship in the CCD can be solved by applying the pattern of existing UN organs, or another formula concordant with the democratic principle of the sovereign equality of nations. This relatively modest change would not, and could not, affect the role which the USA and the USSR are called upon to play in bringing about disarmament by virtue of their political and military standing in the world.

Additional structural innovations may be required to enable the negotiating machinery, be it the CCD or a new body,[34] to perform its functions properly. These could include permanent sub-committees to deal with several issues simultaneously. However, in addition to new working methods, it is essential to define in more precise terms than hitherto the tasks of the negotiators and to establish a concrete agenda for their work. This will become possible when a coherent programme of disarmament has been agreed upon at the highest possible level, specifying consecutive steps to be taken in a logical and politically realistic order.

V. Conclusions

The idea of controlling the weapons of war has a strong appeal in a world troubled by tension, insecurity and the growing threat of annihilation. In and

---

[34] In January 1978, the French government proposed that the CCD should be replaced by a new negotiating forum.

of itself, arms control cannot remove the motives for acquiring arms, but it may help to reduce suspicion and improve relations among states; to minimize the risks of war by accident or miscalculation, or even by design; to narrow the disparity between heavily and lightly armed states; to mitigate the scope of destruction and suffering in armed conflicts; to save resources for economic and social development; to diminish the dangers to the human environment; and to pave the way towards a more secure world. For these reasons arms control has become part and parcel of multilateral diplomacy and a focus of international attention.

It is sometimes argued that unilateral cuts or restraints in the acquisition of arms are preferable to formal international agreements. The arguments run as follows: unilateral decisions arouse less bureaucratic opposition within the countries concerned than do inter-state treaties; in the process of negotiations each side usually tries to improve its bargaining position through the development or deployment of weapons that it would not otherwise have undertaken, thereby stimulating arms competition rather than abating it; and arms control agreements may sometimes provide justification or an excuse for embarking on new weapon programmes which are not covered by the agreements.

Unilateral measures are certainly feasible where states perceive no specific military threat and can take action without requiring reciprocity. Unilateral cuts in arms could also be made by states with substantial "over-kill" capacity, which would apply, in the first place, to the USA and the USSR. However, significant unilateral cuts are politically unlikely for most nations. Normally, a country embarking on arms reductions would expect similar responses from other nations. Reciprocal restraints assumed without formal treaty commitments—and there are many areas where this could be done without risk to the security of respective nations—would usefully supplement the present, more conventional means of achieving arms control, but could not replace them. Limitations resulting from parallel moves would need to be codified in treaties to become durable and enforceable. A treaty defines the range of prohibited activities and gives the prohibition the force of law. It inhibits certain government decisions and neutralizes those forces within each state which would otherwise urge new arms acquisitions. Moreover, abrogation of a legally binding commitment is more complicated and hazardous than reversing a unilateral undertaking.

The arms control treaties hitherto reached have made a contribution to better understanding among nations, but have failed in a most essential respect: they have not halted the arms race or reduced the military potential of states. The choice of arms control measures has been haphazard; in many cases, the weapons prohibited have had little, if any, military importance, and the outlawed activities have never been seriously contemplated as methods of war. Negotiations have not kept pace with advancing military technology and rising levels of armaments. It may well be that the very tactic of discussing small, "easy-to-achieve", unrelated steps meant to produce incremental effects, is fallacious and needs to be revised in favour of a more integrated approach.

One could conceive of comprehensive, balanced "packages" of measures, comprising quantitative across-the-board reductions and qualitative limitations of both conventional and non-conventional armaments, as well as restrictions on the deployment and transfer of weapons. The significance of such packages would be enhanced if they provided for prohibitions of certain specific categories of arms, since the clandestine or speedy development of a conventional or nuclear weapon capability could hardly be made from a zero base, that is, after the destruction of stockpiles and the cessation of production. Also, no-first-use or even unconditional no-use undertakings might usefully be included since there is less incentive to develop or maintain weapons with an uncertain future. Cuts in military expenditures could be effected simultaneously with cuts in arms manufacture or other military activity. This would be beneficial not only from the economic point of view but also as an additional check that the agreed measures were actually implemented.

An integrated approach might well improve the security of states in a more equitable way, and give better guarantees against unilateral advantages, than piecemeal arms control. This implies that the main emphasis ought to be placed on multilateral negotiations. The United Nations provides a natural framework for such negotiations.

Arms control, even when comprehensive in scope, presupposes the continued existence of national military establishments. It does not require radical changes in the present world order, because it makes no claim to abolish war. However, the ultimate goal of all peaceful endeavours is to abolish the use of force in inter-state relations by eliminating the very instruments of war. Complete world-wide disarmament would require international structures guaranteeing the security of states and allowing them to relinquish the prerogative of providing for their own defence. The necessary institutions of a lasting peace—the building blocs of a new political order—could gradually develop, beginning with an effective machinery for keeping and enforcing peace and settling international disputes, simultaneously with meaningful, comprehensive arms control measures.

References

1. UN document S/C. 3/SC. 3/7/Rev.1.
2. UN General Assembly resolution 41(I).
3. *Nature,* Vol. 269, 20 October 1977, p. 639.
4. London Press Service, Verbatim Service VS 216/14, 14 October 1977.
5. *New York Times,* 18 August 1976.

6. UN document A/RES/1884(XVIII).
7. Disarmament Conference document CCD/476.
8. Final Declaration of the Review Conference of the parties to the Treaty on the Non-Proliferation of Nuclear Weapons, Review Conference document NPT/CONF/35/I, Annex I.
9. *World Armaments and Disarmament, SIPRI Yearbook 1977* (Stockholm, Almqvist & Wiksell, 1977, Stockholm International Peace Research Institute).
10. UN Security Council resolution No. 255.
11. UN document S/PV.1430.
12. Disarmament Conference document CCD/PV.655.
13. Disarmament Conference document CCD/PV.659.
14. Disarmament Conference document CCD/PV.666.
15. Disarmament Conference documents ENDC/PV.2; ENDC/30; ENDC/70; ENDC/2/Rev. 1 and Corr. 1; and UN document A.C.1/867.
16. UN document A/RES/2603A/XXIV.
17. US Executive Order 11850, Renunciation of Certain Uses in War of Chemical Herbicides and Riot Control Agents, April 8, 1975, 40 Federal Register 16187.
18. Conference of Government Experts on the Use of Certain Conventional Weapons (Lucerne, 24.9–18.10 1974), Report, International Committee of the Red Cross, Geneva 1975; Conference of Government Experts on the Use of Certain Conventional Weapons (Second Session—Lugano, 28.1–26.2 1976), Report, International Committee of the Red Cross, Geneva 1976.
19. *Krasnaya Zvezda*, 24 September 1977; and *U.S. News and World Report*, 14 November 1977.
20. Disarmament Conference document ENDC/2.
21. Disarmament Conference document ENDC/30.
22. UN General Assembly resolution 31/90.
23. *Arms Control and Disarmament Agreements*, Texts and History of Negotiations (US Arms Control and Disarmament Agency, Washington, June 1977).
24. Report to the Preparatory Committee for the NPT Review Conference, 19 August 1974, NPT/PC.II/9.
25. *International Court of Justice, Reports of Judgments*, Advisory Opinions and Orders, 1951.
26. UN document A/RES/502(VI).
27. UN document A/RES/1403(XIV).
28. UN document A/RES/1722(XVI).
29. Disarmament Conference document ENDC/1/Add.1.
30. Disarmament Conference document ENDC/PV.390.
31. Disarmament Conference document ENDC/1.

2. Multilateral arms control agreements

This chapter reproduces in full, or in part, those documents agreed to by more than two states and which relate to arms control in the broad sense of this term (see the discussion in the Introduction). It consists of two sections: section I contains the texts of the pre-World War II agreements relevant to the topics discussed in Chapter 1, while section II consists of a comprehensive collection of such agreements concluded during the post-World War II period.

Each agreement is followed by a list of parties, with the exception of the 1925 Geneva Protocol and the eight major post-war treaties (that is, the Antarctic Treaty, the Partial Test Ban Treaty, the Outer Space Treaty, the Treaty of Tlatelolco, the Non-Proliferation Treaty, the Sea-Bed Treaty, the BW Convention, and the ENMOD Convention), since the parties to these agreements are listed in the presentation of the status of their implementation in Chapter 3.

I. Selected pre-World War II agreements

THE DECLARATION OF ST. PETERSBURG

Signed on 29 November*/11 December 1868.
Entered into force on 29 November*/11 December 1868.

Upon the invitation of the Imperial Cabinet of Russia, an international military commission having been assembled at St. Petersburg in order to consider the desirability of forbidding the use of certain projectiles in time of war among civilized nations, and this commission having fixed by a common accord the technical limits within which the necessities of war ought to yield to the demands of humanity, the undersigned have been authorized by the orders of their Governments to declare as follows:

Considering that the progress of civilization should have the effect of alleviating, as much as possible the calamities of war:

That the only legitimate object which states should endeavor to accomplish during war is to weaken the military force of the enemy;

That for this purpose, it is sufficient to disable the greatest possible number of men;

That this object would be exceeded by the employment of arms which uselessly aggravate the sufferings of disabled men, or render their death inevitable;

That the employment of such arms would, therefore, be contrary to the laws of humanity;

The contracting parties engage, mutually, to renounce, in case of war among themselves, the employment by their military or naval forces, of any projectile of less weight than four hundred grammes, which is explosive, or is charged with fulminating or inflammable substances.

They agree to invite all the states which have not taken part in the deliberations of the International Military Commission, assembled at St. Petersburg, by sending delegates thereto, to accede to the present engagement.

This engagement is obligatory only upon the contracting or acceding parties thereto, in case of war between two or more of themselves; it is not applicable with regard to non-contracting powers, or powers that shall not have acceded to it.

It will also cease to be obligatory from the moment when, in a war between contracting or acceding parties, a non-contracting party, or a non-acceding party, shall join one of the belligerents.

The contracting or acceding parties reserve to themselves the right to come to an understanding, hereafter, whenever a precise proposition shall be drawn up, in view of future improvements which may be effected in the armament of troops, in order to maintain the principles which they have established, and to reconcile the necessities of war with the laws of humanity.

Done at St. Petersburg, November 29 (December 11), 1868.

---

* Date according to the Gregorian Calendar.

Source: "Official Documents", *Supplement to the American Journal of International Law*, Vol. I, published for the American Society of International Law (Baker, Voorhis & Co., New York, 1907).

The Declaration of St. Petersburg has been signed or acceded to by Austria-Hungary, Baden, Bavaria, Belgium, Brazil, Denmark, France, Great Britain, Greece, Italy, Netherlands, Persia, Portugal, Prussia and the North German Confederation, Russia, Sweden and Norway, Switzerland, Turkey, and Württemberg.

DECLARATION (IV,2) CONCERNING ASPHYXIATING GASES

Signed at The Hague on 29 July 1899.
Entered into force on 4 September 1900.
Depositary: Netherlands government.

The undersigned, plenipotentiaries of the Powers represented at the International Peace Conference at The Hague, duly authorized to that effect by their Governments, inspired by the sentiments which found expression in the Declaration of St. Petersburg of the 29th November (11th December), 1868,
Declare as follows:
The contracting Powers agree to abstain from the use of projectiles the sole object of which is the diffusion of asphyxiating or deleterious gases.
The present Declaration is only binding on the contracting Powers in the case of a war between two or more of them.
It shall cease to be binding from the time when, in a war between the contracting Powers, one of the belligerents shall be joined by a non-contracting Power.
The present Declaration shall be ratified as soon as possible.
The ratifications shall be deposited at The Hague.
A *procès-verbal* shall be drawn up on the receipt of each ratification, a copy of which, duly certified, shall be sent through the diplomatic channel to all the contracting Powers.
The non-signatory Powers can adhere to the present Declaration. For this purpose they must make their adhesion known to the contracting Powers by means of a written notification addressed to the Netherland Government, and by it communicated to all the other contracting Powers.
In the event of one of the high contracting Parties denouncing the present Declaration, such denunciation shall not take effect until a year after the notification made in writing to the Government of the Netherlands, and forthwith communicated by it to all the other contracting Powers.
This denunciation shall only affect the notifying Power.

In faith of which the plenipotentiaries have signed the present Declaration, and affixed their seals thereto.
Done at The Hague, the 29th July, 1899, in a single copy, which shall be kept in the archives of the Netherland Government, and copies of which, duly certified, shall be sent by the diplomatic channel to the contracting Powers.

Source: Scott, J. B. (Ed.), *The Hague Conventions and Declarations of 1899 and 1907*, 2nd ed. (Oxford University Press, New York, 1915).

This Declaration has been ratified or acceded to by: Austria-Hungary, Belgium, Bulgaria, China, Denmark, Ethiopia, France, Germany, Great Britain, Greece, Italy, Japan, Luxembourg, Mexico, Montenegro, Netherlands, Nicaragua, Persia, Portugal, Romania, Russia, Serbia, Siam, Spain, Sweden and Norway, Switzerland, and Turkey.

DECLARATION (IV,3) CONCERNING EXPANDING BULLETS

Signed at The Hague on 29 July 1899.
Entered into force on 4 September 1900.
Depositary: Netherlands government.

The undersigned, plenipotentiaries of the Powers represented at the International Peace Conference at The Hague, duly authorized to that effect by their Governments, inspired by the sentiments which found expression in the Declaration of St. Petersburg of the 29th November (11th December), 1868,
Declare as follows:
The contracting Parties agree to abstain from the use of bullets which expand or flatten easily in the human body, such as bullets with a hard envelope which does not entirely cover the core or is pierced with incisions.
The present Declaration is only binding for the contracting Powers in the case of a war between two or more of them.
It shall cease to be binding from the time when, in a war between the contracting Powers, one of the belligerents is joined by a non-contracting Power.
The present Declaration shall be ratified as soon as possible.
The ratification shall be deposited at The Hague.
A *procès-verbal* shall be drawn up on the receipt of each ratification, a copy of which, duly certified, shall be sent through the diplomatic channel to all the contracting Powers.
The non-signatory Powers may adhere to the present Declaration. For this purpose they must make their adhesion known to the contracting Powers by means of a written notification addressed to the Netherland Government, and by it communicated to all the other contracting Powers.
In the event of one of the high contracting Parties denouncing the present Declaration, such denunciation shall not take effect until a year after the notification made in writing to the Netherland Government, and forthwith communicated by it to all the other contracting Powers.
This denunciation shall only affect the notifying Power.

In faith of which the plenipotentiaries have signed the present Declaration, and have affixed their seals thereto.
Done at The Hague, the 29th July, 1899, in a single copy, which shall be kept in the archives of the Netherland Government, and of which copies, duly certified, shall be sent through the diplomatic channel to the contracting Powers.

Source: Scott, J. B. (Ed.), *The Hague Conventions and Declarations of 1899 and 1907*, 2nd ed. (Oxford University Press, New York, 1915).

This Declaration has been ratified or acceded to by: Austria-Hungary, Belgium, Bulgaria, China, Denmark, Ethiopia, France, Germany, Great Britain, Greece, Italy, Japan, Luxembourg, Mexico, Montenegro, Netherlands, Nicaragua, Persia, Portugal, Romania, Russia, Serbia, Siam, Spain, Sweden and Norway, Switzerland, and Turkey.

CONVENTION (IV) RESPECTING THE LAWS AND CUSTOMS OF WAR ON LAND

Signed at The Hague on 18 October 1907.
Entered into force on 26 January 1910.
Depositary: Netherlands government.

His Majesty the German Emperor, King of Prussia; [etc.]:

Seeing that, while seeking means to preserve peace and prevent armed conflicts between nations, it is likewise necessary to bear in mind the case where the appeal to arms has been brought about by events which their care was unable to avert;

Animated by the desire to serve, even in this extreme case, the interests of humanity and the ever progressive needs of civilization;

Thinking it important, with this object, to revise the general laws and customs of war, either with a view to defining them with greater precision or to confining them within such limits as would mitigate their severity as far as possible;

Have deemed it necessary to complete and explain in certain particulars the work of the First Peace Conference, which, following on the Brussels Conference of 1874, and inspired by the ideas dictated by a wise and generous forethought, adopted provisions intended to define and govern the usages of war on land.

According to the views of the high contracting Parties, these provisions, the wording of which has been inspired by the desire to diminish the evils of war, as far as military requirements permit, are intended to serve as a general rule of conduct for the belligerents in their mutual relations and in their relations with the inhabitants.

It has not, however, been found possible at present to concert regulations covering all the circumstances which arise in practice;

On the other hand, the high contracting Parties clearly do not intend that unforeseen cases should, in the absence of a written undertaking, be left to the arbitrary judgment of military commanders.

Until a more complete code of the laws of war has been issued, the high contracting Parties deem it expedient to declare that, in cases not included in the Regulations adopted by them, the inhabitants and the belligerents remain under the protection and the rule of the principles of the law of nations, as they result from the usages established among civilized peoples, from the laws of humanity, and the dictates of the public conscience.

They declare that it is in this sense especially that Articles 1 and 2 of the Regulations adopted must be understood.

The high contracting Parties, wishing to conclude a fresh Convention to this effect, have appointed the following as their plenipotentiaries:
[Here follow the names of plenipotentiaries.]
Who, after having deposited their full powers, found in good and due form, have agreed upon the following:

Article 1

The contracting Powers shall issue instructions to their armed land forces which shall be in conformity with the Regulations respecting the laws and customs of war on land, annexed to the present Convention.

Article 2

The provisions contained in the Regulations referred to in Article 1, as well as in the present Convention, do not apply except between contracting Powers, and then only if all the belligerents are parties to the Convention.

Article 3

A belligerent party which violates the provisions of the said Regulations shall, if the case demands, be liable to pay compensation. It shall be responsible for all acts committed by persons forming part of its armed forces.

Article 4

The present Convention, duly ratified, shall as between the contracting Powers, be substituted for the Convention of the 29th July 1899, respecting the laws and customs of war on land.

The Convention of 1899 remains in force as between the Powers which signed it, and which do not also ratify the present Convention.

Article 5

The present Convention shall be ratified as soon as possible.

The ratifications shall be deposited at The Hague.

The first deposit of ratifications shall be recorded in a *procès-verbal* signed by the Representatives of the Powers which take part therein and by the Netherland Minister for Foreign Affairs.

The subsequent deposits of ratifications shall be made by means of a written notification, addressed to the Netherland Government and accompanied by the instrument of ratification.

A duly certified copy of the *procès-verbal* relative to the first deposit of ratifications, of the notifications mentioned in the preceding paragraph, as well as of the instruments of ratification, shall be immediately sent by the Netherland Government, through the diplomatic channel, to the Powers invited to the Second Peace Conference, as well as to the other Powers which have adhered to the Convention. In the cases contemplated in the preceding paragraph the said Government shall at the same time inform them of the date on which it received the notification.

Article 6

Non-signatory Powers may adhere to the present Convention.

The Power which desires to adhere notifies in writing its intention to the Netherland Government, forwarding to it the act of adhesion, which shall be deposited in the archives of the said Government.

This Government shall at once transmit to all the other Powers a duly certified copy of the notification as well as of the act of adhesion, mentioning the date on which it received the notification.

Article 7

The present Convention shall come into force, in the case of the Powers which were a party to the first deposit of ratifications, sixty days after the date of the *procès-verbal* of this deposit, and, in the case of the Powers which ratify subsequently or which adhere, sixty days after the notification of their ratification or of their adhesion has been received by the Netherland Government.

Article 8

In the event of one of the contracting Powers wishing to denounce the present Convention, the denunciation shall be notified in writing to the Netherland Government, which shall at once communicate a duly certified copy of the notification to all the other Powers, informing them of the date on which it was received.

The denunciation shall only have effect in regard to the notifying Power, and one year after the notification has reached the Netherland Government.

Article 9

A register kept by the Netherland Ministry of Foreign Affairs shall give the date of the deposit of ratifications made in virtue of Article 5, paragraphs 3 and 4, as well as the date on which the notifications of adhesion (Article 6, paragraph 2), or of denunciation (Article 8, paragraph 1) were received.

Each contracting Power is entitled to have access to this register and to be supplied with duly certified extracts.

In faith whereof the plenipotentiaries have appended their signatures to the present Convention.

Done at The Hague, the 18th October, 1907, in a single copy, which shall remain deposited in the archives of the Netherland Government, and duly certified copies of which shall be sent, through the diplomatic channel, to the Powers which have been invited to the Second Peace Conference.

ANNEX TO THE CONVENTION

Regulations respecting the laws and customs of war on land

EXTRACTS:

. . .

SECTION II. HOSTILITIES

Chapter I. Means of injuring the enemy, sieges, and bombardments

Article 22

The right of belligerents to adopt means of injuring the enemy is not unlimited.

Article 23

In addition to the prohibitions provided by special Conventions, it is especially forbidden—

(*a*) To employ poison or poisoned weapons;

(*b*) To kill or wound treacherously individuals belonging to the hostile nation or army;

(*c*) To kill or wound an enemy who, having laid down his arms, or having no longer means of defence, has surrendered at discretion;

(*d*) To declare that no quarter will be given;

(*e*) To employ arms, projectiles, or material calculated to cause unnecessary suffering;

(*f*) To make improper use of a flag of truce, of the national flag or of the military insignia and uniform of the enemy, as well as the distinctive badges of the Geneva Convention;*

(*g*) To destroy or seize the enemy's property, unless such destruction or seizure be imperatively demanded by the necessities of war;

(*h*) To declare abolished, suspended, or inadmissible in a court of law the rights and actions of the nationals of the hostile party.

A belligerent is likewise forbidden to compel the nationals of the hostile party to take part in the operations of war directed against their own country, even if they were in the belligerent's service before the commencement of the war.

Article 24

Ruses of war and the employment of measures necessary for obtaining information about the enemy and the country are considered permissible.

Article 25

The attack or bombardment, by whatever means, of towns, villages, dwellings, or buildings which are undefended is prohibited.

Article 26

The officer in command of an attacking force must, before commencing a bombardment, except in cases of assault, do all in his power to warn the authorities.

Article 27

In sieges and bombardments all necessary steps must be taken to spare, as far as possible, buildings dedicated to religion, art, science, or charitable purposes, historic monuments, hospitals, and places where the sick and wounded are collected, provided they are not being used at the time for military purposes.

It is the duty of the besieged to indicate the presence of such buildings or places by distinctive and visible signs, which shall be notified to the enemy beforehand.

Article 28

The pillage of a town or place, even when taken by assault, is prohibited.

. . .

---

* The Red Cross Convention of 22 August 1864 for the amelioration of the condition of the wounded in armies in the field.

Source: Scott, J. B. (Ed.), *The Hague Conventions and Declarations of 1899 and 1907*, 2nd ed. (Oxford University Press, New York, 1915).

This Convention has been ratified or acceded to by: Austria-Hungary, Belgium, Bolivia, Brazil, China, Cuba, Denmark, Dominican Republic, El Salvador, Ethiopia, Finland, France, Germany, Great Britain, Guatemala, Haiti, Japan, Liberia, Luxembourg, Mexico, Netherlands, Nicaragua, Norway, Panama, Poland, Portugal, Romania, Russia, Siam, Sweden, Switzerland, and United States.

Many provisions of this Convention are identical to the provisions included in Convention (II) with respect to the laws and customs of war on land, signed at The Hague on 29 July 1899. The 1899 Convention was ratified or acceded to by: Argentina, Austria-Hungary, Belgium, Bolivia, Brazil, Bulgaria, Chile,

China, Colombia, Cuba, Denmark, Dominican Republic, Ecuador, El Salvador, France, Germany, Great Britain, Greece, Guatemala, Haiti, Honduras, Italy, Japan, Korea, Luxembourg, Mexico, Montenegro, Netherlands, Nicaragua, Norway, Panama, Paraguay, Persia, Peru, Portugal, Romania, Russia, Serbia, Siam, Spain, Sweden, Switzerland, Turkey, United States, Uruguay, and Venezuela.

States which ratified the 1899 Convention, but did not ratify the 1907 Convention, remain formally bound by the former in their relations with the other parties thereto. As between the parties to the 1907 Convention, this Convention has replaced the 1899 Convention.

CONVENTION (VIII) RELATIVE TO THE LAYING OF AUTOMATIC SUBMARINE CONTACT MINES

Signed at The Hague on 18 October 1907.
Entered into force on 26 January 1910.
Depositary: Netherlands government.

His Majesty the German Emperor, King of Prussia; [etc.]:
Inspired by the principle of the freedom of sea routes, the common highway of all nations;
Seeing that, although the existing position of affairs makes it impossible to forbid the employment of automatic submarine contact mines, it is nevertheless desirable to restrict and regulate their employment in order to mitigate the severity of war and to ensure, as far as possible, to peaceful navigation the security to which it is entitled, despite the existence of war;
Until such time as it is found possible to formulate rules on the subject which shall ensure to the interests involved all the guarantees desirable;
Have resolved to conclude a Convention for this purpose, and have appointed the following as their plenipotentiaries:
[Here follow the names of plenipotentiaries.]
Who, after having deposited their full powers, found in good and due form, have agreed upon the following provisions:

Article 1

It is forbidden—
1. To lay unanchored automatic contact mines, except when they are so constructed as to become harmless one hour at most after the person who laid them ceases to control them;
2. To lay anchored automatic contact mines which do not become harmless as soon as they have broken loose from their moorings;
3. To use torpedoes which do not become harmless when they have missed their mark.

Article 2

It is forbidden to lay automatic contact mines off the coast and ports of the enemy, with the sole object of intercepting commercial shipping.

Article 3

When anchored automatic contact mines are employed, every possible precaution must be taken for the security of peaceful shipping.
The belligerents undertake to do their utmost to render these mines harmless within a limited time, and, should they cease to be under surveillance, to notify the danger zones as soon as military exigencies permit, by a notice addressed to ship owners, which must also be communicated to the Governments through the diplomatic channel.

Article 4

Neutral Powers which lay automatic contact mines off their coasts must observe the same rules and take the same precautions as are imposed on belligerents.
The neutral Power must inform ship owners, by a notice issued in advance, where automatic contact mines have been laid. This notice must be communicated at once to the Governments through the diplomatic channel.

Article 5

At the close of the war, the contracting Powers undertake to do their utmost to remove the mines which they have laid, each Power removing its own mines.
As regards anchored automatic contact mines laid by one of the belligerents off the coast of the other, their position must be notified to the other party by the Power which laid them, and each Power must proceed with the least possible delay to remove the mines in its own waters.

Article 6

The contracting Powers which do not at present own perfected mines of the pattern contemplated in the present Convention, and which, consequently, could not at present carry out the rules laid down in Articles 1 and 3, undertake to convert the *matériel* of their mines as soon as possible, so as to bring it into conformity with the foregoing requirements.

Article 7

The provisions of the present Convention do not apply except between contracting Powers, and then only if all the belligerents are parties to the Convention.

Article 8

The present Convention shall be ratified as soon as possible.
The ratifications shall be deposited at The Hague.
The first deposit of ratifications shall be recorded in a *procès-verbal* signed by the representatives of the Powers which take part therein and by the Netherland Minister for Foreign Affairs.
The subsequent deposits of ratifications shall be made by means of a written notification addressed to the Netherland Government and accompanied by the instrument of ratification.
A duly certified copy of the *procès-verbal* relative to the first deposit of ratifications, of the notifications mentioned in the preceding paragraph, as well as of the instruments of ratification, shall be at once sent, by the Netherland Government, through the diplomatic channel, to the Powers invited to the Second Peace Conference, as

Article 9

Non-signatory Powers may adhere to the present Convention.

The Power which desires to adhere notifies in writing its intention to the Netherland Government, transmitting to it the act of adhesion, which shall be deposited in the archives of the said Government.

This Government shall at once transmit to all the other Powers a duly certified copy of the notification as well as of the act of adhesion, stating the date on which it received the notification.

Article 10

The present Convention shall come into force, in the case of the Powers which were a party to the first deposit of ratifications, sixty days after the date of the *procès-verbal* of this deposit, and, in the case of the Powers which ratify subsequently or adhere, sixty days after the notification of their ratification or of their adhesion has been received by the Netherland Government.

Article 11

The present Convention shall remain in force for seven years, dating from the sixtieth day after the date of the first deposit of ratifications.

Unless denounced, it shall continue in force after the expiration of this period.

The denunciation shall be notified in writing to the Netherland Government, which shall at once communicate a duly certified copy of the notification to all the Powers, informing them of the date on which it was received.

The denunciation shall only have effect in regard to the notifying Power, and six months after the notification has reached the Netherland Government.

Article 12

The contracting Powers undertake to reopen the question of the employment of automatic contact mines six months before the expiration of the period contemplated in the first paragraph of the preceding article, in the event of the question not having been already reopened and settled by the Third Peace Conference.

If the contracting Powers conclude a fresh Convention relative to the employment of mines, the present Convention shall cease to be applicable from the moment it comes into force.

Article 13

A register kept by the Netherland Ministry for Foreign Affairs shall give the date of the deposit of ratifications made in virtue of Article 8, paragraphs 3 and 4, as well as the date on which the notifications of adhesion (Article 9, paragraph 2) or of denunciation (Article 11, paragraph 3) have been received.

Each contracting Power is entitled to have access to this register and to be supplied with duly certified extracts from it.

In faith whereof the plenipotentiaries have appended their signatures to the present Convention.

Done at The Hague, the 18th October, 1907, in a single copy, which shall remain deposited in the archives of the Netherland Government, and duly certified copies of which shall be sent, through the diplomatic channel, to the Powers which have been invited to the Second Peace Conference.

Source: Scott, J. B. (Ed.), *The Hague Conventions and Declarations of 1899 and 1907*, 2nd. ed. (Oxford University Press, New York, 1915).

This Convention has been ratified or acceded to by: Austria-Hungary, Belgium, Brazil, China, Denmark, El Salvador, Ethiopia, Finland, France, Germany, Great Britain, Guatemala, Haiti, Japan, Liberia, Luxembourg, Mexico, Netherlands, Nicaragua, Norway, Panama, Romania, Siam, Switzerland, and United States.

CONVENTION (IX) CONCERNING BOMBARDMENT BY NAVAL FORCES IN TIME OF WAR

Signed at The Hague on 18 October 1907.
Entered into force on 26 January 1910.
Depositary: Netherlands government.

His Majesty the German Emperor, King of Prussia; [etc.]:

Animated by the desire to realize the wish expressed by the First Peace Conference respecting the bombardment by naval forces of undefended ports, towns, and villages;

Whereas it is expedient that bombardments by naval forces should be subject to rules of general application which would safeguard the rights of the inhabitants and assure the preservation of the more important buildings, by applying as far as possible to this operation of war the principles of the Regulation of 1899 respecting the laws and customs of land war;

Actuated, accordingly, by the desire to serve the interests of humanity and to diminish the severity and disasters of war;

Have resolved to conclude a Convention to this effect, and have, for this purpose, appointed the following as their plenipotentiaries:

[Here follow the names of the plenipotentiaries.]

Who, after depositing their full powers, found in good and due form, have agreed upon the following provisions:

Chapter I. The Bombardment of Undefended Ports, Towns, Villages, Dwellings, or Buildings

Article 1

The bombardment by naval forces of undefended ports, towns, villages, dwellings, or buildings is forbidden.

A place cannot be bombarded solely because automatic submarine contact mines are anchored off the harbor.

Article 2

Military works, military or naval establishments, depots of arms or war *matériel*, workshops or plant which could be utilized for the needs of the hostile fleet or army, and the ships of war in the harbor, are not, however, included in this prohibition. The commander of a naval force may destroy them with artillery, after a summons followed by a reasonable time of waiting, if all other means are impossible, and when the local authorities have not themselves destroyed them within the time fixed.

He incurs no responsibility for any unavoidable damage which may be caused by a bombardment under such circumstances.

If for military reasons immediate action is necessary, and no delay can be allowed the enemy, it is understood that the prohibition to bombard the undefended town holds good, as in the case given in paragraph 1, and that the commander shall take all due measures in order that the town may suffer as little harm as possible.

Article 3

After due notice has been given, the bombardment of undefended ports, towns, villages, dwellings, or buildings may be commenced, if the local authorities, after a formal summons has been made to them, decline to comply with requisitions for provisions or supplies necessary for the immediate use of the naval force before the place in question.

These requisitions shall be in proportion to the resources of the place. They shall only be demanded in the name of the commander of the said naval force, and they shall, as far as possible, be paid for in cash; if not, they shall be evidenced by receipts.

Article 4

Undefended ports, towns, villages, dwellings, or buildings may not be bombarded on account of failure to pay money contributions.

Chapter II. General Provisions

Article 5

In bombardments by naval forces all the necessary measures must be taken by the commander to spare as far as possible sacred edifices, buildings used for artistic, scientific, or charitable purposes, historic monuments, hospitals, and places where the sick or wounded are collected, on the understanding that they are not used at the same time for military purposes.

It is the duty of the inhabitants to indicate such monuments, edifices, or places by visible signs, which shall consist of large, stiff rectangular panels divided diagonally into two colored triangular portions, the upper portion black, the lower portion white.

Article 6

If the military situation permits, the commander of the attacking naval force, before commencing the bombardment, must do his utmost to warn the authorities.

Article 7

A town or place, even when taken by storm, may not be pillaged.

Chapter III. Final Provisions

Article 8

The provisions of the present Convention do not apply except between contracting Powers, and then only if all the belligerents are parties to the Convention.

Article 9

The present Convention shall be ratified as soon as possible.

The ratifications shall be deposited at The Hague.

The first deposit of ratifications shall be recorded in a *procès-verbal* signed by the representatives of the Powers which take part therein and by the Netherland Minister of Foreign Affairs.

The subsequent deposits of ratifications shall be made by means of a written notification addressed to the Netherland Government and accompanied by the instrument of ratification.

A duly certified copy of the *procès-verbal* relative to the first deposit of ratifications, of the notifications mentioned in the preceding paragraph, as well as of the instruments of ratification, shall be at once sent by the Netherland Government, through the diplomatic channel, to the Powers invited to the Second Peace Conference, as well as to the other Powers which have adhered to the Convention. In the cases contemplated in the preceding paragraph, the said Government shall inform them at the same time of the date on which it received the notification.

Article 10

Non-signatory Powers may adhere to the present Convention.

The Power which desires to adhere shall notify its intention to the Netherland Government, forwarding to it the act of adhesion, which shall be deposited in the archives of the said Government.

This Government shall immediately forward to all the other Powers a duly certified copy of the notification, as well as of the act of adhesion, mentioning the date on which it received the notification.

Article 11

The present Convention shall come into force, in the case of the Powers which were a party to the first deposit of ratifications, sixty days after the date of the *procès-verbal* of that deposit, and, in the case of the Powers which ratify subsequently or which adhere, sixty days after the notification of their ratification or of their adhesion has been received by the Netherland Government.

Article 12

In the event of one of the contracting Powers wishing to denounce the present Convention, the denunciation shall be notified in writing to the Netherland Government, which shall at once communicate a duly certified copy of the notification to all the other Powers informing them of the date on which it was received.

The denunciation shall only have effect in regard to the notifying Power, and one year after the notification has reached the Netherland Government.

Article 13

A register kept by the Netherland Minister for Foreign Affairs shall give the date of the deposit of ratifications made in virtue of Article 9, paragraphs 3 and 4, as well as the date on which the notifications of adhesion (Article 10, paragraph 2) or of denunciation (Article 12, paragraph 1) have been received.

Each contracting Power is entitled to have access to this register and to be supplied with duly certified extracts from it.

In faith whereof the plenipotentiaries have appended their signatures to the present Convention.

Done at The Hague, the 18th October, 1907, in a single copy, which shall remain deposited in the archives of the Netherland Government, and duly certified copies of which shall be sent, through the diplomatic channel, to the Powers which have been invited to the Second Peace Conference.

Source: Scott, J. B. (Ed.), *The Hague Conventions and Declarations of 1899 and 1907*, 2nd. ed. (Oxford University Press, New York, 1915).

This Convention has been ratified or acceded to by: Austria-Hungary, Belgium, Bolivia, Brazil, China, Cuba, Denmark, El Salvador, Ethiopia, Finland, France, Germany, Great Britain, Guatemala, Haiti, Japan, Liberia, Luxembourg, Mexico, Netherlands, Nicaragua, Norway, Panama, Poland, Portugal, Romania, Russia, Siam, Spain, Sweden, Switzerland, and United States.

DECLARATION (XIV) PROHIBITING THE DISCHARGE OF PROJECTILES AND EXPLOSIVES FROM BALLOONS

Signed at The Hague on 18 October 1907.
Entered into force on 27 November 1909.
Depositary: Netherlands government.

The undersigned, plenipotentiaries of the Powers invited to the Second International Peace Conference at The Hague, duly authorized to that effect by their Governments, inspired by the sentiments which found expression in the Declaration of St. Petersburg of the 29th November (11th December), 1868, and being desirous of renewing the declaration of The Hague of the 29th July, 1899, which has now expired,*

Declare:

The contracting Powers agree to prohibit, for a period extending to the close of the Third Peace Conference, the discharge of projectiles and explosives from balloons or by other new methods of a similar nature.

The present Declaration is only binding on the contracting Powers in case of war between two or more of them.

It shall cease to be binding from the time when, in a war between the contracting Powers, one of the belligerents is joined by a non-contracting Power.

The present Declaration shall be ratified as soon as possible.

The ratifications shall be deposited at The Hague.

A *procès-verbal* shall be drawn up recording the receipt of the ratifications, of which a duly certified copy shall be sent, through the diplomatic channel, to all the contracting Powers.

Non-signatory Powers may adhere to the present Declaration. To do so, they must make known their adhesion to the contracting Powers by means of a written notification, addressed to the Netherland Government, and communicated by it to all the other contracting Powers.

In the event of one of the high contracting Parties denouncing the present Declaration, such denunciation shall not take effect until a year after the notification made in writing to the Netherland Government, and forthwith communicated by it to all the other contracting Powers.

This denunciation shall only have effect in regard to the notifying Power.

In faith whereof the plenipotentiaries have appended their signatures to the present Declaration.

Done at The Hague, the 18th October, 1907, in a single copy, which shall remain deposited in the archives of the Netherland Government, and duly certified copies of which shall be sent, through the diplomatic channel, to the contracting Powers.

---

* Declaration (IV,1) to prohibit for the term of five years the launching of projectiles and explosives from balloons, and other new methods of a similar nature, signed at The Hague on 29 July 1899.

Source: Scott, J. B. (Ed.), *The Hague Conventions and Declarations of 1899 and 1907*, 2nd. ed. (Oxford University Press, New York, 1915).

This Declaration has been ratified or acceded to by: Belgium, Bolivia, Brazil, China, El Salvador, Ethiopia, Finland, Great Britain, Haiti, Liberia, Luxembourg, Netherlands, Nicaragua, Norway, Panama, Portugal, Siam, Switzerland, and United States.

COVENANT OF THE LEAGUE OF NATIONS

Signed on 28 June 1919.
Entered into force on 10 January 1920.

EXTRACTS:

. . .

Article 8

1. The Members of the League recognise that the maintenance of peace requires the reduction of national armaments to the lowest point consistent with national safety and the enforcement by common action of international obligations.

2. The Council, taking account of the geographical situation and circumstances of each State, shall formulate plans for such reduction for the consideration and action of the several Governments.

3. Such plans shall be subject to reconsideration and revision at least every ten years.

4. After these plans have been adopted by the several

Governments, the limits of armaments therein fixed shall not be exceeded without the concurrence of the Council.

5. The Members of the League agree that the manufacture by private enterprise of munitions and implements of war is open to grave objections. The Council shall advise how the evil effects attendant upon such manufacture can be prevented, due regard being had to the necessities of those Members of the League which are not able to manufacture the munitions and implements of war necessary for their safety.

6. The Members of the League undertake to interchange full and frank information as to the scale of their armaments, their military, naval and air programmes and the condition of such of their industries as are adaptable to warlike purposes.

Article 9

A permanent Commission shall be constituted to advise the Council on the execution of the provisions of Articles 1 and 8 and on military, naval and air questions generally.

. . .

Source: *Essential Facts about the League of Nations*, 9th ed., revised (Geneva, 1938).

Members of the League of Nations as of 31 December 1937: Afghanistan, Albania, Argentina, Australia, Austria, Belgium, Bolivia, Bulgaria, Canada, Chile, China, Colombia, Cuba, Czechoslovakia, Denmark, Dominican Republic, Ecuador, Egypt, El Salvador, Estonia, Ethiopia, Finland, France, Greece, Guatemala, Haiti, Honduras, Hungary, India, Iran, Iraq, Ireland, Italy, Latvia, Liberia, Lithuania, Luxembourg, Mexico, Netherlands, New Zealand, Nicaragua, Norway, Panama, Peru, Poland, Portugal, Romania, Siam, Spain, Sweden, Switzerland, Turkey, South Africa, Union of Soviet Socialist Republics, United Kingdom, Uruguay, Venezuela, and Yugoslavia.

TREATY REGULATING THE STATUS OF SPITSBERGEN AND CONFERRING THE SOVEREIGNTY OF NORWAY

Signed at Paris on 9 February 1920.
Entered into force on 14 August 1925.
Depositary: French government.

EXTRACTS:

The President of the United States of America; His Majesty the King of Great Britain and Ireland and of the British Dominions beyond the Seas, Emperor of India; His Majesty the King of Denmark; the President of the French Republic; His Majesty the King of Italy; His Majesty the Emperor of Japan; His Majesty the King of Norway; Her Majesty the Queen of the Netherlands; His Majesty the King of Sweden,

Desirous, while recognising the sovereignty of Norway over the Archipelago of Spitsbergen, including Bear Island, of seeing these territories provided with an equitable régime, in order to assure their development and peaceful utilisation,

Have appointed as their respective Plenipotentiaries with a view to concluding a Treaty to this effect:
. . .

Who, having communicated their full powers, found in good and due form, have agreed as follows:

Article 1

The High Contracting Parties undertake to recognise, subject to the stipulations of the present Treaty, the full and absolute sovereignty of Norway over the Archipelago of Spitsbergen, comprising, with Bear Island or Beeren-Eiland, all the Islands situated between 10° and 35° longitude east of Greenwich and between 74° and 81° latitude North, especially West Spitsbergen, North-East Land, Barents Island, Edge Island, Wiche Islands, Hope Island or Hopen-Eiland, and Prince Charles Foreland, together with all islands great or small, and rocks appertaining thereto.

Article 2

Ships and nationals of all the High Contracting Parties shall enjoy equally the rights of fishing and hunting in the territories specified in Article 1 and in their territorial waters.

Norway shall be free to maintain, take or decree suitable measures to ensure the preservation and, if necessary, the reconstitution of the fauna and flora of the said regions, and their territorial waters; it being clearly understood that these measures shall always be applicable equally to the nationals of all the High Contracting Parties without any exemption, privilege or favour whatsoever, direct or indirect to the advantage of any one of them.

Occupiers of land whose rights have been recognised in accordance with the terms of Articles 6 and 7 will enjoy the exclusive right of hunting on their own land: (1) in the neighbourhood of their habitations, houses, stores, factories and installations, constructed for the purpose of developing their property, under conditions laid down by the local police regulations; (2) within a radius of 10 kilometres round the headquarters of their place of business or works; and in both cases, subject always to the observance of regulations made by the Norwegian Government in accordance with the conditions laid down in the present Article.

Article 3

The nationals of all the High Contracting Parties shall have equal liberty of access and entry for any reason or object whatever to the waters, fjords and ports of the territories specified in Article 1; subject to the observance of local laws and regulations, they may carry on there without impediment all maritime, industrial, mining and commercial operations on a footing of absolute equality.

They shall be admitted under the same conditions of equality to the exercise and practice of all maritime, industrial, mining or commercial enterprises both on land and in the territorial waters, and no monopoly shall be established on any account or for any enterprise whatever.

Notwithstanding any rules relating to coasting trade which may be in force in Norway, ships of the High Contracting Parties going to or coming from the territories specified in Article 1 shall have the right to put into Norwegian ports on their outward or homeward voyage for the purpose of taking on board or disembarking passengers or cargo going to or coming from the said territories, or for any other purpose.

It is agreed that in every respect and especially with regard to exports, imports and transit traffic, the nationals of all the High Contracting Parties, their ships and goods shall not be subject to any charges or restrictions whatever which are not borne by the nationals, ships or goods which enjoy in Norway the treatment of the most favoured nation; Norwegian nationals, ships or goods being for this purpose assimilated to those of the other High Contracting Parties, and not treated more favourably in any respect.

No charge or restriction shall be imposed on the exportation of any goods to the territories of any of the Contracting Powers other or more onerous than on the exportation of similar goods to the territory of any other Contracting Power (including Norway) or to any other destination.

Article 4

All public wireless telegraphy stations established or to be established by, or with the authorisation of, the Norwegian Government within the territories referred to in Article 1 shall always be open on a footing of absolute equality to communications from ships of all flags and from nationals of the High Contracting Parties, under the conditions laid down in the Wireless Telegraphy Convention of July 5, 1912, or in the subsequent International Convention which may be concluded to replace it.

Subject to international obligations arising out of a state of war, owners of landed property shall always be at liberty to establish and use for their own purposes wireless telegraphy installations, which shall be free to communicate on private business with fixed or moving wireless stations, including those on board ships and aircraft.

Article 5

The High Contracting Parties recognise the utility of establishing an international meteorological station in the territories specified in Article 1, the organisation of which shall form the subject of a subsequent Convention.

Conventions shall also be concluded laying down the conditions under which scientific investigations may be conducted in the said territories.

Article 6

Subject to the provisions of the present Article, acquired rights of nationals of the High Contracting Parties shall be recognised.

Claims arising from taking possession or from occupation of land before the signature of the present Treaty shall be dealt with in accordance with the Annex hereto, which will have the same force and effect as the present Treaty.

Article 7

With regard to methods of acquisition, enjoyment and exercise of the right of ownership of property, including mineral rights, in the territories specified in Article 1, Norway undertakes to grant to all nationals of the High Contracting Parties treatment based on complete equality and in conformity with the stipulations of the present Treaty.

Expropriation may be resorted to only on grounds of public utility and on payment of proper compensation.

Article 8

Norway undertakes to provide for the territories specified in Article 1 mining regulations which, especially from the point of view of imposts, taxes or charges of any kind, and of general or particular labour conditions, shall exclude all privileges, monopolies or favours for the benefit of the State or of the nationals of any one of the High Contracting Parties, including Norway, and shall guarantee to the paid staff of all categories the remuneration and protection necessary for their physical, moral and intellectual welfare.

Taxes, dues and duties levied shall be devoted exclusively to the said territories and shall not exceed what is required for the object in view.

So far, particularly, as the exportation of minerals is concerned, the Norwegian Government shall have the right to levy an export duty which shall not exceed 1 per cent of the maximum value of the minerals exported up to 100,000 tons, and beyond that quantity the duty will be proportionately diminished. The value shall be fixed at the end of the navigation season by calculating the average free on board price obtained.

Three months before the date fixed for their coming into force, the draft mining regulations shall be communicated by the Norwegian Government to the other Contracting Powers. If during this period one or more of the said Powers propose to modify these regulations before they are applied, such proposals shall be communicated by the Norwegian Government to the other Contracting Powers in order that they may be submitted to examination and the decision of a Commission composed of one representative of each of the said Powers. This Commission shall meet at the invitation of the Norwegian Government and shall come to a decision within a period of three months from the date of its first meeting. Its decisions shall be taken by a majority.

Article 9

Subject to the rights and duties resulting from the admission of Norway to the League of Nations, Norway undertakes not to create nor to allow the establishment of any naval base in the territories specified in Article 1 and not to construct any fortification in the said territories, which may never be used for warlike purposes.

Article 10

Until the recognition by the High Contracting Parties of a Russian Government shall permit Russia to adhere to the present Treaty, Russian nationals and companies shall enjoy the same rights as nationals of the High Contracting Parties.

Claims in the territories specified in Article 1 which they may have to put forward shall be presented under the conditions laid down in the present Treaty (Article 6 and Annex) through the intermediary of the Danish Government, who declare their willingness to lend their good offices for this purpose.

The present treaty, of which the French and English texts are both authentic, shall be ratified.

Ratifications shall be deposited at Paris as soon as possible.

Powers of which the seat of the Government is outside Europe may confine their action to informing the Government of the French Republic, through their diplomatic representative at Paris, that their ratification has been given, and in this case, they shall transmit the instrument as soon as possible.

The present Treaty will come into force, in so far as the stipulations of Article 8 are concerned, from the date of its ratification by all the signatory Powers; and in all other respects on the same date as the mining regulations provided for in that Article.

Third Powers will be invited by the Government of the French Republic to adhere to the present Treaty duly ratified. This adhesion shall be effected by a communication addressed to the French Government, which will undertake to notify the other Contracting Parties.

In witness whereof the above-named Plenipotentiaries have signed the present Treaty.

Done at Paris, the ninth day of February, 1920, in duplicate, one copy to be transmitted to the Government of His Majesty the King of Norway, and one deposited in the archives of the French Republic; authenticated copies will be transmitted to the other Signatory Powers.

ANNEX

1

(1) Within three months from the coming into force of the present Treaty, notification of all claims to land which had been made to any Government before the signature of the present Treaty must be sent by the Government of the claimant to a Commissioner charged to examine such claims. The Commissioner will be a judge or jurisconsult of Danish nationality possessing the necessary qualifications for the task, and shall be nominated by the Danish Government.

(2) The notification must include a precise delimitation of the land claimed and be accompanied by a map on a scale of not less than 1/1,000,000 on which the land claimed is clearly marked.

(3) The notification must be accompanied by the deposit of a sum of one penny for each acre (40 ares) of land claimed, to defray the expenses of the examination of the claims.

(4) The Commissioner will be entitled to require from the claimants any further documents or information which he may consider necessary.

(5) The Commissioner will examine the claims so notified. For this purpose he will be entitled to avail himself of such expert assistance as he may consider necessary, and in case of need to cause investigations to be carried out on the spot.

(6) The remuneration of the Commissioner will be fixed by agreement between the Danish Government and the other Governments concerned. The Commissioner will fix the remuneration of such assistants as he considers it necessary to employ.

(7) The Commissioner, after examining the claims, will prepare a report showing precisely the claims which he is of opinion should be recognised at once and those which, either because they are disputed or for any other reason, he is of opinion should be submitted to arbitration as hereinafter provided. Copies of this report will be forwarded by the Commissioner to the Governments concerned.

(8) If the amount of the sums deposited in accordance with clause (3) is insufficient to cover the expenses of the examination of the claims, the Commissioner will, in every case where he is of opinion that a claim should be recognised, at once state what further sum the claimant should be required to pay. This sum will be based on the amount of the land to which the claimant's title is recognised.

If the sums deposited in accordance with clause (3) exceed the expenses of the examination the balance will be devoted to the cost of the arbitration hereinafter provided for.

(9) Within three months from the date of the report referred to in clause (7) of this paragraph, the Norwegian Government shall take the necessary steps to confer upon claimants whose claims have been recognised by the Commissioner a valid title securing to them the exclusive property in the land in question, in accordance with the laws and regulations in force or to be enforced in the territories specified in Article 1 of the present Treaty, and subject to the mining regulations referred to in Article 8 of the present Treaty.

In the event, however, of a further payment being required in accordance with clause (8) of this paragraph, a provisional title only will be delivered, which title will become definitive on payment by the claimant, within such reasonable period as the Norwegian Government may fix, of the further sum required of him.

2

Claims which for any reason the Commissioner referred to in clause (1) of the preceding paragraph has not recognised as valid will be settled in accordance with the following provisions:

(1) Within three months from the date of the report referred to in clause (7) of the preceding paragraph, each of the Governments whose nationals have been found to possess claims which have not been recognised will appoint an arbitrator.

The Commissioner will be the President of the Tribunal so constituted. In cases of equal division of opinion, he shall have the deciding vote. He will nominate a Secretary to receive the documents referred to in clause (2) of this paragraph and to make the necessary arrangements for the meeting of the Tribunal.

(2) Within one month from the appointment of the Secretary referred to in clause (1) the claimants concerned will send to him through the intermediary of their respective Governments statements indicating precisely their claims and accompanied by such documents and arguments as they may wish to submit in support thereof.

(3) Within two months from the appointment of the Secretary referred to in clause (1) the Tribunal shall meet at Copenhagen for the purpose of dealing with the claims which have been submitted to it.

(4) The language of the Tribunal shall be English. Documents or arguments may be submitted to it by the interested parties in their own language, but in that case must be accompanied by an English translation.

(5) The claimants shall be entitled, if they so desire, to be heard by the Tribunal either in person or by counsel,

and the Tribunal shall be entitled to call upon the claimants to present such additional explanations, documents or arguments as it may think necessary.

(6) Before the hearing of any case the Tribunal shall require from the parties a deposit or security for such sum as it may think necessary to cover the share of each party in the expenses of the Tribunal. In fixing the amount of such sum the Tribunal shall base itself principally on the extent of the land claimed. The Tribunal shall also have power to demand a further deposit from the parties in cases where special expense is involved.

(7) The honorarium of the arbitrators shall be calculated per month, and fixed by the Governments concerned. The salary of the Secretary and any other persons employed by the Tribunal shall be fixed by the President.

(8) Subject to the provisions of this Annex the Tribunal shall have full power to regulate its own procedure.

(9) In dealing with the claims the Tribunal shall take into consideration:—
(a) Any applicable rules of International Law;
(b) The general principles of justice and equity;
(c) The following circumstances:—
  (i) The date on which the land claimed was first occupied by the claimant or his predecessors in title;
  (ii) The date on which the claim was notified to the Government of the claimant;
  (iii) The extent to which the claimant or his predecessors in title have developed and exploited the land claimed. In this connection the Tribunal shall take into account the extent to which the claimants may have been prevented from developing their undertakings by conditions or restrictions resulting from the war of 1914–19.

(10) All the expenses of the Tribunal shall be divided among the claimants in such proportion as the Tribunal shall decide. If the amount of the sums paid in accordance with clause (6) is larger than the expenses of the Tribunal, the balance shall be returned to the parties whose claims have been recognised in such proportion as the Tribunal shall think fit.

(11) The decisions of the Tribunal shall be communicated by it to the Governments concerned, including in every case the Norwegian Government.

The Norwegian Government shall within three months from the receipt of each decision take the necessary steps to confer upon the claimants whose claims have been recognised by the Tribunal a valid title to the land in question, in accordance with the laws and regulations in force or to be enforced in the territories specified in Article 1, and subject to the mining regulations referred to in Article 8 of the present Treaty. Nevertheless, the titles so conferred will only become definitive on the payment by the claimant concerned, within such reasonable period as the Norwegian Government may fix, of his share of the expenses of the Tribunal.

3

Any claims which are not notified to the Commissioner in accordance with clause (1) of paragraph 1, or which not having been recognised by him are not submitted to the Tribunal in accordance with paragraph 2, will be finally extinguished.

Source: *Treaty Series No. 18* (HMSO, London, 1924).

The Spitsbergen Treaty has been ratified or acceded to by: Afghanistan, Albania, Argentina, Australia, Austria, Belgium, Bulgaria, Canada, Chile, China, Czechoslovakia, Denmark, Dominican Republic, Egypt, Estonia, Finland, France, Germany, Greece, Hungary, India, Italy, Japan, Monaco, Netherlands, New Zealand, Norway, Poland, Portugal, Romania, Saudi Arabia, South Africa, Spain, Sweden, Switzerland, Union of Soviet Socialist Republics, United Kingdom, United States, Venezuela, and Yugoslavia.

PROTOCOL FOR THE PROHIBITION OF THE USE IN WAR OF ASPHYXIATING, POISONOUS OR OTHER GASES, AND OF BACTERIOLOGICAL METHODS OF WARFARE

Signed at Geneva on 17 June 1925.
Entered into force on 8 February 1928.
Depositary: French government.

The Undersigned plenipotentiaries, in the name of their respective Governments:

Whereas the use in war of asphyxiating, poisonous or other gases, and of all analogous liquids materials or devices, has been justly condemned by the general opinion of the civilised world; and

Whereas the prohibition of such use has been declared in Treaties to which the majority of Powers of the world are Parties; and

To the end that this prohibition shall be universally accepted as a part of International Law, binding alike the conscience and the practice of nations;

Declare:

That the High Contracting Parties, so far as they are not already Parties to Treaties prohibiting such use, accept this prohibition, agree to extend this prohibition to the use of bacteriological methods of warfare and agree to be bound as between themselves according to the terms of this declaration.

The High Contracting Parties will exert every effort to induce other States to accede to the present Protocol. Such accession will be notified to the Government of the French Republic, and by the latter to all signatory and acceding Powers, and will take effect on the date of the notification by the Government of the French Republic.

The present Protocol, of which the French and English texts are both authentic, shall be ratified as soon as possible. It shall bear to-day's date.

The ratifications of the present Protocol shall be addressed to the Government of the French Republic, which will at once notify the deposit of such ratification to each of the signatory and acceding Powers.

The instruments of ratification of and accession to the present Protocol will remain deposited in the archives of the Government of the French Republic.

The present Protocol will come into force for each signatory Power as from the date of deposit of its ratification, and, from that moment, each Power will be bound as regards other Powers which have already deposited their ratifications.

  In witness whereof the Plenipotentiaries have signed the present Protocol.

  Done at Geneva in a single copy, the seventeenth day of June, One Thousand Nine Hundred and Twenty-Five.

Source: *League of Nations Treaty Series,* Vol. XCIV (Lausanne, 1929).

Number of parties as of 31 December 1977: 99.

For the list of states which have signed, ratified, acceded or succeeded to the Geneva Protocol, see pages 145–49.

II. The post-World War II agreements

CHARTER OF THE UNITED NATIONS

Signed on 26 June 1945.
Entered into force on 24 October 1945.

EXTRACTS:
. . .
Article 11

1. The General Assembly may consider the general principles of cooperation in the maintenance of international peace and security, including the principles governing disarmament and the regulation of armaments, and may make recommendations with regard to such principles to the Members or to the Security Council or to both.

. . .
Article 26

In order to promote the establishment and maintenance of international peace and security with the least diversion for armaments of the world's human and economic resources, the Security Council shall be responsible for formulating, with the assistance of the Military Staff Committee referred to in Article 47, plans to be submitted to the Members of the United Nations for the establishment of a system for the regulation of armaments.

. . .
Article 47

1. There shall be established a Military Staff Committee to advise and assist the Security Council on all questions relating to the Security Council's military requirements for the maintenance of international peace and security, the employment and command of forces placed at its disposal, the regulation of armaments, and possible disarmament.

. . .

Source: *Charter of the United Nations and Statute of the International Court of Justice*, OPI/239–26285 (United Nations Office of Public Information, New York, November 1966).

Number of UN member states as of 31 December 1977: 149.

For the list of UN member states, see Appendix A.

CONVENTION ON THE PREVENTION AND PUNISHMENT OF THE CRIME OF GENOCIDE

Adopted by the UN General Assembly on 9 December 1948.
Entered into force on 12 January 1951.
Depositary: the UN Secretary-General.

The Contracting Parties,
Having considered the declaration made by the General Assembly of the United Nations in its resolution 96 (I) dated 11 December 1946 that genocide is a crime under international law, contrary to the spirit and aims of the United Nations and condemned by the civilized world;
Recognizing that at all periods of history genocide has inflicted great losses on humanity; and
Being convinced that, in order to liberate mankind from such an odious scourge, international co-operation is required.
Hereby agree as hereinafter provided:

Article I
The Contracting Parties confirm that genocide, whether committed in time of peace or in time of war, is a crime under international law which they undertake to prevent and to punish.

Article II
In the present Convention, genocide means any of the following acts committed with intent to destroy, in whole or in part, a national, ethnical, racial or religious group, as such:
(*a*) Killing members of the group;
(*b*) Causing serious bodily or mental harm to members of the group;
(*c*) Deliberately inflicting on the group conditions of life calculated to bring about its physical destruction in whole or in part;
(*d*) Imposing measures intended to prevent births within the group;
(*e*) Forcibly transferring children of the group to another group.

Article III
The following acts shall be punishable:
(*a*) Genocide;
(*b*) Conspiracy to commit genocide;
(*c*) Direct and public incitement to commit genocide;
(*d*) Attempt to commit genocide;
(*e*) Complicity in genocide.

Article IV
Persons committing genocide or any of the other acts enumerated in article III shall be punished, whether they are constitutionally responsible rulers, public officials or private individuals.

Article V

The Contracting Parties undertake to enact, in accordance with their respective Constitutions, the necessary legislation to give effect to the provisions of the present Convention and, in particular, to provide effective penalties for persons guilty of genocide or of any of the other acts enumerated in article III.

Article VI

Person charged with genocide or any of the other acts enumerated in article III shall be tried by a competent tribunal of the State in the territory of which the act was committed, or by such international penal tribunal as may have jurisdiction with respect to those Contracting Parties which shall have accepted its jurisdiction.

Article VII

Genocide and the other acts enumerated in article III shall not be considered as political crimes for the purpose of extradition.

The Contracting Parties pledge themselves in such cases to grant extradition in accordance with their laws and treaties in force.

Article VIII

Any Contracting Party may call upon the competent organs of the United Nations to take such action under the Charter of the United Nations as they consider appropriate for the prevention and suppression of acts of genocide or any of the other acts enumerated in article III.

Article IX

Disputes between the Contracting Parties relating to the interpretation, application or fulfilment of the present Convention, including those relating to the responsibility of a State for genocide or for any of the other acts enumerated in article III, shall be submitted to the International Court of Justice at the request of any of the parties to the dispute.

Article X

The present Convention, of which the Chinese, English, French, Russian and Spanish texts are equally authentic, shall bear the date of 9 December 1948.

Article XI

The present Convention shall be open until 31 December 1949 for signature on behalf of any Member of the United Nations and of any non-member State to which an invitation to sign has been addressed by the General Assembly.

The present Convention shall be ratified, and the instruments of ratification shall be deposited with the Secretary-General of the United Nations.

After 1 January 1950 the present Convention may be acceded to on behalf of any Member of the United Nations and of any non-member State which has received an invitation as aforesaid.

Instruments of accession shall be deposited with the Secretary-General of the United Nations.

Article XII

Any Contracting Party may at any time, by notification addressed to the Secretary-General of the United Nations, extend the application of the present Convention to all or any of the territories for the conduct of whose foreign relations that Contracting Party is responsible.

Article XIII

On the day when the first twenty instruments of ratification or accession have been deposited, the Secretary-General shall draw up a *procès-verbal* and transmit a copy thereof to each Member of the United Nations and to each of the non-member States contemplated in article XI.

The present Convention shall come into force on the ninetieth day following the date of deposit of the twentieth instrument of ratification or accession.

Any ratification or accession effected subsequent to the latter date shall become effective on the ninetieth day following the deposit of the instrument of ratification or accession.

Article XIV

The present Convention shall remain in effect for a period of ten years as from the date of its coming into force.

It shall thereafter remain in force for successive periods of five years for such Contracting Parties as have not denounced it at least six months before the expiration of the current period.

Denunciation shall be effected by a written notification addressed to the Secretary-General of the United Nations.

Article XV

If, as a result of denunciations, the number of Parties to the present Convention should become less than sixteen, the Convention shall cease to be in force as from the date on which the last of these denunciations shall become effective.

Article XVI

A request for the revision of the present Convention may be made at any time by any Contracting Party by means of a notification in writing addressed to the Secretary-General.

The General Assembly shall decide upon the steps, if any, to be taken in respect of such request.

Article XVII

The Secretary-General of the United Nations shall notify all Members of the United Nations and the non-member States contemplated in article XI of the following:

(*a*) Signatures, ratifications and accessions received in accordance with article XI;

(*b*) Notifications received in accordance with article XII;

(*c*) The date upon which the present Convention comes into force in accordance with article XIII;

(*d*) Denunciations received in accordance with article XIV;

(*e*) The abrogation of the Convention in accordance with article XV;

(*f*) Notifications received in accordance with article XVI.

Article XVIII

The original of the present Convention shall be deposited in the archives of the United Nations.

A certified copy of the Convention shall be transmitted to each Member of the United Nations and to each of the non-member States contemplated in article XI.

Article XIX

The present Convention shall be registered by the Secretary-General of the United Nations on the date of its coming into force.

Source: *Treaty Series*, Vol. 78 (United Nations, New York, 1951).

The following states have ratified, acceded or succeeded to the Genocide Convention: Afghanistan, Albania, Algeria, Argentina, Australia, Austria, Bahamas, Belgium, Brazil, Bulgaria, Burma, Byelorussia, Canada, Chile, Colombia, Costa Rica, Cuba, Czechoslovakia, Denmark, Ecuador, Egypt, El Salvador, Ethiopia, Fiji, Finland, France, German Democratic Republic, Federal Republic of Germany, Ghana, Greece, Guatemala, Haiti, Honduras, Hungary, Iceland, India, Iran, Iraq, Ireland, Israel, Italy, Jamaica, Jordan, Democratic Kampuchea, Lao People's Democratic Republic, Lebanon, Lesotho, Liberia, Mali, Mexico, Monaco, Mongolia, Morocco, Nepal, Netherlands, Nicaragua, Norway, Pakistan, Panama, Peru, Philippines, Poland, Republic of Korea (South), Republic of South Viet-Nam,* Romania, Rwanda, Saudi Arabia, Spain, Sri Lanka, Sweden, Syria, Tonga, Tunisia, Turkey, Ukraine, Union of Soviet Socialist Republics, United Kingdom, Upper Volta, Uruguay, Venezuela, Yugoslavia, and Zaire.

* On 2 July 1976, the single state of the Socialist Republic of Viet Nam was proclaimed.

GENEVA CONVENTION RELATIVE TO THE PROTECTION OF CIVILIAN PERSONS IN TIME OF WAR

Signed at Geneva on 12 August 1949.
Entered into force on 21 October 1950.
Depositary: Swiss Federal Council.

EXTRACTS:

The undersigned Plenipotentiaries of the Governments represented at the Diplomatic Conference held at Geneva from April 21 to August 12, 1949 for the purpose of establishing a Convention for the Protection of Civilian Persons in Time of War, have agreed as follows:

Part I. General provisions

Article 1

The High Contracting Parties undertake to respect and to ensure respect for the present Convention in all circumstances.

Article 2

In addition to the provisions which shall be implemented in peace time, the present Convention shall apply to all cases of declared war or of any other armed conflict which may arise between two or more of the High Contracting Parties, even if the state of war is not recognised by one of them.

The Convention shall also apply to all cases of partial or total occupation of the territory of a High Contracting Party, even if the said occupation meets with no armed resistance.

Although one of the Powers in conflict may not be a party to the present Convention, the Powers who are parties thereto shall remain bound by it in their mutual relations. They shall furthermore be bound by the Convention in relation to the said Power, if the latter accepts and applies the provisions thereof.

Article 3

In the case of armed conflict not of an international character occurring in the territory of one of the High Contracting Parties, each Party to the conflict shall be bound to apply, as a minimum, the following provisions:

(1) Persons taking no active part in the hostilities, including members of armed forces who have laid down their arms and those placed *hors de combat* by sickness, wounds, detention, or any other cause, shall in all circumstances be treated humanely, without any adverse distinction founded on race, colour, religion or faith, sex, birth or wealth, or any other similar criteria.

To this end, the following acts are and shall remain prohibited at any time and in any place whatsoever with respect to the above-mentioned persons:

(*a*) violence to life and person, in particular murder of all kinds, mutilation, cruel treatment and torture;

(*b*) taking of hostages;

(*c*) outrages upon personal dignity, in particular humiliating and degrading treatment;

(*d*) the passing of sentences and the carrying out of executions without previous judgment pronounced by a regularly constituted court, affording all the judicial guarantees which are recognized as indispensable by civilized peoples.

(2) The wounded and sick shall be collected and cared for.

An impartial humanitarian body, such as the International Committee of the Red Cross, may offer its services to the Parties to the conflict.

The Parties to the conflict should further endeavour to bring into force, by means of special agreements, all or part of the other provisions of the present Convention.

The application of the preceding provisions shall not affect the legal status of the Parties to the conflict.

Article 4

Persons protected by the Convention are those who, at a given moment and in any manner whatsoever, find themselves, in case of a conflict or occupation, in the hands of a Party to the conflict or Occupying Power of which they are not nationals.

Nationals of a State which is not bound by the Convention are not protected by it. Nationals of a neutral State who find themselves in the territory of a belligerent State, and nationals of a co-belligerent State, shall not be regarded as protected persons while the State of which they are nationals has normal diplomatic representation in the State in whose hands they are.

The provisions of Part II are, however, wider in application, as defined in Article 13.

Persons protected by the Geneva Convention for the Amelioration of the Condition of the Wounded and Sick in Armed Forces in the Field of August 12, 1949, or by the Geneva Convention for the Amelioration of the Condition of Wounded, Sick and Shipwrecked Members of Armed

Forces at Sea of August 12, 1949, or by the Geneva Convention relative to the Treatment of Prisoners of War of August 12, 1949 shall not be considered as protected persons within the meaning of the present Convention.

. . .

Part II. General protection of populations against certain consequences of war

Article 13

The provisions of Part II cover the whole of the populations of the countries in conflict, without any adverse distinction based, in particular, on race, nationality, religion or political opinion, and are intended to alleviate the sufferings caused by war.

Article 14

In time of peace, the High Contracting Parties and, after the outbreak of hostilities, the Parties thereto, may establish in their own territory and, if the need arises, in occupied areas, hospital and safety zones and localities so organized as to protect from the effects of war, wounded, sick and aged persons, children under fifteen, expectant mothers and mothers of children under seven.

Upon the outbreak and during the course of hostilities, the Parties concerned may conclude agreements on mutual recognition of the zones and localities they have created. They may for this purpose implement the provisions of the Draft Agreement annexed to the present Convention, with such amendments as they may consider necessary.

The Protecting Powers and the International Committee of the Red Cross are invited to lend their good offices in order to facilitate the institution and recognition of these hospital and safety zones and localities.

Article 15

Any Party to the conflict may, either direct or through a neutral State or some humanitarian organization, propose to the adverse Party to establish, in the regions where fighting is taking place, neutralized zones intended to shelter from the effects of war the following persons, without distinction:

(*a*) wounded and sick combatants or noncombatants;

(*b*) civilian persons who take no part in hostilities, and who, while they reside in the zones, perform no work of a military character.

When the Parties concerned have agreed upon the geographical position, administration, food supply and supervision of the proposed neutralized zone, a written agreement shall be concluded and signed by the representatives of the Parties to the conflict. The agreement shall fix the beginning and the duration of the neutralization of the zone.

Article 16

The wounded and sick, as well as the infirm, and expectant mothers, shall be the object of particular protection and respect.

As far as military considerations allow, each Party to the conflict shall facilitate the steps taken to search for the killed and wounded, to assist the shipwrecked and other persons exposed to grave danger, and to protect them against pillage and ill-treatment.

Article 17

The Parties to the conflict shall endeavour to conclude local agreements for the removal from besieged or encircled areas, of wounded, sick, infirm, and aged persons, children and maternity cases, and for the passage of ministers of all religions, medical personnel and medical equipment on their way to such areas.

Article 18

Civilian hospitals organized to give care to the wounded and sick, the infirm and maternity cases, may in no circumstances be the object of attack, but shall at all times be respected and protected by the Parties to the conflict.

States which are Parties to a conflict shall provide all civilian hospitals with certificates showing that they are civilian hospitals and that the buildings which they occupy are not used for any purpose which would deprive these hospitals of protection in accordance with Article 19.

Civilian hospitals shall be marked by means of the emblem provided for in Article 38 of the Geneva Convention for the Amelioration of the Condition of the Wounded and Sick in Armed Forces in the Field of August 12, 1949, but only if so authorized by the State.

The Parties to the conflict shall, in so far as military considerations permit, take the necessary steps to make the distinctive emblems indicating civilian hospitals clearly visible to the enemy land, air and naval forces in order to obviate the possibility of any hostile action.

In view of the dangers to which hospitals may be exposed by being close to military objectives, it is recommended that such hospitals be situated as far as possible from such objectives.

Article 19

The protection to which civilian hospitals are entitled shall not cease unless they are used to commit, outside their humanitarian duties, acts harmful to the enemy. Protection may, however, cease only after due warning has been given, naming, in all appropriate cases, a reasonable time limit, and after such warning has remained unheeded.

The fact that sick or wounded members of the armed forces are nursed in these hospitals, or the presence of small arms and ammunition taken from such combatants and not yet handed to the proper service, shall not be considered to be acts harmful to the enemy.

Article 20

Persons regularly and solely engaged in the operation and administration of civilian hospitals, including the personnel engaged in the search for, removal and transporting of and caring for wounded and sick civilians, the infirm and maternity cases, shall be respected and protected.

In occupied territory and in zones of military operations, the above personnel shall be recognizable by means of an identity card certifying their status, bearing the photograph of the holder and embossed with the stamp of the responsible authority, and also by means of a stamped, water-resistant armlet which they shall wear on the left arm while carrying out their duties. This armlet shall be issued by the State and shall bear the emblem provided for in Article 38 of the Geneva Convention for the Amelioration of the Condition of the Wounded and Sick in Armed Forces in the Field of August 12, 1949.

Other personnel who are engaged in the operation and administration of civilian hospitals shall be entitled to respect and protection and to wear the armlet, as provided in and under the conditions prescribed in this Article, while they are employed on such duties. The identity card shall state the duties on which they are employed.

The management of each hospital shall at all times hold at the disposal of the competent national or occupying authorities an up-to-date list of such personnel.

Article 21

Convoys of vehicles or hospital trains on land or specially provided vessels on sea, conveying wounded and sick civilians, the infirm and maternity cases, shall be respected and protected in the same manner as the hospitals provided for in Article 18, and shall be marked, with the consent of the State, by the display of the distinctive emblem provided for in Article 38 of the Geneva Convention for the Amelioration of the Condition of the Wounded and Sick in Armed Forces in the Field of August 12, 1949.

Article 22

Aircraft exclusively employed for the removal of wounded and sick civilians, the infirm and maternity cases, or for the transport of medical personnel and equipment shall not be attacked, but shall be respected while flying at heights, times and on routes specifically agreed upon between all the Parties to the conflict concerned.

They may be marked with the distinctive emblem provided for in Article 38 of the Geneva Convention for the Amelioration of the Condition of the Wounded and Sick in Armed Forces in the Field of August 12, 1949.

Unless agreed otherwise, flights over enemy or enemy occupied territory are prohibited.

Such aircraft shall obey every summons to land. In the event of a landing thus imposed, the aircraft with its occupants may continue its flight after examination, if any.

. . .

Article 146

The High Contracting Parties undertake to enact any legislation necessary to provide effective penal sanctions for persons committing, or ordering to be committed, any of the grave breaches of the present Convention defined in the following Article.

Each High Contracting Party shall be under the obligation to search for persons alleged to have committed, or to have ordered to be committed, such grave breaches, and shall bring such persons, regardless of their nationality, before its own courts. It may also, if it prefers, and in accordance with the provisions of its own legislation, hand such persons over for trial to another High Contracting Party concerned, provided such High Contracting Party has made out a *prima facie* case.

Each High Contracting Party shall take measures necessary for the suppression of all acts contrary to the provisions of the present Convention other than the grave breaches defined in the following Article.

In all circumstances, the accused persons shall benefit by safeguards of proper trial and defence, which shall not be less favourable than those provided by Article 105 and those following of the Geneva Convention relative to the Treatment of Prisoners of War of August 12, 1949.

Article 147

Grave breaches to which the preceding Article relates shall be those involving any of the following acts, if committed against persons or property protected by the present Convention: wilful killing, torture or inhuman treatment, including biological experiments, wilfully causing great suffering or serious injury to body or health, unlawful deportation or transfer or unlawful confinement of a protected person, compelling a protected person to serve in the forces of a hostile Power, or wilfully depriving a protected person of the rights of fair and regular trial prescribed in the present Convention, taking of hostages and extensive destruction and appropriation of property, not justified by military necessity and carried out unlawfully and wantonly.

Article 148

No High Contracting Party shall be allowed to absolve itself or any other High Contracting Party of any liability incurred by itself or by another High Contracting Party in respect of breaches referred to in the preceding Article.

Article 149

At the request of a Party to the conflict, an enquiry shall be instituted, in a manner to be decided between the interested Parties, concerning any alleged violation of the Convention.

If agreement has not been reached concerning the procedure for the enquiry, the Parties should agree on the choice of an umpire who will decide upon the procedure to be followed.

Once the violation has been established, the Parties to the conflict shall put an end to it and shall repress it with the least possible delay.

. . .

Article 151

The present Convention, which bears the date of this day, is open to signature until February 12, 1950, in the name of the Powers represented at the Conference which opened at Geneva on April 21, 1949.

Article 152

The present Convention shall be ratified as soon as possible and the ratifications shall be deposited at Berne.

A record shall be drawn up of the deposit of each instrument of ratification and certified copies of this record shall be transmitted by the Swiss Federal Council to all the Powers in whose name the Convention has been signed, or whose accession has been notified.

Article 153

The present Convention shall come into force six months after not less than two instruments of ratification have been deposited.

Thereafter, it shall come into force for each High Contracting Party six months after the deposit of the instrument of ratification.

Article 154

In the relations between the Powers who are bound by The Hague Conventions respecting the Laws and Customs of War on Land, whether that of July 29, 1899, or that of October 18, 1907, and who are parties to the present Convention, this last Convention shall be supplementary to Sections II and III of the Regulations annexed to the above mentioned Conventions of The Hague.

Article 155

From the date of its coming into force, it shall be open to any Power in whose name the present Convention has not been signed, to accede to this Convention.

Article 156

Accessions shall be notified in writing to the Swiss Federal Council, and shall take effect six months after the date on which they are received.

The Swiss Federal Council shall communicate the accessions to all the Powers in whose name the Convention has been signed, or whose accession has been notified.

Article 157

The situations provided for in Articles 2 and 3 shall give immediate effect to ratifications deposited and accessions notified by the Parties to the conflict before or after the beginning of hostilities or occupation. The Swiss Federal Council shall communicate by the quickest method any ratifications or accessions received from Parties to the conflict.

Article 158

Each of the High Contracting Parties shall be at liberty to denounce the present Convention.

The denunciation shall be notified in writing to the Swiss Federal Council, which shall transmit it to the Governments of all the High Contracting Parties.

The denunciation shall take effect one year after the notification thereof has been made to the Swiss Federal Council. However, a denunciation of which notification has been made at a time when the denouncing Power is involved in a conflict shall not take effect until peace has been concluded, and until after operations connected with the release, repatriation and reestablishment of the persons protected by the present Convention have been terminated.

The denunciation shall have effect only in respect of the denouncing Power. It shall in no way impair the obligations which the Parties to the conflict shall remain bound to fulfil by virtue of the principles of the law of nations, as they result from the usages established among civilized peoples, from the laws of humanity and the dictates of the public conscience.

Article 159

The Swiss Federal Council shall register the present Convention with the Secretariat of the United Nations. The Swiss Federal Council shall also inform the Secretariat of the United Nations of all ratifications, accessions and denunciations received by it with respect to the present Convention.

In witness whereof the undersigned, having deposited their respective full powers, have signed the present Convention.

Done at Geneva this twelfth day of August, 1949, in the English and French languages. The original shall be deposited in the archives of the Swiss Confederation. The Swiss Federal Council shall transmit certified copies thereof to each of the signatory and acceding states.

Source: *Sveriges överenskommelser med främmande makter, 1959* [Sweden's Agreements with Foreign Powers], No. 14–17 (Swedish Foreign Office, Stockholm, 1959).

The following states ratified, acceded or succeeded to this convention (Geneva Convention IV): Afghanistan, Albania, Algeria, Argentina, Australia, Austria, Bahrain, Bangladesh, Barbados, Belgium, Botswana, Brazil, Bulgaria, Burundi, Byelorussia, Cameroon, Canada, Central African Republic, Chad, Chile, China, Colombia, People's Republic of Congo, Costa Rica, Cuba, Cyprus, Czechoslovakia, Dahomey, Denmark, Dominican Republic, Ecuador, Egypt, El Salvador, Ethiopia, Fiji, Finland, France, Gabon, Gambia, German Democratic Republic, Federal Republic of Germany, Ghana, Greece, Guatemala, Guinea-Bissau, Guyana, Haiti, Holy See, Honduras, Hungary, Iceland, India, Indonesia, Iran, Iraq, Ireland, Israel, Italy, Ivory Coast, Jamaica, Japan, Jordan, Kenya, Khmer Republic, Democratic People's Republic of Korea (North), Republic of Korea (South), Kuwait, Laos, Lebanon, Lesotho, Liberia, Libya, Liechtenstein, Luxembourg, Madagascar, Malawi, Malaysia, Mali, Malta, Mauritania, Mauritius, Mexico, Monaco, Mongolia, Morocco, Nepal, Netherlands, New Zealand, Nicaragua, Niger, Nigeria, Norway, Oman, Pakistan, Panama, Paraguay, Peru, Philippines, Poland, Portugal, Romania, Rwanda, San Marino, Saudi Arabia, Senegal, Sierra Leone, Singapore, Somalia, South Africa, Spain, Sri Lanka, Sudan, Swaziland, Sweden, Switzerland, Syrian Arab Republic, Tanzania, Thailand, Togo, Trinidad and Tobago, Tunisia, Turkey, Uganda, Ukraine, Union of Soviet Socialist Republics, United Arab Emirates, United Kingdom, United States, Upper Volta, Uruguay, Venezuela, Democratic Republic of Viet Nam,* Republic of Viet Nam,* Provisional Revolutionary Government of the Republic of South Vietnam,* Yemen, Yugoslavia, Zaire, and Zambia.

Geneva Convention IV was worked out at the Diplomatic Conference held from 21 April to 12 August 1949. Other conventions adopted at the same time:
Convention (I) for the amelioration of the condition of the wounded and sick in armed forces in the field.
Convention (II) for the amelioration of the condition of the wounded, sick and shipwrecked members of armed forces at sea.
Convention (III) relative to the treatment of prisoners of war.

* On 2 July 1976, the single state of the Socialist Republic of Viet Nam was proclaimed.

STATUTE OF THE INTERNATIONAL ATOMIC ENERGY AGENCY

Opened for signature on 26 October 1956.
Entered into force on 29 July 1957.

EXTRACTS:

. . .

Article III. *Functions*

A. The Agency is authorized:

. . .

5. To establish and administer safeguards designed to ensure that special fissionable and other materials, ser-

vices, equipment, facilities, and information made available by the Agency or at its request or under its supervision or control are not used in such a way as to further any military purpose; and to apply safeguards, at the request of the parties, to any bilateral or multilateral arrangement, or at the request of a State, to any of that State's activities in the field of atomic energy.

. . .

Article XII. *Agency safeguards*

. . .

B. The Agency shall, as necessary, establish a staff of inspectors. The staff of inspectors shall have the responsibility of examining all operations conducted by the Agency itself to determine whether the Agency is complying with the health and safety measures prescribed by it for application to projects subject to its approval, supervision or control, and whether the Agency is taking adequate measures to prevent the source and special fissionable materials in its custody or used or produced in its own operations from being used in furtherance of any military purpose. The Agency shall take remedial action forthwith to correct any non-compliance or failure to take adequate measures.

C. ... The inspectors shall report any non-compliance to the Director General who shall thereupon transmit the report to the Board of Governors. The Board shall call upon the recipient State or States to remedy forthwith any non-compliance which it finds to have occurred. The Board shall report the non-compliance to all members and to the Security Council and General Assembly of the United Nations. In the event of failure of the recipient State or States to take fully corrective action within a reasonable time, the Board may take one or both of the following measures: direct curtailment or suspension of assistance being provided by the Agency or by a member, and call for the return of materials and equipment made available to the recipient member or group of members. The Agency may also, in accordance with article XIX, suspend any non-complying member from the exercise of the privileges and rights of membership.

. . .

Source: *Statute* (IAEA, Vienna, March 1967).

The following states were members of the IAEA as of December 1977: Afghanistan, Albania, Algeria, Argentina, Australia, Austria, Bangladesh, Belgium, Bolivia, Brazil, Bulgaria, Burma, Byelorussia, United Republic of Cameroon, Canada, Chile, Colombia, Costa Rica, Cuba, Cyprus, Czechoslovakia, Denmark, Dominican Republic, Ecuador, Egypt, El Salvador, Ethiopia, Finland, France, Gabon, German Democratic Republic, Federal Republic of Germany, Ghana, Greece, Guatemala, Haiti, Holy See, Hungary, Iceland, India, Indonesia, Iran, Iraq, Ireland, Israel, Italy, Ivory Coast, Jamaica, Japan, Jordan, Democratic Kampuchea, Kenya, Democratic People's Republic of Korea (North), Republic of Korea (South), Kuwait, Lebanon, Liberia, Libya, Liechtenstein, Luxembourg, Madagascar, Malaysia, Mali, Mauritius, Mexico, Monaco, Mongolia, Morocco, Netherlands, New Zealand, Nicaragua, Niger, Nigeria, Norway, Pakistan, Panama, Paraguay, Peru, Philippines, Poland, Portugal, Qatar, Romania, Saudi Arabia, Senegal, Sierra Leone, Singapore, South Africa, Spain, Sri Lanka, Sudan, Sweden, Switzerland, Syria, United Republic of Tanzania, Thailand, Tunisia, Turkey, Uganda, Ukraine, Union of Soviet Socialist Republics, United Arab Emirates, United Kingdom, United States, Uruguay, Venezuela, Viet Nam, Yugoslavia, Zaire, and Zambia.

THE ANTARCTIC TREATY

Signed at Washington on 1 December 1959.
Entered into force on 23 June 1961.
Depositary: US government.

The Governments of Argentina, Australia, Belgium, Chile, the French Republic, Japan, New Zealand, Norway, the Union of South Africa, the Union of Soviet Socialist Republics, the United Kingdom of Great Britain and Northern Ireland, and the United States of America,

Recognizing that it is in the interest of all mankind that Antarctica shall continue forever to be used exclusively for peaceful purposes and shall not become the scene or object of international discord;

Acknowledging the substantial contributions to scientific knowledge resulting from international cooperation in scientific investigation in Antarctica;

Convinced that the establishment of a firm foundation for the continuation and development of such cooperation on the basis of freedom of scientific investigation in Antarctica as applied during the International Geophysical Year accords with the interests of science and the progress of all mankind;

Convinced also that a treaty ensuring the use of Antarctica for peaceful purposes only and the continuance of international harmony in Antarctica will further the purposes and principles embodied in the Charter of the United Nations;

Have agreed as follows:

Article I

1. Antarctica shall be used for peaceful purposes only. There shall be prohibited, *inter alia,* any measures of a military nature, such as the establishment of military bases and fortifications, the carrying out of military maneuvers, as well as the testing of any type of weapons.

2. The present Treaty shall not prevent the use of military personnel or equipment for scientific research or for any other peaceful purpose.

Article II

Freedom of scientific investigation in Antarctica and cooperation toward that end, as applied during the International Geophysical Year, shall continue, subject to the provisions of the present Treaty.

Article III

1. In order to promote international cooperation in scientific investigation in Antarctica, as provided for in Article II of the present Treaty, the Contracting Parties agree that, to the greatest extent feasible and practicable:

(*a*) information regarding plans for scientific programs in Antarctica shall be exchanged to permit maximum economy and efficiency of operations;

(*b*) scientific personnel shall be exchanged in Antarctica between expeditions and stations;

(*c*) scientific observations and results from Antarctica shall be exchanged and made freely available.

2. In implementing this Article, every encouragement shall be given to the establishment of cooperative working relations with those Specialized Agencies of the United Nations and other international organizations having a scientific or technical interest in Antarctica.

Article IV

1. Nothing contained in the present Treaty shall be interpreted as:

(a) a renunciation by any Contracting Party of previously asserted rights of or claims to territorial sovereignty in Antarctica;

(b) a renunciation or diminution by any Contracting Party of any basis of claim to territorial sovereignty in Antarctica which it may have whether as a result of its activities or those of its nationals in Antarctica, or otherwise;

(c) prejudicing the position of any Contracting Party as regards its recognition or non-recognition of any other State's right of or claim or basis of claim to territorial sovereignty in Antarctica.

2. No acts or activities taking place while the present Treaty is in force shall constitute a basis for asserting, supporting or denying a claim to territorial sovereignty in Antarctica or create any rights of sovereignty in Antarctica. No new claim, or enlargement of an existing claim, to territorial sovereignty in Antarctica shall be asserted while the present Treaty is in force.

Article V

1. Any nuclear explosions in Antarctica and the disposal there of radioactive waste material shall be prohibited.

2. In the event of the conclusion of international agreements concerning the use of nuclear energy, including nuclear explosions and the disposal of radioactive waste material, to which all of the Contracting Parties whose representatives are entitled to participate in the meetings provided for under Article IX are parties, the rules established under such agreements shall apply in Antarctica.

Article VI

The provisions of the present Treaty shall apply to the area south of 60° South Latitude, including all ice shelves, but nothing in the present Treaty shall prejudice or in any way affect the rights, or the exercise of the rights, of any State under international law with regard to the high seas within that area.

Article VII

1. In order to promote the objectives and ensure the observance of the provisions of the present Treaty, each Contracting Party whose representatives are entitled to participate in the meetings referred to in Article IX of the Treaty shall have the right to designate observers to carry out any inspection provided for by the present Article. Observers shall be nationals of the Contracting Parties which designate them. The names of observers shall be communicated to every other Contracting Party having the right to designate observers, and like notice shall be given of the termination of their appointment.

2. Each observer designated in accordance with the provisions of paragraph 1 of this Article shall have complete freedom of access at any time to any or all areas of Antarctica.

3. All areas of Antarctica, including all stations, installations and equipment within those areas, and all ships and aircraft at points of discharging or embarking cargoes or personnel in Antarctica, shall be open at all times to inspection by any observers designated in accordance with paragraph 1 of this Article.

4. Aerial observation may be carried out at any time over any or all areas of Antarctica by any of the Contracting Parties having the right to designate observers.

5. Each Contracting Party shall, at the time when the present Treaty enters into force for it, inform the other Contracting Parties, and thereafter shall give them notice in advance, of

(a) all expeditions to and within Antarctica, on the part of its ships or nationals, and all expeditions to Antarctica organized in or proceeding from its territory;

(b) all stations in Antarctica occupied by its nationals; and

(c) any military personnel or equipment intended to be introduced by it into Antarctica subject to the conditions prescribed in paragraph 2 of Article I of the present Treaty.

Article VIII

1. In order to facilitate the exercise of their functions under the present Treaty, and without prejudice to the respective positions of the Contracting Parties relating to jurisdiction over all other persons in Antarctica, observers designated under paragraph 1 of Article VII and scientific personnel exchanged under subparagraph 1 (b) of Article III of the Treaty, and members of the staffs accompanying any such persons, shall be subject only to the jurisdiction of the Contracting Party of which they are nationals in respect of all acts or omissions occurring while they are in Antarctica for the purpose of exercising their functions.

2. Without prejudice to the provisions of paragraph 1 of this Article, and pending the adoption of measures in pursuance of subparagraph 1 (e) of Article IX, the Contracting Parties concerned in any case of dispute with regard to the exercise of jurisdiction in Antarctica shall immediately consult together with a view to reaching a mutually acceptable solution.

Article IX

1. Representatives of the Contracting Parties named in the preamble to the present Treaty shall meet at the City of Canberra within two months after the date of entry into force of the Treaty, and thereafter at suitable intervals and places, for the purpose of exchanging information, consulting together on matters of common interest pertaining to Antarctica, and formulating and considering, and recommending to their Governments, measures in furtherance of the principles and objectives of the Treaty, including measures regarding:

(a) use of Antarctica for peaceful purposes only;

(b) facilitation of scientific research in Antarctica;

(c) facilitation of international scientific cooperation in Antarctica;

(d) facilitation of the exercise of the rights of inspection provided for in Article VII of the Treaty;

(e) questions relating to the exercise of jurisdiction in Antarctica;

(f) preservation and conservation of living resources in Antarctica.

2. Each Contracting Party which has become a party to the present Treaty by accession under Article XIII shall be entitled to appoint representatives to participate in the meetings referred to in paragraph 1 of the present Article, during such time as that Contracting Party demon-

strates its interest in Antarctica by conducting substantial scientific research activity there, such as the establishment of a scientific station or the despatch of a scientific expedition.

3. Reports from the observers referred to in Article VII of the present Treaty shall be transmitted to the representatives of the Contracting Parties participating in the meetings referred to in paragraph 1 of the present Article.

4. The measures referred to in paragraph 1 of this Article shall become effective when approved by all the Contracting Parties whose representatives were entitled to participate in the meetings held to consider those measures.

5. Any or all of the rights established in the present Treaty may be exercised as from the date of entry into force of the Treaty whether or not any measures facilitating the exercise of such rights have been proposed, considered or approved as provided in this Article.

Article X

Each of the Contracting Parties undertakes to exert appropriate efforts, consistent with the Charter of the United Nations, to the end that no one engages in any activity in Antarctica contrary to the principles or purposes of the present Treaty.

Article XI

1. If any dispute arises between two or more of the Contracting Parties concerning the interpretation or application of the present Treaty, those Contracting Parties shall consult among themselves with a view to having the dispute resolved by negotiation, inquiry, mediation, conciliation, arbitration, judicial settlement or other peaceful means of their own choice.

2. Any dispute of this character not so resolved shall, with the consent, in each case, of all parties to the dispute, be referred to the International Court of Justice for settlement; but failure to reach agreement on reference to the International Court shall not absolve parties to the dispute from the responsibility of continuing to seek to resolve it by any of the various peaceful means referred to in paragraph 1 of this Article.

Article XII

1. (a) The present Treaty may be modified or amended at any time by unanimous agreement of the Contracting Parties whose representatives are entitled to participate in the meetings provided for under Article IX. Any such modification or amendment shall enter into force when the depositary Government has received notice from all such Contracting Parties that they have ratified it.

(b) Such modification or amendment shall thereafter enter into force as to any other Contracting Party when notice of ratification by it has been received by the depositary Government. Any such Contracting Party from which no notice of ratification is received within a period of two years from the date of entry into force of the modification or amendment in accordance with the provisions of subparagraph 1(a) of this Article shall be deemed to have withdrawn from the present Treaty on the date of the expiration of such period.

2. (a) If after the expiration of thirty years from the date of entry into force of the present Treaty, any of the Contracting Parties whose representatives are entitled to participate in the meetings provided for under Article IX so requests by a communication addressed to the depositary Government, a Conference of all the Contracting Parties shall be held as soon as practicable to review the operation of the Treaty.

(b) Any modification or amendment to the present Treaty which is approved at such a Conference by a majority of the Contracting Parties there represented, including a majority of those whose representatives are entitled to participate in the meetings provided for under Article IX, shall be communicated by the depositary Government to all the Contracting Parties immediately after the termination of the Conference and shall enter into force in accordance with the provisions of paragraph 1 of the present Article.

(c) If any such modification or amendment has not entered into force in accordance with the provisions of subparagraph 1(a) of this Article within a period of two years after the date of its communication to all the Contracting Parties, any Contracting Party may at any time after the expiration of that period give notice to the depositary Government of its withdrawal from the present Treaty; and such withdrawal shall take effect two years after the receipt of the notice by the depositary Government.

Article XIII

1. The present Treaty shall be subject to ratification by the signatory States. It shall be open for accession by any State which is a Member of the United Nations, or by any other State which may be invited to accede to the Treaty with the consent of all the Contracting Parties whose representatives are entitled to participate in the meetings provided for under Article IX of the Treaty.

2. Ratification of or accession to the present Treaty shall be effected by each State in accordance with its constitutional processes.

3. Instruments of ratification and instruments of accession shall be deposited with the Government of the United States of America, hereby designated as the depositary Government.

4. The depositary Government shall inform all signatory and acceding States of the date of each deposit of an instrument of ratification or accession, and the date of entry into force of the Treaty and of any modification or amendment thereto.

5. Upon the deposit of instruments of ratification by all the signatory States, the present Treaty shall enter into force for those States and for States which have deposited instruments of accession. Thereafter the Treaty shall enter into force for any acceding State upon the deposit of its instrument of accession.

6. The present Treaty shall be registered by the depositary Government pursuant to Article 102 of the Charter of the United Nations.

Article XIV

The present Treaty, done in the English, French, Russian and Spanish languages, each version being equally authentic, shall be deposited in the archives of the Government of the United States of America, which shall transmit duly certified copies thereof to the Governments of the signatory and acceding States.

In witness whereof, the undersigned Plenipotentiaries, duly authorized, have signed the present Treaty.
Done at Washington this first day of December, one thousand nine hundred and fifty-nine.

Source: *Treaty Series, Treaties and international agreements registered or filed and recorded with the Secretariat of the United Nations,* Vol. 402 (United Nations, New York, 1962).

Number of parties as of 31 December 1977: 19.

For the list of states which have signed, ratified or acceded to the Antarctic Treaty, see pages 152–94.

JOINT STATEMENT OF AGREED PRINCIPLES FOR DISARMAMENT NEGOTIATIONS

Made on 20 September 1961.

Having conducted an extensive exchange of views on disarmament pursuant to their agreement announced in the General Assembly on 30 March 1961,

Noting with concern that the continuing arms race is a heavy burden for humanity and is fraught with dangers for the cause of world peace,

Reaffirming their adherence to all the provisions of the General Assembly resolution 1378 (XIV) of 20 November 1959,

Affirming that to facilitate the attainment of general and complete disarmament in a peaceful world it is important that all States abide by existing international agreements, refrain from any actions which might aggravate international tensions, and that they seek settlement of all disputes by peaceful means,

The United States and the USSR have agreed to recommend the following principles as the basis for future multilateral negotiations on disarmament and to call upon other States to co-operate in reaching early agreement on general and complete disarmament in a peaceful world in accordance with these principles.

1. The goal of negotiations is to achieve agreement on a programme which will ensure that (a) disarmament is general and complete and war is no longer an instrument for settling international problems, and (b) such disarmament is accompanied by the establishment of reliable procedures for the peaceful settlement of disputes and effective arrangements for the maintenance of peace in accordance with the principles of the United Nations Charter.

2. The programme for general and complete disarmament shall ensure that States will have at their disposal only those non-nuclear armaments, forces, facilities, and establishments as are agreed to be necessary to maintain internal order and protect the personal security of citizens; and that States shall support and provide agreed manpower for a United Nations peace force.

3. To this end, the programme for general and complete disarmament shall contain the necessary provisions, with respect to the military establishment of every nation, for:

(a) Disbanding of armed forces, dismantling of military establishments, including bases, cessation of the production of armaments as well as their liquidation or conversion to peaceful uses;

(b) Elimination of all stockpiles of nuclear, chemical, bacteriological, and other weapons of mass destruction and cessation of the production of such weapons;

(c) Elimination of all means of delivery of weapons of mass destruction;

(d) Abolishment of the organization and institutions designed to organize the military effort of States, cessation of military training, and closing of all military training institutions;

(e) Discontinuance of military expenditures.

4. The disarmament programme should be implemented in an agreed sequence, by stages until it is completed, with each measure and stage carried out within specified time-limits. Transition to a subsequent stage in the process of disarmament should take place upon a review of the implementation of measures included in the preceding stage and upon a decision that all such measures have been implemented and verified and that any additional verification arrangements required for measures in the next stage are, when appropriate, ready to operate.

5. All measures of general and complete disarmament should be balanced so that at no stage of the implementation of the treaty could any State or group of States gain military advantage and that security is ensured equally for all.

6. All disarmament measures should be implemented from beginning to end under such strict and effective international control as would provide firm assurance that all parties are honouring their obligations. During and after the implementation of general and complete disarmament, the most thorough control should be exercised, the nature and extent of such control depending on the requirements for verification of the disarmament measures being carried out in each stage. To implement control over and inspection of disarmament, an International Disarmament Organization including all parties to the agreement should be created within the framework of the United Nations. This International Disarmament Organization and its inspectors should be assured unrestricted access without veto to all places as necessary for the purpose of effective verification.

7. Progress in disarmament should be accompanied by measures to strengthen institutions for maintaining peace and the settlement of international disputes by peaceful means. During and after the implementation of the programme of general and complete disarmament, there should be taken, in accordance with the principles of the United Nations Charter, the necessary measures to maintain international peace and security, including the obligation of States to place at the disposal of the United Nations agreed manpower necessary for an international peace force to be equipped with agreed types of armaments. Arrangements for the use of this force should ensure that the United Nations can effectively deter or suppress any threat or use of arms in violation of the purposes and principles of the United Nations.

8. States participating in the negotiations should seek to achieve and implement the widest possible agreement at the earliest possible date. Efforts should continue without interruption until agreement upon the total programme has been achieved, and efforts to ensure early agreement on and implementation of measures of disarmament should be undertaken without prejudicing progress on agreement on the total programme and in such a way that these measures would facilitate and form part of that programme.

Source: Official Records of the General Assembly, Fifteenth Session, A/4879, 20 September 1961.

In resolution A/RES/1722 (XVI) of 20 December 1961, approved unanimously, the UN General Assembly welcomed the above joint statement of the governments of the USA and the USSR (the McCloy-Zorin Statement) and recommended that negotiations on general and complete disarmament should be based upon the agreed principles.

LETTER FROM PRESIDENTIAL ADVISER McCLOY TO DEPUTY FOREIGN MINISTER ZORIN: VERIFICATION OF RETAINED FORCES AND ARMAMENTS, 20 SEPTEMBER 1961

Dear Mr. Zorin:

At the 18 September 1961 session of our bilateral discussions on disarmament you indicated that the draft of a joint statement of agreed principles which I submitted to you on behalf of the United States Government on 14 September 1961 would be acceptable to the Government of the Soviet Union provided the following clause were omitted from paragraph 6:

"Such verification should ensure that not only agreed limitations or reductions take place but also that retained armed forces and armaments do not exceed agreed levels at any stage."

This sentence expresses a key element in the United States position which we believe is implicit in the entire joint statement of agreed principles that whenever an agreement stipulates that at a certain point certain levels of forces and armaments may be retained, the verification machinery must have all the rights and powers necessary to ensure that those levels are not exceeded.

It appears from your statements that the Soviet Union will be unwilling to agree to a joint statement of agreed principles unless the above-mentioned clause is omitted therefrom. My Government has authorized me to inform you that, in the interest of progress toward resuming disarmament negotiations, it is willing to remove the above-mentioned sentence from paragraph 6 of the joint statement of agreed principles since it is an item to which the Soviet Union has not agreed.

This is done upon the express understanding that the substantive position of the United States Government as outlined in the above-quoted sentence and in our memorandum of 14 September 1961 remains unchanged, and is in no sense prejudiced by the exclusion of this sentence from the joint statement of agreed principles.

The United States continues to adhere to and will continue to advance the principle contained in the omitted sentence as a necessary element in any comprehensive disarmament negotiations or agreement.

Very truly yours,

John J. McCloy

Source: UN document A/4880, 20 September 1961.

LETTER FROM DEPUTY FOREIGN MINISTER ZORIN TO PRESIDENTIAL ADVISER McCLOY, 20 SEPTEMBER 1961

Dear Mr. McCloy,

I have received your letter of 20 September 1961, in which you express a reservation with regard to the position which the United States of America intends to adopt in subsequent negotiations on disarmament.

According to the agreement which we reached in the course of a bilateral exchange of views, the United States agreed not to include, in the joint statement by the Governments of the USSR and the United States on the principles for disarmament negotiations, the proposal with which you are conversant and the adoption of which would imply acceptance of the concept of the establishment of control over armaments instead of control over disarmament. In your letter you say that this proposal "expresses a key element in the United States position".

In this connexion I must state that, as you know, the position of the USSR on the question of control over general and complete disarmament has been thoroughly and clearly explained in the statements of the Soviet Government and its leader N. S. Khrushchev. The Soviet Union favours the most thorough and strict international control over the measures of general and complete disarmament. While strongly advocating effective control over disarmament and wishing to facilitate as much as possible the achievement of agreement on this control, the Soviet Union is at the same time resolutely opposed to the establishment of control over armaments.

It appears from your letter that the United States is trying to establish control over the armed forces and armaments retained by States at any given stage of disarmament. However, such control, which in fact means control over armaments, would turn into an international system of legalized espionage, which would naturally be unacceptable to any State concerned for its security and the interests of preserving peace throughout the world. The position of the United States on this question, if it insists on the proposal described above, will inevitably complicate agreement on a programme of general and complete disarmament, on the general principles of which we have agreed.

The Soviet Union will continue to make every effort towards the earliest preparation of a treaty on general and complete disarmament under effective international control.

I have the honour to be, etc.

V. Zorin
Permanent Representative of the USSR
to the United Nations

Source: UN document A/4887, 25 September 1961.

TREATY BANNING NUCLEAR WEAPON TESTS IN THE ATMOSPHERE, IN OUTER SPACE AND UNDER WATER

Signed at Moscow on 5 August 1963.
Entered into force on 10 October 1963.
Depositaries: UK, US and Soviet governments.

The Governments of the United States of America, the United Kingdom of Great Britain and Northern Ireland, and the Union of Soviet Socialist Republics, hereinafter referred to as the "Original Parties",

Proclaiming as their principal aim the speediest possible achievement of an agreement on general and complete disarmament under strict international control in accordance with the objectives of the United Nations which would put an end to the armaments race and eliminate the incentive to the production and testing of all kinds of weapons, including nuclear weapons,

Seeking to achieve the discontinuance of all test explosions of nuclear weapons for all time, determined to continue negotiations to this end, and desiring to put an end to the contamination of man's environment by radioactive substances,

Have agreed as follows:

Article I

1. Each of the Parties to this Treaty undertakes to prohibit, to prevent, and not to carry out any nuclear weapon test explosion, or any other nuclear explosion, at any place under its jurisdiction or control:

(*a*) in the atmosphere; beyond its limits, including outer space; or under water, including territorial waters or high seas; or

(*b*) in any other environment if such explosion causes radioactive debris to be present outside the territorial limits of the State under whose jurisdiction or control such explosion is conducted. It is understood in this connection that the provisions of this subparagraph are without prejudice to the conclusion of a treaty resulting in the permanent banning of all nuclear test explosions, including all such explosions underground, the conclusion of which, as the Parties have stated in the Preamble to this Treaty, they seek to achieve.

2. Each of the Parties to this Treaty undertakes furthermore to refrain from causing, encouraging, or in any way participating in, the carrying out of any nuclear weapon test explosion, or any other nuclear explosion, anywhere which would take place in any of the environments described, or have the effect referred to, in paragraph 1 of this Article.

Article II

1. Any Party may propose amendments to this Treaty. The text of any proposed amendment shall be submitted to the Depositary Governments which shall circulate it to all Parties to this Treaty. Thereafter, if requested to do so by one-third or more of the Parties, the Depositary Governments shall convene a conference, to which they shall invite all the Parties, to consider such amendment.

2. Any amendment to this Treaty must be approved by a majority of the votes of all the Parties to this Treaty, including the votes of all of the Original Parties. The amendment shall enter into force for all Parties upon the deposit of instruments of ratification by a majority of all the Parties, including the instruments of ratification of all of the Original Parties.

Article III

1. This Treaty shall be open to all States for signature. Any State which does not sign this Treaty before its entry into force in accordance with paragraph 3 of this Article may accede to it at any time.

2. This Treaty shall be subject to ratification by signatory States. Instruments of ratification and instruments of accession shall be deposited with the Governments of the Original Parties—the United States of America, the United Kingdom of Great Britain and Northern Ireland, and the Union of Soviet Socialist Republics—which are hereby designated the Depositary Governments.

3. This Treaty shall enter into force after its ratification by all the Original Parties and the deposit of their instruments of ratification.

4. For States whose instruments of ratification or accession are deposited subsequent to the entry into force of this Treaty, it shall enter into force on the date of the deposit of their instruments of ratification or accession.

5. The Depositary Governments shall promptly inform all signatory and acceding States of the date of each signature, the date of deposit of each instrument of ratification of and accession to this Treaty, the date of its entry into force, and the date of receipt of any requests for conferences or other notices.

6. This Treaty shall be registered by the Depositary Governments pursuant to Article 102 of the Charter of the United Nations.

Article IV

This Treaty shall be of unlimited duration.

Each Party shall in exercising its national sovereignty have the right to withdraw from the Treaty if it decides that extraordinary events, related to the subject matter of this Treaty, have jeopardized the supreme interests of its country. It shall give notice of such withdrawal to all other Parties to the Treaty three months in advance.

Article V

This Treaty, of which the English and Russian texts are equally authentic, shall be deposited in the archives of the Depositary Governments. Duly certified copies of this Treaty shall be transmitted by the Depositary Governments to the Governments of the signatory and acceding States.

In witness whereof the undersigned, duly authorized, have signed this Treaty.

Done in triplicate at the city of Moscow the fifth day of August, one thousand nine hundred and sixty-three.

Source: *Treaty Series,* Vol. 480 (United Nations, New York, 1963).

Number of parties as of 31 December 1977: 108.

For the list of states which have signed, ratified, acceded or succeeded to the Partial Test Ban Treaty, see pages 152–94.

TREATY ON PRINCIPLES GOVERNING THE ACTIVITIES OF STATES IN THE EXPLORATION AND USE OF OUTER SPACE, INCLUDING THE MOON AND OTHER CELESTIAL BODIES

Signed at London, Moscow and Washington on 27 January 1967.
Entered into force on 10 October 1967.
Depositaries: UK, US and Soviet governments.

The States Parties to this Treaty,

Inspired by the great prospects opening up before mankind as a result of man's entry into outer space,

Recognizing the common interest of all mankind in the progress of the exploration and use of outer space for peaceful purposes,

Believing that the exploration and use of outer space should be carried on for the benefit of all peoples irrespective of the degree of their economic or scientific development,

Desiring to contribute to broad international co-operation in the scientific as well as the legal aspects of the exploration and use of outer space for peaceful purposes,

Believing that such co-operation will contribute to the development of mutual understanding and to the strengthening of friendly relations between States and peoples,

Recalling resolution 1962 (XVIII), entitled "Declaration of Legal Principles Governing the Activities of States in the Exploration and Use of Outer Space", which was adopted unanimously by the United Nations General Assembly on 13 December 1963,

Recalling resolution 1884 (XVIII), calling upon States to refrain from placing in orbit around the earth any objects carrying nuclear weapons or any other kinds of weapons of mass destruction or from installing such weapons on celestial bodies, which was adopted unanimously by the United Nations General Assembly on 17 October 1963,

Taking account of United Nations General Assembly resolution 110 (II) of 3 November 1947, which condemned propaganda designed or likely to provoke or encourage any threat to the peace, breach of the peace or act of aggression, and considering that the aforementioned resolution is applicable to outer space,

Convinced that a Treaty on Principles Governing the Activities of States in the Exploration and Use of Outer Space, including the Moon and Other Celestial Bodies, will further the Purposes and Principles of the Charter of the United Nations,

Have agreed on the following:

Article I

The exploration and use of outer space, including the moon and other celestial bodies, shall be carried out for the benefit and in the interests of all countries, irrespective of their degree of economic or scientific development, and shall be the province of all mankind.

Outer space, including the moon and other celestial bodies, shall be free for exploration and use by all States without discrimination of any kind, on a basis of equality and in accordance with international law, and there shall be free access to all areas of celestial bodies.

There shall be freedom of scientific investigation in outer space, including the moon and other celestial bodies, and States shall facilitate and encourage international co-operation in such investigation.

Article II

Outer space, including the moon and other celestial bodies, is not subject to national appropriation by claim of sovereignty, by means of use or occupation, or by any other means.

Article III

States Parties to the Treaty shall carry on activities in the exploration and use of outer space, including the moon and other celestial bodies, in accordance with international law, including the Charter of the United Nations, in the interest of maintaining international peace and security and promoting international co-operation and understanding.

Article IV

States Parties to the Treaty undertake not to place in orbit around the earth any objects carrying nuclear weapons or any other kinds of weapons of mass destruction, instal such weapons on celestial bodies, or station such weapons in outer space in any other manner.

The moon and other celestial bodies shall be used by all States Parties to the Treaty exclusively for peaceful purposes. The establishment of military bases, installations and fortifications, the testing of any type of weapons and the conduct of military manœuvres on celestial bodies shall be forbidden. The use of military personnel for scientific research or for any other peaceful purposes shall not be prohibited. The use of any equipment or facility necessary for peaceful exploration of the moon and other celestial bodies shall also not be prohibited.

Article V

States Parties to the Treaty shall regard astronauts as envoys of mankind in outer space and shall render to them all possible assistance in the event of accident, distress, or emergency landing on the territory of another State Party or on the high seas. When astronauts make such a landing, they shall be safely and promptly returned to the State of registry of their space vehicle.

In carrying on activities in outer space and on celestial bodies, the astronauts of one State Party shall render all possible assistance to the astronauts of other States Parties.

States Parties to the Treaty shall immediately inform the other States Parties to the Treaty or the Secretary-General of the United Nations of any phenomena they discover in outer space, including the moon and other celestial bodies, which could constitute a danger to the life or health of astronauts.

Article VI

States Parties to the Treaty shall bear international responsibility for national activities in outer space, including the moon and other celestial bodies, whether such activities are carried on by governmental agencies or by nongovernmental entities, and for assuring that national activities are carried out in conformity with the provisions set forth in the present Treaty. The activities of non-governmental entities in outer space, including the moon and other celestial bodies, shall require authorization and continuing supervision by the appropriate State Party to the Treaty. When activities are carried on in outer space, including the moon and other celestial bodies, by an international organization, responsibility for compliance with this Treaty shall be borne both by the international organization and by the States Parties to the Treaty participating in such organization.

Article VII

Each State Party to the Treaty that launches or procures the launching of an object into outer space, including the moon and other celestial bodies, and each State Party from whose territory or facility an object is launched, is internationally liable for damage to another State Party to the Treaty or to its natural or juridical persons by such object or its component parts on the Earth, in air space or in outer space, including the moon and other celestial bodies.

Article VIII

A State Party to the Treaty on whose registry an object launched into outer space is carried shall retain jurisdiction and control over such object, and over any personnel thereof, while in outer space or on a celestial body. Ownership of objects launched into outer space, including objects landed or constructed on a celestial body, and of their component parts, is not affected by their presence in outer space or on a celestial body or by their return to the Earth. Such objects or component parts found beyond the limits of the State Party to the Treaty on whose registry they are carried shall be returned to that State Party, which shall, upon request, furnish identifying data prior to their return.

Article IX

In the exploration and use of outer space, including the moon and other celestial bodies, States Parties to the Treaty shall be guided by the principle of co-operation and mutual assistance and shall conduct all their activities in outer space, including the moon and other celestial bodies, with due regard to the corresponding interests of all other States Parties to the Treaty. States Parties to the Treaty shall pursue studies of outer space, including the moon and other celestial bodies, and conduct exploration of them so as to avoid their harmful contamination and also adverse changes in the environment of the Earth resulting from the introduction of extraterrestrial matter and, where necessary, shall adopt appropriate measures for this purpose. If a State Party to the Treaty has reason to believe that an activity or experiment planned by it or its nationals in outer space, including the moon and other celestial bodies, would cause potentially harmful interference with activities of other States Parties in the peaceful exploration and use of outer space, including the moon and other celestial bodies, it shall undertake appropriate international consultations before proceeding with any such activity or experiment. A State Party to the Treaty which has reason to believe that an activity or experiment planned by another State Party in outer space, including the moon and other celestial bodies, would cause potentially harmful interference with activities in the peaceful exploration and use of outer space, including the moon and other celestial bodies, may request consultation concerning the activity or experiment.

Article X

In order to promote international co-operation in the exploration and use of outer space, including the moon and other celestial bodies, in conformity with the purposes of this Treaty, the States Parties to the Treaty shall consider on a basis of equality any requests by other States Parties to the Treaty to be afforded an opportunity to observe the flight of space objects launched by these States.

The nature of such an opportunity for observation and the conditions under which it could be afforded shall be determined by agreement between the States concerned.

Article XI

In order to promote international co-operation in the peaceful exploration and use of outer space, States Parties to the Treaty conducting activities in outer space, including the moon and other celestial bodies, agree to inform the Secretary-General of the United Nations as well as the public and the international scientific community, to the greatest extent feasible and practicable, of the nature, conduct, locations and results of such activities. On receiving the said information, the Secretary-General of the United Nations should be prepared to disseminate it immediately and effectively.

Article XII

All stations, installations, equipment and space vehicles on the moon and other celestial bodies shall be open to representatives of other States Parties to the Treaty on a basis of reciprocity. Such representatives shall give reasonable advance notice of a projected visit, in order that appropriate consultations may be held and that maximum precautions may be taken to assure safety and to avoid interference with normal operations in the facility to be visited.

Article XIII

The provisions of this Treaty shall apply to the activities of States Parties to the Treaty in the exploration and use of outer space, including the moon and other celestial bodies, whether such activities are carried on by a single State Party to the Treaty or jointly with other States, including cases where they are carried on within the framework of international inter-governmental organizations.

Any practical questions arising in connexion with activities carried on by international inter-governmental organizations in the exploration and use of outer space, including the moon and other celestial bodies, shall be resolved by the States Parties to the Treaty either with the appropriate international organization or with one or more States members of that international organization, which are Parties to this Treaty.

Article XIV

1. This Treaty shall be open to all States for signature. Any State which does not sign this Treaty before its entry into force in accordance with paragraph 3 of this Article may accede to it at any time.
2. This Treaty shall be subject to ratification by signatory States. Instruments of ratification and instruments of accession shall be deposited with the Governments of the United Kingdom of Great Britain and Northern Ireland, the Union of Soviet Socialist Republics and the United States of America, which are hereby designated the Depositary Governments.
3. This Treaty shall enter into force upon the deposit of instruments of ratification by five Governments including the Governments designated as Depositary Governments under this Treaty.
4. For States whose instruments of ratification or accession are deposited subsequent to the entry into force of this Treaty, it shall enter into force on the date of the deposit of their instruments of ratification or accession.
5. The Depositary Governments shall promptly inform all signatory and acceding States of the date of each signature, the date of deposit of each instrument of ratification of and accession to this Treaty, the date of its entry into force and other notices.
6. This Treaty shall be registered by the Depositary Governments pursuant to Article 102 of the Charter of the United Nations.

Article XV

Any State Party to the Treaty may propose amendments to this Treaty. Amendments shall enter into force for each State Party to the Treaty accepting the amendments upon their acceptance by a majority of the States Parties to the Treaty and thereafter for each remaining State Party to the Treaty on the date of acceptance by it.

Article XVI

Any State Party to the Treaty may give notice of its withdrawal from the Treaty one year after its entry into force by written notification to the Depositary Governments. Such withdrawal shall take effect one year from the date of receipt of this notification.

Article XVII

This Treaty, of which the English, Russian, French, Spanish and Chinese texts are equally authentic, shall be deposited in the archives of the Depositary Governments. Duly certified copies of this Treaty shall be transmitted by the Depositary Governments to the Governments of the signatory and acceding States.

In witness whereof the undersigned, duly authorised, have signed this Treaty.

Done in triplicate, at the cities of London, Moscow and Washington, the twenty-seventh day of January, one thousand nine hundred and sixty-seven.

Source: *Treaty Series,* Vol. 610 (United Nations, New York, 1970).

Number of parties as of 31 December 1977: 77.

For the list of states which have signed, ratified, acceded or succeeded to the Outer Space Treaty, see pages 152–94.

TREATY FOR THE PROHIBITION OF NUCLEAR WEAPONS IN LATIN AMERICA

Signed at Mexico, Federal District, on 14 February 1967.

The Treaty enters into force for each state that has ratified it when the requirements specified in the Treaty have been met, that is, that all states in the region which were in existence when the Treaty was opened for signature, deposit the instruments of ratification; that Protocols I and II be signed and ratified by those states to which they apply; and that agreements on safeguards be concluded with the IAEA. The signatory states have the right to waive, wholly or in part, those requirements.

The Treaty came into force on 22 April 1968 as between Mexico and El Salvador, on behalf of which instruments of ratification, with annexed declarations wholly waiving the above requirements, were deposited on 20 September 1967 and 22 April 1968, respectively.

The Protocols enter into force for the states that have ratified them on the date of the deposit of their instruments of ratification.

Depositary: Government of Mexico.

Preamble

In the name of their peoples and faithfully interpreting their desires and aspirations, the Governments of the States which sign the Treaty for the Prohibition of Nuclear Weapons in Latin America,

Desiring to contribute, so far as lies in their power, towards ending the armaments race, especially in the field of nuclear weapons, and towards strengthening a world at peace, based on the sovereign equality of States, mutual respect and good neighbourliness,

Recalling that the United Nations General Assembly, in its Resolution 808 (IX), adopted unanimously as one of the three points of a coordinated programme of disarmament "the total prohibition of the use and manufacture of nuclear weapons and weapons of mass destruction of every type",

Recalling that militarily denuclearized zones are not an end in themselves but rather a means for achieving general and complete disarmament at a later stage,

Recalling United Nations General Assembly Resolution

1911 (XVIII), which established that the measures that should be agreed upon for the denuclearization of Latin America should be taken "in the light of the principles of the Charter of the United Nations and of regional agreements",

Recalling United Nations General Assembly Resolution 2028 (XX), which established the principle of an acceptable balance of mutual responsibilities and duties for the nuclear and non-nuclear powers, and

Recalling that the Charter of the Organization of American States proclaims that it is an essential purpose of the Organization to strengthen the peace and security of the hemisphere,

Convinced:

That the incalculable destructive power of nuclear weapons has made it imperative that the legal prohibition of war should be strictly observed in practice if the survival of civilization and of mankind itself is to be assured,

That nuclear weapons, whose terrible effects are suffered, indiscriminately and inexorably, by military forces and civilian population alike, constitute, through the persistence of the radioactivity they release, an attack on the integrity of the human species and ultimately may even render the whole earth uninhabitable,

That general and complete disarmament under effective international control is a vital matter which all the peoples of the world equally demand,

That the proliferation of nuclear weapons, which seems inevitable unless States, in the exercise of their sovereign rights, impose restrictions on themselves in order to prevent it, would make any agreement on disarmament enormously difficult and would increase the danger of the outbreak of a nuclear conflagration,

That the establishment of militarily denuclearized zones is closely linked with the maintenance of peace and security in the respective regions,

That the military denuclearization of vast geographical zones, adopted by the sovereign decision of the States comprised therein, will exercise a beneficial influence on other regions where similar conditions exist,

That the privileged situation of the signatory States, whose territories are wholly free from nuclear weapons, imposes upon them the inescapable duty of preserving that situation both in their own interests and for the good of mankind,

That the existence of nuclear weapons in any country of Latin America would make it a target for possible nuclear attacks and would inevitably set off, throughout the region, a ruinous race in nuclear weapons which would involve the unjustifiable diversion, for warlike purposes, of the limited resources required for economic and social development,

That the foregoing reasons, together with the traditional peace-loving outlook of Latin America, give rise to an inescapable necessity that nuclear energy should be used in that region exclusively for peaceful purposes, and that the Latin American countries should use their right to the greatest and most equitable possible access to this new source of energy in order to expedite the economic and social development of their peoples,

Convinced finally:

That the military denuclearization of Latin America—being understood to mean the undertaking entered into internationally in this Treaty to keep their territories forever free from nuclear weapons—will constitute a measure which will spare their peoples from the squandering of their limited resources on nuclear armaments and will protect them against possible nuclear attacks on their territories, and will also constitute a significant contribution towards preventing the proliferation of nuclear-weapons and a powerful factor for general and complete disarmament, and

That Latin America, faithful to its tradition of universality, must not only endeavour to banish from its homelands the scourge of a nuclear war, but must also strive to promote the well-being and advancement of its peoples, at the same time co-operating in the fulfilment of the ideals of mankind, that is to say, in the consolidation of a permanent peace based on equal rights, economic fairness and social justice for all, in accordance with the principles and purposes set forth in the Charter of the United Nations and in the Charter of the Organization of American States,

Have agreed as follows:

Article 1. *Obligations*

1. The Contracting Parties hereby undertake to use exclusively for peaceful purposes the nuclear material and facilities which are under their jurisdiction, and to prohibit and prevent in their respective territories:

(*a*) The testing, use, manufacture, production or acquisition by any means whatsoever of any nuclear weapons, by the Parties themselves, directly or indirectly, on behalf of anyone else or in any other way, and

(*b*) The receipt, storage, installation, deployment and any form of possession of any nuclear weapons, directly or indirectly, by the Parties themselves, by anyone on their behalf or in any other way.

2. The Contracting Parties also undertake to refrain from engaging in, encouraging or authorizing, directly or indirectly, or in any way participating in the testing, use, manufacture, production, possession or control of any nuclear weapon.

Article 2. *Definition of the Contracting Parties*

For the purposes of this Treaty, the Contracting Parties are those for whom the Treaty is in force.

Article 3. *Definition of territory*

For the purposes of this Treaty, the term "territory" shall include the territorial sea, air space and any other space over which the State exercises sovereignty in accordance with its own legislation.

Article 4. *Zone of application*

1. The zone of application of this Treaty is the whole of the territories for which the Treaty is in force.

2. Upon fulfilment of the requirements of article 28, paragraph 1, the zone of application of this Treaty shall also be that which is situated in the western hemisphere within the following limits (except the continental part of the territory of the United States of America and its territorial waters): starting at a point located at 35° north latitude, 75° west longitude; from this point directly southward to a point at 30° north latitude, 75° west longitude; from there, directly eastward to a point at 30° north latitude, 50° west longitude; from there, along a loxodromic

line to a point at 5° north latitude, 20° west longitude; from there, directly southward to a point at 60° south latitude, 20° west longitude; from there, directly westward to a point at 60° south latitude, 115° west longitude; from there, directly northward to a point at 0 latitude, 115° west longitude; from there, along a loxodromic line to a point at 35° north latitude, 150° west longitude; from there, directly eastward to a point at 35° north latitude, 75° west longitude.

Article 5. *Definition of nuclear weapons*

For the purposes of this Treaty, a nuclear weapon is any device which is capable of releasing nuclear energy in an uncontrolled manner and which has a group of characteristics that are appropriate for use for warlike purposes. An instrument that may be used for the transport or propulsion of the device is not included in this definition if it is separable from the device and not an indivisible part thereof.

Article 6. *Meeting of signatories*

At the request of any of the signatory States or if the Agency established by article 7 should so decide, a meeting of all the signatories may be convoked to consider in common questions which may affect the very essence of this instrument, including possible amendments to it. In either case, the meeting will be convoked by the General Secretary.

Article 7. *Organization*

1. In order to ensure compliance with the obligations of this Treaty, the Contracting Parties hereby establish an international organization to be known as the Agency for the Prohibition of Nuclear Weapons in Latin America, hereinafter referred to as "the Agency". Only the Contracting Parties shall be affected by its decisions.
2. The Agency shall be responsible for the holding of periodic or extraordinary consultations among Member States on matters relating to the purposes, measures and procedures set forth in this Treaty and to the supervision of compliance with the obligations arising therefrom.
3. The Contracting Parties agree to extend to the Agency full and prompt co-operation in accordance with the provisions of this Treaty, of any agreements they may conclude with the Agency and of any agreements the Agency may conclude with any other international organization or body.
4. The headquarters of the Agency shall be in Mexico City.

Article 8. *Organs*

1. There are hereby established as principal organs of the Agency a General Conference, a Council and a Secretariat.
2. Such subsidiary organs as are considered necessary by the General Conference may be established within the purview of this Treaty.

Article 9. *The General Conference*

1. The General Conference, the supreme organ of the Agency, shall be composed of all the Contracting Parties; it shall hold regular sessions every two years, and may also hold special sessions whenever this Treaty so provides or, in the opinion of the Council, the circumstances so require.
2. The General Conference:

(*a*) May consider and decide on any matters or questions covered by this Treaty, within the limits thereof, including those referring to powers and functions of any organ provided for in this Treaty;

(*b*) Shall establish procedures for the control system to ensure observance of this Treaty in accordance with its provisions;

(*c*) Shall elect the Members of the Council and the General Secretary;

(*d*) May remove the General Secretary from office if the proper functioning of the Agency so requires;

(*e*) Shall receive and consider the biennial and special reports submitted by the Council and the General Secretary.

(*f*) Shall initiate and consider studies designed to facilitate the optimum fulfilment of the aims of this Treaty, without prejudice to the power of the General Secretary independently to carry out similar studies for submission to and consideration by the Conference.

(*g*) Shall be the organ competent to authorize the conclusion of agreements with Governments and other international organizations and bodies.

3. The General Conference shall adopt the Agency's budget and fix the scale of financial contributions to be paid by Member States, taking into account the systems and criteria used for the same purpose by the United Nations.
4. The General Conference shall elect its officers for each session and may establish such subsidiary organs as it deems necessary for the performance of its functions.
5. Each Member of the Agency shall have one vote. The decisions of the General Conference shall be taken by a two-thirds majority of the Members present and voting in the case of matters relating to the control system and measures referred to in article 20, the admission of new Members, the election or removal of the General Secretary, adoption of the budget and matters related thereto. Decisions on other matters, as well as procedural questions and also determination of which questions must be decided by a two-thirds majority, shall be taken by a simple majority of the Members present and voting.
6. The General Conference shall adopt its own rules of procedure.

Article 10. *The Council*

1. The Council shall be composed of five Members of the Agency elected by the General Conference from among the Contracting Parties, due account being taken of equitable geographic distribution.
2. The Members of the Council shall be elected for a term of four years. However, in the first election three will be elected for two years. Outgoing Members may not be re-elected for the following period unless the limited number of States for which the Treaty is in force so requires.
3. Each Member of the Council shall have one representative.
4. The Council shall be so organized as to be able to function continuously.
5. In addition to the functions conferred upon it by this Treaty and to those which may be assigned to it by the General Conference, the Council shall, through the General Secretary, ensure the proper operation of the contro

system in accordance with the provisions of this Treaty and with the decisions adopted by the General Conference.

6. The Council shall submit an annual report on its work to the General Conference as well as such special reports as it deems necessary or which the General Conference requests of it.

7. The Council shall elect its officers for each session.

8. The decisions of the Council shall be taken by a simple majority of its Members present and voting.

9. The Council shall adopt its own rules of procedure.

Article 11. *The Secretariat*

1. The Secretariat shall consist of a General Secretary, who shall be the chief administrative officer of the Agency, and of such staff as the Agency may require. The term of office of the General Secretary shall be four years and he may be re-elected for a single additional term. The General Secretary may not be a national of the country in which the Agency has its headquarters. In case the office of General Secretary becomes vacant, a new election shall be held to fill the office for the remainder of the term.

2. The staff of the Secretariat shall be appointed by the General Secretary, in accordance with rules laid down by the General Conference.

3. In addition to the functions conferred upon him by this Treaty and to those which may be assigned to him by the General Conference,—the General Secretary shall ensure, as provided by article 10, paragraph 5, the proper operation of the control system established by this Treaty, in accordance with the provisions of the Treaty and the decisions taken by the General Conference.

4. The General Secretary shall act in that capacity in all meetings of the General Conference and of the Council and shall make an annual report to both bodies on the work of the Agency and any special reports requested by the General Conference or the Council or which the General Secretary may deem desirable.

5. The General Secretary shall establish the procedures for distributing to all Contracting Parties information received by the Agency from governmental sources and such information from non-governmental sources as may be of interest to the Agency.

6. In the performance of their duties the General Secretary and the staff shall not seek or receive instructions from any Government or from any other authority external to the Agency and shall refrain from any action which might reflect on their position as international officials responsible only to the Agency; subject to their responsibility to the Agency, they shall not disclose any industrial secrets or other confidential information coming to their knowledge by reason of their official duties in the Agency.

7. Each of the Contracting Parties undertakes to respect the exclusively international character of the responsibilities of the General Secretary and the staff and not to seek to influence them in the discharge of their responsibilities.

Article 12. *Control system*

1. For the purpose of verifying compliance with the obligations entered into by the Contracting Parties in accordance with article 1, a control system shall be established which shall be put into effect in accordance with the provisions of articles 13–18 of this Treaty.

2. The control system shall be used in particular for the purpose of verifying:

(*a*) That devices, services and facilities intented for peaceful uses of nuclear energy are not used in the testing or manufacture of nuclear weapons;

(*b*) That none of the activities prohibited in article 1 of this Treaty are carried out in the territory of the Contracting Parties with nuclear materials or weapons introduced from abroad, and

(*c*) That explosions for peaceful purposes are compatible with article 18 of this Treaty.

Article 13. *IAEA safeguards*

Each Contracting Party shall negotiate multilateral or bilateral agreements with the International Atomic Energy Agency for the application of its safeguards to its nuclear activities. Each Contracting Party shall initiate negotiations within a period of 180 days after the date of the deposit of its instrument of ratification of this Treaty. These agreements shall enter into force, for each Party, not later than eighteen months after the date of the initiation of such negotiations except in case of unforeseen circumstances or *force majeure*.

Article 14. *Reports of the Parties*

1. The Contracting Parties shall submit to the Agency and to the International Atomic Energy Agency, for their information, semi-annual reports stating that no activity prohibited under this Treaty has occurred in their respective territories.

2. The Contracting Parties shall simultaneously transmit to the Agency a copy of any report they may submit to the International Atomic Energy Agency which relates to matters that are the subject of this Treaty and to the application of safeguards.

3. The Contracting Parties shall also transmit to the Organization of American States, for its information, any reports that may be of interest to it, in accordance with the obligations established by the Inter-American System.

Article 15. *Special reports requested by the General Secretary*

1. With the authorization of the Council, the General Secretary may request any of the Contracting Parties to provide the Agency with complementary or supplementary information regarding any event or circumstance connected with compliance with this Treaty, explaining his reasons. The Contracting Parties undertake to co-operate promptly and fully with the General Secretary.

2. The General Secretary shall inform the Council and the Contracting Parties forthwith of such requests and of the respective replies.

Article 16. *Special inspections*

1. The International Atomic Energy Agency and the Council established by this Treaty have the power of carrying out special inspections in the following cases:

(*a*) In the case of the International Atomic Energy Agency, in accordance with the agreements referred to in article 13 of this Treaty;

(*b*) In the case of the Council:

(*i*) When so requested, the reasons for the request being stated, by any Party which suspects that some activity prohibited by this Treaty has been carried out or is about to be carried out, either in the territory of any other Party or in any other place on such latter Party's behalf, the Council shall immediately arrange for such an inspection in accordance with article 10, paragraph 5;

(ii) When requested by any Party which has been suspected of or charged with having violated this Treaty, the Council shall immediately arrange for the special inspection requested in accordance with article 10, paragraph 5.

The above requests will be made to the Council through the General Secretary.

2. The costs and expenses of any special inspection carried out under paragraph 1, sub-paragraph (b), sections (i) and (ii) of this article shall be borne by the requesting Party or Parties, except where the Council concludes on the basis of the report on the special inspection that, in view of the circumstances existing in the case, such costs and expenses should be borne by the Agency.

3. The General Conference shall formulate the procedures for the organization and execution of the special inspections carried out in accordance with paragraph 1, sub-paragraph (b), sections (i) and (ii) of this article.

4. The Contracting Parties undertake to grant the inspectors carrying out such special inspections full and free access to all places and all information which may be necessary for the performance of their duties and which are directly and intimately connected with the suspicion of violation of this Treaty. If so requested by the authorities of the Contracting Party in whose territory the inspection is carried out, the inspectors designated by the General Conference shall be accompanied by representatives of said authorities, provided that this does not in any way delay or hinder the work of the inspectors.

5. The Council shall immediately transmit to all the Parties, through the General Secretary, a copy of any report resulting from special inspections.

6. Similarly, the Council shall send through the General Secretary to the Secretary-General of the United Nations, for transmission to the United Nations Security Council and General Assembly, and to the Council of the Organization of American States, for its information, a copy of any report resulting from any special inspection carried out in accordance with paragraph 1, sub-paragraph (b), sections (i) and (ii) of this article.

7. The Council may decide, or any Contracting Party may request, the convening of a special session of the General Conference for the purpose of considering the reports resulting from any special inspection. In such a case, the General Secretary shall take immediate steps to convene the special session requested.

8. The General Conference, convened in special session under this article, may make recommendations to the Contracting Parties and submit reports to the Secretary-General of the United Nations to be transmitted to the United Nations Security Council and the General Assembly.

Article 17. *Use of nuclear energy for peaceful purposes*

Nothing in the provisions of this Treaty shall prejudice the rights of the Contracting Parties, in conformity with this Treaty, to use nuclear energy for peaceful purposes, in particular for their economic development and social progress.

Article 18. *Explosions for peaceful purposes*

1. The Contracting Parties may carry out explosions of nuclear devices for peaceful purposes—including explosions which involve devices similar to those used in nuclear weapons—or collaborate with third parties for the same purpose, provided that they do so in accordance with the provisions of this article and the other articles of the Treaty, particularly articles 1 and 5.

2. Contracting Parties intending to carry out, or to cooperate in carrying out, such an explosion shall notify the Agency and the International Atomic Energy Agency, as far in advance as the circumstances require, of the date of the explosion and shall at the same time provide the following information:

(a) The nature of the nuclear device and the source from which it was obtained;

(b) The place and purpose of the planned explosion;

(c) The procedures which will be followed in order to comply with paragraph 3 of this article;

(d) The expected force of the device, and

(e) The fullest possible information on any possible radioactive fall-out that may result from the explosion or explosions, and measures which will be taken to avoid danger to the population, flora, fauna and territories of any other Party or Parties.

3. The General Secretary and the technical personnel designated by the Council and the International Atomic Energy Agency may observe all the preparations, including the explosion of the device, and shall have unrestricted access to any area in the vicinity of the site of the explosion in order to ascertain whether the device and the procedures followed during the explosion are in conformity with the information supplied under paragraph 2 of this article and the other provisions of this Treaty.

4. The Contracting Parties may accept the collaboration of third parties for the purpose set forth in paragraph 1 of the present article, in accordance with paragraphs 2 and 3 thereof.

Article 19. *Relations with other international organizations*

1. The Agency may conclude such agreements with the International Atomic Energy Agency as are authorized by the General Conference and as it considers likely to facilitate the efficient operation of the control system established by this Treaty.

2. The Agency may also enter into relations with any international organization or body, especially any which may be established in the future to supervise disarmament or measures for the control of armaments in any part of the world.

3. The Contracting Parties may, if they see fit, request the advice of the Inter-American Nuclear Energy Commission on all technical matters connected with the application of this Treaty with which the Commission is competent to deal under its Statute.

Article 20. *Measures in the event of violation of the Treaty*

1. The General Conference shall take note of all cases in which, in its opinion, any Contracting Party is not complying fully with its obligations under this Treaty and shall draw the matter to the attention of the Party concerned, making such recommendations as it deems appropriate.

2. If, in its opinion, such non-compliance constitutes a violation of this Treaty which might endanger peace and security, the General Conference shall report thereon stimultaneously to the United Nations Security Council and the General Assembly through the Secretary-General of the United Nations, and to the Council of the Organization of American States. The General Conference shall likewise report to the International Atomic Energy Agency for such purposes as are relevant in accordance with its Statute.

Article 21. *United Nations and Organization of American States*

None of the provisions of this Treaty shall be construed as impairing the rights and obligations of the Parties under the Charter of the United Nations or, in the case of States Members of the Organization of American States, under existing regional treaties.

Article 22. *Privileges and immunities*

1. The Agency shall enjoy in the territory of each of the Contracting Parties such legal capacity and such privileges and immunities as may be necessary for the exercise of its functions and the fulfilment of its purposes.

2. Representatives of the Contracting Parties accredited to the Agency and officials of the Agency shall similarly enjoy such privileges and immunities as are necessary for the performance of their functions.

3. The Agency may conclude agreements with the Contracting Parties with a view to determining the details of the application of paragraphs 1 and 2 of this article.

Article 23. *Notification of other agreements*

Once this Treaty has entered into force, the Secretariat shall be notified immediately of any international agreement concluded by any of the Contracting Parties on matters with which this Treaty is concerned; the Secretariat shall register it and notify the other Contracting Parties.

Article 24. *Settlement of disputes*

Unless the Parties concerned agree on another mode of peaceful settlement, any question or dispute concerning the interpretation or application of this Treaty which is not settled shall be referred to the International Court of Justice with the prior consent of the Parties to the controversy.

Article 25. *Signature*

1. This Treaty shall be open indefinitely for signature by:

(*a*) All the Latin American Republics, and

(*b*) All other sovereign States situated in their entirety south of latitude 35° north in the western hemisphere; and, except as provided in paragraph 2 of this article, all such States which become sovereign, when they have been admitted by the General Conference.

2. The General Conference shall not take any decision regarding the admission of a political entity part or all of whose territory is the subject, prior to the date when this Treaty is opened for signature, of a dispute or claim between an extra-continental country and one or more Latin American States, so long as the dispute has not been settled by peaceful means.

Article 26. *Ratification and deposit*

1. This Treaty shall be subject to ratification by signatory States in accordance with their respective constitutional procedures.

2. This Treaty and the instruments of ratification shall be deposited with the Government of the Mexican United States, which is hereby designated the Depositary Government.

3. The Depositary Government shall send certified copies of this Treaty to the Governments of signatory States and shall notify them of the deposit of each instrument of ratification.

Article 27. *Reservations*

This Treaty shall not be subject to reservations.

Article 28. *Entry into force*

1. Subject to the provisions of paragraph 2 of this article, this Treaty shall enter into force among the States that have ratified it as soon as the following requirements have been met:

(*a*) Deposit of the instruments of ratification of this Treaty with the Depositary Government by the Governments of the States mentioned in article 25 which are in existence on the date when this Treaty is opened for signature and which are not affected by the provisions of article 25, paragraph 2;

(*b*) Signature and ratification of Additional Protocol I annexed to this Treaty by all extra-continental or continental States having *de jure* or *de facto* international responsibility for territories situated in the zone of application of the Treaty;

(*c*) Signature and ratification of the Additional Protocol II annexed to this Treaty by all powers possessing nuclear weapons;

(*d*) Conclusion of bilateral or multilateral agreements on the application of the Safeguards System of the International Atomic Energy Agency in accordance with article 13 of this Treaty.

2. All signatory States shall have the imprescriptible right to waive, wholly or in part, the requirements laid down in the preceding paragraph. They may do so by means of a declaration which shall be annexed to their respective instrument of ratification and which may be formulated at the time of deposit of the instrument or subsequently. For those States which exercise this right, this Treaty shall enter into force upon deposit of the declaration, or as soon as those requirements have been met which have not been expressly waived.

3. As soon as this Treaty has entered into force in accordance with the provisions of paragraph 2 for eleven States, the Depositary Government shall convene a preliminary meeting of those States in order that the Agency may be set up and commence its work.

4. After the entry into force of this Treaty for all countries of the zone, the rise of a new power possessing nuclear weapons shall have the effect of suspending the execution of this Treaty for those countries which have ratified it without waiving requirements of paragraph 1, sub-paragraph (*c*) of this article, and which request such suspension; the Treaty shall remain suspended until the new power, on its own initiative or upon request by the General Conference, ratifies the annexed Additional Protocol II.

Article 29. *Amendments*

1. Any Contracting Party may propose amendments to this Treaty and shall submit its proposals to the Council through the General Secretary, who shall transmit them to all the other Contracting Parties and, in addition, to all other signatories in accordance with article 6. The Council, through the General Secretary, shall immediately following the meeting of signatories convene a special session of the General Conference to examine the proposals made, for the adoption of which a two-thirds majority of the Contracting Parties present and voting shall be required.

2. Amendments adopted shall enter into force as soon as the requirements set forth in article 28 of this Treaty have been complied with.

Article 30. *Duration and denunciation*

1. This Treaty shall be of a permanent nature and shall remain in force indefinitely, but any Party may denounce it by notifying the General Secretary of the Agency if, in the opinion of the denouncing State, there have arisen or may arise circumstances connected with the content of this Treaty or of the annexed Additional Protocols I and II which affect its supreme interests or the peace and security of one or more Contracting Parties.

2. The denunciation shall take effect three months after the delivery to the General Secretary of the Agency of the notification by the Government of the signatory State concerned. The General Secretary shall immediately communicate such notification to the other Contracting Parties and to the Secretary-General of the United Nations for the information of the United Nations Security Council and the General Assembly. He shall also communicate it to the Secretary-General of the Organization of American States.

Article 31. *Authentic texts and registration*

This Treaty, of which the Spanish, Chinese, English, French, Portuguese and Russian texts are equally authentic, shall be registered by the Depositary Government in accordance with article 102 of the United Nations Charter. The Depositary Government shall notify the Secretary-General of the United Nations of the signatures, ratifications and amendments relating to this Treaty and shall communicate them to the Secretary-General of the Organization of American States for its information.

Transitional Article

Denunciation of the declaration referred to in article 28, paragraph 2, shall be subject to the same procedures as the denunciation of this Treaty, except that it will take effect on the date of delivery of the respective notification.

In witness whereof the undersigned Plenipotentiaries, having deposited their full powers, found in good and due form, sign this Treaty on behalf of their respective Governments.

Done at Mexico, Distrito Federal, on the Fourteenth day of February, one thousand nine hundred and sixty-seven.

ADDITIONAL PROTOCOL I

The undersigned Plenipotentiaries, furnished with full powers by their respective Governments,

Convinced that the Treaty for the Prohibition of Nuclear Weapons in Latin America, negotiated and signed in accordance with the recommendations of the General Assembly of the United Nations in Resolution 1911 (XVIII) of 27 November 1963, represents an important step towards ensuring the non-proliferation of nuclear weapons,

Aware that the non-proliferation of nuclear weapons is not an end in itself but, rather, a means of achieving general and complete disarmament at a later stage, and

Desiring to contribute, so far as lies in their power, towards ending the armaments race, especially in the field of nuclear weapons, and towards strengthening a world at peace, based on mutual respect and sovereign equality of States,

Have agreed as follows:

Article 1

To undertake to apply the statute of denuclearization in respect of warlike purposes as defined in articles 1, 3, 5 and 13 of the Treaty for the Prohibition of Nuclear Weapons in Latin America in territories for which, *de jure* or *de facto*, they are internationally responsible and which lie within the limits of the geographical zone established in that Treaty.

Article 2

The duration of this Protocol shall be the same as that of the Treaty for the Prohibition of Nuclear Weapons in Latin America of which this Protocol is an annex, and the provisions regarding ratification and denunciation contained in the Treaty shall be applicable to it.

Article 3

This Protocol shall enter into force, for the States which have ratified it, on the date of the deposit of their respective instruments of ratification.

In witness whereof the undersigned Plenipotentiaries, having deposited their full powers, found in good and due form, sign this Protocol on behalf of their respective Governments.

ADDITIONAL PROTOCOL II

The undersigned Plenipotentiaries, furnished with full powers by their respective Governments,

Convinced that the Treaty for the Prohibition of Nuclear Weapons in Latin America, negotiated and signed in accordance with the recommendations of the General Assembly of the United Nations in Resolution 1911 (XVIII) of 27 November 1963, represents an important step towards ensuring the non-proliferation of nuclear weapons,

Aware that the non-proliferation of nuclear weapons is not an end in itself but, rather, a means of achieving general and complete disarmament at a later stage, and

Desiring to contribute, so far as lies in their power, towards ending the armaments race, especially in the field of nuclear weapons, and towards promoting and strengthening a world at peace, based on mutual respect and sovereign equality of States,

Have agreed as follows:

Article 1

The statute of denuclearization of Latin America in respect of warlike purposes, as defined, delimited and set forth in the Treaty for the Prohibition of Nuclear Weapons in Latin America of which this instrument is an annex, shall be fully respected by the Parties to this Protocol in all its express aims and provisions.

Article 2

The Governments represented by the undersigned Plenipotentiaries undertake, therefore, not to contribute in any way to the performance of acts involving a violation of the obligations of article 1 of the Treaty in the territories to which the Treaty applies in accordance with article 4 thereof.

Article 3

The Governments represented by the undersigned Plenipotentiaries also undertake not to use or threaten to use nuclear weapons against the Contracting Parties of the Treaty for the Prohibition of Nuclear Weapons in Latin America.

Article 4

The duration of this Protocol shall be the same as that of the Treaty for the Prohibition of Nuclear Weapons in Latin America of which this Protocol is an annex, and the definitions of territory and nuclear weapons set forth in articles 3 and 5 of the Treaty shall be applicable to this Protocol, as well as the provisions regarding ratification, reservations, denunciation, authentic texts and registration contained in articles 26, 27, 30 and 31 of the Treaty.

Article 5

This Protocol shall enter into force, for the States which have ratified it, on the date of the deposit of their respective instruments of ratification.

In witness whereof, the undersigned Plenipotentiaries, having deposited their full powers, found to be in good and due form, hereby sign this Additional Protocol on behalf of their respective Governments.

Source: *Treaty Series,* Vol. 634 (United Nations, New York, 1970).

Number of parties to the Treaty as of 31 December 1977: 22.
Number of parties to Protocol I as of 31 December 1977: 2.
Number of parties to Protocol II as of 31 December 1977: 4.

For the list of states which have signed and ratified the Treaty of Tlatelolco, and of those which have signed and ratified Additional Protocols I and II, see pages 152–94.

SECURITY COUNCIL RESOLUTION ON SECURITY ASSURANCES TO NON-NUCLEAR WEAPON STATES

Adopted on 19 June 1968.

The Security Council,

Noting with appreciation the desire of a large number of States to subscribe to the treaty on the Non-Proliferation of Nuclear Weapons, and thereby to undertake not to receive the transfer from any transferor whatsoever of nuclear weapons or other nuclear explosive devices or of control over such weapons or explosive devices directly, or indirectly; not to manufacture or otherwise acquire nuclear weapons or other nuclear explosive devices; and not to seek or receive any assistance in the manufacture of nuclear weapons or other nuclear explosive devices,

Taking into consideration the concern of certain of these States that, in conjunction with their adherence to the Treaty on the Non-Proliferation of Nuclear Weapons, appropriate measures be undertaken to safeguard their security,

Bearing in mind that any aggression accompanied by the use of nuclear weapons would endanger the peace and security of all States,

1. *Recognizes* that aggression with nuclear weapons or the threat of such aggression against a non-nuclear-weapon State would create a situation in which the Security Council, and above all its nuclear-weapon State permanent members, would have to act immediately in accordance with their obligations under the United Nations Charter;

2. *Welcomes* the intention expressed by certain States that they will provide or support immediate assistance, in accordance with the Charter, to any non-nuclear-weapon State Party to the Treaty on the Non-Proliferation of Nuclear Weapons that is a victim of an act or an object of a threat of aggression in which nuclear weapons are used;

3. *Reaffirms* in particular the inherent right, recognized under Article 51 of the Charter, of individual and collective self-defense if an armed attack occurs against a Member of the United Nations, until the Security Council has taken measures necessary to maintain international peace and security.

Source: UN document S/RES/225 (1968), 19 June 1968.

The Security Council approved this resolution by a vote of 10 to 0, with 5 abstentions. It was supported by Canada, Republic of China (Taiwan), Denmark, Ethiopia, Hungary, Paraguay, Senegal, UK, USA and USSR. The following countries abstained: Algeria, Brazil, France, India and Pakistan.

TREATY ON THE NON-PROLIFERATION OF NUCLEAR WEAPONS

Signed at London, Moscow and Washington on 1 July 1968.
Entered into force on 5 March 1970.
Depositaries: UK, US and Soviet governments.

The States concluding this Treaty, hereinafter referred to as the "Parties to the Treaty",

Considering the devastation that would be visited upon all mankind by a nuclear war and the consequent need to make every effort to avert the danger of such a war and to take measures to safeguard the security of peoples,

Believing that the proliferation of nuclear weapons would seriously enhance the danger of nuclear war,

In conformity with resolutions of the United Nations General Assembly calling for the conclusion of an agreement on the prevention of wider dissemination of nuclear weapons,

Undertaking to cooperate in facilitating the application of International Atomic Energy Agency safeguards on peaceful nuclear activities,

Expressing their support for research, development and other efforts to further the application, within the framework of the International Atomic Energy Agency safeguards system, of the principle of safeguarding effectively the flow of source and special fissionable materials by use of instruments and other techniques at certain strategic points,

Affirming the principle that the benefits of peaceful applications of nuclear technology, including any technological by-products which may be derived by nuclear-weapon States from the development of nuclear explosive devices, should be available for peaceful purposes to all Parties to the Treaty, whether nuclear-weapon or non-nuclear-weapon States,

Convinced that, in furtherance of this principle, all Parties to the Treaty are entitled to participate in the fullest possible exchange of scientific information for, and to contribute alone or in cooperation with other States to, the further development of the applications of atomic energy for peaceful purposes,

Declaring their intention to achieve at the earliest possible date the cessation of the nuclear arms race and to undertake effective measures in the direction of nuclear disarmament,

Urging the cooperation of all States in the attainment of this objective,

Recalling the determination expressed by the Parties to the 1963 Treaty banning nuclear weapon tests in the atmosphere, in outer space and under water in its Preamble to seek to achieve the discontinuance of all test explosions of nuclear weapons for all time and to continue negotiations to this end,

Desiring to further the easing of international tension and the strengthening of trust between States in order to facilitate the cessation of the manufacture of nuclear weapons, the liquidation of all their existing stockpiles, and the elimination from national arsenals of nuclear weapons and the means of their delivery pursuant to a treaty on general and complete disarmament under strict and effective international control,

Recalling that, in accordance with the Charter of the United Nations, States must refrain in their international relations from the threat or use of force against the territorial integrity or political independence of any State, or in any other manner inconsistent with the Purposes of the United Nations, and that the establishment and maintenance of international peace and security are to be promoted with the least diversion for armaments of the world's human and economic resources,

Have agreed as follows:

Article I

Each nuclear-weapon State Party to the Treaty undertakes not to transfer to any recipient whatsoever nuclear weapons or other nuclear explosive devices or control over such weapons or explosive devices directly, or indirectly; and not in any way to assist, encourage, or induce any non-nuclear-weapon State to manufacture or otherwise acquire nuclear weapons or other nuclear explosive devices, or control over such weapons or explosive devices.

Article II

Each non-nuclear-weapon State Party to the Treaty undertakes not to receive the transfer from any transferor whatsoever of nuclear weapons or other nuclear explosive devices or of control over such weapons or explosive devices directly, or indirectly; not to manufacture or otherwise acquire nuclear weapons or other nuclear explosive devices; and not to seek or receive any assistance in the manufacture of nuclear weapons or other nuclear explosive devices.

Article III

1. Each non-nuclear-weapon State Party to the Treaty undertakes to accept safeguards, as set forth in an agreement to be negotiated and concluded with the International Atomic Energy Agency in accordance with the Statute of the International Atomic Energy Agency and the Agency's safeguards system, for the exclusive purpose of verification of the fulfillment of its obligations assumed under this Treaty with a view to preventing diversion of nuclear energy from peaceful uses to nuclear weapons or other nuclear explosive devices. Procedures for the safeguards required by this article shall be followed with respect to source or special fissionable material whether it is being produced, processed or used in any principal nuclear facility or is outside any such facility. The safeguards required by this article shall be applied on all source or special fissionable material in all peaceful nuclear activities within the territory of such State, under its jurisdiction, or carried out under its control anywhere.

2. Each State Party to the Treaty undertakes not to provide: (a) source or special fissionable material, or (b) equipment or material especially designed or prepared for the processing, use or production of special fissionable material, to any non-nuclear-weapon State for peaceful purposes, unless the source or special fissionable material shall be subject to the safeguards required by this article.

3. The safeguards required by this article shall be implemented in a manner designed to comply with article IV of this Treaty, and to avoid hampering the economic or technological development of the Parties or international cooperation in the field of peaceful nuclear activities, including the international exchange of nuclear material and equipment for the processing, use or production of nuclear material for peaceful purposes in accordance with the pro-

visions of this article and the principle of safeguarding set forth in the Preamble of the Treaty.

4. Non-nuclear-weapon States Party to the Treaty shall conclude agreements with the International Atomic Energy Agency to meet the requirements of this article either individually or together with other States in accordance with the Statute of the International Atomic Energy Agency. Negotiation of such agreements shall commence within 180 days from the original entry into force of this Treaty. For States depositing their instruments of ratification or accession after the 180-day period, negotiation of such agreements shall commence not later than the date of such deposit. Such agreements shall enter into force not later than eighteen months after the date of initiation of negotiations.

Article IV

1. Nothing in this Treaty shall be interpreted as affecting the inalienable right of all the Parties to the Treaty to develop research, production and use of nuclear energy for peaceful purposes without discrimination and in conformity with articles I and II of this Treaty.

2. All the Parties to the Treaty undertake to facilitate, and have the right to participate in, the fullest possible exchange of equipment, materials and scientific and technological information for the peaceful uses of nuclear energy. Parties to the Treaty in a position to do so shall also cooperate in contributing alone or together with other States or international organizations to the further development of the applications of nuclear energy for peaceful purposes, especially in the territories of non-nuclear-weapon States Party to the Treaty, with due consideration for the needs of the developing areas of the world.

Article V

Each Party to the Treaty undertakes to take appropriate measures to ensure that, in accordance with this Treaty, under appropriate international observation and through appropriate international procedures, potential benefits from any peaceful applications of nuclear explosions will be made available to non-nuclear-weapon States Party to the Treaty on a non-discriminatory basis and that the charge to such Parties for the explosive devices used will be as low as possible and exclude any charge for research and development. Non-nuclear-weapon States Party to the Treaty shall be able to obtain such benefits, pursuant to a special international agreement or agreements, through an appropriate international body with adequate representation of non-nuclear-weapon States. Negotiations on this subject shall commence as soon as possible after the Treaty enters into force. Non-nuclear-weapon States Party to the Treaty so desiring may also obtain such benefits pursuant to bilateral agreements.

Article VI

Each of the Parties to the Treaty undertakes to pursue negotiations in good faith on effective measures relating to cessation of the nuclear arms race at an early date and to nuclear disarmament, and on a treaty on general and complete disarmament under strict and effective international control.

Article VII

Nothing in this Treaty affects the right of any group of States to conclude regional treaties in order to assure the total absence of nuclear weapons in their respective territories.

Article VIII

1. Any Party to the Treaty may propose amendments to this Treaty. The text of any proposed amendment shall be submitted to the Depositary Governments which shall circulate it to all Parties to the Treaty. Thereupon, if requested to do so by one-third or more of the Parties to the Treaty, the Depositary Governments shall convene a conference, to which they shall invite all the Parties to the Treaty, to consider such an amendment.

2. Any amendment to this Treaty must be approved by a majority of the votes of all the Parties to the Treaty, including the votes of all nuclear-weapon States Party to the Treaty and all other Parties which, on the date the amendment is circulated, are members of the Board of Governors of the International Atomic Energy Agency. The amendment shall enter into force for each Party that deposits its instrument of ratification of the amendment upon the deposit of such instruments of ratification by a majority of all the Parties, including the instruments of ratification of all nuclear-weapon States Party to the Treaty and all other Parties which, on the date the amendment is circulated, are members of the Board of Governors of the International Atomic Energy Agency. Thereafter, it shall enter into force for any other Party upon the deposit of its instrument of ratification of the amendment.

3. Five years after the entry into force of this Treaty, a conference of Parties to the Treaty shall be held in Geneva, Switzerland, in order to review the operation of this Treaty with a view to assuring that the purposes of the Preamble and the provisions of the Treaty are being realized. At intervals of five years thereafter, a majority of the Parties to the Treaty may obtain, by submitting a proposal to this effect to the Depositary Governments, the convening of further conferences with the same objective of reviewing the operation of the Treaty.

Article IX

1. This Treaty shall be open to all States for signature. Any State which does not sign the Treaty before its entry into force in accordance with paragraph 3 of this article may accede to it at any time.

2. This Treaty shall be subject to ratification by signatory States. Instruments of ratification and instruments of accession shall be deposited with the Governments of the United States of America, the United Kingdom of Great Britain and Northern Ireland and the Union of Soviet Socialist Republics, which are hereby designated the Depositary Governments.

3. This Treaty shall enter into force after its ratification by the States, the Governments of which are designated Depositaries of the Treaty, and forty other States signatory to this Treaty and the deposit of their instruments of ratification. For the purposes of this Treaty, a nuclear-weapon State is one which has manufactured and exploded a nuclear weapon or other nuclear explosive device prior to January 1, 1967.

4. For States whose instruments of ratification or accession are deposited subsequent to the entry into force of this Treaty, it shall enter into force on the date of the deposit of their instruments of ratification or accession.

5. The Depositary Governments shall promptly inform

all signatory and acceding States of the date of each signature, the date of deposit of each instrument of ratification or of accession, the date of the entry into force of this Treaty, and the date of receipt of any requests for convening a conference or other notices.

6. This Treaty shall be registered by the Depositary Governments pursuant to article 102 of the Charter of the United Nations.

Article X

1. Each Party shall in exercising its national sovereignty have the right to withdraw from the Treaty if it decides that extraordinary events, related to the subject matter of this Treaty, have jeopardized the supreme interests of its country. It shall give notice of such withdrawal to all other Parties to the Treaty and to the United Nations Security Council three months in advance. Such notice shall include a statement of the extraordinary events it regards as having jeopardized its supreme interests.

2. Twenty-five years after the entry into force of the Treaty, a conference shall be convened to decide whether the Treaty shall continue in force indefinitely, or shall be extended for an additional fixed period or periods. This decision shall be taken by a majority of the Parties to the Treaty.

Article XI

This Treaty, the English, Russian, French, Spanish and Chinese texts of which are equally authentic, shall be deposited in the archives of the Depositary Governments. Duly certified copies of this Treaty shall be transmitted by the Depositary Governments to the Governments of the signatory and acceding States.

Source: *United States Treaties and Other International Agreements*, Vol. 21, Part 1 (US Department of State, Washington, 1970).

Number of parties as of 31 December 1977: 103.

For the list of states which have signed, ratified, acceded or succeeded to the Non-Proliferation Treaty, see pages 152–94.

TREATY ON THE PROHIBITION OF THE EMPLACEMENT OF NUCLEAR WEAPONS AND OTHER WEAPONS OF MASS DESTRUCTION ON THE SEABED AND THE OCEAN FLOOR AND IN THE SUBSOIL THEREOF

Signed at London, Moscow and Washington on 11 February 1971.
Entered into force on 18 May 1972.
Depositaries: UK, US and Soviet governments.

The States Parties to this Treaty,

Recognizing the common interest of mankind in the progress of the exploration and use of the seabed and the ocean floor for peaceful purposes,

Considering that the prevention of a nuclear arms race on the seabed and the ocean floor serves the interests of maintaining world peace, reduces international tensions and strengthens friendly relations among States,

Convinced that this Treaty constitutes a step towards the exclusion of the seabed, the ocean floor and the subsoil thereof from the arms race,

Convinced that this Treaty constitutes a step towards a treaty on general and complete disarmament under strict and effective international control, and determined to continue negotiations to this end,

Convinced that this Treaty will further the purposes and principles of the Charter of the United Nations, in a manner consistent with the principles of international law and without infringing the freedoms of the high seas,

Have agreed as follows:

Article I

1. The States Parties to this Treaty undertake not to emplant or emplace on the seabed and the ocean floor and in the subsoil thereof beyond the outer limit of a seabed zone, as defined in article II, any nuclear weapons or any other types of weapons of mass destruction as well as structures, launching installations or any other facilities specifically designed for storing, testing or using such weapons.

2. The undertakings of paragraph 1 of this article shall also apply to the seabed zone referred to in the same paragraph, except that within such seabed zone, they shall not apply either to the coastal State or to the seabed beneath its territorial waters.

3. The States Parties to this Treaty undertake not to assist, encourage or induce any State to carry out activities referred to in paragraph 1 of this article and not to participate in any other way in such actions.

Article II

For the purpose of this Treaty, the outer limit of the seabed zone referred to in article I shall be coterminous with the twelve-mile outer limit of the zone referred to in part II of the Convention on the Territorial Sea and the Contiguous Zone, signed at Geneva on April 29, 1958, and shall be measured in accordance with the provisions of part I, section II, of that Convention and in accordance with international law.

Article III

1. In order to promote the objectives of and insure compliance with the provisions of this Treaty, each State Party to the Treaty shall have the right to verify through observation the activities of other States Parties to the Treaty on the seabed and the ocean floor and in the subsoil thereof beyond the zone referred to in article I, provided that observation does not interfere with such activities.

2. If after such observation reasonable doubts remain concerning the fulfillment of the obligations assumed under the Treaty, the State Party having such doubts and the State Party that is responsible for the activities giving rise to the doubts shall consult with a view to removing the doubts. If the doubts persist, the State Party having such doubts shall notify the other States Parties, and the Parties concerned shall cooperate on such further procedures for verification as may be agreed, including appropriate in-

spection of objects, structures, installations or other facilities that reasonably may be expected to be of a kind described in article I. The Parties in the region of the activities, including any coastal State, and any other Party so requesting, shall be entitled to participate in such consultation and cooperation. After completion of the further procedures for verification, an appropriate report shall be circulated to other Parties by the Party that initiated such procedures.

3. If the State responsible for the activities giving rise to the reasonable doubts is not identifiable by observation of the object, structure, installation or other facility, the State Party having such doubts shall notify and make appropriate inquiries of States Parties in the region of the activities and of any other State Party. If it is ascertained through these inquiries that a particular State Party is responsible for the activities, that State Party shall consult and cooperate with other Parties as provided in paragraph 2 of this article. If the identity of the State responsible for the activities cannot be ascertained through these inquiries, then further verification procedures, including inspection, may be undertaken by the inquiring State Party, which shall invite the participation of the Parties in the region of the activities, including any coastal State, and of any other Party desiring to cooperate.

4. If consultation and cooperation pursuant to paragraphs 2 and 3 of this article have not removed the doubts concerning the activities and there remains a serious question concerning fulfillment of the obligations assumed under this Treaty, a State Party may, in accordance with the provisions of the Charter of the United Nations, refer the matter to the Security Council, which may take action in accordance with the Charter.

5. Verification pursuant to this article may be undertaken by any State Party using its own means, or with the full or partial assistance of any other State Party, or through appropriate international procedures within the framework of the United Nations and in accordance with its Charter.

6. Verification activities pursuant to this Treaty shall not interfere with activities of other States Parties and shall be conducted with due regard for rights recognized under international law, including the freedoms of the high seas and the rights of coastal States with respect to the exploration and exploitation of their continental shelves.

Article IV

Nothing in this Treaty shall be interpreted as supporting or prejudicing the position of any State Party with respect to existing international conventions, including the 1958 Convention on the Territorial Sea and the Contiguous Zone, or with respect to rights or claims which such State Party may assert, or with respect to recognition or non-recognition of rights or claims asserted by any other State, related to waters off its coasts, including, *inter alia*, territorial seas and contiguous zones, or to the seabed and the ocean floor, including continental shelves.

Article V

The Parties to this Treaty undertake to continue negotiations in good faith concerning further measures in the field of disarmament for the prevention of an arms race on the seabed, the ocean floor and the subsoil thereof.

Article VI

Any State Party may propose amendments to this Treaty. Amendments shall enter into force for each State Party accepting the amendments upon their acceptance by a majority of the States Parties to the Treaty and, thereafter, for each remaining State Party on the date of acceptance by it.

Article VII

Five years after the entry into force of this Treaty, a conference of Parties to the Treaty shall be held at Geneva, Switzerland, in order to review the operation of this Treaty with a view to assuring that the purposes of the preamble and the provisions of the Treaty are being realized. Such review shall take into account any relevant technological developments. The review conference shall determine, in accordance with the views of a majority of those Parties attending, whether and when an additional review conference shall be convened.

Article VIII

Each State Party to this Treaty shall in exercising its national sovereignty have the right to withdraw from this Treaty if it decides that extraordinary events related to the subject matter of this Treaty have jeopardized the supreme interests of its country. It shall give notice of such withdrawal to all other States Parties to the Treaty and to the United Nations Security Council three months in advance. Such notice shall include a statement of the extraordinary events it considers to have jeopardized its supreme interests.

Article IX

The provisions of this Treaty shall in no way affect the obligations assumed by States Parties to the Treaty under international instruments establishing zones free from nuclear weapons.

Article X

1. This Treaty shall be open for signature to all States. Any State which does not sign the Treaty before its entry into force in accordance with paragraph 3 of this article may accede to it at any time.

2. This Treaty shall be subject to ratification by signatory States. Instruments of ratification and of accession shall be deposited with the Governments of the United States of America, the United Kingdom of Great Britain and Northern Ireland, and the Union of Soviet Socialist Republics, which are hereby designated the Depositary Governments.

3. This Treaty shall enter into force after the deposit of instruments of ratification by twenty-two Governments, including the Governments designated as Depositary Governments of this Treaty.

4. For States whose instruments of ratification or accession are deposited after the entry into force of this Treaty, it shall enter into force on the date of the deposit of their instruments of ratification or accession.

5. The Depositary Governments shall promptly inform the Governments of all signatory and acceding States of the date of each signature, of the date of deposit of each instrument of ratification or of accession, of the date of the entry into force of this Treaty, and of the receipt of other notices.

6. This Treaty shall be registered by the Depositary Governments pursuant to Article 102 of the Charter of the United Nations.

Article XI

This Treaty, the English, Russian, French, Spanish and Chinese texts of which are equally authentic, shall be deposited in the archives of the Depositary Governments. Duly certified copies of this Treaty shall be transmitted by the Depositary Governments to the Governments of the States signatory and acceding thereto.

Source: *Treaties and Other International Acts*, Series 7337 (US Government Printing Office, Washington).

Number of parties as of 31 December 1977: 65.

For the list of states which have signed, ratified or acceded to the Sea-Bed Treaty, see pages 152–94.

THE STRUCTURE AND CONTENT OF AGREEMENTS BETWEEN THE AGENCY AND STATES REQUIRED IN CONNECTION WITH THE TREATY ON THE NON-PROLIFERATION OF NUCLEAR WEAPONS

Agreed on 10 March 1971.

On 20 April 1971, the IAEA Board of Governors authorized the Director General to use the material reproduced below as the basis for negotiating safeguards agreements between the IAEA and non-nuclear weapon states parties to the NPT.

PART I

Basic undertaking

1. The Agreement should contain, in accordance with Article III.1 of the Treaty on the Non-Proliferation of Nuclear Weapons, an undertaking by the State to accept safeguards, in accordance with the terms of the Agreement, on all source or special fissionable material in all peaceful nuclear activities within its territory, under its jurisdiction or carried out under its control anywhere, for the exclusive purpose of verifying that such material is not diverted to nuclear weapons or other nuclear explosive devices.

Application of safeguards

2. The Agreement should provide for the Agency's right and obligation to ensure that safeguards will be applied, in accordance with the terms of the Agreement, on all source or special fissionable material in all peaceful nuclear activities within the territory of the State, under its jurisdiction or carried out under its control anywhere, for the exclusive purpose of verifying that such material is not diverted to nuclear weapons or other nuclear explosive devices.

Co-operation between the Agency and the State

3. The Agreement should provide that the Agency and the State shall co-operate to facilitate the implementation of the safeguards provided for therein.

Implementation of safeguards

4. The Agreement should provide that safeguards shall be implemented in a manner designed:

(a) To avoid hampering the economic and technological development of the State or international co-operation in the field of peaceful nuclear activities, including international exchange of *nuclear material;*

(b) To avoid undue interference in the State's peaceful nuclear activities, and in particular in the operation of *facilities;* and

(c) To be consistent with prudent management practices required for the economic and safe conduct of nuclear activities.

5. The Agreement should provide that the Agency shall take every precaution to protect commercial and industrial secrets and other confidential information coming to its knowledge in the implementation of the Agreement. The Agency shall not publish or communicate to any State, organization or person any information obtained by it in connection with the implementation of the Agreement, except that specific information relating to such implementation in the State may be given to the Board of Governors and to such Agency staff members as require such knowledge by reason of their official duties in connection with safeguards, but only to the extent necessary for the Agency to fulfil its responsibilities in implementing the Agreement. Summarized information on *nuclear material* being safeguarded by the Agency under the Agreement may be published upon decision of the Board if the States directly concerned agree.

6. The Agreement should provide that in implementing safeguards pursuant thereto the Agency shall take full account of technological developments in the field of safeguards, and shall make every effort to ensure optimum cost-effectiveness and the application of the principle of safeguarding effectively the flow of *nuclear material* subject to safeguards under the Agreement by use of instruments and other techniques at certain *strategic points* to the extent that present or future technology permits. In order to ensure optimum cost-effectiveness, use should be made, for example, of such means as:

(a) Containment as a means of defining *material balance areas* for accounting purposes;

(b) Statistical techniques and random sampling in evaluating the flow of *nuclear material;* and

(c) Concentration of verification procedures on those stages in the nuclear fuel cycle involving the production, processing, use or storage of *nuclear material* from which nuclear weapons or other nuclear explosive devices could readily be made, and minimization of verification procedures in respect of other *nuclear material*, on condition that this does not hamper the Agency in applying safeguards under the Agreement.

National system of accounting for and control of nuclear material

7. The Agreement should provide that the State shall establish and maintain a system of accounting for and control of all *nuclear material* subject to safeguards under the

Agreement, and that such safeguards shall be applied in such a manner as to enable the Agency to verify, in ascertaining that there has been no diversion of *nuclear material* from peaceful uses to nuclear weapons or other nuclear explosive devices, findings of the State's system. The Agency's verification shall include, inter alia, independent measurements and observations conducted by the Agency in accordance with the procedures specified in Part II below. The Agency, in its verification, shall take due account of the technical effectiveness of the State's system.

Provisions of information to the Agency

8. The Agreement should provide that to ensure the effective implementation of safeguards thereunder the Agency shall be provided, in accordance with the provisions set out in Part II below, with information concerning *nuclear material* subject to safeguards under the Agreement and the features of *facilities* relevant to safeguarding such material. The Agency shall require only the minimum amount of information and data consistent with carrying out its responsibilities under the Agreement. Information pertaining to *facilities* shall be the minimum necessary for safeguarding *nuclear material* subject to safeguards under the Agreement. In examining design information, the Agency shall, at the request of the State, be prepared to examine on premises of the State design information which the State regards as being of particular sensitivity. Such information would not have to be physically transmitted to the Agency provided that it remained available for ready further examination by the Agency on premises of the State.

Agency inspectors

9. The Agreement should provide that the State shall take the necessary steps to ensure that Agency inspectors can effectively discharge their functions under the Agreement. The Agency shall secure the consent of the State to the designation of Agency inspectors to that State. If the State, either upon proposal of a designation or at any other time after a designation has been made, objects to the designation, the Agency shall propose to the State an alternative designation or designations. The repeated refusal of a State to accept the designation of Agency inspectors which would impede the inspections conducted under the Agreement would be considered by the Board upon referral by the Director General with a view to appropriate action. The visits and activities of Agency inspectors shall be so arranged as to reduce to a minimum the possible inconvenience and disturbance to the State and to the peaceful nuclear activities inspected, as well as to ensure protection of industrial secrets or any other confidential information coming to the inspectors' knowledge.

Privileges and immunities

10. The Agreement should specify the privileges and immunities which shall be granted to the Agency and its staff in respect of their functions under the Agreement. In the case of a State party to the Agreement on the Privileges and Immunities of the Agency, the provisions thereof, as in force for such State, shall apply. In the case of other States, the privileges and immunities granted should be such as to ensure that:

(a) The Agency and its staff will be in a position to discharge their functions under the Agreement effectively; and

(b) No such State will be placed thereby in a more favourable position than States party to the Agreement on the Privileges and Immunities of the Agency.

Termination of safeguards
Consumption or dilution of nuclear material

11. The Agreement should provide that safeguards shall terminate on *nuclear material* subject to safeguards thereunder upon determination by the Agency that it has been consumed, or has been diluted in such a way that it is no longer usable for any nuclear activity relevant from the point of view of safeguards, or has become practically irrecoverable.

Transfer of nuclear material out of the State

12. The Agreement should provide, with respect to *nuclear material* subject to safeguards thereunder, for notification of transfers of such material out of the State, in accordance with the provisions set out in paragraphs 92–94 below. The Agency shall terminate safeguards under the Agreement on *nuclear material* when the recipient State has assumed responsibility therefor, as provided for in paragraph 91. The Agency shall maintain records indicating each transfer and, where applicable, the re-application of safeguards to the transferred *nuclear material*.

Provisions relating to nuclear material to be used in non-nuclear activities

13. The Agreement should provide that if the State wishes to use *nuclear material* subject to safeguards thereunder in non-nuclear activities, such as the production of alloys or ceramics, it shall agree with the Agency on the circumstances under which the safeguards on such *nuclear material* may be terminated.

Non-application of safeguards to nuclear material to be used in non-peaceful activities

14. The Agreement should provide that if the State intends to exercise its discretion to use *nuclear material* which is required to be safeguarded thereunder in a nuclear activity which does not require the application of safeguards under the Agreement, the following procedures will apply:

(a) The State shall inform the Agency of the activity, making it clear:

(i) That the use of the *nuclear material* in a non-proscribed military activity will not be in conflict with an undertaking the State may have given and in respect of which Agency safeguards apply, that the *nuclear material* will be used only in a peaceful nuclear activity; and

(ii) That during the period of non-application of safeguards the *nuclear material* will not be used for the production of nuclear weapons or other nuclear explosive devices;

(b) The State and the Agency shall make an arrangement so that, only while the *nuclear material* is in such an activity, the safeguards provided for in the Agreement will not be applied. The arrangement shall identify, to the extent possible, the period or circumstances during which safeguards will not be applied. In any event, the safeguards provided for in the Agreement shall again apply as soon as the *nuclear material* is reintroduced into a peaceful nuclear activity. The Agency shall be kept informed of the total quantity and composition of such unsafeguarded *nuclear material* in the State and of any exports of such material; and

(c) Each arrangement shall be made in agreement with the Agency. The Agency's agreement shall be given as promptly as possible; it shall only relate to the temporal and procedural provisions, reporting arrangements, etc., but shall not involve any approval or classified knowledge of the military activity or relate to the use of the *nuclear material* therein.

Finance

15. The Agreement should contain one of the following sets of provisions:

(a) An agreement with a Member of the Agency should provide that each party thereto shall bear the expenses it incurs in implementing its responsibilities thereunder. However, if the State or persons under its jurisdiction incur extraordinary expenses as a result of a specific request by the Agency, the Agency shall reimburse such expenses provided that it has agreed in advance to do so. In any case the Agency shall bear the cost of any additional measuring or sampling which inspectors may request; or

(b) An agreement with a party not a Member of the Agency should in application of the provisions of Article XIV.C of the Statute, provide that the party shall reimburse fully to the Agency the safeguards expenses the Agency incurs thereunder. However, if the party or persons under its jurisdiction incur extraordinary expenses as a result of a specific request by the Agency, the Agency shall reimburse such expenses provided that it has agreed in advance to do so.

Third party liability for nuclear damage

16. The Agreement should provide that the State shall ensure that any protection against third party liability in respect of nuclear damage, including any insurance or other financial security, which may be available under its laws or regulations shall apply to the Agency and its officials for the purpose of the implementation of the Agreement, in the same way as that protection applies to nationals of the State.

International responsibility

17. The Agreement should provide that any claim by one party thereto against the other in respect of any damage, other than damage arising out of a nuclear incident, resulting from the implementation of safeguards under the Agreement, shall be settled in accordance with international law.

Measures in relation to verification of non-diversion

18. The Agreement should provide that if the Board, upon report of the Director General, decides that an action by the State is essential and urgent in order to ensure verification that *nuclear material* subject to safeguards under the Agreement is not diverted to nuclear weapons or other nuclear explosive devices the Board shall be able to call upon the State to take the required action without delay, irrespective of whether procedures for the settlement of a dispute have been invoked.

19. The Agreement should provide that if the Board upon examination of relevant information reported to it by the Director General finds that the Agency is not able to verify that there has been no diversion of *nuclear material* required to be safeguarded under the Agreements to nuclear weapons or other nuclear explosive devices, it may make the reports provided for in paragraph C of Article XII of the Statute and may also take, where applicable, the other measures provided for in that paragraph. In taking such action the Board shall take account of the degree of assurance provided by the safeguards measures that have been applied and shall afford the State every reasonable opportunity to furnish the Board with any necessary reassurance.

Interpretation and application of the Agreement and settlement of disputes

20. The Agreement should provide that the parties thereto shall, at the request of either, consult about any question arising out of the interpretation or application thereof.

21. The Agreement should provide that the State shall have the right to request that any question arising out of the interpretation or application thereof be considered by the Board; and that the State shall be invited by the Board to participate in the discussion of any such question by the Board.

22. The Agreement should provide that any dispute arising out of the interpretation or application thereof except a dispute with regard to a finding by the Board under paragraph 19 above or an action taken by the Board pursuant to such a finding which is not settled by negotiation or another procedure agreed to by the parties should, on the request of either party, be submitted to an arbitral tribunal composed as follows: each party would designate one arbitrator, and the two arbitrators so designated would elect a third, who would be the Chairman. If, within 30 days of the request for arbitration, either party has not designated an arbitrator, either party to the dispute may request the President of the International Court of Justice to appoint an arbitrator. The same procedure would apply if, within 30 days of the designation or appointment of the second arbitrator, the third arbitrator had not been elected. A majority of the members of the arbitral tribunal would constitute a quorum, and all decisions would require the concurrence of two arbitrators. The arbitral procedure would be fixed by the tribunal. The decisions of the tribunal would be binding on both parties.

Final clauses

Amendment of the Agreement

23. The Agreement should provide that the parties thereto shall, at the request of either of them, consult each other on amendment of the Agreement. All amendments shall require the agreement of both parties. It might additionally be provided, if convenient to the State, that the agreement of the parties on amendments to Part II of the Agreement could be achieved by recourse to a simplified procedure. The Director General shall promptly inform all Member States of any amendment to the Agreement.

Suspension of application of Agency safeguards under other agreements

24. Where applicable and where the State desires such a provision to appear, the Agreement should provide that the application of Agency safeguards in the State under

other safeguards agreements with the Agency shall be suspended while the Agreement is in force. If the State has received assistance from the Agency for a project, the State's undertaking in the Project Agreement not to use items subject thereto in such a way as to further any military purpose shall continue to apply.

Entry into force and duration

25. The Agreement should provide that it shall enter into force on the date on which the Agency receives from the State written notification that the statutory and constitutional requirements for entry into force have been met. The Director General shall promptly inform all Member States of the entry into force.

26. The Agreement should provide for it to remain in force as long as the State is party to the Treaty on the Non-Proliferation of Nuclear Weapons.

PART II

Introduction

27. The Agreement should provide that the purpose of Part II thereof is to specify the procedures to be applied for the implementation of the safeguards provisions of Part I.

Objective of safeguards

28. The Agreement should provide that the objective of safeguards is the timely detection of diversion of significant quantities of *nuclear material* from peaceful nuclear activities to the manufacture of nuclear weapons or of other nuclear explosive devices or for purposes unknown, and deterrence of such diversion by the risk of early detection.

29. To this end the Agreement should provide for the use of material accountancy as a safeguards measure of fundamental importance, with containment and surveillance as important complementary measures.

30. The Agreement should provide that the technical conclusion of the Agency's verification activities shall be a statement, in respect of each *material balance area*, of the amount of *material unaccounted for* over a specific period, giving the limits of accuracy of the amounts stated.

National system of accounting for and control of nuclear material

31. The Agreement should provide that pursuant to paragraph 7 above the Agency, in carrying out its verification activities, shall make full use of the State's system of accounting for and control of all *nuclear material* subject to safeguards under the Agreement, and shall avoid unnecessary duplication of the State's accounting and control activities.

32. The Agreement should provide that the State's system of accounting for and control of all *nuclear material* subject to safeguards under the Agreement shall be based on a structure of material balance areas, and shall make provision as appropriate and specified in the Subsidiary Arrangements for the establishment of such measures as:

(a) A measurement system for the determination of the quantities of *nuclear material* received, produced, shipped, lost or otherwise removed from inventory, and the quantities on inventory;

(b) The evaluation of precision and accuracy of measurements and the estimation of measurement uncertainty;

(c) Procedures for identifying, reviewing and evaluating differences in shipper/receiver measurements;

(d) Procedures for taking a *physical inventory;*

(e) Procedures for the evaluation of accumulations of unmeasured inventory and unmeasured losses;

(f) A system of records and reports showing, for each *material balance area,* the inventory of *nuclear material* and the changes in that inventory including receipts into and transfers out of the *material balance area;*

(g) Provisions to ensure that the accounting procedures and arrangements are being operated correctly; and

(h) Procedures for the submission of reports to the Agency in accordance with paragraphs 59–69 below.

Starting point of safeguards

33. The Agreement should provide that safeguards shall not apply thereunder to material in mining or ore processing activities.

34. The Agreement should provide that:

(a) When any material containing uranium or thorium which has not reached the stage of the nuclear fuel cycle described in subparagraph (c) below is directly or indirectly exported to a non-nuclear-weapon State, the State shall inform the Agency of its quantity, composition and destination, unless the material is exported for specifically non-nuclear purposes;

(b) When any material containing uranium or thorium which has not reached the stage of the nuclear fuel cycle described in sub-paragraph (c) below is imported, the State shall inform the Agency of its quantity and composition, unless the material is imported for specifically non-nuclear purposes; and

(c) When any *nuclear material* of a composition and purity suitable for fuel fabrication or for being isotopically enriched leaves the plant or the process stage in which it has been produced, or when such *nuclear material,* or any other *nuclear material* produced at a later stage in the nuclear fuel cycle, is imported into the State, the *nuclear material* shall become subject to the other safeguards procedures specified in the Agreement.

Termination of safeguards

35. The Agreement should provide that safeguards shall terminate on *nuclear material* subject to safeguards thereunder under the conditions set forth in paragraph 11 above. Where the conditions of that paragraph are not met, but the State considers that the recovery of safeguarded *nuclear material* from residues is not for the time being practicable or desirable, the Agency and the State shall consult on the appropriate safeguards measures to be applied. It should further be provided that safeguards shall terminate on *nuclear material* subject to safeguards under the Agreement under the conditions set forth in paragraph 13 above, provided that the State and the Agency agree that such *nuclear material* is practicably irrecoverable.

Exemptions from safeguards

36. The Agreement should provide that the Agency shall, at the request of the State, exempt *nuclear material* from safeguards, as follows:

(a) Special fissionable material, when it is used in gram quantitites or less as a sensing component in instruments;
(b) *Nuclear material,* when it is used in non-nuclear activities in accordance with paragraph 13 above, if such *nuclear material* is recoverable; and
(c) Plutonium with an isotopic concentration of plutonium-238 exceeding 80%.

37. The Agreement should provide that *nuclear material* that would otherwise be subject to safeguards shall be exempted from safeguards at the request of the State, provided that *nuclear material* so exempted in the State may not at any time exceed:
(a) One kilogram in total of special fissionable material, which may consist of one or more of the following:
  (i) Plutonium;
  (ii) Uranium with an *enrichment* of 0.2 (20%) and above, taken account of by multiplying its weight by its *enrichment;* and
  (iii) Uranium with an *enrichment* below 0.2 (20%) and above that of natural uranium, taken account of by multiplying its weight by five times the square of its *enrichment;*
(b) Ten metric tons in total of natural uranium and depleted uranium with an *enrichment* above 0.005 (0.5%);
(c) Twenty metric tons of depleted uranium with an *enrichment* of 0.005 (0.5%) or below; and
(d) Twenty metric tons of thorium;
or such greater amounts as may be specified by the Board of Governors for uniform application.

38. The Agreement should provide that if exempted *nuclear material* is to be processed or stored together with safeguarded *nuclear material,* provision should be made for the re-application of safeguards thereto.

Subsidiary arrangements

39. The Agreement should provide that the Agency and the State shall make Subsidiary Arrangements which shall specify in detail, to the extent necessary to permit the Agency to fulfil its responsibilities under the Agreement in an effective and efficient manner, how the procedures laid down in the Agreement are to be applied. Provision should be made for the possibility of an extension or change of the Subsidiary Arrangements by agreement between the Agency and the State without amendment of the Agreement.

40. It should be provided that the Subsidiary Arrangements shall enter into force at the same time as, or as soon as possible after, the entry into force of the Agreement. The State and the Agency shall make every effort to achieve their entry into force within 90 days of the entry into force of the Agreement, a later date being acceptable only with the agreement of both parties. The State shall provide the Agency promptly with the information required for completing the Subsidiary Arrangements. The Agreement should also provide that, upon its entry into force, the Agency shall ben entitled to apply the procedures laid down therein in respect of the *nuclear material* listed in the inventory provided for in paragraph 41 below.

Inventory

41. The Agreement should provide that, on the basis of the initial report referred to in paragraph 62 below, the Agency shall establish a unified inventory of all *nuclear material* in the State subject to safeguards under the Agreement, irrespective of its origin, and maintain this inventory on the basis of subsequent reports and of the results of its verification activities. Copies of the inventory shall be made available to the State at agreed intervals.

Design information

General

42. Pursuant to paragraph 8 above, the Agreement should stipulate that design information in respect of existing *facilities* shall be provided to the Agency during the discussion of the Subsidiary Arrangements, and that the time limits for the provision of such information in respect of new *facilities* shall be specified in the Subsidiary Arrangements. It should further be stipulated that such information shall be provided as early as possible before *nuclear material* is introduced into a new *facility*.

43. The Agreement should specify that the design information in respect of each *facility* to be made available to the Agency shall include, when applicable:
(a) Identification of the *facility,* stating its general character, purpose, nominal capacity and geographic location, and the name and address to be used for routine business purposes;
(b) Description of the general arrangement of the *facility* with reference, to the extent feasible, to the form, location and flow of *nuclear material* and to the general layout of important items of equipment which use, produce or process *nuclear material;*
(c) Description of features of the *facility* relating to material accountancy, containment and surveillance; and
(d) Description of the existing and proposed procedures at the *facility* for *nuclear material* accountancy and control, with special reference to *material balance areas* established by the operator, measurements of flow and procedures for *physical inventory* taking.

44. The Agreement should further provide that other information relevant to the application of safeguards shall be made available to the Agency in respect of each *facility,* in particular on organizational responsibility for material accountancy and control. It should also be provided that the State shall make available to the Agency supplementary information on the health and safety procedures which the Agency shall observe and with which the inspectors shall comply at the *facility*.

45. The Agreement should stipulate that design information in respect of a modification relevant for safeguards purposes shall be provided for examination sufficiently in advance for the safeguards procedures to be adjusted when necessary.

Purposes of examination of design information

46. The Agreement should provide that the design information made available to the Agency shall be used for the following purposes:
(a) To identify the features of *facilities* and *nuclear material* relevant to the application of safeguards to *nuclear material* in sufficient detail to facilitate verification;
(b) To determine *material balance areas* to be used for Agency accounting purposes and to select those *strategic points* which are *key measurement points* and which will be used to determine the *nuclear material* flows and inventories; in determining such *material balance areas* the Agency shall, inter alia, use the following criteria:
  (i) The size of the *material balance area* should be

related to the accuracy with which the material balance can be established;

(ii) In determining the *material balance area* advantage should be taken of any opportunity to use containment and surveillance to help ensure the completeness of flow measurements and thereby simplify the application of safeguards and concentrate measurement efforts at *key measurement points;*

(iii) A number of *material balance areas* in use at a *facility* or at distinct sites may be combined in one *material balance area* to be used for Agency accounting purposes when the Agency determines that this is consistent with its verification requirements; and

(iv) If the State so requests, a special *material balance area* around a process step involving commercially sensitive information may be established;

(c) To establish the nominal timing and procedures for taking of *physical inventory* for Agency accounting purposes;

(d) To establish the records and reports requirements and records evaluation procedures;

(e) To establish requirements and procedures for verification of the quantity and location of *nuclear material;* and

(f) To select appropriate combinations of containment and surveillance methods and techniques and the *strategic points* at which they are to be applied.

It should further be provided that the results of the examination of the design information shall be included in the Subsidiary Arrangements.

Re-examination of design information

47. The Agreement should provide that design information shall be re-examined in the light of changes in operating conditions, of developments in safeguards technology or of experience in the application of verification procedures, with a view to modifying the action the Agency has taken pursuant to paragraph 46 above.

Verification of design information

48. The Agreement should provide that the Agency, in co-operation with the State, may send inspectors to *facilities* to verify the design information provided to the Agency pursuant to paragraphs 42–45 above for the purposes stated in paragraph 46.

Information in respect of nuclear material outside facilities

49. The Agreement should provide that the following information concerning *nuclear material* customarily used outside *facilities* shall be provided as applicable to the Agency:

(a) General description of the use of the *nuclear material,* its geographic location, and the user's name and address for routine business purposes; and

(b) General description of the existing and proposed procedures for *nuclear material* accountancy and control, including organizational responsibility for material accountancy and control.

The Agreement should further provide that the Agency shall be informed on a timely basis of any change in the information provided to it under this paragraph.

50. The Agreement should provide that the information made available to the Agency in respect of *nuclear material* customarily used outside *facilities* may be used, to the extent relevant, for the purposes set out in sub-paragraphs 46(b)–(f) above.

Records system

General

51. The Agreement should provide that in establishing a national system of accounting for and control of *nuclear material* as referred to in paragraph 7 above, the State shall arrange that records are kept in respect of each *material balance area*. Provision should also be made that the Subsidiary Arrangements shall describe the records to be kept in respect of each *material balance area*.

52. The Agreement should provide that the State shall make arrangements to facilitate the examination of records by inspectors, particularly if the records are not kept in English, French, Russian or Spanish.

53. The Agreement should provide that the records shall be retained for at least five years.

54. The Agreement should provide that the records shall consist, as appropriate, of:

(a) Accounting records of all *nuclear material* subject to safeguards under the Agreement; and

(b) Operating records for *facilities* containing such *nuclear material*.

55. The Agreement should provide that the system of measurements on which the records used for the preparation of reports are based shall either conform to the latest international standards or be equivalent in quality to such standards.

Accounting records

56. The Agreement should provide that the accounting records shall set forth the following in respect of each *material balance area:*

(a) All *inventory changes,* so as to permit a determination of the *book inventory* at any time;

(b) All measurement results that are used for determination of the *physical inventory;* and

(c) All *adjustments* and *corrections* that have been made in respect of *inventory changes, book inventories* and *physical inventories.*

57. The Agreement should provide that for all *inventory changes* and *physical inventories* the records shall show, in respect of each *batch* of *nuclear material:* material identification, *batch data* and *source data.* Provision should further be included that records shall account for uranium, thorium and plutonium separately in each *batch* of *nuclear material.* Furthermore, the date of the *inventory change* and, when appropriate, the originating *material balance area* and the receiving *material balance area* or the recipient, shall be indicated for each *inventory change.*

Operating records

58. The Agreement should provide that the operating records shall set forth as appropriate in respect of each *material balance area:*

(a) Those operating data which are used to establish changes in the quantities and composition of *nuclear material;*

(b) The data obtained from the calibration of tanks and instruments and from sampling and analyses, the procedures to control the quality of measurements and the derived estimates of random and systematic error;

(c) The description of the sequence of the actions taken in preparing for, and in taking, a *physical inventory*, in order to ensure that it is correct and complete; and

(d) The description of the action taken in order to ascertain the cause and magnitude of any accidental or unmeasured loss that might occur.

Reports system
General

59. The Agreement should specify that the State shall provide the Agency with reports as detailed in paragraphs 60–69 below in respect of *nuclear material* subject to safeguards thereunder.

60. The Agreement should provide that reports shall be made in English, French, Russian or Spanish, except as otherwise specified in the Subsidiary Arrangements.

61. The Agreement should provide that reports shall be based on the records kept in accordance with paragraphs 51–58 above and shall consist, as appropriate, of accounting reports and special reports.

Accounting reports

62. The Agreement should stipulate that the Agency shall be provided with an initial report on all *nuclear material* which is to be subject to safeguards thereunder. It should also be provided that the initial report shall be dispatched by the State to the Agency within 30 days of the last day of the calendar month in which the Agreement enters into force, and shall reflect the situation as of the last day of that month.

63. The Agreement should stipulate that for each *material balance area* the State shall provide the Agency with the following accounting reports:

(a) *Inventory change* reports showing changes in the inventory of *nuclear material*. The reports shall be dispatched as soon as possible and in any event within 30 days after the end of the month in which the *inventory changes* occurred or were established; and

(b) Material balance reports showing the material balance based on a *physical inventory* of *nuclear material* actually present in the *material balance area*. The reports shall be dispatched as soon as possible and in any event within 30 days after the *physical inventory* has been taken.

The reports shall be based on data available as of the date of reporting and may be corrected at a later date as required.

64. The Agreement should provide that *inventory change* reports shall specify identification and *batch data* for each *batch* of *nuclear material*, the date of the *inventory change* and, as appropriate, the originating *material balance area* and the receiving *material balance area* or the recipient. These reports shall be accompanied by concise notes:

(a) Explaining the *inventory changes*, on the basis of the operating data contained in the operating records provided for under subparagraph 58(a) above; and

(b) Describing, as specified in the Subsidiary Arrangements, the anticipated operational programme, particularly the taking of a *physical inventory*.

65. The Agreement should provide that the State shall report each *inventory change, adjustment* and *correction* either periodically in a consolidated list or individually. The *inventory changes* shall be reported in terms of *batches;* small amounts, such as analytical samples, as specified in the Subsidiary Arrangements, may be combined and reported as one *inventory change*.

66. The Agreement should stipulate that the Agency shall provide the State with semi-annual statements of *book inventory* of *nuclear material* subject to safeguards, for each *material balance area*, as based on the *inventory change* reports for the period covered by each such statement.

67. The Agreement should specify that the material balance reports shall include the following entries, unless otherwise agreed by the Agency and the State:

(a) Beginning *physical inventory;*
(b) *Inventory changes* (first increases, then decreases);
(c) Ending *book inventory;*
(d) *Shipper/receiver differences;*
(e) Adjusted ending *book inventory;*
(f) Ending *physical inventory;* and
(g) *Material unaccounted for.*

A statement of the *physical inventory*, listing all *batches* separately and specifying material identification and *batch data* for each *batch*, shall be attached to each material balance report.

Special reports

68. The Agreement should provide that the State shall make special reports without delay:

(a) If any unusual incident or circumstances lead the State to believe that there is or may have been loss of *nuclear material* that exceeds the limits to be specified for this purpose in the Subsidiary Arrangements; or

(b) If the containment has unexpectedly changed from that specified in the Subsidiary Arrangements to the extent that unauthorized removal of *nuclear material* has become possible.

Amplification and clarification of reports

69. The Agreement should provide that at the Agency's request the State shall supply amplifications or clarifications of any report, in so far as relevant for the purpose of safeguards.

Inspections
General

70. The Agreement should stipulate that the Agency shall have the right to make inspections as provided for in paragraphs 71–82 below.

Purposes of inspections

71. The Agreement should provide that the Agency may make ad hoc inspections in order to:

(a) Verify the information contained in the initial report on the *nuclear material* subject to safeguards under the Agreement;

(b) Identify and verify changes in the situation which have occurred since the date of the initial report; and

(c) Identify, and if possible verify the quantity and composition of, *nuclear material* in accordance with paragraphs 93 and 96 below, before its transfer out of or upon its transfer into the State.

72. The Agreement should provide that the Agency may make routine inspections in order to:

(a) Verify that reports are consistent with records;

(b) Verify the location, identity, quantity and composition of all *nuclear material* subject to safeguards under the Agreement; and

(c) Verify information on the possible causes of *material unaccounted for, shipper/receiver differences* and uncertainties in the *book inventory*.

73. The Agreement should provide that the Agency may make special inspections subject to the procedures laid down in paragraph 77 below:

(a) In order to verify the information contained in special reports; or

(b) If the Agency considers that information made available by the State, including explanations from the State and information obtained from routine inspections, is not adequate for the Agency to fulfil its responsibilities under the Agreement.

An inspection shall be deemed to be special when it is either additional to the routine inspection effort provided for in paragraphs 78–82 below, or involves access to information or locations in addition to the access specified in paragraph 76 for ad hoc and routine inspections, or both.

Scope of inspections

74. The Agreement should provide that for the purposes stated in paragraphs 71–73 above the Agency may:

(a) Examine the records kept pursuant to paragraphs 51–58;

(b) Make independent measurements of all *nuclear material* subject to safeguards under the Agreement;

(c) Verify the functioning and calibration of instruments and other measuring and control equipment;

(d) Apply and make use of surveillance and containment measures; and

(e) Use other objective methods which have been demonstrated to be technically feasible.

75. It should further be provided that within the scope of paragraph 74 above the Agency shall be enabled:

(a) To observe that samples at *key measurement points* for material balance accounting are taken in accordance with procedures which produce representative samples, to observe the treatment and analysis of the samples and to obtain duplicates of such samples;

(b) To observe that the measurements of *nuclear material* at *key measurement points* for material balance accounting are representative, and to observe the calibration of the instruments and equipment involved;

(c) To make arrangements with the State that, if necessary:

(i) Additional measurements are made and additional samples taken for the Agency's use;

(ii) The Agency's standard analytical samples are analysed;

(iii) Appropriate absolute standards are used in calibrating instruments and other equipment; and

(iv) Other calibrations are carried out;

(d) To arrange to use its own equipment for independent measurement and surveillance, and if so agreed and specified in the Subsidiary Arrangements, to arrange to install such equipment;

(e) To apply its seals and other identifying and tamper-indicating devices to containments, if so agreed and specified in the Subsidiary Arrangements; and

(f) To make arrangements with the State for the shipping of samples taken for the Agency's use.

Access for inspections

76. The Agreement should provide that:

(a) For the purposes specified in sub-paragraphs 71(a) and (b) above and until such time as the *strategic points* have been specified in the Subsidiary Arrangements, the Agency's inspectors shall have access to any location where the initial report or any inspections carried out in connection with it indicate that *nuclear material* is present;

(b) For the purposes specified in sub-paragraph 71(c) above the inspectors shall have access to any location of which the Agency has been notified in accordance with sub-paragraphs 92(c) or 95(c) below;

(c) For the purposes specified in paragraph 72 above the Agency's inspectors shall have access only to the *strategic points* specified in the Subsidiary Arrangements and to the records maintained pursuant to paragraphs 51–58; and

(d) In the event of the State concluding that any unusual circumstances require extended limitations on access by the Agency, the State and the Agency shall promptly make arrangements with a view to enabling the Agency to discharge its safeguards responsibilities in the light of these limitations. The Director General shall report each such arrangement to the Board.

77. The Agreement should provide that in circumstances which may lead to special inspections for the purposes specified in paragraph 73 above the State and the Agency shall consult forthwith. As a result of such consultations the Agency may make inspections in addition to the routine inspection effort provided for in paragraphs 78–82 below, and may obtain access in agreement with the State to information or locations in addition to the access specified in paragraph 76 above for ad hoc and routine inspections. Any disagreement concerning the need for additional access shall be resolved in accordance with paragraphs 21 and 22; in case action by the State is essential and urgent, paragraph 18 above shall apply.

Frequency and intensity of routine inspections

78. The Agreement should provide that the number, intensity, duration and timing of routine inspections shall be kept to the minimum consistent with the effective implementation of the safeguards procedures set forth therein, and that the Agency shall make the optimum and most economical use of available inspection resources.

79. The Agreement should provide that in the case of *facilities* and *material balance areas* outside *facilities* with a content or *annual throughput*, whichever is greater, of *nuclear material* not exceeding five *effective kilograms*, routine inspections shall not exceed one per year. For other *facilities* the number, intensity, duration, timing and mode of inspections shall be determined on the basis that in the maximum or limiting case the inspection régime shall be no more intensive than is necessary and sufficient to maintain continuity of knowledge of the flow and inventory of *nuclear material*.

80. The Agreement should provide that the maximum routine inspection effort in respect of *facilities* with a content or *annual throughput* of *nuclear material* exceeding five *effective kilograms* shall be determined as follows:

(a) For reactors and sealed stores, the maximum total of routine inspection per year shall be determined by allowing one sixth of a *man-year of inspection* for each such *facility* in the State;

(b) For other *facilities* involving plutonium or uranium enriched to more than 5%, the maximum total of routine inspection per year shall be determined by allowing for each such *facility* $30 \times \sqrt{E}$ man-days of inspection per year, where E is the inventory or *annual throughput* of *nuclear material*, whichever is greater, expressed in *effective kilograms*. The maximum established for any such *facility* shall not, however, be less than 1.5 *man-years of inspection;* and

(c) For all other *facilities*, the maximum total of routine inspection per year shall be determined by allowing for each such *facility* one third of a *man-year of inspection* plus $0.4 \times E$ man-days of inspection per year, where E is the inventory or *annual throughput* of *nuclear material*, whichever is greater, expressed in *effective kilograms*.

The Agreement should further provide that the Agency and the State may agree to amend the maximum figures specified in this paragraph upon determination by the Board that such amendment is reasonable.

81. Subject to paragraphs 78–80 above the criteria to be used for determining the actual number, intensity, duration, timing and mode of routine inspections of any *facility* shall include:

(a) The form of *nuclear material*, in particular, whether the material is in bulk form or contained in a number of separate items; its chemical composition and, in the case of uranium, whether it is of low or high *enrichment;* and its accessibility;

(b) The effectiveness of the State's accounting and control system, including the extent to which the operators of *facilities* are functionally independent of the State's accounting and control system; the extent to which the measures specified in paragraph 32 above have been implemented by the State; the promptness of reports submitted to the Agency; their consistency with the Agency's independent verification; and the amount and accuracy of the *material unaccounted for*, as verified by the Agency;

(c) Characteristics of the State's nuclear fuel cycle, in particular, the number and types of *facilities* containing *nuclear material* subject to safeguards, the characteristics of such *facilities* relevant to safeguards, notably the degree of containment; the extent to which the design of such *facilities* facilitates verification of the flow and inventory of *nuclear material;* and the extent to which information from different *material balance areas* can be correlated;

(d) International interdependence, in particular, the extent to which *nuclear material* is received from or sent to other States for use or processing; any verification activity by the Agency in connection therewith; and the extent to which the State's nuclear activities are interrelated with those of other States; and

(e) Technical developments in the field of safeguards, including the use of statistical techniques and random sampling in evaluating the flow of *nuclear material*.

82. The Agreement should provide for consultation between the Agency and the State if the latter considers that the inspection effort is being deployed with undue concentration on particular *facilities*.

Notice of inspections

83. The Agreement should provide that the Agency shall give advance notice to the State before arrival of inspectors at *facilities* or *material balance areas* outside *facilities*, as follows:

(a) For ad hoc inspections pursuant to sub-paragraph 71(c) above, at least 24 hours, for those pursuant to sub-paragraphs 71(a) and (b), as well as the activities provided for in paragraph 48, at least one week;

(b) For special inspections pursuant to paragraph 73 above, as promptly as possible after the Agency and the State have consulted as provided for in paragraph 77, it being understood that notification of arrival normally will constitute part of the consultations; and

(c) For routine inspections pursuant to paragraph 72 above, at least 24 hours in respect of the *facilities* referred to in sub-paragraph 80(b) and sealed stores containing plutonium or uranium enriched to more than 5%, and one week in all other cases.

Such notice of inspections shall include the names of the inspectors and shall indicate the *facilities* and the *material balance areas* outside *facilities* to be visited and the periods during which they will be visited. If the inspectors are to arrive from outside the State the Agency shall also give advance notice of the place and time of their arrival in the State.

84. However, the Agreement should also provide that, as a supplementary measure, the Agency may carry out without advance notification a portion of the routine inspections pursuant to paragraph 80 above in accordance with the principle of random sampling. In performing any unannounced inspections, the Agency shall fully take into account any operational programme provided by the State pursuant to paragraph 64(b). Moreover, whenever practicable, and on the basis of the operational programme, it shall advise the State periodically of its general programme of announced and unannounced inspections, specifying the general periods when inspections are foreseen. In carrying out any unannounced inspections, the Agency shall make every effort to minimize any practical difficulties for *facility* operators and the State, bearing in mind the relevant provisions of paragraphs 44 above and 89 below. Similarly the State shall make every effort to facilitate the task of the inspectors.

Designation of inspectors

85. The Agreement should provide that:

(a) The Director General shall inform the State in writing of the name, qualifications, nationality, grade and such other particulars as may be relevant, of each Agency official he proposes for designation as an inspector for the State;

(b) The State shall inform the Director General within 30 days of the receipt of such a proposal whether it accepts the proposal;

(c) The Director General may designate each official who has been accepted by the State as one of the inspectors for the State, and shall inform the State of such designations; and

(d) The Director General, acting in response to a request by the State or on his own initiative, shall immediately inform the State of the withdrawal of the designation of any official as an inspector for the State.

The Agreement should also provide, however, that in respect of inspectors needed for the purposes stated in paragraph 48 above and to carry out ad hoc inspections pursuant to sub-paragraphs 71(a) and (b) the designation procedures shall be completed if possible within 30 days after the entry into force of the Agreement. If such designation appears impossible within this time limit, inspectors for such purposes shall be designated on a temporary basis.

86. The Agreement should provide that the State shall grant or renew as quickly as possible appropriate visas, where required, for each inspector designated for the State.

Conduct and visits of inspectors

87. The Agreement should provide that inspectors, in exercising their functions under paragraphs 48 and 71–75 above, shall carry out their activities in a manner designed to avoid hampering or delaying the construction, commissioning or operation of *facilities*, or affecting their safety. In particular inspectors shall not operate any *facility* themselves or direct the staff of a *facility* to carry out any operation. If inspectors consider that in pursuance of paragraphs 74 and 75, particular operations in a *facility* should be carried out by the operator, they shall make a request therefor.

88. When inspectors require services available in the State, including the use of equipment, in connection with the performance of inspections, the State shall facilitate the procurement of such services and the use of such equipment by inspectors.

89. The Agreement should provide that the State shall have the right to have inspectors accompanied during their inspections by representatives of the State, provided that inspectors shall not thereby be delayed or otherwise impeded in the exercise of their functions.

Statements on the Agency's verification activities

90. The Agreement should provide that the Agency shall inform the State of:

(a) The results of inspections, at intervals to be specified in the Subsidiary Arrangements; and

(b) The conclusions it has drawn from its verification activites in the State, in particular by means of statements in respect of each *material balance area*, which shall be made as soon as possible after a *physical inventory* has been taken and verified by the Agency and a material balance has been struck.

International transfers
General

91. The Agreement should provide that *nuclear material* subject or required to be subject to safeguards thereunder which is transferred internationally shall, for purposes of the Agreement, be regarded as being the responsibility of the State:

(a) In the case of import, from the time that such responsibility ceases to lie with the exporting State, and no later than the time at which the *nuclear material* reaches its destination; and

(b) In the case of export, up to the time at which the recipient State assumes such responsibility, and no later than the time at which the *nuclear material* reaches its destination.

The Agreement should provide that the States concerned shall make suitable arrangements to determine the point at which the transfer of responsibility will take place. No State shall be deemed to have such responsibility for *nuclear material* merely by reason of the fact that the *nuclear material* is in transit on or over its territory or territorial waters, or that it is being transported under its flag or in its aircraft.

Transfers out of the State

92. The Agreement should provide that any intended transfer out of the State of safeguarded *nuclear material* in an amount exceeding one *effective kilogram*, or by successive shipments to the same State within a period of three months each of less than one *effective kilogram* but exceeding in total one *effective kilogram*, shall be notified to the Agency after the conclusion of the contractual arrangements leading to the transfer and normally at least two weeks before the *nuclear material* is to be prepared for shipping. The Agency and the State may agree on different procedures for advance notification. The notification shall specify:

(a) The identification and, if possible, the expected quantity and composition of the *nuclear material* to be transferred, and the *material balance area* from which it will come;

(b) The State for which the *nuclear material* is destined;

(c) The dates on and locations at which the *nuclear material* is to be prepared for shipping;

(d) The approximate dates of dispatch and arrival of the *nuclear material;* and

(e) At what point of the transfer the recipient State will assume responsibility for the *nuclear material*, and the probable date on which this point will be reached.

93. The Agreement should further provide that the purpose of this notification shall be to enable the Agency if necessary to identify, and if possible verify the quantity and composition of, *nuclear material* subject to safeguards under the Agreement before it is transferred out of the State and, if the Agency so wishes or the State so requests, to affix seals to the *nuclear material* when it has been prepared for shipping. However, the transfer of the *nuclear material* shall not be delayed in any way by any action taken or contemplated by the Agency pursuant to this notification.

94. The Agreement should provide that, if the *nuclear material* will not be subject to Agency safeguards in the recipient State, the exporting State shall make arrangements for the Agency to receive, within three months of the time when the recipient State accepts responsibility for the *nuclear material* from the exporting State, confirmation by the recipient State of the transfer.

Transfers into the State

95. The Agreement should provide that the expected transfer into the State of *nuclear material* required to be subject to safeguards in an amount greater than one *effective kilogram*, or by successive shipments from the same State within a period of three months each of less than one *effective kilogram* but exceeding in total one *effective kilogram*, shall be notified to the Agency as much in advance as possible of the expected arrival of the *nuclear material*, and in any case not later than the date on which the recipient State assumes responsibility therefor. The Agency and the State may agree on different procedures for advance notification. The notification shall specify:

(a) The identification and, if possible, the expected quantity and composition of the *nuclear material;*

(b) At what point of the transfer responsibility for the *nuclear material* will be assumed by the State for the purposes of the Agreement, and the probable date on which this point will be reached; and

(c) The expected date of arrival, the location to which the *nuclear material* is to be delivered and the date on which it is intended that the *nuclear material* should be unpacked.

96. The Agreement should provide that the purpose of this notification shall be to enable the Agency if necessary to identify, and if possible verify the quantity and composition of, *nuclear material* subject to safeguards which has been transferred into the State, by means of inspection of the consignment at the time it is unpacked. However, unpacking shall not be delayed by any action taken or contemplated by the Agency pursuant to this notification.

Special reports

97. The Agreement should provide that in the case of international transfers a special report as envisaged in paragraph 68 above shall be made if any unusual incident or circumstances lead the State to believe that there is or may have been loss of *nuclear material*, including the occurrence of significant delay during the transfer.

Definitions

98. "Adjustment" means an entry into an accounting record or a report showing a *shipper/receiver difference* or *material unaccounted for*.

99. "Annual throughput" means, for the purposes of paragraphs 79 and 80 above, the amount of *nuclear material* transferred annually out of a *facility* working at nominal capacity.

100. "Batch" means a portion of *nuclear material* handled as a unit for accounting purposes at a *key measurement point* and for which the composition and quantity are defined by a single set of specifications or measurements. The *nuclear material* may be in bulk form or contained in a number of separate items.

101. "Batch data" means the total weight of each element of *nuclear material* and, in the case of plutonium and uranium, the isotopic composition when appropriate. The units of account shall be as follows:

(a) Grams of contained plutonium;

(b) Grams of total uranium and grams of contained uranium-235 plus uranium-233 for uranium enriched in these isotopes; and

(c) Kilograms of contained thorium, natural uranium or depleted uranium.

For reporting purposes the weights of individual items in the *batch* shall be added together before rounding to the nearest unit.

102. "Book inventory" of a *material balance area* means the algebraic sum of the most recent *physical inventory* of that *material balance area* and of all *inventory changes* that have occurred since that *physical inventory* was taken.

103. "Correction" means an entry into an accounting record or a report to rectify an identified mistake or to reflect an improved measurement of a quantity previously entered into the record or report. Each correction must identify the entry to which it pertains.

104. "Effective kilogram" means a special unit used in safeguarding *nuclear material*. The quantity in "effective kilograms" is obtained by taking:

(a) For plutonium, its weight in kilograms;

(b) For uranium with an *enrichment* of 0.01 (1 %) and above, its weight in kilograms multiplied by the square of its *enrichment*;

(c) For uranium with an *enrichment* below 0.01 (1 %) and above 0.005 (0.5 %), its weight in kilograms multiplied by 0.0001; and

(d) For depleted uranium with an *enrichment* of 0.005 (0.5 %) or below, and for thorium, its weight in kilograms multiplied by 0.00005.

105. "Enrichment" means the ratio of the combined weight of the isotopes uranium-233 and uranium-235 to that of the total uranium in question.

106. "Facility" means:

(a) A reactor, a critical facility, a conversion plant, a fabrication plant, a reprocessing plant, an isotope separation plant or a separate storage installation; or

(b) Any location where *nuclear material* in amounts greater than one *effective kilogram* is customarily used.

107. "Inventory change" means an increase or decrease, in terms of *batches,* of *nuclear material* in a *material balance area;* such a change shall involve one of the following:

(a) Increases:

(i) Import;

(ii) Domestic receipt: receipts from other *material balance areas*, receipts from a non-safeguarded (non-peaceful) activity or receipts at the starting point of safeguards;

(iii) Nuclear production: production of special fissionable material in a reactor; and

(iv) De-exemption: reapplication of safeguards on *nuclear material* previously exempted therefrom on account of its use or quantity.

(b) Decreases:

(i) Export;

(ii) Domestic shipment: shipments to other *material balance areas* or shipments for a non-safeguarded (non-peaceful) activity;

(iii) Nuclear loss: loss of *nuclear material* due to its transformation into other element(s) or isotope(s) as a result of nuclear reactions;

(iv) Measured discard: *nuclear material* which has been measured, or estimated on the basis of measurements, and disposed of in such a way that it is not suitable for further nuclear use;

(v) Retained waste: *nuclear material* generated from processing or from an operational accident, which is deemed to be unrecoverable for the time being but which is stored;

(vi) Exemption: exemption of *nuclear material* from safeguards on account of its use or quantity; and

(vii) Other loss: for example, accidental loss (that is, irretrievable and inadvertent loss of *nuclear material* as the result of an operational accident) or theft.

108. "Key measurement point" means a location where *nuclear material* appears in such a form that it may be measured to determine material flow or inventory. "Key measurement points" thus include, but are not limited to, the inputs and outputs (including measured discards) and storages in *material balance areas*.

109. "Man-year of inspection" means, for the purposes of paragraph 80 above, 300 man-days of inspection, a man-day being a day during which a single inspector has access to a *facility* at any time for a total of not more than eight hours.

110. "Material balance area" means an area in or outside of a *facility* such that:

(a) The quantity of *nuclear material* in each transfer

into or our of each "material balance area" can be determined; and

(b) The *physical inventory* of *nuclear material* in each "material balance area" can be determined when necessary, in accordance with specified procedures,

in order that the material balance for Agency safeguards purposes can be established.

111. "Material unaccounted for" means the difference between *book inventory* and *physical inventory*.

112. "Nuclear material" means any source or any special fissionable material as defined in Article XX of the Statute. The term source material shall not be interpreted as applying to ore or ore residue. Any determination by the Board under Article XX of the Statute after the entry into force of this Agreement which adds to the materials considered to be source material or special fissionable material shall have effect under this Agreement only upon acceptance by the State.

113. "Physical inventory" means the sum of all the measured or derived estimates of *batch* quantities of *nuclear material* on hand at a given time within a *material balance area*, obtained in accordance with specified procedures.

114. "Shipper/receiver difference" means the difference between the quantity of *nuclear material* in a *batch* as stated by the shipping *material balance area* and as measured at the receiving *material balance area*.

115. "Source data" means those data, recorded during measurement or calibration or used to derive empirical relationships, which identify *nuclear material* and provide *batch data*. "Source data" may include, for example, weight of compounds, conversion factors to determine weight of element, specific gravity, element concentration, isotopic ratios, relationship between volume and manometer readings and relationship between plutonium produced and power generated.

116. "Strategic point" means a location selected during examination of design information where, under normal conditions and when combined with the information from all "strategic points" taken together, the information necessary and sufficient for the implementation of safeguards measures is obtained and verified; a "strategic point" may include any location where key measurements related to material balance accountancy are made and where containment and surveillance measures are executed.

Source: IAEA document INFCIRC/153 (IAEA, Vienna, 1971).

Number of NPT safeguards agreements with the IAEA in force as of 31 December 1977: 55.

For the list of states which have concluded NPT safeguards agreements, see pages 152–94.

CONVENTION ON THE PROHIBITION OF THE DEVELOPMENT, PRODUCTION AND STOCKPILING OF BACTERIOLOGICAL (BIOLOGICAL) AND TOXIN WEAPONS AND ON THEIR DESTRUCTION

Signed at London, Moscow and Washington on 10 April 1972.
Entered into force on 26 March 1975.
Depositaries: UK, US and Soviet governments.

The States Parties to this Convention,

Determined to act with a view to achieving effective progress towards general and complete disarmament, including the prohibition and elimination of all types of weapons of mass destruction, and convinced that the prohibition of the development, production and stockpiling of chemical and bacteriological (biological) weapons and their elimination, through effective measures, will facilitate the achievement of general and complete disarmament under strict and effective international control,

Recognizing the important significance of the Protocol for the Prohibition of the Use in War of Asphyxiating, Poisonous or Other Gases, and of Bacteriological Methods of Warfare, signed at Geneva on June 17, 1925, and conscious also of the contribution which the said Protocol has already made, and continues to make, to mitigating the horrors of war,

Reaffirming their adherence to the principles and objectives of that Protocol and calling upon all States to comply strictly with them,

Recalling that the General Assembly of the United Nations has repeatedly condemned all actions contrary to the principles and objectives of the Geneva Protocol of June 17, 1925,

Desiring to contribute to the strengthening of confidence between peoples and the general improvement of the international atmosphere,

Desiring also to contribute to the realization of the purposes and principles of the Charter of the United Nations,

Convinced of the importance and urgency of eliminating from the arsenals of States, through effective measures, such dangerous weapons of mass destruction as those using chemical or bacteriological (biological) agents,

Recognizing that an agreement on the prohibition of bacteriological (biological) and toxin weapons represents a first possible step towards the achievement of agreement on effective measures also for the prohibition of the development, production and stockpiling of chemical weapons, and determined to continue negotiations to that end,

Determined, for the sake of all mankind, to exclude completely the possibility of bacteriological (biological) agents and toxins being used as weapons,

Convinced of the importance and urgency of eliminat-conscience of mankind and that no effort should be spared to minimize this risk,

Have agreed as follows:

Article I

Each State Party to this Convention undertakes never in any circumstances to develop, produce, stockpile or otherwise acquire or retain:

(1) Microbial or other biological agents, or toxins whatever their origin or method of production, of types and in quantitites that have no justification for prophylactic, protective or other peaceful purposes;

(2) Weapons, equipment or means of delivery designed to use such agents or toxins for hostile purposes or in armed conflict.

Article II

Each State Party to this Convention undertakes to destroy, or to divert to peaceful purposes, as soon as possible but not later than nine months after the entry into force of the Convention, all agents, toxins, weapons, equipment and means of delivery specified in article I of the Convention, which are in its possession or under its jurisdiction or control. In implementing the provisions of this article all necessary safety precautions shall be observed to protect populations and the environment.

Article III

Each State Party to this Convention undertakes not to transfer to any recipient whatsoever, directly or indirectly, and not in any way to assist, encourage, or induce any State, group of States or international organizations to manufacture or otherwise acquire any of the agents, toxins, weapons, equipment or means of delivery specified in article I of the Convention.

Article IV

Each State Party to this Convention shall, in accordance with its constitutional processes, take any necessary measures to prohibit and prevent the development, production, stockpiling, acquisition or retention of the agents, toxins, weapons, equipment and means of delivery specified in article I of the Convention, within the territory of such State, under its jurisdiction or under its control anywhere.

Article V

The States Parties to this Convention undertake to consult one another and to cooperate in solving any problems which may arise in relation to the objective of, or in the application of the provisions of, the Convention. Consultation and cooperation pursuant to this article may also be undertaken through appropriate international procedures within the framework of the United Nations and in accordance with its Charter.

Article VI

(1) Any State Party to this Convention which finds that any other State Party is acting in breach of obligations deriving from the provisions of the Convention may lodge a complaint with the Security Council of the United Nations. Such a complaint should include all possible evidence confirming its validity, as well as a request for its consideration by the Security Council.

(2) Each State Party to this Convention undertakes to cooperate in carrying out any investigation which the Security Council may initiate, in accordance with the provisions of the Charter of the United Nations, on the basis of the complaint received by the Council. The Security Council shall inform the States Parties to the Convention of the results of the investigation.

Article VII

Each State Party to this Convention undertakes to provide or support assistance, in accordance with the United Nations Charter, to any Party to the Convention which so requests, if the Security Council decides that such Party has been exposed to danger as a result of violation of the Convention.

Article VIII

Nothing in this Convention shall be interpreted as in any way limiting or detracting from the obligations assumed by any State under the Protocol for the Prohibition of the Use in War of Asphyxiating, Poisonous or Other Gases, and of Bacteriological Methods of Warfare, signed at Geneva on June 17, 1925.

Article IX

Each State Party to this Convention affirms the recognized objective of effective prohibition of chemical weapons and, to this end, undertakes to continue negotiations in good faith with a view to reaching early agreement on effective measures for the prohibition of their development, production and stockpiling and for their destruction, and on appropriate measures concerning equipment and means of delivery specifically designed for the production or use of chemical agents for weapons purposes.

Article X

(1) The States Parties to this Convention undertake to facilitate, and have the right to participate in, the fullest possible exchange of equipment, materials and scientific and technological information for the use of bacteriological (biological) agents and toxins for peaceful purposes. Parties to the Convention in a position to do so shall also cooperate in contributing individually or together with other States or international organizations to the further development and application of scientific discoveries in the field of bacteriology (biology) for prevention of disease, or for other peaceful purposes.

(2) This Convention shall be implemented in a manner designed to avoid hampering the economic or technological development of States Parties to the Convention or international cooperation in the field of peaceful bacteriological (biological) activities, including the international exchange of bacteriological (biological) agents and toxins and equipment for the processing, use or production of bacteriological (biological) agents and toxins for peaceful purposes in accordance with the provisions of the Convention.

Article XI

Any State Party may propose amendments to this Convention. Amendments shall enter into force for each State Party accepting the amendments upon their acceptance by a majority of the States Parties to the Convention and thereafter for each remaining State Party on the date of acceptance by it.

Article XII

Five years after the entry into force of this Convention, or earlier if it is requested by a majority of Parties to the Convention by submitting a proposal to this effect to the Depositary Governments, a conference of States Parties to the Convention shall be held at Geneva, Switzerland, to review the operation of the Convention, with a view to assuring that the purposes of the preamble and the provisions of the Convention, including the provisions concerning negotiations on chemical weapons, are being realized. Such review shall take into account any new scientific and technological developments relevant to the Convention.

Article XIII

(1) This Convention shall be of unlimited duration.

(2) Each State Party to this Convention shall in exercising its national sovereignty have the right to withdraw from the Convention if it decides that extraordinary events, related to the subject matter of the Convention, have jeopardized the supreme interests of its country. It shall give notice of such withdrawal to all other States Parties to the Convention and to the United Nations Security Council three months in advance. Such notice shall include a statement of the extraordinary events it regards as having jeopardized its supreme interests.

Article XIV

(1) This Convention shall be open to all States for signature. Any State which does not sign the Convention before its entry into force in accordance with paragraph (3) of this Article may accede to it at any time.

(2) This Convention shall be subject to ratification by signatory States. Instruments of ratification and instruments of accession shall be deposited with the Governments of the United States of America, the United Kingdom of Great Britain and Northern Ireland and the Union of Soviet Socialist Republics, which are hereby designated the Depositary Governments.

(3) This Convention shall enter into force after the deposit of instruments of ratification by twenty-two Governments, including the Governments designated as Depositaries of the Convention.

(4) For States whose instruments of ratification or accession are deposited subsequent to the entry into force of this Convention, it shall enter into force on the date of the deposit of their instruments of ratification or accession.

(5) The Depositary Governments shall promptly inform all signatory and acceding States of the date of each signature, the date of deposit of each instrument of ratification or of accession and the date of the entry into force of this Convention, and of the receipt of other notices.

(6) This Convention shall be registered by the Depositary Governments pursuant to Article 102 of the Charter of the United Nations.

Article XV

This Convention, the English, Russian, French, Spanish and Chinese texts of which are equally authentic, shall be deposited in the archives of the Depositary Governments. Duly certified copies of the Convention shall be transmitted by the Depositary Governments to the Governments of the signatory and acceding States.

Source: *Treaties and Other International Acts,* Series 8062 (US Government Printing Office, Washington).

Number of parties as of 31 December 1977: 76.

For the list of states which have signed, ratified or acceded to the BW Convention, see pages 152–94.

AGREEMENT BETWEEN BELGIUM, DENMARK, THE FEDERAL REPUBLIC OF GERMANY, IRELAND, ITALY, LUXEMBOURG, THE NETHERLANDS, THE EUROPEAN ATOMIC ENERGY COMMUNITY AND THE INTERNATIONAL ATOMIC ENERGY AGENCY IN IMPLEMENTATION OF ARTICLE III, (1) AND (4) OF THE TREATY ON THE NON-PROLIFERATION OF NUCLEAR WEAPONS

Signed on 5 April 1973.
Entered into force on 21 February 1977.

Whereas the Kingdom of Belgium, the Kingdom of Denmark, the Federal Republic of Germany, Ireland, the Italian Republic, the Grand Duchy of Luxembourg and the Kingdom of the Netherlands (hereinafter referred to as "the States") are signatories of the Treaty on the Non-Proliferation of Nuclear Weapons (hereinafter referred to as "the Treaty") opened for signature at London, Moscow and Washington on 1 July 1968 and which entered into force on 5 March 1970;

Recalling that pursuant to Article IV(1) of the Treaty nothing in the Treaty shall be interpreted as affecting the inalienable right of all the Parties to the Treaty to develop research, production and use of nuclear energy for peaceful purposes without discrimination and in conformity with Articles I and II of the Treaty;

Recalling that according to Article IV(2) of the Treaty all the Parties to the Treaty undertake to facilitate, and have the right to participate in, the fullest possible exchange of equipment, materials and scientific and technological information for the peaceful uses of nuclear energy;

Recalling further that under the terms of the same paragraph the Parties to the Treaty in a position to do so shall also co-operate in contributing alone or together with other States or international organisations to the further development of the applications of nuclear energy for peaceful purposes, especially in the territories of non-nuclear-weapon States Party to the Treaty;

Whereas Article III(1) of the Treaty provides that each non-nuclear-weapon State Party to the Treaty undertakes to accept safeguards, as set forth in an agreement to be negotiated and concluded with the International Atomic Energy Agency (hereinafter referred to as "the Agency") in accordance with the Statute of the Agency (hereinafter referred to as "the Statute") and the Agency's safeguards system, for the exclusive purpose of verification of the fulfilment of its obligations assumed under this Treaty with a view to preventing diversion of nuclear energy from peaceful uses to nuclear weapons or other nuclear explosive devices;

Whereas Article III(4) provides that non-nuclear-weapon States Party to the Treaty shall conclude agreements with the Agency to meet the requirements of the said Article either individually or together with other States in accordance with the Statute;

Whereas the States are Members of the European Atomic Energy Community (EURATOM) (hereinafter referred to as "the Community") and have assigned to institutions common to the European Communities regulatory, executive and judicial powers which these institutions exercise in their own right in those areas for which they are competent and which may take effect directly within the legal systems of the Member States;

Whereas within this institutional framework, the Community has in particular the task of ensuring, through appropriate safeguards, that nuclear materials are not diverted to purposes other than those for which they were intended, and will, from the time of the entry into force of the Treaty within the territories of the States, thus be required to satisfy itself through the system of safeguards established by the EURATOM Treaty, that source and special fissionable material in all peaceful nuclear activities within the territories of the States is not diverted to nuclear weapons or other nuclear explosive devices;

Whereas these safeguards include notification to the Community of the basic technical characteristics of nuclear facilities, maintenance and submission of operating records to permit nuclear materials accounting for the Community as a whole, inspections by officials of the Community, and a system of sanctions;

Whereas the Community has the task of establishing with other countries and with international organisations relations which may promote progress in the use of nuclear energy for peaceful purposes and is expressly authorised to assume special safeguards obligations in an agreement with a third State or an international organisation;

Whereas the Agency's international safeguards system referred to in the Treaty comprises, in particular, provisions for the submission of design information to the Agency, the maintenance of records, the submission of reports on all nuclear material subject to safeguards to the Agency, inspections carried out by the Agency's inspectors, requirements for the establishment and maintenance of a system of accounting for and control of nuclear material by a State, and measures in relation to verification of non-diversion;

Whereas the Agency, in the light of its statutory responsibilities and its relationship to the General Assembly and the Security Council of the United Nations, has the responsibility to assure the international community that effective safeguards are being applied under the Treaty;

Noting that the States which were Members of the Community when they signed the Treaty, made it known on that occasion that safeguards provided for in Article III(1) of the Treaty would have to be set out in a verification agreement between the Community, the States and the Agency and defined in such a way that the rights and obligations of the States and the Community would not be affected;

Whereas the Board of Governors of the Agency (hereinafter referred to as "the Board") has approved a comprehensive set of model provisions for the structure and content of agreements between the Agency and States required in connection with the Treaty to be used as the basis for negotiating safeguards agreements between the Agency and non-nuclear-weapon States Party to the Treaty;

Whereas the Agency is authorised under Article III. A. 5 of the Statute, to apply safeguards, at the request of the parties, to any bilateral or multilateral arrangement, or at the request of a State, to any of that State's activities in the field of atomic energy;

Whereas it is the desire of the Agency, the Community and the States to avoid unnecessary duplication of safeguards activities;

Now, therefore, the Agency, the Community and the States have agreed as follows:

PART I.

Basic undertaking

Article 1

The States undertake, pursuant to Article III(1) of the Treaty, to accept safeguards, in accordance with the terms of this Agreement, on all source or special fissionable material in all peaceful nuclear activities within their territories, under their jurisdiction or carried out under their control anywhere, for the exclusive purpose of verifying that such material is not diverted to nuclear weapons or other nuclear explosive devices.

Application of safeguards

Article 2

The Agency shall have the right and the obligation to ensure that safeguards will be applied, in accordance with the terms of this Agreement, on all source or special fissionable material in all peaceful nuclear activities within the territories of the States, under their jurisdiction or carried out under their control anywhere for the exclusive purpose of verifying that such material is not diverted to nuclear weapons or other nuclear explosive devices.

Article 3

(a) The Community undertakes, in applying its safeguards on source and special fissionable material in all peaceful nuclear activities within the territories of the States, to co-operate with the Agency, in accordance with the terms of this Agreement, with a view to ascertaining that such source and special fissionable material is not diverted to nuclear weapons or other nuclear explosive devices.

(b) The Agency shall apply its safeguards, in accordance with the terms of this Agreement, in such a manner as to enable it to verify, in ascertaining that there has been no diversion of nuclear material from peaceful uses to nuclear weapons or other nuclear explosive devices, findings of the Community's system of safeguards. The Agency's verification shall include, inter alia, independent measurements and observations conducted by the Agency in accordance with the procedures specified in this Agreement. The Agency, in its verification, shall take due account of the effectiveness of the Community's system of safeguards in accordance with the terms of this Agreement.

Co-operation between the Agency, the Community and the States

Article 4

The Agency, the Community and the States shall co-operate, in so far as each Party is concerned, to facilitate the implementation of the safeguards provided for in this

Agreement and shall avoid unnecessary duplication of safeguards activities.

Implementation of safeguards

Article 5

The safeguards provided for in this Agreement shall be implemented in a manner designed:

(a) To avoid hampering the economic and technological development in the Community or international co-operation in the field of peaceful nuclear activities, including international exchange of nuclear material;

(b) To avoid undue interference in the peaceful nuclear activities in the Community, and in particular in the operation of facilities; and

(c) To be consistent with prudent management practices required for the economic and safe conduct of nuclear activities.

Article 6

(a) The Agency shall take every precaution to protect commercial and industrial secrets and other confidential information coming to its knowledge in the implementation of this Agreement.

(b) (i) The Agency shall not publish or communicate to any State, organisation or person any information obtained by it in connection with the implementation of this Agreement, except that specific information relating to the implementation thereof may be given to the Board and to such Agency staff members as require such knowledge by reason of their official duties in connection with safeguards, but only to the extent necessary for the Agency to fulfil its responsibilities in implementing this Agreement;

(ii) Summarised information on nuclear material subject to safeguards under this Agreement may be published upon decision of the Board if the States directly concerned or the Community, in so far as either Party is individually concerned, agree thereto.

Article 7

(a) In implementing safeguards under this Agreement, full account shall be taken of technological development in the field of safeguards, and every effort shall be made to ensure optimum cost-effectiveness and the application of the principle of safeguarding effectively the flow of nuclear material subject to safeguards under this Agreement by use of instruments and other techniques at certain strategic points to the extent that present or future technology permits.

(b) In order to ensure optimum cost-effectiveness, use shall be made, for example, of such means as:

(i) Containment as a means of defining material balance areas for accounting purposes;

(ii) Statistical techniques and random sampling in evaluating the flow of nuclear material; and

(iii) Concentration of verification procedures on those stages in the nuclear fuel cycle involving the production, processing, use or storage of nuclear material from which nuclear weapons or other nuclear explosive devices could readily be made, and minimisation of verification procedures in respect of other nuclear material, on condition that this does not hamper the implementation of this Agreement.

Provision of information to the Agency

Article 8

(a) In order to ensure the effective implementation of safeguards under this Agreement, the Community shall, in accordance with the provisions set out in this Agreement, provide the Agency with information concerning nuclear material subject to such safeguards and the features of facilities relevant to safeguarding such material.

(b) (i) The Agency shall require only the minimum amount of information and data consistent with carrying out its responsibilities under this Agreement.

(ii) Information pertaining to facilities shall be the minimum necessary for safeguarding nuclear material subject to safeguards under this Agreement.

(c) If the Community so requests, the Agency shall be prepared to examine on premises of the Community design information which the Community regards as being of particular sensitivity. Such information need not be physically transmitted to the Agency provided that it remains readily available for further examination by the Agency on premises of the Community.

Agency inspectors

Article 9

(a) (i) The Agency shall secure the consent of the Community and the States to the designation of Agency inspectors to the States.

(ii) If the Community, either upon proposal of a designation or at any other time after a designation has been made, objects to the designation, the Agency shall propose to the Community and the States an alternative designation or designations.

(iii) If, as a result of the repeated refusal of the Community to accept the designation of Agency inspectors, inspections to be conducted under this Agreement would be impeded, such refusal shall be considered by the Board, upon referral by the Director General of the Agency (hereinafter referred to as "the Director General"), with a view to its taking appropriate action.

(b) The Community and the States concerned shall take the necessary steps to ensure that Agency inspectors can effectively discharge their functions under this Agreement.

(c) The visits and activities of Agency inspectors shall be so arranged as:

(i) To reduce to a minimum the possible inconvenience and disturbance to the Community and the States and to the peaceful nuclear activities inspected; and

(ii) To ensure protection of industrial secrets or any other confidential information coming to the knowledge of Agency inspectors.

Privileges and immunities

Article 10

Each State shall apply to the Agency, including its property, funds and assets, and to its inspectors and other officials, performing functions under this Agreement, the relevant provisions of the Agreement on the Privileges and Immunities of the International Atomic Energy Agency.

Consumption or dilution of nuclear material

Article 11

Safeguards under this Agreement shall terminate on nuclear material upon determination by the Community and the Agency that the material has been consumed, or has been diluted in such a way that it is no longer usable for any nuclear activity relevant from the point of view of safeguards, or has become practically irrecoverable.

Transfer of nuclear material out of the States

Article 12

The Community shall give the Agency notification of transfers of nuclear material subject to safeguards under this Agreement out of the States, in accordance with the provisions of this Agreement. Safeguards under this Agreement shall terminate on nuclear material when the recipient State has assumed responsibility therefor as provided for in this Agreement. The Agency shall maintain records indicating each transfer and, where applicable, the re-application of safeguards to the transferred nuclear material.

Provisions relating to nuclear material to be used in non-nuclear activities

Article 13

Where nuclear material subject to safeguards under this Agreement is to be used in non-nuclear activities, such as the production of alloys or ceramics, the Community shall agree with the Agency, before the material is so used, on the circumstances under which the safeguards under this Agreement on such material may be terminated.

Non-application of safeguards to nuclear material to be used in non-peaceful activities

Article 14

If a State intends to exercise its discretion to use nuclear material which is required to be safeguarded under this Agreement in a nuclear activity which does not require the application of safeguards under this Agreement, the following procedures shall apply:

(a) The Community and the State shall inform the Agency of the activity, and the State shall make it clear:

(i) That the use of the nuclear material in a non-proscribed military activity will not be in conflict with an undertaking the State may have given and in respect of which Agency safeguards apply, that the material will be used only in a peaceful nuclear activity; and

(ii) That during the period of non-application of safeguards under this Agreement the nuclear material will not be used for the production of nuclear weapons or other nuclear explosive devices;

(b) The Agency and the Community shall make an arrangement so that, only while the nuclear material is in such an activity, the safeguards provided for in this Agreement will not be applied. The arrangement shall identify, to the extent possible, the period or circumstances during which such safeguards will not be applied. In any event, the safeguards provided for in this Agreement shall apply again as soon as the nuclear material is reintroduced into a peaceful nuclear activity. The Agency shall be kept informed of the total quantity and composition of such material in the State or in the States concerned and of any transfer of such material out of that State or those States; and

(c) Each arrangement shall be made in agreement with the Agency. Such agreement shall be given as promptly as possible and shall relate only to such matters as, inter alia, temporal and procedural provisions and reporting arrangements, but shall not involve any approval or classified knowledge of the military activity or relate to the use of the nuclear material therein.

Finance

Article 15

The Agency, the Community and the States will bear the expenses incurred by each of them in implementing their respective responsibilities under this Agreement. However, if the Community, the States or persons under their jurisdiction, incur extraordinary expenses as a result of a specific request by the Agency, the Agency shall reimburse such expenses provided that it has agreed in advance to do so. In any case, the Agency shall bear the cost of any additional measuring or sampling which Agency inspectors may request.

Third party liability for nuclear damage

Article 16

The Community and the States shall ensure that any protection against third party liability in respect of nuclear damage, including any insurance or other financial security which may be available under their laws or regulations shall apply to the Agency and its officials for the purpose of the implementation of this Agreement, in the same way as that protection applies to nationals of the States.

International responsibility

Article 17

Any claim by the Community or a State against the Agency or by the Agency against the Community or a State in respect of any damage resulting from the implementation of safeguards under this Agreement, other than damage arising out of a nuclear incident, shall be settled in accordance with international law.

Measures in relation to verification of non-diversion

Article 18

If the Board, upon report of the Director General, decides that an action by the Community or a State, in so far as either Party is individually concerned, is essential and urgent in order to ensure verification that nuclear material subject to safeguards under this Agreement is not diverted to nuclear weapons or other nuclear explosive devices, the Board may call upon the Community or that State to take the required action without delay, irrespective of whether procedures have been invoked pursuant to Article 22 for the settlement of a dispute.

Article 19

If the Board, upon examination of relevant information reported to it by the Director General, finds that the Agency is not able to verify that there has been no diversion of nuclear material required to be safeguarded under this

Agreement, to nuclear weapons or other nuclear explosive devices, it may make the reports provided for in Article XII(C) of the Statute and may also take, where applicable, the other measures provided for in that paragraph. In taking such action, the Board shall take account of the degree of assurance provided by the safeguards measures that have been applied and shall offer the Community or the State, in so far as either Party is individually concerned, every reasonable opportunity to furnish the Board with any necessary reassurance.

Interpretation and application of the Agreement and settlement of disputes

Article 20

At the request of the Agency, the Community or a State, there shall be consultations about any question arising out of the interpretation or application of this Agreement.

Article 21

The Community and the States shall have the right to request that any question arising out of the interpretation or application of this Agreement be considered by the Board. The Board shall invite the Community and the State concerned to participate in the discussion of any such question by the Board.

Article 22

Any dispute arising out of the interpretation or application of this Agreement except a dispute with regard to a finding by the Board under Article 19 or an action taken by the Board pursuant to such a finding, which is not settled by negotiation or another procedure agreed to by the Agency, the Community and the States shall, at the request of any one of them, be submitted to an arbitral tribunal composed of five arbitrators. The Community and the States shall designate two arbitrators and the Agency shall also designate two arbitrators, and the four arbitrators so designated shall elect a fifth, who shall be the Chairman. If, within thirty days of the request for arbitration, the Community and the States, or the Agency, have not designated two arbitrators each, the Community or the Agency may request the President of the International Court of Justice to appoint these arbitrators. The same procedure shall apply if, within thirty days of the designation or appointment of the fourth arbitrator, the fifth arbitrator has not been elected. A majority of the members of the arbitral tribunal shall constitute a quorum, and all decisions shall require the concurrence of at least three arbitrators. The arbitral procedure shall be fixed by the tribunal. The decisions of the tribunal shall be binding on the Agency, the Community, and the States concerned.

Accession

Article 23

(a) This Agreement shall come into force for non-nuclear-weapon States Party to the Treaty which become Members of the Community, upon:
  (i) Notification to the Agency by the State concerned that its procedures with respect to the coming into force of this Agreement have been completed; and
  (ii) Notification to the Agency by the Community that it is in a position to apply its safeguards in respect of that State for the purposes of this Agreement.

(b) Where the State concerned has concluded other agreements with the Agency for the application of Agency safeguards, upon the coming into force of this Agreement for that State, the application of Agency safeguards under such agreements shall be suspended while this Agreement is in force; provided, however, that the State's undertaking in those agreements not to use items which are subject thereto in such a way as to further any military purpose shall continue to apply.

Amendment of the Agreement

Article 24

(a) The Agency, the Community and the States shall, at the request of any one of them, consult on amendment to this Agreement.

(b) All amendments shall require the agreement of the Agency, the Community and the States.

(c) The Director General shall promptly inform all Member States of the Agency of any amendment to this Agreement.

Entry into force and duration

Article 25

(a) This Agreement shall enter into force on the date upon which the Agency receives from the Community and the States written notification that their own requirements for entry into force have been met. The Director General shall promptly inform all Member States of the Agency of the entry into force of this Agreement.

(b) This Agreement shall remain in force as long as the States are Parties to the Treaty.

Protocol

Article 26

The Protocol attached to this Agreement shall be an integral part thereof. The term "Agreement" as used in this instrument means the Agreement and the Protocol together.

PART II

Introduction

Article 27

The purpose of this part of the Agreement is to specify, as required, the procedures to be applied in the implementation of the safeguards provisions of Part I.

Objective of safeguards

Article 28

The objective of the safeguards procedures set forth in this Agreement is the timely detection of diversion of significant quantities of nuclear material from peaceful nuclear activities to the manufacture of nuclear weapons or of other nuclear explosive devices or for purposes unknown, and deterrence of such diversion by the risk of early detection.

Article 29

For the purpose of achieving the objective set forth in Article 28, material accountancy shall be used as a safeguards measure of fundamental importance, with containment and surveillance as important complementary measures.

Article 30

The technical conclusion of the Agency's verification activities shall be a statement, in respect of each material balance area, of the amount of material unaccounted for over a specific period, and giving the limits of accuracy of the amounts stated.

The Community's system of safeguards

Article 31

Pursuant to Article 3, the Agency, in carrying out its verification activities, shall make full use of the Community's system of safeguards.

Article 32

The Community's system of accounting for and control of nuclear material under this Agreement shall be based on a structure of material balance areas. The Community, in applying its safeguards, will make use of and, to the extent necessary, make provision for, as appropriate and specified in the Subsidiary Arrangements such measures as:

(a) A measurement system for the determination of the quantities of nuclear material received, produced, shipped, lost or otherwise removed from inventory, and the quantities on inventory;
(b) The evaluation of precision and accuracy of measurements and the estimation of measurement uncertainty;
(c) Procedures for identifying, reviewing and evaluating differences in shipper/receiver measurements;
(d) Procedures for taking a physical inventory;
(e) Procedures for the evaluation of accumulations of unmeasured inventory and unmeasured losses;
(f) A system of records and reports showing, for each material balance area, the inventory of nuclear material and the changes in that inventory including receipts into and transfers out of the material balance area;
(g) Provisions to ensure that the accounting procedures and arrangements are being operated correctly; and
(h) Procedures for the provision of reports to the Agency in accordance with Articles 59 to 65 and 67 to 69.

Article 33

Safeguards under this Agreement shall not apply to material in mining or ore processing activities.

Article 34

(a) When any material containing uranium or thorium which has not reached the stage of the nuclear fuel cycle described in paragraph (c) is directly or indirectly exported to a non-nuclear-weapon State not Party to this Agreement, the Community shall inform the Agency of its quantity, composition and destination, unless the material is exported for specifically non-nuclear purposes;
(b) When any material containing uranium or thorium which has not reached the stage of the nuclear fuel cycle described in paragraph (c) is imported into the States, the Community shall inform the Agency of its quantity and composition, unless the material is imported for specifically non-nuclear purposes; and
(c) When any nuclear material of a composition and purity suitable for fuel fabrication or for isotopic enrichment leaves the plant or the process stage in which it has been produced, or when such nuclear material, or any other nuclear material produced at a later stage in the nuclear fuel cycle, is imported into the States, the nuclear material shall become subject to the other safeguards procedures specified in this Agreement.

Termination of safeguards

Article 35

(a) Safeguards under this Agreement shall terminate on nuclear material, under the conditions set forth in Article 11. Where the conditions of that Article are not met, but the Community considers that the recovery of nuclear material subject to safeguards under this Agreement from residues is not for the time being practicable or desirable, the Agency and the Community shall consult on the appropriate safeguards measures to be applied.

(b) Safeguards under this Agreement shall terminate on nuclear material, under the conditions set forth in Article 13, provided that the Agency and the Community agree that such nuclear material is practicably irrecoverable.

Exemptions from safeguards

Article 36

At the request of the Community, the Agency shall exempt nuclear material from safeguards under this Agreement, as follows:

(a) Special fissionable material, when it is used in gram quantities or less as a sensing component in instruments;
(b) Nuclear material, when it is used in non-nuclear activities in accordance with Article 13, if such nuclear material is recoverable; and
(c) Plutonium with an isotopic concentration of plutonium-238 exceeding 80%.

Article 37

At the request of the Community the Agency shall exempt from safeguards under this Agreement nuclear material that would otherwise be subject to such safeguards, provided that the total quantity of nuclear material which has been exempted in the States in accordance with this Article may not at any time exceed:

(a) One kilogram in total of special fissionable material, which may consist of one or more of the following:
  (i) Plutonium;
  (ii) Uranium with an enrichment of 0.2 (20%) and above, taken account of by multiplying its weight by its enrichment; and
  (iii) Uranium with an enrichment below 0.2 (20%) and above that of natural uranium, taken account of by multiplying its weight by five times the square of its enrichment;
(b) Ten metric tons in total of natural uranium and depleted uranium with an enrichment above 0.005 (0.5%);
(c) Twenty metric tons of depleted uranium with an enrichment of 0.005 (0.5%) or below; and

(d) Twenty metric tons of thorium;
or such greater amounts as may be specified by the Board for uniform application.

Article 38

If exempted nuclear material is to be processed or stored together with nuclear material subject to safeguards under this Agreement, provision shall be made for the re-application of such safeguards thereto.

Subsidiary arrangements

Article 39

The Community shall make Subsidiary Arrangements with the Agency which shall specify in detail, to the extent necessary to permit the Agency to fulfil its responsibilities under this Agreement in an effective and efficient manner, how the procedures laid down in this Agreement are to be applied. The Subsidiary Arrangements may be extended or changed by agreement between the Agency and the Community without amendment of this Agreement.

Article 40

The Subsidiary Arrangements shall enter into force at the same time as, or as soon as possible after, the entry into force of this Agreement. The Agency, the Community and the States shall make every effort to achieve their entry into force within ninety days of the entry into force of this Agreement; an extension of that period shall require agreement between the Agency, the Community and the States. The Community shall provide the Agency promptly with the information required for completing the Subsidiary Arrangements. Upon the entry into force of this Agreement, the Agency shall have the right to apply the procedures laid down therein in respect of the nuclear material listed in the inventory provided for in Article 41, even if the Subsidiary Arrangements have not yet entered into force.

Inventory

Article 41

On the basis of the initial report referred to in Article 62, the Agency shall establish a unified inventory of all nuclear material in the States subject to safeguards under this Agreement, irrespective of its origin, and shall maintain this inventory on the basis of subsequent reports and of the results of its verification activities. Copies of the inventory shall be made available to the Community at intervals to be agreed.

Design information

General provisions
Article 42

Pursuant to Article 8, design information in respect of existing facilities shall be provided to the Agency by the Community during the discussion of the Subsidiary Arrangements. The time limits for the provision of design information in respect of the new facilities shall be specified in the Subsidiary Arrangements and such information shall be provided as early as possible before nuclear material is introduced into a new facility.

Article 43

The design information to be provided to the Agency shall include, in respect of each facility, when applicable:

(a) The identification of the facility, stating its general character, purpose, nominal capacity and geographic location, and the name and address to be used for routine business purposes;

(b) A description of the general arrangement of the facility with reference, to the extent feasible, to the form, location and flow of nuclear material and to the general layout of important items of equipment which use, produce or process nuclear material;

(c) A description of features of the facility relating to material accountancy, containment and surveillance; and

(d) A description of the existing and proposed procedures at the facility for nuclear material accountancy and control, with special reference to material balance areas established by the operator, measurements of flow and procedures for physical inventory taking.

Article 44

Other information relevant to the application of safeguards under this Agreement shall also be provided to the Agency in respect of each facility, if so specified in the Subsidiary Arrangements. The Community shall provide the Agency with supplementary information on the health and safety procedures which the Agency shall observe and with which Agency inspectors shall comply at the facility.

Article 45

The Agency shall be provided by the Community with design information in respect of a modification relevant for purposes of safeguards under this Agreement, for examination, and shall be informed of any change in the information provided to it under Article 44, sufficiently in advance for the safeguards procedures to be applied under this Agreement to be adjusted when necessary.

Article 46. *Purpose of examination of design information*

The design information provided to the Agency shall be used for the following purposes:

(a) To identify the features of facilities and nuclear material relevant to the application of safeguards to nuclear material in sufficient detail to facilitate verification;

(b) To determine material balance areas to be used for accounting purposes under this Agreement and to select those strategic points which are key measurement points and which will be used to determine flow and inventory of nuclear material; in determining such material balance areas the following criteria shall, inter alia, be used:

(i) The size of the material balance area shall be related to the accuracy with which the material balance can be established;

(ii) In determining the material balance area advantage shall be taken of any opportunity to use containment and surveillance to help ensure the completeness of flow measurements and thereby to simplify the application of safeguards and to concentrate measurement efforts at key measurement points;

(iii) A special material balance area may be established at the request of the Community or of the State concerned around a process step involving commercially sensitive information;

(c) To establish the nominal timing and procedures for taking of physical inventory of nuclear material for accounting purposes under this Agreement;
(d) To establish the records and reports requirements and records evaluation procedures;
(e) To establish requirements and procedures for verification of the quantity and location of nuclear material; and
(f) To select appropriate combinations of containment and surveillance methods and techniques and the strategic points at which they are to be applied.

The results of the examination of the design information, as agreed upon between the Agency and the Community, shall be included in the Subsidiary Arrangements.

Article 47. *Re-examination of design information*

Design information shall be re-examined in the light of changes in operating conditions, of developments in safeguards technology or of the experience in the application of verification procedures, with a view to modifying action taken pursuant to Article 46.

Article 48. *Verification of design information*

The Agency, in co-operation with the Community and the State concerned may send inspectors to facilities to verify the design information provided to the Agency pursuant to Articles 42 to 45 for the purpose stated in Article 46.

Information in respect of nuclear material outside facilities

Article 49

The Agency shall be provided by the Community with the following information when nuclear material is to be customarily used outside facilities, as applicable:
(a) A general description of the use of the nuclear material, its geographic location, and the user's name and address for routine business purposes; and
(b) A general description of the existing and proposed procedures for nuclear material accountancy and control, as specified in the Subsidiary Arrangements.

The Agency shall be informed by the Community, on a timely basis, of any change in the information provided to it under this Article.

Article 50

The information provided to the Agency pursuant to Article 49 may be used, to the extent relevant, for the purposes set out in Article 46(b) to (f).

Records system

General provisions

Article 51

The Community shall arrange that records are kept in respect of each material balance area. The records to be kept shall be described in the Subsidiary Arrangements.

Article 52

The Community shall make arrangements to facilitate the examination of records by Agency inspectors, particularly if the records are not kept in English, French, Russian or Spanish.

Article 53

Records shall be retained for at least five years.

Article 54

Records shall consist, as appropriate, of:
(a) Accounting records of all nuclear material subject to safeguards under this Agreement; and
(b) Operating records for facilities containing such nuclear material.

Article 55

The system of measurements on which the records used for the preparation of reports are based shall either conform to the latest international standards or be equivalent in quality to such standards.

Accounting records

Article 56

The accounting records shall set forth the following in respect of each material balance area:
(a) All inventory changes, so as to permit a determination of the book inventory at any time;
(b) All measurement results that are used for determination of the physical inventory; and
(c) All adjustments and corrections that have been made in respect of inventory changes, book inventories and physical inventories.

Article 57

For all inventory changes and physical inventories the records shall show, in respect of each batch of nuclear material: material identification, batch data and source data. The records shall account for uranium, thorium and plutonium separately in each batch of nuclear material. For each inventory change, the date of the inventory change and, when appropriate, the originating material balance area and the receiving material balance area or the recipient, shall be indicated.

Article 58. *Operating records*

The operating records shall set forth, as appropriate, in respect of each material balance area:
(a) Those operating data which are used to establish changes in the quantities and composition of nuclear material;
(b) The data obtained from the calibration of tanks and instruments and from sampling and analyses, the procedures to control the quality of measurements and the derived estimates of random and systematic error;
(c) A description of the sequence of the actions taken in preparing for, and in taking, a physical inventory, in order to ensure that it is correct and complete; and
(d) A description of the actions taken in order to ascertain the cause and magnitude of any accidental or unmeasured loss that might occur.

Reports system

General provisions

Article 59

The Community shall provide the Agency with reports as detailed in Articles 60 to 65 and 67 to 69 in respect of nuclear material subject to safeguards under this Agreement.

Article 60

Reports shall be made in English, French, Russian or Spanish, except as otherwise specified in the Subsidiary Arrangements.

Article 61

Reports shall be based on the records kept in accordance with Articles 51 and 58 and shall consist, as appropriate, of accounting reports and special reports.

Accounting reports

Article 62

The Agency shall be provided by the Community with an initial report on all nuclear material subject to safeguards under this Agreement. The initial report shall be dispatched to the Agency within thirty days of the last day of the calendar month in which this Agreement enters into force, and shall reflect the situation as of the last day of that month.

Article 63

The Community shall provide the Agency with the following accounting reports for each material balance area:

(a) Inventory change reports showing all changes in the inventory of nuclear material. The reports shall be dispatched as soon as possible and in any event within the time limits specified in the Subsidiary Arrangements; and

(b) Material balance reports showing the material balance based on a physical inventory of nuclear material actually present in the material balance area. The reports shall be dispatched as soon as possible and in any event within the time limits specified in the Subsidiary Arrangements.

The reports shall be based on data available as of the date of reporting and may be corrected at a later date, as required.

Article 64

Inventory change reports shall specify identification and batch data for each batch of nuclear material, the date of the inventory change and, as appropriate, the originating material balance area and the receiving material balance area or the recipient. These reports shall be accompanied by concise notes:

(a) Explaining the inventory changes, on the basis of the operating data contained in the operating records provided for under Article 58(a); and

(b) Describing, as specified in the Subsidiary Arrangements, the anticipated operational programme, particularly the taking of a physical inventory.

Article 65

The Community shall report each inventory change, adjustment and correction, either periodically in a consolidated list or individually. Inventory changes shall be reported in terms of batches. As specified in the Subsidiary Arrangements, small changes in inventory of nuclear material, such as transfers of analytical samples, may be combined in one batch and reported as one inventory change.

Article 66

The Agency shall provide the Community, for the use of the interested parties, with semi-annual statements of book inventory of nuclear material subject to safeguards under this Agreement, for each material balance area, as based on the inventory change reports for the period covered by each such statement.

Article 67

Material balance reports shall include the following entries unless otherwise agreed by the Agency and the Community:

(a) Beginning physical inventory;
(b) Inventory changes (first increases, then decreases);
(c) Ending book inventory;
(d) Shipper/receiver differences;
(e) Adjusted ending book inventory;
(f) Ending physical inventory; and
(g) Material unaccounted for.

A statement of the physical inventory, listing all batches separately and specifying material identification and batch data for each batch, shall be attached to each material balance report.

Article 68. *Special reports*

The Community shall make special reports without delay:

(a) If any unusual incident or circumstances lead the Community to believe that there is or may have been loss of nuclear material that exceeds the limits specified for this purpose in the Subsidiary Arrangements; or

(b) If the containment has unexpectedly changed from that specified in the Subsidiary Arrangements to the extent that unauthorized removal of nuclear material has become possible.

Article 69. *Amplification and clarification of reports*

If the Agency so requests, the Community shall provide it with amplifications or clarifications of any report, in so far as relevant for the purpose of safeguards under this Agreement.

Inspections

Article 70. *General provisions*

The Agency shall have the right to make inspections as provided for in this Agreement.

Purpose of inspections

Article 71

The Agency may make ad hoc inspections in order to:

(a) Verify the information contained in the initial report on the nuclear material subject to safeguards under this Agreement and identify and verify changes in the situation which have occurred between the date of the initial report and the date of the entry into force of the Subsidiary Arrangements in respect of a given facility; and

(b) Identify, and if possible verify the quantity and composition of nuclear material subject to safeguards under this Agreement in accordance with Articles 93 and 96, before its transfer out of or upon its transfer into the States except for transfers within the Community.

Article 72

The Agency may make routine inspections in order to:

(a) Verify that reports are consistent with records;

(b) Verify the location, identity, quantity and composition of all nuclear material subject to safeguards under this Agreement; and

(c) Verify information on the possible causes of material unaccounted for, shipper/receiver differences and uncertainties in the book inventory.

Article 73

Subject to the procedures laid down in Article 77, the Agency may make special inspections:
 (a) In order to verify the information contained in special reports; or
 (b) If the Agency considers that information made available by the Community including explanations from the Community and information obtained from routine inspections, is not adequate for the Agency to fulfil its responsibilities under this Agreement.

An inspection shall be deemed to be special when it is either additional to the routine inspection effort provided for in this Agreement or involves access to information or locations in addition to the access specified in Article 76 for ad hoc and routine inspections, or both.

Scope of inspections

Article 74

For the purposes specified in Articles 71 to 73, the Agency may:
 (a) Examine the records kept pursuant to Articles 51 to 58;
 (b) Make independent measurements of all nuclear material subject to safeguards under this Agreement;
 (c) Verify the functioning and calibration of instruments and other measuring and control equipment;
 (d) Apply and make use of surveillance and containment measures; and
 (e) Use other objective methods which have been demonstrated to be technically feasible.

Article 75

Within the scope of Article 74, the Agency shall be enabled:
 (a) To observe that samples at key measurement points for material balance accountancy are taken in accordance with procedures which produce representative samples, to observe the treatment and analysis of the samples and to obtain duplicates of such samples;
 (b) To observe that the measurements of nuclear material at key measurement points for material balance accountancy are representative, and to observe the calibration of the instruments and equipment involved;
 (c) To make arrangements with the Community and to the extent necessary with the State concerned that, if necessary:
  (i) Additional measurements are made and additional samples taken for the Agency's use;
  (ii) The Agency's standard analytical samples are analysed;
  (iii) Appropriate absolute standards are used in calibrating instruments and other equipment; and
  (iv) Other calibrations are carried out;
 (d) To arrange to use its own equipment for independent measurement and surveillance, and if so agreed and specified in the Subsidiary Arrangements to arrange to install such equipment;
 (e) To apply its seals and other identifying and tamper-indicating devices to containments, if so agreed and specified in the Subsidiary Arrangements; and

 (f) To make arrangements with the Community or the State concerned for the shipping of samples taken for the Agency's use.

Access for inspections

Article 76

(a) For the purposes specified in Article 71(a) and until such time as the strategic points have been specified in the Subsidiary Arrangements, the Agency inspectors shall have access to any location where the initial report or any inspections carried out in connection with it indicate that nuclear material subject to safeguards under this Agreement is present;
 (b) For the purposes specified in Article 71(b) the Agency inspectors shall have access to any location of which the Agency has been notified in accordance with Articles 92(d)(iii) or 95(d)(iii);
 (c) For the purposes specified in Article 72 the inspectors shall have access only to the strategic points specified in the Subsidiary Arrangements and to the records maintained pursuant to Articles 51 to 58; and
 (d) In the event of the Community concluding that any unusual circumstances require extended limitations on access by the Agency, the Community and the Agency shall promptly make arrangements with a view to enabling the Agency to discharge its safeguards responsibilities in the light of these limitations. The Director General shall report each such arrangement to the Board.

Article 77

In the circumstances which may lead to special inspections for the purposes specified in Article 73 the Community and the Agency shall consult forthwith. As a result of such consultations the Agency may:
 (a) Make inspections in addition to the routine inspection effort provided for in this Agreement; and
 (b) Obtain access, in agreement with the Community, to information or locations in additions to those specified in Article 76. Any disagreement shall be resolved in accordance with Articles 21 and 22. In case action by the Community or a State, in so far as either Party is individually concerned, is essential and urgent, Article 18 shall apply.

Frequency and intensity of routine inspections

Article 78

The number, intensity and duration of routine inspections, applying optimum timing, shall be kept to the minimum consistent with the effective implementation of the safeguards procedures set forth in this Agreement, and optimum and most economical use of available inspection resources under the Agreement shall be made.

Article 79

The Agency may carry out one routine inspection per year in respect of facilities and material balance areas outside facilities with a content or annual throughput, whichever is greater, of nuclear material not exceeding five effective kilograms.

Article 80

The number, intensity, duration, timing and mode of routine inspections in respect of facilities with a content or annual throughput of nuclear material exceeding five effective kilograms shall be determined on the basis that in the maximum or limiting case the inspection regime shall be no more intensive than is necessary and sufficient to maintain continuity of knowledge of the flow and inventory of nuclear material, and the maximum routine inspection effort in respect of such facilities shall be determined as follows:

(a) For reactors and sealed storage installations the maximum total of routine inspection per year shall be determined by allowing one sixth of a man-year of inspection for each such facility;

(b) For facilities, other than reactors or sealed storage installations, involving plutonium or uranium enriched to more than 5%, the maximum total of routine inspection per year shall be determined by allowing for each such facility $30 \times \sqrt{E}$ man-days of inspection per year, where E is the inventory or annual throughput of nuclear material, whichever is greater, expressed in effective kilograms. The maximum established for any such facility shall not, however, be less than 1.5 man-years of inspection; and

(c) For facilities not covered by paragraphs (a) or (b), the maximum total of routine inspection per year shall be determined by allowing for each such facility one third of a man-year of inspection plus $0.4 \times E$ man-days of inspection per year, where E is the inventory or annual throughput of nuclear material, whichever is greater, expressed in effective kilograms.

The Parties to this Agreement may agree to amend the figures for the maximum inspection effort specified in this Article, upon determination by the Board that such amendment is reasonable.

Article 81

Subject to Articles 78 to 80 the criteria to be used for determining the actual number, intensity, duration, timing and mode of routine inspections in respect of any facility shall include:

(a) *The form of the nuclear material,* in particular, whether the nuclear material is in bulk form or contained in a number of separate items; its chemical composition and, in the case of uranium, whether it is of low or high enrichment; and its accessibility;

(b) *The effectiveness of the Community's safeguards,* including the extent to which the operators of facilities are functionally independent of the Community's safeguards; the extent to which the measures specified in Article 32 have been implemented by the Community; the promptness of reports provided to the Agency; their consistency with the Agency's independent verification; and the amount and accuracy of the material unaccounted for, as verified by the Agency;

(c) *Characteristics of the nuclear fuel cycle in the States,* in particular, the number and types of facilities containing nuclear material subject to safeguards under this Agreement, the characteristics of such facilities relevant to safeguards under this Agreement, notably the degree of containment; the extent to which the design of such facilities facilitates verification of the flow and inventory of nuclear material; and the extent to which information from different material balance areas can be correlated;

(d) *International interdependence,* in particular, the extent to which nuclear material is received from or sent to other States for use or processing; any verification activities by the Agency in connection therewith; and the extent to which the nuclear activities in each State are interrelated with those in other States; and

(e) *Technical developments in the field of safeguards,* including the use of statistical techniques and random sampling in evaluating the flow of nuclear material.

Article 82

The Agency and the Community shall consult if the latter considers that the inspection effort is being deployed with undue concentration on particular facilities.

Notice of inspections

Article 83

The Agency shall give advance notice to the Community and to the States concerned before arrival of Agency inspectors at facilities or material balance areas outside facilities, as follows:

(a) For ad hoc inspections pursuant to Article 71(b), at least 24 hours; for those pursuant to Article 71(a) as well as the activities provided for in Article 48, at least one week;

(b) For special inspections pursuant to Article 73, as promptly as possible after the Agency and the Community have consulted as provided for in Article 77, it being understood that notification of arrival normally will constitute part of the consultations; and

(c) For routine inspections pursuant to Article 72, at least 24 hours in respect of the facilities referred to in Article 80(b) and sealed storage installations containing plutonium or uranium enriched to more than 5%, and one week in all other cases.

Such notice of inspections shall include the names of the Agency inspectors and shall indicate the facilities and the material balance areas outside facilities to be visited and the period during which they will be visited. If the Agency inspectors are to arrive from outside the States, the Agency shall also give advance notice of the place and time of their arrival in the States.

Article 84

Notwithstanding the provisions of Article 83, the Agency may, as a supplementary measure, carry out without advance notification a portion of the routine inspections pursuant to Article 80 in accordance with the principle of random sampling. In performing any unannounced inspections, the Agency shall fully take into account any operational programme provided to it pursuant to Article 64(b). Moreover, whenever practicable, and on the basis of the operational programme it shall advise the Community and the State concerned periodically of its general programme of announced and unannounced inspections, specifying the general periods when inspections are foreseen. In carrying out any unannounced inspections, the Agency shall make every effort to minimize any practical difficulties for the Community and the State concerned and for facility operators, bearing in mind the relevant provisions of Articles 44 and 89. Similarly the Community and the State concerned shall make every effort to facilitate the task of Agency inspectors.

Designation of Agency inspectors

Article 85

The following procedures shall apply to the designation of Agency inspectors:

(a) The Director General shall inform the Community and the States in writing of the name, qualifications, nationality, grade and such other particulars as may be relevant, of each Agency official he proposes for designation as an Agency inspector for the States;

(b) The Community shall inform the Director General within thirty days of the receipt of such a proposal whether the proposal is accepted;

(c) The Director General may designate each official who has been accepted by the Community and the States as one of the Agency inspectors for the States, and shall inform the Community and the States of such designations; and

(d) The Director General, acting in response to a request by the Community or on his own initiative, shall immediately inform the Community and the States of the withdrawal of the designation of any official as an Agency inspector for the States.

However, in respect of Agency inspectors needed for the activities provided for in Article 48 and to carry out ad hoc inspections pursuant to Article 71(a) the designation procedures shall be completed if possible within thirty days after the entry into force of this Agreement. If such designation appears impossible within this time limit, Agency inspectors for such purposes shall be designated on a temporary basis.

Article 86

The States shall grant or renew as quickly as possible appropriate visas, where required, for each Agency inspector designated pursuant to Article 85.

Conduct and visits of Agency inspectors

Article 87

Agency inspectors, in exercising their functions under Articles 48 and 71 to 75, shall carry out their activities in a manner designed to avoid hampering or delaying the construction, commissioning or operation of facilities, or affecting their safety. In particular, Agency inspectors shall not operate any facility themselves or direct the staff of a facility to carry out any operation. If Agency inspectors consider that in pursuance of Articles 74 and 75, particular operations in a facility should be carried out by the operator, they shall make a request therefor.

Article 88

When Agency inspectors require services available in a State, including the use of equipment, in connection with the performance of inspections, the State concerned and the Community shall facilitate the procurement of such services and the use of such equipment by Agency inspectors.

Article 89

The Community and the States concerned shall have the right to have Agency inspectors accompanied during their inspections by its inspectors and their representatives respectively, provided that Agency inspectors shall not thereby be delayed or otherwise impeded in the exercise of their functions.

Statement on the Agency's verification activities

Article 90

The Agency shall inform the Community for the use of the interested parties of:

(a) The results of its inspections, at intervals to be specified in the Subsidiary Arrangements; and

(b) The conclusions it has drawn from its verification activities.

Transfers into or out of the States

Article 91

General provisions

Nuclear material subject or required to be subject to safeguards under this Agreement which is transferred into or out of the States shall, for purposes of this Agreement, be regarded as being the responsibility of the Community and of the State concerned:

(a) In the case of transfers into the States, from the time that such responsibility ceases to lie with the State from which the material is transferred, and no later than the time at which the material reaches its destination; and

(b) In the case of transfers out of the States up to the time at which the recipient State has such responsibility, and no later than the time at which the nuclear material reaches its destination.

The point at which the transfer of responsibility will take place shall be determined in accordance with suitable arrangements to be made by the Community and the State concerned, on the one hand, and the State to which or from which the nuclear material is transferred, on the other hand. Neither the Community nor a State shall be deemed to have such responsibility for nuclear material merely by reason of the fact that the nuclear material is in transit on or over a State's territory, or that it is being transported on a ship under a State's flag or in the aircraft of a State.

Transfers out of the States

Article 92

(a) The Community shall notify the Agency of any intended transfer out of the States of nuclear material subject to safeguards under this Agreement if the shipment exceeds one effective kilogram, or, for facilities which normally transfer significant quantities to the same State in shipments each not exceeding one effective kilogram, if so specified in the Subsidiary Arrangements.

(b) Such notification shall be given to the Agency after the conclusion of the contractual arrangements leading to the transfer and within the time limit specified in the Subsidiary Arrangements.

(c) The Agency and the Community may agree on different procedures for advance notification.

(d) The notification shall specify:

(i) The identification and, if possible, the expected quantity and the composition of the nuclear material to be transferred, and the material balance area from which it will come;

(ii) The State for which the nuclear material is destined;

(iii) The dates on and locations at which the nuclear material is to be prepared for shipping;

(iv) The approximate dates of dispatch and arrival of the nuclear material; and

(v) At what point of the transfer the recipient State will assume responsibility for the nuclear material for the purpose of this Agreement, and the probable date on which that point will be reached.

Article 93

The notification referred to in Article 92 shall be such as to enable the Agency to make, if necessary, an ad hoc inspection to identify, and if possible verify the quantity and composition of the nuclear material before it is transferred out of the States, except for transfers within the Community and, if the Agency so wishes or the Community so requests, to affix seals to the nuclear material when it has been prepared for shipping. However, the transfer of the nuclear material shall not be delayed in any way by any action taken or contemplated by the Agency pursuant to such a notification.

Article 94

If nuclear material will not be subject to Agency safeguards in the recipient State the Community shall make arrangements for the Agency to receive within three months of the time when the recipient State accepts responsibility for the nuclear material, confirmation by the recipient State of the transfer.

Transfers into the States

Article 95

(a) The Community shall notify the Agency of any expected transfer into the States of nuclear material required to be subject to safeguards under this Agreement if the shipment exceeds one effective kilogram, or, for facilities to which significant quantities are normally transferred from the same State in shipments each not exceeding one effective kilogram, if so specified in the Subsidiary Arrangements.

(b) The Agency shall be notified as much in advance as possible of the expected arrival of the nuclear material, and in any case within the time limits specified in the Subsidiary Arrangements.

(c) The Agency and the Community may agree on different procedures for advance notification.

(d) The notification shall specify:
 (i) The identification and, if possible, the expected quantity and composition of the nuclear material;
 (ii) At what point of the transfer the Community and the State concerned will have responsibility for the nuclear material for the purpose of this Agreement, and the probable date on which that point will be reached; and
 (iii) The expected date of arrival, the location where, and the date on which, the nuclear material is intended to be unpacked.

Article 96

The notification referred to in Article 95 shall be such as to enable the Agency to make, if necessary, an ad hoc inspection to identify, and if possible verify the quantity and composition of, the nuclear material transferred into the States, except for transfers within the Community, at the time the consignment is unpacked. However, unpacking shall not be delayed by any action taken or contemplated by the Agency pursuant to such a notification.

Article 97

Special reports

The Community shall make a special report as envisaged in Article 68 if any unusual incident or circumstances lead the Community to believe that there is or may have been loss of nuclear material, including the occurrence of significant delay, during a transfer into or out of the States.

Definitions

Article 98

For the purposes of this Agreement:

1. A. *Community* means both:
   (a) The legal person created by the Treaty establishing the European Atomic Energy Community (EURATOM), Party to this Agreement; and
   (b) The territories to which the EURATOM Treaty applies.
   B. *States* means the non-nuclear-weapon States Members of the Community, Party to this Agreement.

2. A. *Adjustment* means an entry into an accounting record or a report showing a shipper/receiver difference or material unaccounted for.
   B. *Annual throughput* means, for the purposes of Articles 79 and 80, the amount of nuclear material transferred annually out of a facility working at nominal capacity.
   C. *Batch* means a portion of nuclear material handled as a unit for accounting purposes at a key measurement point and for which the composition and quantity are defined by a single set of specifications or measurements. The nuclear material may be in bulk form or contained in a number of separate items.
   D. *Batch data* means the total weight of each element of nuclear material and, in the case of plutonium and uranium, the isotopic composition when appropriate. The units of account shall be as follows:
   (a) Grams of contained plutonium;
   (b) Grams of total uranium and grams of contained uranium-235 plus uranium-233 for uranium enriched in these isotopes; and
   (c) Kilograms of contained thorium, natural uranium or depleted uranium.
   For reporting purposes the weights of individual items in the batch shall be added together before rounding to the nearest unit.
   E. *Book inventory* of a material balance area means the algebraic sum of the most recent physical inventory of that material balance area and of all inventory changes that have occurred since that physical inventory was taken.
   F. *Correction* means an entry into an accounting record or a report to rectify an identified mistake or to reflect an improved measurement of a quantity previously entered into the record or report. Each correction must identify the entry to which it pertains.
   G. *Effective kilogram* means a special unit used in

safeguarding nuclear material. The quantity in effective kilograms is obtained by taking:
(a) For plutonium, its weight in kilograms;
(b) For uranium with an enrichment of 0.01 (1%) and above, its weight in kilograms multiplied by the square of its enrichment;
(c) For uranium with an enrichment below 0.01 (1%) and above 0.005 (0.5%), its weight in kilograms multiplied by 0.0001; and
(d) For depleted uranium with an enrichment of 0.005 (0.5%) or below, and for thorium, its weight in kilograms multiplied by 0.00005.

H. *Enrichment* means the ratio of the combined weight of the isotopes uranium-233 and uranium-235 to that of the total uranium in question.

I. *Facility* means:
(a) A reactor, a critical facility, a conversion plant, a fabrication plant, a reprocessing plant, an isotope separation plant or a separate storage installation; or
(b) Any location where nuclear material in amounts greater than one effective kilogram is customarily used.

J. *Inventory change* means an increase or decrease, in terms of batches, of nuclear material in a material balance area; such a change shall involve one of the following:
(a) Increases:
　(i) Import;
　(ii) Domestic receipt: receipts from within the States: from other material balance areas; from a non-safeguarded (non-peaceful) activity; at the starting point of safeguards;
　(iii) Nuclear production: production of special fissionable material in a reactor; and
　(iv) De-exemption: reapplication of safeguards on nuclear material previously exempted therefrom on account of its use or quantity.
(b) Decreases:
　(i) Export;
　(ii) Domestic shipment: shipments within the States to other material balance areas or for a non-safeguarded (non-peaceful) activity;
　(iii) Nuclear loss: loss of nuclear material due to its transformation into other element(s) or isotope(s) as a result of nuclear reactions;
　(iv) Measured discard: nuclear material which has been measured, or estimated on the basis of measurements, and disposed of in such a way that it is not suitable for further nuclear use;
　(v) Retained waste: nuclear material generated from processing or from an operational accident, which is deemed to be unrecoverable for the time being but which is stored;
　(vi) Exemption: exemption of nuclear material from safeguards on account of its use or quantity; and
　(vii) Other loss: for example, accidental loss (that is, irretrievable and inadvertent loss of nuclear material as the result of an operational accident) or theft.

K. *Key measurement point* means a location where nuclear material appears in such a form that it may be measured to determine material flow or inventory. Key measurement points thus include, but are not limited to, the inputs and outputs (including measured discards) and storages in material balance areas.

L. *Man-year of inspection* means, for the purposes of Article 80, 300 man-days of inspection, a man-day being a day during which a single inspector has access to a facility at any time for a total of not more than eight hours.

M. *Material balance area* means an area in or outside of a facility such that:
(a) The quantity of nuclear material in each transfer into or out of each material balance area can be determined; and
(b) The physical inventory of nuclear material in each material balance area can be determined when necessary in accordance with specified procedures,
in order that the material balance for Agency safeguards purposes can be established.

N. *Material unaccounted for* means the difference between book inventory and physical inventory.

O. *Nuclear material* means any source or any special fissionable material as defined in Article XX of the Statute. The term "source material" shall not be interpreted as applying to ore or ore residue. Any determination by the Board under Article XX of the Statute after the entry into force of this Agreement which adds to the materials considered to be source material or special fissionable material shall have effect under this Agreement only upon acceptance by the Community and the States.

P. *Physical inventory* means the sum of all the measured or derived estimates of batch quantities of nuclear material on hand at a given time within a material balance area, obtained in accordance with specified procedures.

Q. *Shipper/receiver difference* means the difference between the quantity of nuclear material in a batch as stated by the shipping material balance area and as measured at the receiving material balance area.

R. *Source data* means those data, recorded during measurement or calibration or used to derive empirical relationships, which identify nuclear material and provide batch data. Source data may include, for example, weight of compounds, conversion factors to determine weight of element, specific gravity, element concentration, isotopic ratios, relationship between volume and manometer readings and relationship between plutonium produced and power generated.

S. *Strategic point* means a location selected during examination of design information where, under normal conditions and when combined with the information from all strategic points taken together, the information necessary and sufficient for the implementation of safeguards measures is obtained and verified; a strategic point may include any location where key measurements related to material balance accountancy are made and where containment and surveillance measures are executed.

PROTOCOL

Article 1
This Protocol amplifies certain provisions of the Agreement and, in particular, specifies the conditions and means according to which co-operation in the application of the safeguards provided for under the Agreement shall be implemented in such a way as to avoid unnecessary duplication of the Community's safeguards activities.

Article 2
The Community shall collect the information on facilities and on nuclear material outside facilities to be provided to the Agency under the Agreement on the basis of the agreed indicative questionnaire annexed to the Subsidiary Arrangements.

Article 3
The Agency and the Community shall carry out jointly the examination of design information provided for in Article 46(a) to (f) of the Agreement and shall include the agreed results thereof in the Subsidiary Arrangements. The verification of design information provided for in Article 48 of the Agreement shall be carried out by the Agency in co-operation with the Community.

Article 4
When providing the Agency with the information referred to in Article 2 of this Protocol, the Community shall also transmit information on the inspection methods which it proposes to use and the complete proposals, including estimates of inspection efforts for the routine inspection activities, for Attachments to the Subsidiary Arrangements for facilities and material balance areas outside facilities.

Article 5
The preparation of the Attachments to the Subsidiary Arrangements shall be performed together by the Community and the Agency.

Article 6
The Community shall collect the reports from the operators, keep centralised accounts on the basis of these reports and proceed with the technical and accounting control and analysis of the information received.

Article 7
Upon completion of the tasks referred to in Article 6 of this Protocol the Community shall, on a monthly basis, produce and provide the Agency with the inventory change reports within the time limits specified in the Subsidiary Arrangements.

Article 8
Further, the Community shall transmit to the Agency the material balance reports and physical inventory listings with frequency depending on the frequency of physical inventory taking as specified in the Subsidiary Arrangements.

Article 9
The form and format of reports referred to in Articles 7 and 8 of this Protocol, as agreed between the Agency and the Community, shall be specified in the Subsidiary Arrangements.

Article 10
The routine inspection activities of the Community and of the Agency, including the inspections referred to in Article 84 of the Agreement, for the purposes of the Agreement, shall be co-ordinated pursuant to the provisions of Articles 11 to 23 of this Protocol.

Article 11
Subject to Articles 79 and 80 of the Agreement, in determining the actual number, intensity, duration, timing and mode of the Agency inspections in respect of each facility, account shall be taken of the inspection effort carried out by the Community in the framework of its multinational system of safeguards pursuant to the provisions of this Protocol.

Article 12
Inspection efforts under the Agreement for each facility shall be determined by the use of the criteria of Article 81 of the Agreement. Such criteria shall be implemented by using the rules and methods set forth in the Subsidiary Arrangements which have been used for the calculation of the inspection efforts in respect of specific examples attached to the Subsidiary Arrangements. These rules and methods shall be reviewed from time to time, pursuant to Article 7 of the Agreement, to take into account new technological developments in the field of safeguards and experience gained.

Article 13
Such inspection efforts, expressed as agreed estimates of the actual inspection efforts to be applied, shall be set out in the Subsidiary Arrangements together with relevant descriptions of verification approaches and scopes of inspections to be carried out by the Community and by the Agency. These inspection efforts shall constitute, under normal operating conditions and under the conditions set out below, the actual maximum inspection efforts at the facility under the Agreement:

(a) The continued validity of the information on Community safeguards provided for in Article 32 of the Agreement, as specified in the Subsidiary Arrangements;

(b) The continued validity of the information provided to the Agency in accordance with Article 2 of this Protocol;

(c) The continued provision by the Community of the reports pursuant to Articles 60 and 61, 63 to 65 and 67 to 69 of the Agreement, as specified in the Subsidiary Arrangements;

(d) The continued application of the co-ordination arrangements for inspections pursuant to Articles 10 to 23 of this Protocol, as specified in the Subsidiary Arrangements; and

(e) The application by the Community of its inspection effort with respect to the facility, as specified in the Subsidiary Arrangements, pursuant to this Article.

Article 14
(a) Subject to the conditions of Article 13 of this Protocol, the Agency inspections shall be carried out simultaneously with the inspection activities of the Community. Agency inspectors shall be present during the performance of certain of the Community inspections.

(b) Subject to the provisions of paragraph (a), whenever the Agency can achieve the purposes of its routine inspections set out in the Agreement, the Agency inspectors shall implement the provisions of Articles 74 and 75 of the Agreement through the observation of the inspection activities of the Community inspectors, provided, however, that:

(i) With respect to inspection activities of Agency inspectors to be implemented other than through the observation of the inspection activities of the Community inspectors, which can be foreseen, these shall be specified in the Subsidiary Arrangements; and

(ii) In the course of an inspection, Agency inspectors may carry out inspection activities other than through the observation of the inspection activities of the Community inspectors where they find this to be essential and urgent, if the Agency could not otherwise achieve the purposes of its routine inspections and this was unforeseeable.

Article 15

The general scheduling and planning of the Community inspections under the Agreement shall be established by the Community in co-operation with the Agency.

Article 16

Arrangements for the presence of Agency inspectors during the performance of certain of the Community inspections shall be agreed in advance by the Agency and the Community for each type of facility, and to the extent necessary, for individual facilities.

Article 17

In order to enable the Agency to decide, based on requirements for statistical sampling, as to its presence at a particular Community inspection, the Community shall provide the Agency with an advance statement of the numbers, types and contents of items to be inspected according to the information available to the Community from the operator of the facility.

Article 18

Technical procedures in general for each type of facility and, to the extent necessary, for individual facilities, shall be agreed in advance by the Agency and the Community, in particular with respect to:

(a) The determination of techniques for random selection of statistical samples; and

(b) The checking and identification of standards.

Article 19

The co-ordination arrangements for each type of facility set out in the Subsidiary Arrangements shall serve as a basis for the co-ordination arrangements to be specified in each Facility Attachment.

Article 20

The specific co-ordination actions on matters specified in the Facility Attachments pursuant to Article 19 of this Protocol shall be taken between Community and Agency officials designated for that purpose.

Article 21

The Community shall transmit to the Agency its working papers for those inspections at which Agency inspectors were present and inspection reports for all Community inspections performed under the Agreement.

Article 22

The samples of nuclear material for the Agency shall be drawn from the same randomly selected batches of items as for the Community and shall be taken together with Community samples, except when the maintenance of or reduction to the lowest practical level of the Agency inspection effort requires independent sampling by the Agency, as agreed in advance and specified in the Subsidiary Arrangements.

Article 23

The frequencies of physical inventories to be taken by facility operators and to be verified for safeguards purposes will be in accordance with those laid down as guidelines in the Subsidiary Arrangements. If additional activities under the Agreement in relation to physical inventories are considered to be essential, they will be discussed in the Liaison Committee provided for in Article 25 of this Protocol and agreed before implementation.

Article 24

Whenever the Agency can achieve the purposes of its ad hoc inspections set out in the Agreement through observation of the inspection activities of Community inspectors, it shall do so.

Article 25

(a) With a view to facilitating the application of the Agreement and of this Protocol, a Liaison Committee shall be established, composed of representatives of the Community and of the Agency.

(b) The Committee shall meet at least once a year:

(i) To review, in particular, the performance of the co-ordination arrangements provided for in this Protocol, including agreed estimates of inspection efforts;

(ii) To examine the development of safeguards methods and techniques; and

(iii) To consider any questions which have been referred to it by the periodic meetings referred to in paragraph (c).

(c) The Committee shall meet periodically at a lower level to discuss, in particular and to the extent necessary, for individual facilities, the operation of the co-ordination arrangements provided for in this Protocol, including, in the light of technical and operational developments, updating of agreed estimates of inspection efforts with respect to changes in throughput, inventory and facility operational programmes, and the application of inspection procedures in different types of routine inspection activities and, in general terms, statistical sampling requirements. Any questions which could not be settled would be referred to the meetings mentioned in paragraph (b).

(d) Without prejudice to urgent actions which might be required under the Agreement, should problems arise in the application of Article 13 of this Protocol, in particular when the Agency considered that the conditions specified therein had not been met, the Committee would meet as soon as possible at the suitable level in order to assess the situation and to discuss the measures to be taken. If a problem could not be settled, the Committee may make appropriate proposals to the Parties, in particular with the view to modifying the estimates of inspection efforts for routine inspection activities.

(e) The Committee shall elaborate proposals, as necessary, with respect to questions which require the agreement of the Parties.

Done at Brussels in duplicate, on the fifth day of April in the year one thousand nine hundred and seventy-three in the English and French languages, both texts being equally authentic.

Source: IAEA document INFCIRC/193/Add. 1, 18 April 1977.

DECLARATION OF AYACUCHO

Signed at Lima, Peru, on 9 December 1974.

EXTRACTS:

Being assembled in the city of Lima at the invitation of the President of Peru, Major-General Juan Velasco Alvarado, to commemorate the one hundred and fiftieth anniversary of the Battle of Ayacucho, we, the Heads of State and Government of Bolivia, Panama, Peru and Venezuela and the Representatives of the Heads of State of Argentina, Chile, Colombia and Ecuador, recognize the deep historical significance of that feat of arms, which was decisive in the saga of the emancipation of the American continent and which brought to its close a fundamental stage in the process of forging liberty for our peoples.

. . .

We reiterate our adherence to the principles of the legal equality of States, their territorial integrity, self-determination of peoples, ideological pluralism, respect for human rights, non-intervention and international cooperation, good faith in the fulfilment of obligations, the peaceful settlement of international disputes, and the prohibition of the threat or use of force and of armed aggression of economic or financial aggression in relations between States.

We condemn and repudiate the colonial situations which still exist in Latin America and which must be promptly eradicated because they are a potential threat to peace in the region. Our efforts are pledged to the attainment of that goal.

We undertake to promote and support the building of a lasting order of international peace and co-operation and to create the conditions which will make possible the effective limitation of armaments and an end to their acquisition for offensive purposes, so that all possible resources may be devoted to the economic and social development of every country in Latin America.

. . .

Source: UN document A/10044, 28 January 1975.

DOCUMENT ON CONFIDENCE-BUILDING MEASURES AND CERTAIN ASPECTS OF SECURITY AND DISARMAMENT, INCLUDED IN THE FINAL ACT OF THE CONFERENCE ON SECURITY AND CO-OPERATION IN EUROPE

Signed at Helsinki on 1 August 1975.
The original of the Final Act was transmitted to the government of Finland, which retains it in its archives.

The participating States,

Desirous of eliminating the causes of tension that may exist among them and thus of contributing to the strengthening of peace and security in the world:

Determined to strengthen confidence among them and thus to contribute to increasing stability and security in Europe;

Determined further to refrain in their mutual relations, as well as in their international relations in general, from the threat or use of force against the territorial integrity or political independence of any State, or in any other manner inconsistent with the purposes of the United Nations and with the Declaration on Principles Guiding Relations between Participating States as adopted in this Final Act;

Recognizing the need to contribute to reducing the dangers of armed conflict and of misunderstanding or miscalculation of military activities which could give rise to apprehension, particularly in a situation where the participating States lack clear and timely information about the nature of such activities;

Taking into account considerations relevant to efforts aimed at lessening tension and promoting disarmament;

Recognizing that the exchange of observers by invitation at military manœuvres will help to promote contacts and mutual understanding;

Having studied the question of prior notification of major military movements in the context of confidence-building;

Recognizing that there are other ways in which individual States can contribute further to their common objectives;

Convinced of the political importance of prior notification of major military manœuvres for the promotion of mutual understanding and the strengthening of confidence, stability and security;

Accepting the responsibility of each of them to promote these objectives and to implement this measure in accordance with the accepted criteria and modalities, as essentials for the realization of these objectives;

Recognizing that this measure deriving from political decision rests upon a voluntary basis;

Have adopted the following:

I

PRIOR NOTIFICATION OF MAJOR
MILITARY MANŒUVRES

They will notify their major military manœuvres to all other participating States through usual diplomatic channels in accordance with the following provisions:

Notification will be given of major military manœuvres exceeding a total of 25 000 troops, independently or com-

121

bined with any possible air or naval components (in this context the word "troops" includes amphibious and airborne troops). In the case of independent manœuvres of amphibious or airborne troops, or of combined manœuvres involving them, these troops will be included in this total. Furthermore, in the case of combined manœuvres which do not reach the above total but which involve land forces together with significant numbers of either amphibious or airborne troops, or both, notification can also be given.

Notification will be given of major military manœuvres which take place on the territory, in Europe, of any participating State, as well as, if applicable, in the adjoining sea area and air space.

In the case of a participating State whose territory extends beyond Europe, prior notification need be given only of manœuvres which take place in an area within 250 kilometres from its frontier facing or shared with any other European participating State, the participating State need not, however, give notification in cases in which that area is also contiguous to the participating State's frontier facing or shared with a non-European non-participating State.

Notification will be given 21 days or more in advance of the start of the manœuvre or in the case of a manœuvre arranged at shorter notice at the earliest possible opportunity prior to its starting date.

Notification will contain information of the designation, if any, the general purpose of and the States involved in the manœuvre, the type or types and numerical strength of the forces engaged, the area and estimated time-frame of its conduct. The participating States will also, if possible, provide additional relevant information, particularly that related to the components of the forces engaged and the period of involvement of these forces.

Prior notification of other military manœuvres

The participating States recognize that they can contribute further to strengthening confidence and increasing security and stability, and to this end may also notify smaller-scale military manœuvres to other participating States, with special regard for those near the area of such manœuvres.

To the same end, the participating States also recognize that they may notify other military manœuvres conducted by them.

Exchange of observers

The participating States will invite other participating States, voluntarily and on a bilateral basis, in a spirit of reciprocity and goodwill towards all participating States, to send observers to attend military manœuvres.

The inviting State will determine in each case the number of observers, the procedures and conditions of their participation, and give other information which it may consider useful. It will provide appropriate facilities and hospitality.

The invitation will be given as far ahead as is conveniently possible through usual diplomatic channels.

Prior notification of major military movements

In accordance with the Final Recommendations of the Helsinki Consultations the participating States studied the question of prior notification of major military movements as a measure to strengthen confidence.

Accordingly, the participating States recognize that they may, at their own discretion and with a view to contributing to confidence-building, notify their major military movements.

In the same spirit, further consideration will be given by the States participating in the Conference on Security and Co-operation in Europe to the question of prior notification of major military movements, bearing in mind, in particular, the experience gained by the implementation of the measures which are set forth in this document.

Other confidence-building measures

The participating States recognize that there are other means by which their common objectives can be promoted.

In particular, they will, with due regard to reciprocity and with a view to better mutual understanding, promote exchanges by invitation among their military personnel, including visits by military delegations.

In order to make a fuller contribution to their common objective of confidence-building, the participating States, when conducting their military activities in the area covered by the provisions for the prior notification of major military manœuvres, will duly take into account and respect this objective.

They also recognize that the experience gained by the implementation of the provisions set forth above, together with further efforts, could lead to developing and enlarging measures aimed at strengthening confidence.

II

QUESTIONS RELATING TO DISARMAMENT

The participating States recognize the interest of all of them in efforts aimed at lessening military confrontation and promoting disarmament which are designed to complement political détente in Europe and to strengthen their security. They are convinced of the necessity to take effective measures in these fields which by their scope and by their nature constitute steps towards the ultimate achievement of general and complete disarmament under strict and effective international control, and which should result in strengthening peace and security throughout the world.

III

GENERAL CONSIDERATIONS

Having considered the views expressed on various subjects related to the strengthening of security in Europe through joint efforts aimed at promoting détente and disarmament, the participating States, when engaged in such efforts, will, in this context, proceed, in particular, from the following essential considerations:

— The complementary nature of the political and military aspects of security;

— The interrelation between the security of each participating State and security in Europe as a whole and the relationship which exists, in the broader context of world security, between security in Europe and security in the Mediterranean area;

— Respect for the security interests of all States participating in the Conference on Security and Co-operation in Europe inherent in their sovereign equality;

– The importance that participants in negotiating fora see to it that information about relevant developments, progress and results is provided on an appropriate basis to other States participating in the Conference on Security and Co-operation in Europe and, in return, the justified interest of any of those States in having their views considered.

Source: *Konferensen om säkerhet och samarbete i Europa 1973–1975* [Conference on Security and Co-operation in Europe 1973–1975], Ny serie II:29 (Swedish Foreign Office, Stockholm, 1975).

The Final Act was signed by Austria, Belgium, Bulgaria, Canada, Cyprus, Czechoslovakia, Denmark, Finland, France, German Democratic Republic, Federal Republic of Germany, Greece, Holy See, Hungary, Iceland, Ireland, Italy, Liechtenstein, Luxembourg, Malta, Monaco, Netherlands, Norway. Poland, Portugal, Romania, San Marino, Spain, Sweden, Switzerland, Turkey, United Kingdom, United States, Union of Soviet Socialist Republics, and Yugoslavia.

CONVENTION ON THE PROHIBITION OF MILITARY OR ANY OTHER HOSTILE USE OF ENVIRONMENTAL MODIFICATION TECHNIQUES

Signed at Geneva on 18 May 1977.
Not in force on 31 December 1977.
Depositary: UN Secretary-General.

The States Parties to this Convention,

Guided by the interest of consolidating peace, and wishing to contribute to the cause of halting the arms race, and of bringing about general and complete disarmament under strict and effective international control, and of saving mankind from the danger of using new means of warfare,

Determined to continue negotiations with a view to achieving effective progress towards further measures in the field of disarmament,

Recognizing that scientific and technical advances may open new possibilities with respect to modification of the environment,

Recalling the Declaration of the United Nations Conference on the Human Environment, adopted at Stockholm on 16 June 1972,

Realizing that the use of environmental modification techniques for peaceful purposes could improve the interrelationship of man and nature and contribute to the preservation and improvement of the environment for the benefit of present and future generations,

Recognizing, however, that military or any other hostile use of such techniques could have effects extremely harmful to human welfare,

Desiring to prohibit effectively military or any other hostile use of environmental modification techniques in order to eliminate the dangers to mankind from such use, and affirming their willingness to work towards the achievement of this objective,

Desiring also to contribute to the strengthening of trust among nations and to the further improvement of the international situation in accordance with the purposes and principles of the Charter of the United Nations,

Have agreed as follows:

Article I

1. Each State Party to this Convention undertakes not to engage in military or any other hostile use of environmental modification techniques having widespread, long-lasting or severe effects as the means of destruction, damage or injury to any other State Party.

2. Each State Party to this Convention undertakes not to assist, encourage or induce any State, group of States or international organization to engage in activities contrary to the provisions of paragraph 1 of this article.

Article II

As used in article I, the term "environmental modification techniques" refers to any technique for changing—through the deliberate manipulation of natural processes—the dynamics, composition or structure of the earth, including its biota, lithosphere, hydrosphere and atmosphere, or of outer space.

Article III

1. The provisions of this Convention shall not hinder the use of environmental modification techniques for peaceful purposes and shall be without prejudice to the generally recognized principles and applicable rules of international law concerning such use.

2. The States Parties to this Convention undertake to facilitate, and have the right to participate in, the fullest possible exchange of scientific and technological information on the use of environmental modification techniques for peaceful purposes. States Parties in a position to do so shall contribute, alone or together with other States or international organizations, to international economic and scientific co-operation in the preservation, improvement and peaceful utilization of the environment, with due consideration for the needs of the developing areas of the world.

Article IV

Each State Party to this Convention undertakes to take any measures it considers necessary in accordance with its constitutional processes to prohibit and prevent any activity in violation of the provisions of the Convention anywhere under its jurisdiction or control.

Article V

1. The States Parties to this Convention undertake to consult one another and to co-operate in solving any problems which may arise in relation to the objectives of, or in the application of the provisions of, the Convention. Consultation and co-operation pursuant to this article may also be undertaken through appropriate international procedures within the framework of the United Nations and in accordance with its Charter. These international procedures may include the services of appropriate international organizations, as well as of a Consultative Committee of Experts as provided for in paragraph 2 of this article.

2. For the purposes set forth in paragraph 1 of this article, the Depositary shall, within one month of the receipt of a request from any State Party to this Convention, convene a Consultative Committee of Experts. Any State Party may appoint an expert to the Committee whose functions and rules of procedure are set out in the annex, which constitutes an integral part of this Convention. The Committee shall transmit to the Depositary a summary of its findings of fact, incorporating all views and information presented to the Committee during its proceedings. The Depositary shall distribute the summary to all States Parties.

3. Any State Party to this Convention which has reason to believe that any other State Party is acting in breach of obligations deriving from the provisions of the Convention may lodge a complaint with the Security Council of the United Nations. Such a complaint should include all relevant information as well as all possible evidence supporting its validity.

4. Each State Party to this Convention undertakes to co-operate in carrying out any investigation which the Security Council may initiate, in accordance with the provisions of the Charter of the United Nations, on the basis of the complaint received by the Council. The Security Council shall inform the States Parties of the results of the investigation.

5. Each State Party to this Convention undertakes to provide or support assistance, in accordance with the provisions of the Charter of the United Nations, to any State Party which so requests, if the Security Council decides that such Party has been harmed or is likely to be harmed as a result of violation of the Convention.

Article VI

1. Any State Party to this Convention may propose amendments to the Convention. The text of any proposed amendment shall be submitted to the Depositary, who shall promptly circulate it to all States Parties.

2. An amendment shall enter into force for all States Parties to this Convention which have accepted it, upon the deposit with the Depositary of instruments of acceptance by a majority of States Parties. Thereafter it shall enter into force for any remaining State Party on the date of deposit of its instrument of acceptance.

Article VII

This Convention shall be of unlimited duration.

Article VIII

1. Five years after the entry into force of this Convention, a conference of the States Parties to the Convention shall be convened by the Depositary at Geneva, Switzerland. The conference shall review the operation of the Convention with a view to ensuring that its purposes and provisions are being realized, and shall in particular examine the effectiveness of the provisions of paragraph 1 of article I in eliminating the dangers of military or any other hostile use of environmental modification techniques.

2. At intervals of not less than five years thereafter, a majority of the States Parties to this Convention may obtain, by submitting a proposal to this effect to the Depositary, the convening of a conference with the same objectives.

3. If no conference has been convened pursuant to paragraph 2 of this article within ten years following the conclusion of a previous conference, the Depositary shall solicit the views of all States Parties to this Convention, concerning the convening of such a conference. If one third or ten of the States Parties, whichever number is less, respond affirmatively, the Depositary shall take immediate steps to convene the conference.

Article IX

1. This Convention shall be open to all States for signature. Any State which does not sign the Convention before its entry into force in accordance with paragraph 3 of this article may accede to it at any time.

2. This Convention shall be subject to ratification by signatory States. Instruments of ratification or accession shall be deposited with the Secretary-General of the United Nations.

3. This Convention shall enter into force upon the deposit of instruments of ratification by twenty Governments in accordance with paragraph 2 of this article.

4. For those States whose instruments of ratification or accession are deposited after the entry into force of this Convention, it shall enter into force on the date of the deposit of their instruments of ratification or accession.

5. The Depositary shall promptly inform all signatory and acceding States of the date of each signature, the date of deposit of each instrument of ratification or accession and the date of the entry into force of this Convention and of any amendments thereto, as well as of the receipt of other notices.

6. This Convention shall be registered by the Depositary in accordance with Article 102 of the Charter of the United Nations.

Article X

This Convention, of which the English, Arabic, Chinese, French, Russian and Spanish texts are equally authentic, shall be deposited with the Secretary-General of the United Nations, who shall send duly certified copies thereof to the Governments of the signatory and acceding States.

In witness whereof, the undersigned, being duly authorized thereto by their respective Governments, have signed this Convention, opened for signature at Geneva on the eighteenth day of May, one thousand nine hundred and seventy-seven.

ANNEX TO THE CONVENTION

Consultative Committee of Experts

1. The Consultative Committee of Experts shall undertake to make appropriate findings of fact and provide expert views relevant to any problem raised pursuant to paragraph 1 of article V of this Convention by the State Party requesting the convening of the Committee.

2. The work of the Consultative Committee of Experts shall be organized in such a way as to permit it to perform the functions set forth in paragraph 1 of this annex. The Committee shall decide procedural questions relative to the organization of its work, where possible by consensus, but otherwise by a majority of those present and voting. There shall be no voting on matters of substance.

3. The Depositary or his representative shall serve as the Chairman of the Committee.

4. Each expert may be assisted at meetings by one or more advisers.

5. Each expert shall have the right, through the Chairman, to request from States, and from international organizations, such information and assistance as the expert considers desirable for the accomplishment of the Committee's work.

Source: *Convention on the Prohibition of Military or any other Hostile Use of Environmental Modification Techniques* (United Nations, New York, 1977).

Numbers of signatories as of 31 December 1977: 44.

For the list of states which have signed the ENMOD Convention, see pages 152–94.

UNDERSTANDINGS RELATING TO THE CONVENTION ON THE PROHIBITION OF MILITARY OR ANY OTHER HOSTILE USE OF ENVIRONMENTAL MODIFICATION TECHNIQUES, WORKED OUT AT THE CONFERENCE OF THE COMMITTEE ON DISARMAMENT

Understanding relating to Article I

It is the understanding of the Committee that, for the purposes of this Convention, the terms "widespread", "long-lasting" and "severe" shall be interpreted as follows:

(a) "widespread": encompassing an area on the scale of several hundred square kilometers;

(b) "long-lasting": lasting for a period of months, or approximately a season;

(c) "severe": involving serious or significant disruption or harm to human life, natural and economic resources or other assets.

It is further understood that the interpretation set forth above is intended exclusively for this Convention and is not intended to prejudice the interpretation of the same or similar terms if used in connection with any other international agreement.

Understanding relating to Article II

It is the understanding of the Committee that the following examples are illustrative of phenomena that could be caused by the use of environmental modification techniques as defined in Article II of the Convention: earthquakes; tsunamis; an upset in the ecological balance of a region; changes in weather patterns (clouds, precipitation, cyclones of various types and tornadic storms); changes in climate patterns; changes in ocean currents; changes in the state of the ozone layer; and changes in the state of the ionosphere.

It is further understood that all the phenomena listed above, when produced by military or any other hostile use of environmental modification techniques, would result, or could reasonably be expected to result in widespread, long-lasting or severe destruction, damage or injury. Thus, military or any other hostile use of environmental modification techniques as defined in Article II, so as to cause those phenomena as a means of destruction, damage or injury to another State Party, would be prohibited.

It is recognized, moreover, that the list of examples set out above is not exhaustive. Other phenomena which could result from the use of environmental modification techniques as defined in Article II could also be appropriately included. The absence of such phenomena from the list does not in any way imply that the undertaking contained in Article I would not be applicable to those phenomena, provided the criteria set out in that Article were met.

Understanding relating to Article III

It is the understanding of the Committee that this Convention does not deal with the question whether or not a given use of environmental modification techniques for peaceful purposes is in accordance with generally recognized principles and applicable rules of international law.

Understanding relating to Article VIII

It is the understanding of the Committee that a proposal to amend the Convention may also be considered at any Conference of Parties held pursuant to Article VIII. It is further understood that any proposed amendment that is intended for such consideration should, if possible, be submitted to the Depositary no less than 90 days before the commencement of the Conference.

Source: Conference of the Committee on Disarmament document CCD/520, Annex A (Geneva, 1976).

PROTOCOL ADDITIONAL TO THE GENEVA CONVENTIONS OF 12 AUGUST 1949, AND RELATING TO THE PROTECTION OF VICTIMS OF INTERNATIONAL ARMED CONFLICTS (PROTOCOL I)

Signed at Bern on 12 December 1977.
Not in force on 31 December 1977.
Depositary: Swiss Federal Council.

EXTRACTS:

PREAMBLE

The High Contracting Parties,
Proclaiming their earnest wish to see peace prevail among peoples,
Recalling that every State has the duty, in conformity with the Charter of the United Nations, to refrain in its

international relations from the threat or use of force against the sovereignty, territorial integrity or political independence of any State, or in any other manner inconsistent with the purposes of the United Nations,

Believing it necessary nevertheless to reaffirm and develop the provisions protecting the victims of armed conflicts and to supplement measures intended to reinforce their application,

Expressing their conviction that nothing in this Protocol or in the Geneva Conventions of 12 August 1949 can be construed as legitimating or authorizing any act of aggression or any other use of force inconsistent with the Charter of the United Nations,

Reaffirming further that the provisions of the Geneva Conventions of 12 August 1949 and of this Protocol must be fully applied in all circumstances to all persons who are protected by those instruments, without any adverse distinction based on the nature or origin of the armed conflict or on the causes espoused by or attributed to the Parties to the conflict,

Have agreed on the following:

PART I. GENERAL PROVISIONS

Article 1. *General principles and scope of application*

1. The High Contracting Parties undertake to respect and to ensure respect for this Protocol in all circumstances.

2. In cases not covered by this Protocol or by other international agreements, civilians and combatants remain under the protection and authority of the principles of international law derived from established custom, from the principles of humanity and from the dictates of public conscience.

3. This Protocol, which supplements the Geneva Conventions of 12 August 1949 for the protection of war victims, shall apply in the situations referred to in Article 2 common to those Conventions.

4. The situations referred to in the preceding paragraph include armed conflicts in which peoples are fighting against colonial domination and alien occupation and against racist régimes in the exercise of their right of self-determination, as enshrined in the Charter of the United Nations and the Declaration on Principles of International Law concerning Friendly Relations and Co-operation among States in accordance with the Charter of the United Nations.

Article 2. *Definitions*

For the purposes of this Protocol:

(*a*) "First Convention", "Second Convention", "Third Convention" and "Fourth Convention" mean, respectively, the Geneva Convention for the Amelioration of the Condition of the Wounded and Sick in Armed Forces in the Field of 12 August 1949; the Geneva Convention for the Amelioration of the Condition of Wounded, Sick and Shipwrecked Members of Armed Forces at Sea of 12 August 1949; the Geneva Convention relative to the Treatment of Prisoners of War of 12 August 1949; the Geneva Convention relative to the Protection of Civilian Persons in Time of War of 12 August 1949; "the Conventions" means the four Geneva Conventions of 12 August 1949 for the protection of war victims;

(*b*) "rules of international law applicable in armed conflict" means the rules applicable in armed conflict set forth in international agreements to which the Parties to the conflict are Parties and the generally recognized principles and rules of international law which are applicable to armed conflict;

(*c*) "Protecting Power" means a neutral or other State not a Party to the conflict which has been designated by a Party to the conflict and accepted by the adverse Party and has agreed to carry out the functions assigned to a Protecting Power under the Conventions and this Protocol;

(*d*) "substitute" means an organization acting in place of a Protecting Power in accordance with Article 5.

Article 3. *Beginning and end of application*

Without prejudice to the provisions which are applicable at all times:

(*a*) the Conventions and this Protocol shall apply from the beginning of any situation referred to in Article 1 of this Protocol;

(*b*) the application of the Conventions and of this Protocol shall cease, in the territory of Parties to the conflict, on the general close of military operations and, in the case of occupied territories, on the termination of the occupation, except, in either circumstance, for those persons whose final release, repatriation or re-establishment takes place thereafter. These persons shall continue to benefit from the relevant provisions of the Conventions and of this Protocol until their final release, repatriation or re-establishment.

Article 4. *Legal status of the Parties to the conflict*

The application of the Conventions and of this Protocol, as well as the conclusion of the agreements provided for therein, shall not affect the legal status of the Parties to the conflict. Neither the occupation of a territory nor the application of the Conventions and this Protocol shall affect the legal status of the territory in question.

. . .

PART III. METHODS AND MEANS OF WARFARE COMBATANT AND PRISONER-OF-WAR STATUS

Section I. Methods and means of warfare

Article 35. *Basic rules*

1. In any armed conflict, the right of the Parties to the conflict to choose methods or means of warfare is not unlimited.

2. It is prohibited to employ weapons, projectiles and material and methods of warfare of a nature to cause superfluous injury or unnecessary suffering.

3. It is prohibited to employ methods or means of warfare which are intended, or may be expected, to cause widespread, long-term and severe damage to the natural environment.

Article 36. *New weapons*

In the study, development, acquisition or adoption of a new weapon, means or method of warfare, a High Contracting Party is under an obligation to determine whether its employment would, in some or all circumstances, be prohibited by this Protocol or by any other rule of international law applicable to the High Contracting Party.

Article 37. *Prohibition of perfidy*

1. It is prohibited to kill, injure or capture an adversary by resort to perfidy. Acts inviting the confidence of an adversary to lead him to believe that he is entitled to, or is obliged to accord, protection under the rules of international law applicable in armed conflict, with intent to betray that confidence, shall constitute perfidy. The following acts are examples of perfidy:

(*a*) the feigning of an intent to negotiate under a flag of truce or of a surrender;

(*b*) the feigning of an incapacitation by wounds or sickness;

(*c*) the feigning of civilian, non-combatant status; and

(*d*) the feigning of protected status by the use of signs, emblems or uniforms of the United Nations or of neutral or other States not Parties to the conflict.

2. Ruses of war are not prohibited. Such ruses are acts which are intended to mislead an adversary or to induce him to act recklessly but which infringe no rule of international law applicable in armed conflict and which are not perfidious because they do not invite the confidence of an adversary with respect to protection under that law. The following are examples of such ruses: the use of camouflage, decoys, mock operations and misinformation.

Article 38. *Recognized emblems*

1. It is prohibited to make improper use of the distinctive emblem of the red cross, red crescent or red lion and sun or of other emblems, signs or signals provided for by the Conventions or by this Protocol. It is also prohibited to misuse deliberately in an armed conflict other internationally recognized protective emblems, signs or signals, including the flag of truce, and the protective emblem of cultural property.

2. It is prohibited to make use of the distinctive emblem of the United Nations, except as authorized by that Organization.

Article 39. *Emblems of nationality*

1. It is prohibited to make use in an armed conflict of the flags or military emblems, insignia or uniforms of neutral or other States not Parties to the conflict.

2. It is prohibited to make use of the flags or military emblems, insignia or uniforms of adverse Parties while engaging in attacks or in order to shield, favour, protect or impede military operations.

3. Nothing in this Article or in Article 37, paragraph 1(*d*), shall affect the existing generally recognized rules of international law applicable to espionage or to the use of flags in the conduct of armed conflict at sea.

Article 40. *Quarter*

It is prohibited to order that there shall be no survivors, to threaten an adversary therewith or to conduct hostilities on this basis.

Article 41. *Safeguard of an enemy hors de combat*

1. A person who is recognized or who, in the circumstances, should be recognized to be *hors de combat* shall not be made the object of attack.

2. A person is *hors de combat* if:

(*a*) he is in the power of an adverse Party;

(*b*) he clearly expresses an intention to surrender; or

(*c*) he has been rendered unconscious or is otherwise incapacitated by wounds or sickness, and therefore is incapable of defending himself;

provided that in any of these cases he abstains from any hostile act and does not attempt to escape.

3. When persons entitled to protection as prisoners of war have fallen into the power of an adverse Party under unusual conditions of combat which prevent their evacuation as provided for in Part III, Section I, of the Third Convention, they shall be released and all feasible precautions shall be taken to ensure their safety.

Article 42. *Occupants of aircraft*

1. No person parachuting from an aircraft in distress shall be made the object of attack during his descent.

2. Upon reaching the ground in territory controlled by an adverse Party, a person who has parachuted from an aircraft in distress shall be given an opportunity to surrender before being made the object of attack, unless it is apparent that he is engaging in a hostile act.

3. Airborne troops are not protected by this Article.

Section II. Combatant and prisoner-of-war status

Article 43. *Armed forces*

1. The armed forces of a Party to a conflict consist of all organized armed forces, groups and units which are under a command responsible to that Party for the conduct of its subordinates, even if that Party is represented by a government or an authority not recognized by an adverse Party. Such armed forces shall be subject to an internal disciplinary system which, *inter alia,* shall enforce compliance with the rules of international law applicable in armed conflict.

2. Members of the armed forces of a Party to a conflict (other than medical personnel and chaplains covered by Article 33 of the Third Convention) are combatants, that is to say, they have the right to participate directly in hostilities.

3. Whenever a Party to a conflict incorporates a paramilitary or armed law enforcement agency into its armed forces it shall so notify the other Parties to the conflict.

Article 44. *Combatants and prisoners of war*

1. Any combatant, as defined in Article 43, who falls into the power of an adverse Party shall be a prisoner of war.

2. While all combatants are obliged to comply with the rules of international law applicable in armed conflict, violations of these rules shall not deprive a combatant of his right to be a combatant or, if he falls into the power of an adverse Party, of his right to be a prisoner of war, except as provided in paragraphs 3 and 4.

3. In order to promote the protection of the civilian population from the effects of hostilities, combatants are obliged to distinguish themselves from the civilian population while they are engaged in an attack or in a military operation preparatory to an attack. Recognizing, however, that there are situations in armed conflicts where, owing to the nature of the hostilities an armed combatant cannot so distinguish himself, he shall retain his status as a combatant, provided that, in such situations, he carries his arms openly:

(*a*) during each military engagement, and

(*b*) during such time as he is visible to the adversary while he is engaged in a military deployment preceding the launching of an attack in which he is to participate.

Acts which comply with the requirements of this paragraph shall not be considered as perfidious within the meaning of Article 37, paragraph 1 (c).

4. A combatant who falls into the power of an adverse Party while failing to meet the requirements set forth in the second sentence of paragraph 3 shall forfeit his right to be a prisoner of war, but he shall, nevertheless, be given protections equivalent in all respects to those accorded to prisoners of war by the Third Convention and by this Protocol. This protection includes protections equivalent to those accorded to prisoners of war by the Third Convention in the case where such a person is tried and punished for any offences he has committed.

5. Any combatant who falls into the power of an adverse Party while not engaged in an attack or in a military operation preparatory to an attack shall not forfeit his rights to be a combatant and a prisoner of war by virtue of his prior activities.

6. This Article is without prejudice to the right of any person to be a prisoner of war pursuant to Article 4 of the Third Convention.

7. This Article is not intended to change the generally accepted practice of States with respect to the wearing of the uniform by combatants assigned to the regular, uniformed armed units of a Party to the conflict.

8. In addition to the categories of persons mentioned in Article 13 of the First and Second Conventions, all members of the armed forces of a Party to the conflict, as defined in Article 43 of this Protocol, shall be entitled to protection under those Conventions if they are wounded or sick or, in the case of the Second Convention, shipwrecked at sea or in other waters.

Article 45. *Protection of persons who have taken part in hostilities*

1. A person who takes part in hostilities and falls into the power of an adverse Party shall be presumed to be a prisoner of war, and therefore shall be protected by the Third Convention, if he claims the status of prisoner of war, or if he appears to be entitled to such status, or if the Party on which he depends claims such status on his behalf by notification to the detaining Power or to the Protecting Power. Should any doubt arise as to whether any such person is entitled to the status of prisoner of war, he shall continue to have such status and, therefore, to be protected by the Third Convention and this Protocol until such time as his status has been determined by a competent tribunal.

2. If a person who has fallen into the power of an adverse Party is not held as a prisoner of war and is to be tried by that Party for an offence arising out of the hostilities, he shall have the right to assert his entitlement to prisoner-of-war status before a judicial tribunal and to have that question adjudicated. Whenever possible under the applicable procedure, this adjudication shall occur before the trial for the offence. The representatives of the Protecting Power shall be entitled to attend the proceedings in which that question is adjudicated, unless, exceptionally, the proceedings are held *in camera* in the interest of State security. In such a case the detaining Power shall advise the Protecting Power accordingly.

3. Any person who has taken part in hostilities, who is not entitled to prisoner-of-war status and who does not benefit from more favourable treatment in accordance with the Fourth Convention shall have the right at all times to the protection of Article 75 of this Protocol. In occupied territory, any such person, unless he is held as a spy, shall also be entitled, notwithstanding Article 5 of the Fourth Convention, to his rights of communication under that Convention.

Article 46. *Spies*

1. Notwithstanding any other provision of the Conventions or of this Protocol, any member of the armed forces of a Party to the conflict who falls into the power of an adverse Party while engaging in espionage shall not have the right to the status of prisoner of war and may be treated as a spy.

2. A member of the armed forces of a Party to the conflict who, on behalf of that Party and in territory controlled by an adverse Party, gathers or attempts to gather information shall not be considered as engaging in espionage if, while so acting, he is in the uniform of his armed forces.

3. A member of the armed forces of a Party to the conflict who is a resident of territory occupied by an adverse Party and who, on behalf of the Party on which he depends, gathers or attempts to gather information of military value within that territory shall not be considered as engaging in espionage unless he does so through an act of false pretences or deliberately in a clandestine manner. Moreover, such a resident shall not lose his right to the status of prisoner of war and may not be treated as a spy unless he is captured while engaging in espionage.

4. A member of the armed forces of a Party to the conflict who is not a resident of territory occupied by an adverse Party and who has engaged in espionage in that territory shall not lose his right to the status of prisoner of war and may not be treated as a spy unless he is captured before he has rejoined the armed forces to which he belongs.

Article 47. *Mercenaries*

1. A mercenary shall not have the right to be a combatant or a prisoner of war.

2. A mercenary is any person who:

(*a*) is specially recruited locally or abroad in order to fight in an armed conflict;

(*b*) does, in fact, take a direct part in the hostilities;

(*c*) is motivated to take part in the hostilities essentially by the desire for private gain and, in fact, is promised, by or on behalf of a Party to the conflict, material compensation substantially in excess of that promised or paid to combatants of similar ranks and functions in the armed forces of that Party;

(*d*) is neither a national of a Party to the conflict nor a resident of territory controlled by a Party to the conflict;

(*e*) is not a member of the armed forces of a Party to the conflict; and

(*f*) has not been sent by a State which is not a Party to the conflict on official duty as a member of its armed forces.

PART IV. CIVILIAN POPULATION

Section I. General protection against effects of hostilities

Chapter I. Basic rule and field of application

Article 48. *Basic rule*

In order to ensure respect for and protection of the civilian population and civilian objects, the Parties to the conflict shall at all times distinguish between the civilian population and combatants and between civilian objects and military objectives and accordingly shall direct their operations only against military objectives.

Article 49. *Definition of attacks and scope of application*

1. "Attacks" means acts of violence against the adversary, whether in offence or in defence.
2. The provisions of this Protocol with respect to attacks apply to all attacks in whatever territory conducted, including the national territory belonging to a Party to the conflict but under the control of an adverse Party.
3. The provisions of this Section apply to any land, air or sea warfare which may affect the civilian population, individual civilians or civilian objects on land. They further apply to all attacks from the sea or from the air against objectives on land but do not otherwise affect the rules of international law applicable in armed conflict at sea or in the air.
4. The provisions of this Section are additional to the rules concerning humanitarian protection contained in the Fourth Convention, particularly in Part II thereof, and in other international agreements binding upon the High Contracting Parties, as well as to other rules of international law relating to the protection of civilians and civilian objects on land, at sea or in the air against the effects of hostilities.

Chapter II. Civilians and civilian population

Article 50. *Definition of civilians and civilian population*

1. A civilian is any person who does not belong to one of the categories of persons referred to in Article 4 A (1), (2), (3) and (6) of the Third Convention and in Article 43 of this Protocol. In case of doubt whether a person is a civilian, that person shall be considered to be a civilian.
2. The civilian population comprises all persons who are civilians.
3. The presence within the civilian population of individuals who do not come within the definition of civilians does not deprive the population of its civilian character.

Article 51. *Protection of the civilian population*

1. The civilian population and individual civilians shall enjoy general protection against dangers arising from military operations. To give effect to this protection, the following rules, which are additional to other applicable rules of international law, shall be observed in all circumstances.
2. The civilian population as such, as well as individual civilians, shall not be the object of attack. Acts or threats of violence the primary purpose of which is to spread terror among the civilian population are prohibited.
3. Civilians shall enjoy the protection afforded by this Section, unless and for such time as they take a direct part in hostilities.
4. Indiscriminate attacks are prohibited. Indiscriminate attacks are:
   (*a*) those which are not directed at a specific military objective;
   (*b*) those which employ a method or means of combat which cannot be directed at a specific military objective; or
   (*c*) those which employ a method or means of combat the effects of which cannot be limited as required by this Protocol;
   and consequently, in each such case, are of a nature to strike military objectives and civilians or civilian objects without distinction.
5. Among others, the following types of attacks are to be considered as indiscriminate:
   (*a*) an attack by bombardment by any methods or means which treats as a single military objective a number of clearly separated and distinct military objectives located in a city, town, village or other area containing a similar concentration of civilians or civilian objects; and
   (*b*) an attack which may be expected to cause incidental loss of civilian life, injury to civilians, damage to civilian objects, or a combination thereof, which would be excessive in relation to the concrete and direct military advantage anticipated.
6. Attacks against the civilian population or civilians by way of reprisals are prohibited.
7. The presence or movements of the civilian population or individual civilians shall not be used to render certain points or areas immune from military operations, in particular in attempts to shield military objectives from attacks or to shield, favour or impede military operations. The Parties to the conflict shall not direct the movement of the civilian population or individual civilians in order to attempt to shield military objectives from attacks or to shield military operations.
8. Any violation of these prohibitions shall not release the Parties to the conflict from their legal obligations with respect to the civilian population and civilians, including the obligation to take the precautionary measures provided for in Article 57.

Chapter III. Civilian objects

Article 52. *General protection of civilian objects*

1. Civilian objects shall not be the object of attack or reprisals. Civilian objects are all objects which are not military objectives as defined in paragraph 2.
2. Attacks shall be limited strictly to military objectives. In so far as objects are concerned, military objectives are limited to those objects which by their nature, location, purpose or use make an effective contribution to military action and whose total or partial destruction, capture or neutralization, in the circumstances ruling at the time, offers a definite military advantage.
3. In case of doubt whether an object which is normally dedicated to civilian purposes, such as a place of worship, a house or other dwelling or a school, is being used to make an effective contribution to military action, it shall be presumed not to be so used.

Article 53. *Protection of cultural objects and of places of worship*

Without prejudice to the provisions of the Hague Convention for the Protection of Cultural Property in the Event of Armed Conflict of 14 May 1954, and of other relevant international instruments, it is prohibited:

(a) to commit any acts of hostility directed against the historic monuments, works of art or places of worship which constitute the cultural or spiritual heritage of peoples;

(b) to use such objects in support of the military effort;

(c) to make such objects the object of reprisals.

Article 54. *Protection of objects indispensable to the survival of the civilian population*

1. Starvation of civilians as a method of warfare is prohibited.

2. It is prohibited to attack, destroy, remove or render useless objects indispensable to the survival of the civilian population, such as foodstuffs, agricultural areas for the production of foodstuffs, crops, livestock, drinking water installations and supplies and irrigation works, for the specific purpose of denying them for their sustenance value to the civilian population or to the adverse Party, whatever the motive, whether in order to starve out civilians, to cause them to move away, or for any other motive.

3. The prohibitions in paragraph 2 shall not apply to such of the objects covered by it as are used by an adverse Party:

(a) as sustenance solely for the members of its armed forces; or

(b) if not as sustenance, then in direct support of military action, provided, however, that in no event shall actions against these objects be taken which may be expected to leave the civilian population with such inadequate food or water as to cause its starvation or force its movement.

4. These objects shall not be made the object of reprisals.

5. In recognition of the vital requirements of any Party to the conflict in the defence of its national territory against invasion, derogation from the prohibitions contained in paragraph 2 may be made by a Party to the conflict within such territory under its own control where required by imperative military necessity.

Article 55. *Protection of the natural environment*

1. Care shall be taken in warfare to protect the natural environment against widespread, long-term and severe damage. This protection includes a prohibition of the use of methods or means of warfare which are intended or may be expected to cause such damage to the natural environment and thereby to prejudice the health or survival of the population.

2. Attacks against the natural environment by way of reprisals are prohibited.

Article 56. *Protection of works and installations containing dangerous forces*

1. Works or installations containing dangerous forces, namely dams, dykes and nuclear electrical generating stations, shall not be made the object of attack, even where these objects are military objectives, if such attack may cause the release of dangerous forces and consequent severe losses among the civilian population. Other military objectives located at or in the vicinity of these works or installations shall not be made the object of attack if such attack may cause the release of dangerous forces from the works or installations and consequent severe losses among the civilian population.

2. The special protection against attack provided by paragraph 1 shall cease:

(a) for a dam or a dyke only if it is used for other than its normal function and in regular, significant and direct support of military operations and if such attack is the only feasible way to terminate such support;

(b) for a nuclear electrical generating station only if it provides electric power in regular, significant and direct support of military operations and if such attack is the only feasible way to terminate such support;

(c) for other military objectives located at or in the vicinity of these works or installations only if they are used in regular, significant and direct support of military operations and if such attack is the only feasible way to terminate such support.

3. In all cases, the civilian population and individual civilians shall remain entitled to all the protection accorded them by international law, including the protection of the precautionary measures provided for in Article 57. If the protection ceases and any of the works, installations or military objectives mentioned in paragraph 1 is attacked, all practical precautions shall be taken to avoid the release of the dangerous forces.

4. It is prohibited to make any of the works, installations or military objectives mentioned in paragraph 1 the object of reprisals.

5. The Parties to the conflict shall endeavour to avoid locating any military objectives in the vicinity of the works or installations mentioned in paragraph 1. Nevertheless, installations erected for the sole purpose of defending the protected works or installations from attack are permissible and shall not themselves be made the object of attack, provided that they are not used in hostilities except for defensive actions necessary to respond to attacks against the protected works or installations and that their armament is limited to weapons capable only of repelling hostile action against the protected works or installations.

6. The High Contracting Parties and the Parties to the conflict are urged to conclude further agreements among themselves to provide additional protection for objects containing dangerous forces.

7. In order to facilitate the identification of the objects protected by this article, the Parties to the conflict may mark them with a special sign consisting of a group of three bright orange circles placed on the same axis, as specified in Article 16 of Annex I to this Protocol. The absence of such marking in no way relieves any Party to the conflict of its obligations under this Article.

Chapter IV. Precautionary measures

Article 57. *Precautions in attack*

1. In the conduct of military operations, constant care shall be taken to spare the civilian population, civilians and civilian objects.

2. With respect to attacks, the following precautions shall be taken:

(*a*) those who plan or decide upon an attack shall:

   (i) do everything feasible to verify that the objectives to be attacked are neither civilians nor civilian objects and are not subject to special protection but are military objectives within the meaning of paragraph 2 of Article 52 and that it is not prohibited by the provisions of this Protocol to attack them;

   (ii) take all feasible precautions in the choice of means and methods of attack with a view to avoiding, and in any event to minimizing, incidental loss of civilian life, injury to civilians and damage to civilian objects;

   (iii) refrain from deciding to launch any attack which may be expected to cause incidental loss of civilian life, injury to civilians, damage to civilian objects, or a combination thereof, which would be excessive in relation to the concrete and direct military advantage anticipated;

(*b*) an attack shall be cancelled or suspended if it becomes apparent that the objective is not a military one or is subject to special protection or that the attack may be expected to cause incidental loss of civilian life, injury to civilians, damage to civilian objects, or a combination thereof, which would be excessive in relation to the concrete and direct military advantage anticipated;

(*c*) effective advance warning shall be given of attacks which may affect the civilian population, unless circumstances do not permit.

3. When a choice is possible between several military objectives for obtaining a similar military advantage, the objective to be selected shall be that the attack on which may be expected to cause the least danger to civilian lives and to civilian objects.

4. In the conduct of military operations at sea or in the air, each Party to the conflict shall, in conformity with its rights and duties under the rules of international law applicable in armed conflict, take all reasonable precautions to avoid losses of civilian lives and damage to civilian objects.

5. No provision of this Article may be construed as authorizing any attacks against the civilian population, civilians or civilian objects.

Article 58. *Precautions against the effects of attacks*

The Parties to the conflict shall, to the maximum extent feasible:

(*a*) without prejudice to Article 49 of the Fourth Convention, endeavour to remove the civilian population, individual civilians and civilian objects under their control from the vicinity of military objectives;

(*b*) avoid locating military objectives within or near densely populated areas;

(*c*) take the other necessary precautions to protect the civilian population, individual civilians and civilian objects under their control against the dangers resulting from military operations.

Chapter V. Localities and zones under special protection

Articles 59. *Non-defended localitites*

1. It is prohibited for the Parties to the conflict to attack, by any means whatsoever, non-defended localitites.

2. The appropriate authorities of a Party to the conflict may declare as a non-defended locality any inhabited place near or in a zone where armed forces are in contact which is open for occupation by an adverse Party. Such a locality shall fulfil the following conditions:

(*a*) all combatants, as well as mobile weapons and mobile military equipment must have been evacuated;

(*b*) no hostile use shall be made of fixed military installations or establishments;

(*c*) no acts of hostility shall be committed by the authorities or by the population; and

(*d*) no activities in support of military operations shall be undertaken.

3. The presence, in this locality, of persons specially protected under the Conventions and this Protocol, and of police forces retained for the sole purpose of maintaining law and order, is not contrary to the conditions laid down in paragraph 2.

4. The declaration made under paragraph 2 shall be addressed to the adverse Party and shall define and describe, as precisely as possible, the limits of the non-defended locality. The Party to the conflict to which the declaration is addressed shall acknowledge its receipt and shall treat the locality as a non-defended locality unless the conditions laid down in paragraph 2 are not in fact fulfilled, in which event it shall immediately so inform the Party making the declaration. Even if the conditions laid down in paragraph 2 are not fulfilled, the locality shall continue to enjoy the protection provided by the other provisions of this Protocol and the other rules of international law applicable in armed conflict.

5. The Parties to the conflict may agree on the establishment of non-defended localitites even if such localities do not fulfil the conditions laid down in paragraph 2. The agreement should define and describe, as precisely as possible, the limits of the non-defended locality; if necessary, it may lay down the methods of supervision.

6. The Party which is in control of a locality governed by such an agreement shall mark it, so far as possible, by such signs as may be agreed upon with the other Party, which shall be displayed where they are clearly visible, especially on its perimeter and limits and on highways.

7. A locality loses its status as a non-defended locality when it ceases to fulfil the conditions laid down in paragraph 2 or in the agreement referred to in paragraph 5. In such an eventuality, the locality shall continue to enjoy the protection provided by the other provisions of this Protocol and the other rules of international law applicable in armed conflict.

Article 60. *Demilitarized zones*

1. It is prohibited for the Parties to the conflict to extend their military operations to zones on which they have conferred by agreement the status of demilitarized zone, if such extension is contrary to the terms of this agreement.

2. The agreement shall be an express agreement, may be concluded verbally or in writing, either directly or through a Protecting Power or any impartial humanitarian organization, and may consist of reciprocal and concordant declarations. The agreement may be concluded in peacetime, as well as after the outbreak of hostilities, and should define and describe, as precisely as possible, the limits of the demilitarized zone and, if necessary, lay down the methods of supervision.

3. The subject of such an agreement shall normally be any zone which fulfils the following conditions:

(*a*) all combatants, as well as mobile weapons and mobile military equipment, must have been evacuated;

(b) no hostile use shall be made of fixed military installations or establishments;
(c) no acts of hostility shall be committed by the authorities or by the population; and
(d) any activity linked to the military effort must have ceased.

The Parties to the conflict shall agree upon the interpretation to be given to the condition laid down in sub-paragraph (d) and upon persons to be admitted to the demilitarized zone other than those mentioned in paragraph 4.

4. The presence, in this zone, of persons specially protected under the Conventions and this Protocol, and of police forces retained for the sole purpose of maintaining law and order, is not contrary to the conditions laid down in paragraph 3.

5. The Party which is in control of such a zone shall mark it, so far as possible, by such signs as may be agreed upon with the other Party, which shall be displayed where they are clearly visible, especially on its perimeter and limits and on highways.

6. If the fighting draws near to a demilitarized zone, and if the Parties to the conflict have so agreed, none of them may use the zone for purposes related to the conduct of military operations or unilaterally revoke its status.

7. If one of the Parties to the conflict commits a material breach of the provisions of paragraphs 3 or 6, the other Party shall be released from its obligations under the agreement conferring upon the zone the status of demilitarized zone. In such an eventuality, the zone loses its status but shall continue to enjoy the protection provided by the other provisions of this Protocol and the other rules of international law applicable in armed conflict.

Chapter VI. Civil defence

Article 61. *Definitions and scope*

For the purposes of this Protocol:
(a) "civil defence" means the performance of some or all of the undermentioned humanitarian tasks intended to protect the civilian population against the dangers, and to help it to recover from the immediate effects, of hostilities or disasters and also to provide the conditions necessary for its survival. These tasks are:
  (i) warning;
  (ii) evacuation;
  (iii) management of shelters;
  (iv) management of blackout measures;
  (v) rescue;
  (vi) medical services, including first aid, and religious assistance;
  (vii) fire-fighting;
  (viii) detection and marking of danger areas;
  (ix) decontamination and similar protective measures;
  (x) provision of emergency accommodation and supplies;
  (xi) emergency assistance in the restoration and maintenance of order in distressed areas;
  (xii) emergency repair of indispensable public utilities;
  (xiii) emergency disposal of the dead;
  (xiv) assistance in the preservation of objects essential for survival;
  (xv) complementary activities necessary to carry out any of the tasks mentioned above, including, but not limited to, planning and organization;
(b) "civil defence organizations" means those establishments and other units which are organized or authorized by the competent authorities of a Party to the conflict to perform any of the tasks mentioned under sub-paragraph (a), and which are assigned and devoted exclusively to such tasks;
(c) "personnel" of civil defence organizations means those persons assigned by a Party to the conflict exclusively to the performance of the tasks mentioned under sub-paragraph (a), including personnel assigned by the competent authority of that Party exclusively to the administration of these organizations;
(d) "*matériel*" of civil defence organizations means equipment, supplies and transports used by these organizations for the performance of the tasks mentioned under sub-paragraph (a).

Article 62. *General protection*

1. Civilian civil defence organizations and their personnel shall be respected and protected, subject to the provisions of this Protocol, particularly the provisions of this Section. They shall be entitled to perform their civil defence tasks except in case of imperative military necessity.

2. The provisions of paragraph 1 shall also apply to civilians who, although not members of civilian civil defence organizations, respond to an appeal from the competent authorities and perform civil defence tasks under their control.

3. Buildings and *matériel* used for civil defence purposes and shelters provided for the civilian population are covered by Article 52. Objects used for civil defence purposes may not be destroyed or diverted from their proper use except by the Party to which they belong.

Article 63. *Civil defence in occupied territories*

1. In occupied territories, civilian civil defence organizations shall receive from the authorities the facilities necessary for the performance of their tasks. In no circumstances shall their personnel be compelled to perform activities which would interfere with the proper performance of these tasks. The Occupying Power shall not change the structure or personnel of such organizations in any way which might jeopardize the efficient performance of their mission. These organizations shall not be required to give priority to the nationals or interests of that Power.

2. The Occupying Power shall not compel, coerce or induce civilian civil defence organizations to perform their tasks in any manner prejudicial to the interests of the civilian population.

3. The Occupying Power may disarm civil defence personnel for reasons of security.

4. The Occupying Power shall neither divert from their proper use nor requisition buildings or *matériel* belonging to or used by civil defence organizations if such diversion or requisition would be harmful to the civilian population.

5. Provided that the general rule in paragraph 4 continues to be observed, the Occupying Power may requisition or divert these resources, subject to the following particular conditions:
(a) that the buildings or *matériel* are necessary for other needs of the civilian population; and

(b) that the requisition or diversion continues only while such necessity exists.

6. The Occupying Power shall neither divert nor requisition shelters provided for the use of the civilian population or needed by such population.

Article 64. *Civilian civil defence organizations of neutral or other States not Parties to the conflict and international co-ordinating organizations*

1. Articles 62, 63, 65 and 66 shall also apply to the personnel and *matériel* of civilian civil defence organizations of neutral or other States not Parties to the conflict which perform civil defence tasks mentioned in Article 61 in the territory of a Party to the conflict, with the consent and under the control of that Party. Notification of such assistance shall be given as soon as possible to any adverse Party concerned. In no circumstances shall this activity be deemed to be an interference in the conflict. This activity should, however, be performed with due regard to the security interests of the Parties to the conflict concerned.

2. The Parties to the conflict receiving the assistance referred to in paragraph 1 and the High Contracting Parties granting it should facilitate international co-ordination of such civil defence actions when appropriate. In such cases the relevant international organizations are covered by the provisions of this Chapter.

3. In occupied territories, the Occupying Power may only exclude or restrict the activities of civilian civil defence organizations of neutral or other States not Parties to the conflict and of international co-ordinating organizations if it can ensure the adequate performance of civil defence tasks from its own resources or those of the occupied territory.

Article 65. *Cessation of protection*

1. The protection to which civilian civil defence organizations, their personnel, buildings, shelters and *matériel* are entitled shall not cease unless they commit or are used to commit, outside their proper tasks, acts harmful to the enemy. Protection may, however, cease only after a warning has been given setting, whenever appropriate, a reasonable time limit, and after such warning has remained unheeded.

2. The following shall not be considered as acts harmful to the enemy:

(a) that civil defence tasks are carried out under the direction or control of military authorities;

(b) that civilian civil defence personnel co-operate with military personnel in the performance of civil defence tasks, or that some military personnel are attached to civilian civil defence organizations;

(c) that the performance of civil defence tasks may incidentally benefit military victims, particularly those who are hors de combat.

3. It shall also not be considered as an act harmful to the enemy that civilian civil defence personnel bear light individual weapons for the purpose of maintaining order or for self-defence. However, in areas where land fighting is taking place or is likely to take place, the Parties to the conflict shall undertake the appropriate measures to limit these weapons to handguns, such as pistols or revolvers, in order to assist in distinguishing between civil defence personnel and combatants. Although civil defence personnel bear other light individual weapons in such areas, they shall nevertheless be respected and protected as soon as they have been recognized as such.

4. The formation of civilian civil defence organizations along military lines, and compulsory service in them, shall also not deprive them of the protection conferred by this Chapter.

Article 66. *Identification*

1. Each Party to the conflict shall endeavour to ensure that its civil defence organizations, their personnel, buildings and *matériel*, are identifiable while they are exclusively devoted to the performance of civil defence tasks. Shelters provided for the civilian population should be similarly identifiable.

2. Each Party to the conflict shall also endeavour to adopt and implement methods and procedures which will make it possible to recognize civilian shelters as well as civil defence personnel, buildings and *matériel* on which the international distinctive sign of civil defence is displayed.

3. In occupied territories and in areas where fighting is taking place or is likely to take place, civilian civil defence personnel should be recognizable by the international distinctive sign of civil defence and by an identity card certifying their status.

4. The international distinctive sign of civil defence is an equilateral blue triangle on an orange ground when used for the protection of civil defence organizations, their personnel, buildings and *matériel* and for civilian shelters.

5. In addition to the distinctive sign, Parties to the conflict may agree upon the use of distinctive signals for civil defence identification purposes.

6. The application of the provisions of paragraphs 1 to 4 is governed by Chapter V of Annex I to this Protocol.

7. In time of peace, the sign described in paragraph 4 may, with the consent of the competent national authorities, be used for civil defence identification purposes.

8. The High Contracting Parties and the Parties to the conflict shall take the measures necessary to supervise the display of the international distinctive sign of civil defence and to prevent and repress any misuse thereof.

9. The identification of civil defence medical and religious personnel, medical units and medical transports is also governed by Article 18.

Article 67. *Members of the armed forces and military units assigned to civil defence organizations*

1. Members of the armed forces and military units assigned to civil defence organizations shall be respected and protected, provided that:

(a) such personnel and such units are permanently assigned and exclusively devoted to the performance of any of the tasks mentioned in Article 61;

(b) if so assigned, such personnel do not perform any other military duties during the conflict;

(c) such personnel are clearly distinguishable from the other members of the armed forces by prominently displaying the international distinctive sign of civil defence, which shall be as large as appropriate, and such personnel are provided with the identity card referred to in Chapter V of Annex I to this Protocol certifying their status;

(d) such personnel and such units are equipped only with light individual weapons for the purpose of maintaining order or for self-defence. The provisions of Article 65, paragraph 3 shall also apply in this case;

(*e*) such personnel do not participate directly in hostilities, and do not commit, or are not used to commit, outside their civil defence tasks, acts harmful to the adverse Party;

(*f*) such personnel and such units perform their civil defence tasks only within the national territory of their Party.

The non-observance of the conditions stated in (*e*) above by any member of the armed forces who is bound by the conditions prescribed in (*a*) and (*b*) above is prohibited.

2. Military personnel serving within civil defence organizations shall, if they fall into the power of an adverse Party, be prisoners of war. In occupied territory they may, but only in the interest of the civilian population of that territory, be employed on civil defence tasks in so far as the need arises, provided however that, if such work is dangerous, they volunteer for such tasks.

3. The buildings and major items of equipment and transports of military units assigned to civil defence organizations shall be clearly marked with the international distinctive sign of civil defence. This distinctive sign shall be as large as appropriate.

4. The *matériel* and buildings of military units permanently assigned to civil defence organizations and exclusively devoted to the performance of civil defence tasks shall, if they fall into the hands of an adverse Party, remain subject to the laws of war. They may not be diverted from their civil defence purpose so long as they are required for the performance of civil defence tasks, except in case of imperative military necessity, unless previous arrangements have been made for adequate provision for the needs of the civilian population.

Section II. Relief in favour of the civilian population

Article 68. *Field of application*

The provisions of this Section apply to the civilian population as defined in this Protocol and are supplementary to Articles 23, 55, 59, 60, 61 and 62 and other relevant provisions of the Fourth Convention.

Article 69. *Basic needs in occupied territories*

1. In addition to the duties specified in Article 55 of the Fourth Convention concerning food and medical supplies, the Occupying Power shall, to the fullest extent of the means available to it and without any adverse distinction, also ensure the provision of clothing, bedding, means of shelter, other supplies essential to the survival of the civilian population of the occupied territory and objects necessary for religious worship.

2. Relief actions for the benefit of the civilian population of occupied territories are governed by Articles 59, 60, 61, 62, 108, 109, 110 and 111 of the Fourth Convention, and by Article 71 of this Protocol, and shall be implemented without delay.

Section III. Treatment of persons in the power of a party to the conflict

. . .

Article 75. *Fundamental guarantees*

1. In so far as they are affected by a situation referred to in Article 1 of this Protocol, persons who are in the power of a Party to the conflict and who do not benefit from more favourable treatment under the Conventions or under this Protocol shall be treated humanely in all circumstances and shall enjoy, as a minimum, the protection provided by this Article without any adverse distinction based upon race, colour, sex, language, religion or belief, political or other opinion, national or social origin, wealth, birth or other status, or on any other similar criteria. Each Party shall respect the person, honour, convictions and religious practices of all such persons.

2. The following acts are and shall remain prohibited at any time and in any place whatsoever, whether commited by civilian or by military agents:

(*a*) violence to the life, health, or physical or mental well-being of persons, in particular:
    (i) murder
    (ii) torture of all kinds, whether physical or mental;
    (iii) corporal punishment; and
    (iv) mutilation;

(*b*) outrages upon personal dignity, in particular humiliating and degrading treatment, enforced prostitution and any form of indecent assault;

(*c*) the taking of hostages;

(*d*) collective punishments; and

(*e*) threats to commit any of the foregoing acts.

3. Any person arrested, detained or interned for actions related to the armed conflict shall be informed promptly, in a language he understands, of the reasons why these measures have been taken. Except in cases of arrest or detention for penal offences, such persons shall be released with the minimum delay possible and in any event as soon as the circumstances justifying the arrest, detention or internment have ceased to exist.

4. No sentence may be passed and no penalty may be executed on a person found guilty of a penal offence related to the armed conflict except pursuant to a conviction pronounced by an impartial and regularly constituted court respecting the generally recognized principles of regular judicial procedure, which include the following:

(*a*) the procedure shall provide for an accused to be informed without delay of the particulars of the offence alleged against him and shall afford the accused before and during his trial all necessary rights and means of defence;

(*b*) no one shall be convicted of an offence except on the basis of individual penal responsibility;

(*c*) no one shall be accused or convicted of a criminal offence on account of any act or omission which did not constitute a criminal offence under the national or international law to which he was subject at the time when it was committed; nor shall a heavier penalty be imposed than that which was applicable at the time when the criminal offence was committed; if, after the commission of the offence, provision is made by law for the imposition of a lighter penalty, the offender shall benefit thereby;

(*d*) anyone charged with an offence is presumed innocent until proved guilty according to law;

(*e*) anyone charged with an offence shall have the right to be tried in his presence;

(*f*) no one shall be compelled to testify against himself or to confess guilt;

(*g*) anyone charged with an offence shall have the right to examine, or have examined, the witnesses against him and to obtain the attendance and examination of witnesses on his behalf under the same conditions as witnesses against him;

(*h*) no one shall be prosecuted or punished by the same Party for an offence in respect of which a final judgement acquitting or convicting that person has been previously pronounced under the same law and judicial procedure;

(*i*) anyone prosecuted for an offence shall have the right to have the judgement pronounced publicly; and

(*j*) a convicted person shall be advised on conviction of his judicial and other remedies and of the time limits within which they may be exercised.

. . .

PART V. EXECUTION OF THE CONVENTIONS AND OF THIS PROTOCOL

Section I. General provisions

Articles 80. *Measures for execution*

1. The High Contracting Parties and the Parties to the conflict shall without delay take all necessary measures for the execution of their obligations under the Conventions and this Protocol.

2. The High Contracting Parties and the Parties to the conflict shall give orders and instructions to ensure observance of the Conventions and this Protocol, and shall supervise their execution.

. . .

Article 83. *Dissemination*

1. The High Contracting Parties undertake, in time of peace as in time of armed conflict, to disseminate the Conventions and this Protocol as widely as possible in their respective countries and, in particular, to include the study thereof in their programmes of military instruction and to encourage the study thereof by the civilian population, so that those instruments may become known to the armed forces and to the civilian population.

2. Any military or civilian authorities who, in time of armed conflict, assume responsibilities in respect of the application of the Conventions and this Protocol shall be fully acquainted with the text thereof.

Article 84. *Rules of application*

The High Contracting Parties shall communicate to one another, as soon as possible, through the depositary and, as appropriate, through the Protecting Powers, their official translations of this Protocol, as well as the laws and regulations which they may adopt to ensure its application.

Section II. Repression of breaches of the conventions and of this protocol

Article 85. *Repression of breaches of this Protocol*

1. The provisions of the Conventions relating to the repression of breaches and grave breaches, supplemented by this Section, shall apply to the repression of breaches and grave breaches of this Protocol.

2. Acts described as grave breaches in the Conventions are grave breaches of this Protocol if committed against persons in the power of an adverse Party protected by Articles 44, 45 and 73 of this Protocol, or against the wounded, sick and shipwrecked of the adverse Party who are protected by this Protocol, or against those medical or religious personnel, medical units or medical transports which are under the control of the adverse Party and are protected by this Protocol.

3. In addition to the grave breaches defined in Article 11, the following acts shall be regarded as grave breaches of this Protocol, when committed wilfully, in violation of the relevant provisions of this Protocol, and causing death or serious injury to body or health:

(*a*) making the civilian population or individual civilians the object of attack;

(*b*) launching an indiscriminate attack affecting the civilian population or civilian objects in the knowledge that such attack will cause excessive loss of life, injury to civilians or damage to civilian objects, as defined in Article 57, paragraph 2 (*a*) (iii);

(*c*) launching an attack against works or installations containing dangerous forces in the knowledge that such attack will cause excessive loss of life, injury to civilians or damage to civilian objects, as defined in Article 57, paragraph 2 (*a*) (iii);

(*d*) making non-defended localities and demilitarized zones the object of attack;

(*e*) making a person the object of attack in the knowledge that he is *hors de combat;*

(*f*) the perfidious use, in violation of Article 37, of the distinctive emblem of the red cross, red crescent or red lion and sun or of other protective signs recognized by the Conventions or this Protocol.

4. In addition to the grave breaches defined in the preceding paragraphs and in the Conventions, the following shall be regarded as grave breaches of this Protocol, when committed wilfully and in violation of the Conventions or the Protocol;

(*a*) the transfer by the occupying Power of parts of its own civilian population into the territory it occupies, or the deportation or transfer of all or parts of the population of the occupied territory within or outside this territory, in violation of Article 49 of the Fourth Convention;

(*b*) unjustifiable delay in the repatriation of prisoners of war or civilians;

(*c*) practices of *apartheid* and other inhuman and degrading practices involving outrages upon personal dignity, based on racial discrimination;

(*d*) making the clearly-recognized historic monuments, works of art or places of worship which constitute the cultural or spiritual heritage of peoples and to which special protection has been given by special arrangement, for example, within the framework of a competent international organization, the object of attack, causing as a result extensive destruction thereof, where there is no evidence of the violation by the adverse Party of Article 53, subparagraph (*b*), and when such historic monuments, works of art and places of worship are not located in the immediate proximity of military objectives;

(*e*) depriving a person protected by the Conventions or referred to in paragraph 2 of this Article of the rights of fair and regular trial.

5. Without prejudice to the application of the Conventions and of this Protocol, grave breaches of these instruments shall be regarded as war crimes.

Article 86. *Failure to act*

1. The High Contracting Parties and the Parties to the conflict shall repress grave breaches, and take measures necessary to suppress all other breaches, of the Conven-

tions or of this Protocol which result from a failure to act when under a duty to do so.

2. The fact that a breach of the Conventions or of this Protocol was committed by a subordinate does not absolve his superiors from penal or disciplinary responsibility, as the case may be, if they knew, or had information which should have enabled them to conclude in the circumstances at the time, that he was committing or was going to commit such a breach and if they did not take all feasible measures within their power to prevent or repress the breach.

Article 87. *Duty of commanders*

1. The High Contracting Parties and the Parties to the conflict shall require military commanders, with respect to members of the armed forces under their command and other persons under their control, to prevent and, where necessary, to suppress and report to competent authorities breaches of the Conventions and of this Protocol.

2. In order to prevent and suppress breaches, High Contracting Parties and Parties to the conflict shall require that, commensurate with their level of responsibility, commanders ensure that members of the armed forces under their command are aware of their obligations under the Conventions and this Protocol.

3. The High Contracting Parties and Parties to the conflict shall require any commander who is aware that subordinates or other persons under his control are going to commit or have committed a breach of the Conventions or of this Protocol, to initiate such steps as are necessary to prevent such violations of the Conventions of this Protocol, and, where appropriate, to initiate disciplinary or penal action against violators thereof.

. . .

Article 90. *International Fact-Finding Commission*

1. (*a*) International Fact-Finding Commission (hereinafter referred to as "the Commission") consisting of fifteen members of high moral standing and acknowledged impartiality shall be established.

(*b*) When not less than twenty High Contracting Parties have agreed to accept the competence of the Commission pursuant to paragraph 2, the depositary shall then, and at intervals of five years thereafter, convene a meeting of representatives of those High Contracting Parties for the purpose of electing the members of the Commission. At the meeting, the representatives shall elect the members of the Commission by secret ballot from a list of persons to which each of those High Contracting Parties may nominate one person.

(*c*) The members of the Commission shall serve in their personal capacity and shall hold office until the election of new members at the ensuing meeting.

(*d*) At the election, the High Contracting Parties shall ensure that the persons to be elected to the Commission individually possess the qualifications required and that, in the Commission as a whole, equitable geographical representation is assured.

(*e*) In the case of a casual vacancy, the Commission itself shall fill the vacancy, having due regard to the provisions of the preceding sub-paragraphs.

(*f*) The depositary shall make available to the Commission the necessary administrative facilities for the performance of its functions.

2. (*a*) The High Contracting Parties may at the time of signing, ratifying or acceding to the Protocol, or at any other subsequent time, declare that they recognize *ipso facto* and without special agreement, in relation to any other High Contracting Party accepting the same obligation, the competence of the Commission to enquire into allegations by such other Party, as authorized by this Article.

(*b*) The declarations referred to above shall be deposited with the depositary, which shall transmit copies thereof to the High Contracting Parties.

(*c*) The Commission shall be competent to:

(i) enquire into any facts alleged to be a grave breach as defined in the Conventions and this Protocol or other serious violation of the Conventions or of this Protocol;

(ii) facilitate, through its good offices, the restoration of an attitude of respect for the Conventions and this Protocol.

(*d*) In other situations, the Commission shall institute an enquiry at the request of a Party to the conflict only with the consent of the other Party or Parties concerned.

(*e*) Subject to the foregoing provisions of this paragraph, the provisions of Article 52 of the First Convention, Article 53 of the Second Convention, Article 132 of the Third Convention and Article 149 of the Fourth Convention shall continue to apply to any alleged violation of the Conventions and shall extend to any alleged violation of this Protocol.

3. (*a*) Unless otherwise agreed by the Parties concerned, all enquiries shall be undertaken by a Chamber consisting of seven members appointed as follows:

(i) five members of the Commission, not nationals of any Party to the conflict, appointed by the President of the Commission on the basis of equitable representation of the geographical areas, after consultation with the Parties to the conflict;

(ii) two *ad hoc* members, not nationals of any Party to the conflict, one to be appointed by each side.

(*b*) Upon receipt of the request for an enquiry, the President of the Commission shall specify an appropriate time limit for setting up a Chamber. If any *ad hoc* member has not been appointed within the time limit, the President shall immediately appoint such additional members of the Commission as may be necessary to complete the membership of the Chamber.

4. (*a*) The Chamber set up under paragraph 3 to undertake an enquiry shall invite the Parties to the conflict to assist it and to present evidence. The Chamber may also seek such other evidence as it deems appropriate and may carry out an investigation of the situation *in loco*.

(*b*) All evidence shall be fully disclosed to the Parties, which shall have the right to comment on it to the Commission.

(*c*) Each Party shall have the right to challenge such evidence.

5. (*a*) The Commission shall submit to the Parties a report on the findings of fact of the Chamber, with such recommendations as it may deem appropriate.

(*b*) If the Chamber is unable to secure sufficient evidence for factual and impartial findings, the Commission shall state the reasons for that inability.

(*c*) The Commission shall not report its findings publicly, unless all the Parties to the conflict have requested the Commission to do so.

6. The Commission shall establish its own rules, including rules for the presidency of the Commission and the presidency of the Chamber. Those rules shall ensure that the functions of the President of the Commission are exercised at all times and that, in the case of an enquiry, they are exercised by a person who is not a national of a Party to the conflict.

7. The administrative expenses of the Commission shall be met by contributions from the High Contracting Parties which made declarations under paragraph 2, and by voluntary contributions. The Party or Parties to the conflict requesting an enquiry shall advance the necessary funds for expenses incurred by a Chamber and shall be reimbursed by the Party or Parties against which the allegations are made to the extent of fifty percent of the costs of the Chamber. Where there are counter-allegations before the Chamber each side shall advance fifty per cent of the necessary funds.

Article 91. *Responsibility*

A Party to the conflict which violates the provisions of the Conventions or of this Protocol shall, if the case demands, be liable to pay compensation. It shall be responsible for all acts committed by persons forming part of its armed forces.

PART VI. FINAL PROVISIONS

Article 92. *Signature*

This Protocol shall be open for signature by the Parties to the Conventions six months after the signing of the Final Act and will remain open for a period of twelve months.

Article 93. *Ratification*

This Protocol shall be ratified as soon as possible. The instruments of ratification shall be deposited with the Swiss Federal Council, depositary of the Conventions.

Article 94. *Accession*

This Protocol shall be open for accession by any Party to the Conventions which has not signed it. The instruments of accession shall be deposited with the depositary.

Article 95. *Entry into force*

1. This Protocol shall enter into force six months after two instruments of ratification or accession have been deposited.

2. For each Party to the Conventions thereafter ratifying or acceding to this Protocol, it shall enter into force six months after the deposit by such Party of its instrument of ratification or accession.

. . .

Article 99. *Denunciation*

1. In case a High Contracting Party should denounce this Protocol, the denunciation shall only take effect one year after receipt of the instrument of denunciation. If, however, on the expiry of that year the denouncing Party is engaged in one of the situations referred to in Article 1, the denunciation shall not take effect before the end of the armed conflict or occupation and not, in any case, before operations connected with the final release, repatriation or re-establishment of the persons protected by the Conventions or this Protocol have been terminated.

2. The denunciation shall be notified in writing to the depositary, which shall transmit it to all the High Contracting Parties.

3. The denunciation shall have effect only in respect of the denouncing Party.

4. Any denunciation under paragraph 1 shall not affect the obligations already incurred, by reason of the armed conflict, under this Protocol by such denouncing Party in respect of any act committed before this denunciation becomes effective.

. . .

Protocol I was worked out at the Diplomatic Conference which held its sessions in 1974–77. At the same time the Conference adopted a Protocol Additional to the Geneva Conventions of 12 August 1948, and relating to the Protection of Victims of Non-International Armed Conflicts (Protocol II).

By 31 December 1977 the following states had signed Protocol I and Protocol II: Austria, Belgium, Byelorussia, Canada, Chile, Denmark, Ecuador, Egypt, El Salvador, German Democratic Republic, Federal Republic of Germany, Finland, Ghana, Guatemala, Holy See, Honduras, Hungary, Iceland, Iran, Ireland, Italy, Ivory Coast, Jordan, Liechtenstein, Luxembourg, Mongolia, Morocco, Netherlands, Nicaragua, Norway, Pakistan, Panama, Peru, Philippines, Poland, Portugal, Senegal, Sweden, Switzerland, Togo, Tunisia, Ukraine, Union of Soviet Socialist Republics, United Kingdom, United States, Viet Nam, and Yugoslavia.

RESOLUTION 22 OF THE DIPLOMATIC CONFERENCE ON THE REAFFIRMATION AND DEVELOPMENT OF INTERNATIONAL HUMANITARIAN LAW APPLICABLE IN ARMED CONFLICTS

FOLLOW-UP REGARDING PROHIBITION OR RESTRICTION OF USE OF CERTAIN CONVENTIONAL WEAPONS

Adopted on 9 June 1977.

Having met at Geneva for four sessions, in 1974, 1975, 1976 and 1977, and having adopted new humanitarian rules relating to armed conflicts and methods and means of warfare,

Convinced that the suffering of the civilian population and combatants could be significantly reduced if agreements can be attained on the prohibition or restriction for humanitarian reasons of the use of specific conventional weapons, including any which may be deemed to be excessively injurious or to have indiscriminate effects,

Recalling that the issue of prohibitions or restrictions for humanitarian reasons of the use of specific conventional weapons has been the subject of substantive discussion in the *Ad Hoc* Committee on Conventional Weapons of the Conference at all its four sessions, and at the Conferences of Government Experts held under the auspices of the International Committee of the Red Cross in 1974 at Lucerne and in 1976 at Lugano,

Recalling, in this connexion, discussions and relevant resolutions of the General Assembly of the United Nations and appeals made by several Heads of State and Government,

Having concluded, from these discussions, that agreement exists on the desirability of prohibiting the use of conventional weapons, the primary effect of which is to injure by fragments not detectable by X-ray, and that there is a wide area of agreement with regard to landmines and booby-traps.

Having also devoted efforts to the further narrowing down of divergent views on the desirability of prohibiting or restricting the use of incendiary weapons, including napalm,

Having also considered the effects of the use of other conventional weapons, such as small calibre projectiles and certain blast and fragmentation weapons, and having begun the consideration of the possibility of prohibiting or restricting the use of such weapons,

Recognizing that it is important that this work continue and be pursued with the urgency required by evident humanitarian considerations,

Believing that further work should both build upon the areas of agreement thus far identified and include the search for further areas of agreement and should, in each case, seek the broadest possible agreement,

1. *Resolves* to send the report of the *Ad Hoc* Committee and the proposals presented in that Committee to the Governments of States represented at the Conference and to the Secretary-General of the United Nations;

2. *Requests* that serious and early consideration be given to these documents and to the reports of the Conferences of Government Experts of Lucerne and Lugano;

3. *Recommends* that a Conference of Governments should be convened not later than 1979 with a view to reaching:

(*a*) agreements on prohibitions or restrictions on the use of specific conventional weapons including those which may be deemed to be excessively injurious or have indiscriminate effects, taking into account humanitarian and military considerations; and

(*b*) agreement on a mechanism for the review of any such agreements and for the consideration of proposals for further such agreements;

4. *Urges* that consultations be undertaken prior to the consideration of this question at the thirty-second session of the United Nations General Assembly for the purpose of reaching agreement on the steps to be taken in preparation for the Conference;

5. *Recommends* that a consultative meeting of all interested Governments be convened during September/October 1977 for this purpose;

6. *Recommends further* that the States participating in these consultations should consider *inter alia* the establishment of a Preparatory Committee which would seek to establish the best possible basis for the achievement at the Conference of agreements as envisaged in this resolution;

7. *Invites* the General Assembly of the United Nations at its thirty-second session, in the light of the results of the consultations undertaken pursuant to paragraph 4 of this resolution, to take any further action that may be necessary for the holding of the Conference in 1979.

Source: *International Review of the Red Cross,* No. 197–198 (ICRC, Geneva, August–September 1977).

GUIDELINES FOR NUCLEAR TRANSFERS

Agreed to on 21 September 1977 by the Nuclear Supplier Group, and attached to communications addressed on 11 January 1978 to the Director General of the IAEA.

1. The following fundamental principles for safeguards and export controls should apply to nuclear transfers to any non-nuclear-weapon State for peaceful purposes. In this connection, suppliers have defined an export trigger list and agreed on common criteria for technology transfers.

Prohibition on nuclear explosives

2. Suppliers should authorize transfer of items identified in the trigger list only upon formal governmental assurances from recipients explicitly excluding uses which would result in any nuclear explosive device.

Physical protection

3. (*a*) All nuclear materials and facilities identified by the agreed trigger list should be placed under effective physical protection to prevent unauthorized use and handling. The levels of physical protection to be ensured in relation to the type of materials, equipment and facilities, have been agreed by suppliers, taking account of international recommendations.

(*b*) The implementation of measures of physical protection in the recipient country is the responsibility of the Government of that country. However, in order to implement the terms agreed upon amongst suppliers, the levels of physical protection on which these measures have to be based should be the subject of an agreement between supplier and recipient.

(*c*) In each case special arrangements should be made for a clear definition of responsibilities for the transport of trigger list items.

Safeguards

4. Suppliers should transfer trigger list items only when covered by IAEA safeguards, with duration and coverage provisions in conformance with the GOV/1621 guidelines.* Exceptions should be made only after consultation with the parties to this understanding.

5. Suppliers will jointly reconsider their common safeguards requirements, whenever appropriate.

Safeguards triggered by the transfer of certain technology

6. (*a*) The requirements of paragraphs 2, 3 and 4 above should also apply to facilities for reprocessing, enrichment, or heavy-water production, utilizing technology directly transferred by the supplier or derived from transferred facilities, or major critical components thereof.

(b) The transfer of such facilities, or major critical components thereof, or related technology, should require an undertaking (1) that IAEA safeguards apply to any facilities of the same type (i.e. if the design, construction or operating processes are based on the same or similar physical or chemical processes, as defined in the trigger list) constructed during an agreed period in the recipient country and (2) that there should at all times be in effect a safeguards agreement permitting the IAEA to apply Agency safeguards with respect to such facilities identified by the recipient, or by the supplier in consultation with the recipient, as using transferred technology.

Special controls on sensitive exports

7. Suppliers should exercise restraint in the transfer of sensitive facilities, technology and weapons-usable materials. If enrichment or reprocessing facilities, equipment or technology are to be transferred, suppliers should encourage recipients to accept, as an alternative to national plants, supplier involvement and/or other appropriate multinational participation in resulting facilities. Suppliers should also promote international (including IAEA) activities concerned with multinational regional fuel cycle centres.

Special controls on export of enrichment facilities, equipment and technology

8. For a transfer of an enrichment facility, or technology therefor, the recipient nation should agree that neither the transferred facility, nor any facility based on such technology, will be designed or operated for the production of greater than 20% enriched uranium without the consent of the supplier nation, of which the IAEA should be advised.

Controls on supplied or derived weapons-usable material

9. Suppliers recognize the importance, in order to advance the objectives of these Guidelines and to provide opportunities further to reduce the risks of proliferation, of including in agreements on supply of nuclear materials or of facilities which produce weapons-usable material, provisions calling for mutual agreement between the supplier and the recipient on arrangements for reprocessing, storage, alteration, use, transfer or retransfer of any weapons-usable material involved. Suppliers should endeavour to include such provisions whenever appropriate and practicable.

Controls on retransfer

10. (a) Suppliers should transfer trigger list items, including technology defined under paragraph 6, only upon the recipient's assurance that in the case of:
(1) retransfer of such items,
or
(2) transfer of trigger list items derived from facilities originally transferred by the supplier, or with the help of equipment or technology originally transferred by the supplier;
the recipient of the retransfer or transfer will have provided the same assurances as those required by the supplier for the original transfer.

(b) In addition the supplier's consent should be required for: (1) any retransfer of the facilities, major critical components, or technology described in paragraph 6; (2) any transfer of facilities or major critical components derived from those items; (3) any retransfer of heavy water or weapons-usable material.

Supporting activities

Physical security

11. Suppliers should promote international co-operation on the exchange of physical security information, protection of nuclear materials in transit, and recovery of stolen nuclear materials and equipment.

Support for effective IAEA safeguards

12. Suppliers should make special efforts in support of effective implementation of IAEA safeguards. Suppliers should also support the Agency's efforts to assist Member States in the improvement of their national systems of accounting and control of nuclear material and to increase the technical effectiveness of safeguards.

Similarly, they should make every effort to support the IAEA in increasing further the adequacy of safeguards in the light of technical developments and the rapidly growing number of nuclear facilities, and to support appropriate initiatives aimed at improving the effectiveness of IAEA safeguards.

Sensitive plant design features

13. Suppliers should encourage the designers and makers of sensitive equipment to construct it in such a way as to facilitate the application of safeguards.

Consultations

14. (a) Suppliers should maintain contact and consult through regular channels on matters connected with the implementation of these Guidelines.

(b) Suppliers should consult, as each deems appropriate, with other Governments concerned on specific sensitive cases, to ensure that any transfer does not contribute to risks of conflict or instability.

(c) In the event that one or more suppliers believe that there has been a violation of supplier/recipient understandings resulting from these Guidelines, particularly in the case of an explosion of a nuclear device, or illegal termination or violation of IAEA safeguards by a recipient, suppliers should consult promptly through diplomatic channels in order to determine and assess the reality and extent of the alleged violation.

Pending the early outcome of such consultations, suppliers will not act in a manner that could prejudice any measure that may be adopted by other suppliers concerning their current contacts with that recipient.

Upon the findings of such consultations, the suppliers, bearing in mind Article XII of the IAEA Statute, should agree on an appropriate response and possible action which could include the termination of nuclear transfers to that recipient.

15. In considering transfers, each supplier should exercise prudence having regard to all the circumstances of each case, including any risk that technology transfers not covered by paragraph 6, or subsequent retransfers, might result in unsafeguarded nuclear materials.

16. Unanimous consent is required for any changes in these Guidelines, including any which might result from the reconsideration mentioned in paragraph 5.

---

* This is a reference to an IAEA document of 20 August 1973, entitled "The formulation of certain provisions in agreements under the Agency's safeguards system (1965, as provisionally extended in 1966 and 1968)", which recommends that the following two concepts should be reflected in the agreements: (*a*) that the duration of the agreement should be related to the period of actual use of the items in the recipient State; and (*b*) that the provisions for terminating the agreement should be formulated in such a way that the rights and obligations of the parties continue to apply in connection with supplied nuclear material and with special fissionable material produced, processed or used in or in connection with supplied nuclear material, equipment, facilities or non-nuclear material, until such time as the Agency has terminated the application of safeguards thereto.

ANNEX A

Trigger list referred to in Guidelines

PART A. *Material and equipment*

1. Source or special fissionable material as defined in Article XX of the Statute of the International Atomic Energy Agency; provided that items specified in sub-paragraph (a) below, and exports of source or special fissionable material to a given recipient country, within a period of 12 months, below the limits specified in sub-paragraph (b) below, shall not be included:

(*a*) Plutonium with an isotopic concentration of plutonium-238 exceeding 80%.

Special fissionable material when used in gram quantities or less as a sensing component in instruments; and

Source material which the Government is satisfied is to be used only in non-nuclear activities, such as the production of alloys or ceramics;

(*b*) Special fissionable material	50 effective grams;
Natural uranium	500 kilograms;
Depleted uranium	1 000 kilograms; and
Thorium	1 000 kilograms.

2.1. *Reactors and equipment therefor:*

2.1.1. Nuclear reactors capable of operation so as to maintain a controlled self-sustaining fission chain reaction, excluding zero energy reactors, the latter being defined as reactors with a designed maximum rate of production of plutonium not exceeding 100 grams per year.

2.1.2. Reactor pressure vessels:
Metal vessels, as complete units or as major shop-fabricated parts therefor, which are especially designed or prepared to contain the core of a nuclear reactor as defined in paragraph 2.1.1 above and are capable of withstanding the operating pressure of the primary coolant.

2.1.3. Reactor fuel charging and discharging machines: Manipulative equipment especially designed or prepared for inserting or removing fuel in a nuclear reactor as defined in paragraph 2.1.1 above capable of on-load operation or employing technically sophisticated positioning or alignment features to allow complex off-load fuelling operations such as those in which direct viewing of or access to the fuel is not normally available.

2.1.4. Reactor control rods:
Rods especially designed or prepared for the control of the reaction rate in a nuclear reactor as defined in paragraph 2.1.1 above.

2.1.5. Reactor pressure tubes:
Tubes which are especially designed or prepared to contain fuel elements and the primary coolant in a reactor as defined in paragraph 2.1.1 above at an operating pressure in excess of 50 atmospheres.

2.1.6. Zirconium tubes:
Zirconium metal and alloys in the form of tubes or assemblies of tubes, and in quantities exceeding 500 kg per year, especially designed or prepared for use in a reactor as defined in paragraph 2.1.1 above, and in which the relationship of hafnium to zirconium is less than 1:500 parts by weight.

2.1.7. Primary coolant pumps:
Pumps especially designed or prepared for circulating liquid metal as primary coolant for nuclear reactors as defined in paragraph 2.1.1 above.

2.2. *Non-nuclear materials for reactors:*

2.2.1. Deuterium and heavy water:
Deuterium and any deuterium compound in which the ratio of deuterium to hydrogen exceeds 1:5 000 for use in a nuclear reactor as defined in paragraph 2.1.1 above in quantities exceeding 200 kg of deuterium atoms for any one recipient country in any period of 12 months.

2.2.2. Nuclear grade graphite:
Graphite having a purity level better than 5 parts per million boron equivalent and with a density greater than 1.50 grams per cubic centimetre in quantities exceeding 30 metric tons for any one recipient country in any period of 12 months.

2.3.1. Plants for the reprocessing of irradiated fuel elements, and equipment especially designed or prepared therefor.

2.4.1. Plants for the fabrication of fuel elements.

2.5.1. Equipment, other than analytical instruments, especially designed or prepared for the separation of isotopes of uranium.

2.6.1. Plants for the production of heavy water, deuterium and deuterium compounds and equipment especially designed or prepared therefor.

Clarifications of certain of the items on the above list are annexed.

PART B. *Common criteria for technology transfers under paragraph 6 of the Guidelines*

(1) "Technology" means technical data in physical form designated by the supplying country as important to the design, construction, operation, or maintenance of enrichment, reprocessing, or heavy water production facilities or major critical components thereof, but excluding data available to the public, for example, in published books and periodicals, or that which has been made available internationally without restrictions upon its further dissemination.

(2) "Major critical components" are:
(*a*) in the case of an isotope separation plant of the gaseous diffusion type: *diffusion barrier;*
(*b*) in the case of an isotope separation plant of the gas centrifuge type: *gas centrifuge assemblies, corrosion-resistant to* UF_6;
(*c*) in the case of an isotope separation plant of the jet nozzle type: the *nozzle units;*

(d) in the case of an isotope separation plant of the vortex type: *the vortex units.*

(3) For facilities covered by paragraph 6 of the Guidelines for which no major critical component is described in paragraph 2 above, if a supplier nation should transfer in the aggregate a significant fraction of the items essential to the operation of such a facility, together with the knowhow for construction and operation of that facility, that transfer should be deemed to be a transfer of "facilities or major critical components thereof".

(4) The definitions in the preceding paragraphs are solely for the purposes of paragraph 6 of the Guidelines and this Part B, which differ from those applicable to Part A of this trigger list, which should not be interpreted as limited by such definition.

(5) For the purposes of implementing paragraph 6 of the Guidelines, the following facilities should be deemed to be "of the same type (i.e. if their design, construction or operating processes are based on the same or similar physical or chemical processes)":

Where the technology transferred is such as to make possible the construction in the recipient State of a facility of the following type, or major critical components thereof:	The following will be deemed to be facilities of the same type:
(a) an isotope separation plant of the gaseous diffusion type	any other isotope separation plant using the gaseous diffusion process.
(b) an isotope separation plant of the gas centrifuge type	any other isotope separation plant using the gas centrifuge process.
(c) an isotope separation plant of the jet nozzle type	any other isotope separation plant using the jet nozzle process.
(d) an isotope separation plant of the vortex type	any other isotope separation plant using the vortex process.
(e) a fuel reprocessing plant using the solvent extraction process	any other fuel reprocessing plant using the solvent extraction process.
(f) a heavy water plant using the exchange process	any other heavy water plant using the exchange process.
(g) a heavy water plant using the electrolytic process	any other heavy water plant using the electrolytic process.
(h) a heavy water plant using the hydrogen distillation process	any other heavy water plant using the hydrogen distillation process.

Note: In the case of reprocessing, enrichment, and heavy water facilities whose design, construction, or operation processes are based on physical or chemical processes other than those enumerated above, a similar approach would be applied to define facilities "of the same type", and a need to define major critical components of such facilities might arise.

(6) The reference in paragraph 6(b) of the Guidelines to "any facilities of the same type constructed during an agreed period in the recipient's country" is understood to refer to such facilities (or major critical components thereof), the first operation of which commences within a period of at least 20 years from the date of the first operation of (1) a facility which has been transferred or incorporates transferred major critical components or of (2) a facility of the same type built after the transfer of technology. It is understood that during that period there would be a conclusive presumption that any facility of the same type utilized transferred technology. But the agreed period is not intended to limit the duration of the safeguards imposed or the duration of the right to identify facilities as being constructed or operated on the basis of or by the use of transferred technology in accordance with paragraph 6(b) (2) of the Guidelines.

ANNEX

Clarifications of items on the trigger list

A. *Complete nuclear reactors*
(Item 2.1.1 of the trigger list)

1. A "nuclear reactor" basically includes the items within or attached directly to the reactor vessel, the equipment which controls the level of power in the core, and the components which normally contain or come in direct contact with or control the primary coolant of the reactor core.

2. The export of the whole set of major items within this boundary will take place only in accordance with the procedures of the Guidelines. Those individual items within this functionally defined boundary which will be exported only in accordance with the procedures of the Guidelines are listed in paragraphs 2.1.1 to 2.1.5.

The Government reserves to itself the right to apply the procedures of the Guidelines to other items within the functionally defined boundary.

3. It is not intended to exclude reactors which could reasonably be capable of modification to produce significantly more than 100 grams of plutonium per year. Reactors designed for sustained operation at significant power levels, regardless of their capacity for plutonium production, are not considered as "zero energy reactors".

B. *Pressure vessels*

(Item 2.1.2. of the trigger list)

4. A top plate for a reactor pressure vessel is covered by item 2.1.1 as a major shop-fabricated part of a pressure vessel.

5. Reactor internals (e.g. support columns and plates for the core and other vessel internals, control rod guide tubes, thermal shields, baffles, core grid plates, diffuser plates, etc.) are normally supplied by the reactor supplier. In some cases, certain internal support components are included in the fabrication of the pressure vessel. These items are sufficiently critical to the safety and reliability of the operation of the reactor (and, therefore, to the guarantees and liability of the reactor supplier), so that their supply, outside the basic supply arrangement for the reactor itself, would not be common practice. Therefore, although the separate supply of these unique, especially designed and prepared, critical, large and expensive items would not necessarily be considered as falling outside the area of concern, such a mode of supply is considered unlikely.

C. *Reactor control rods*

(Item 2.1.4 of the trigger list)

6. This item includes, in addition to the neutron absorbing part, the support or suspension structures therefor if supplied separately.

D. *Fuel reprocessing plants*

(Item 2.3.1 of the trigger list)

7. A "plant for the reprocessing of irradiated fuel elements" includes the equipment and components which normally come in direct contact with and directly control the irradiated fuel and the major nuclear material and fission product processing streams. The export of the whole set of major items within this boundary will take place only in accordance with the procedures of the Guidelines. In the present state of technology, the following items of equipment are considered to fall within the meaning of the phrase "and equipment especially designed or prepared therefor":

    (a) Irradiated fuel element chopping machines: remotely operated equipment especially designed or prepared for use in a reprocessing plant as identified above and intended to cut, chop or shear irradiated nuclear fuel assemblies, bundles or rods; and

    (b) Critically safe tanks (e.g. small diameter, annular or slab tanks) especially designed or prepared for use in a reprocessing plant as identified above, intended for dissolution of irradiated nuclear fuel and which are capable of withstanding hot, highly corrosive liquid, and which can be remotely loaded and maintained;

8. The Government reserves to itself the right to apply the procedures of the Guidelines to other items within the functionally defined boundary.

E. *Fuel fabrication plants*

(Item 2.4.1 of the trigger list)

9. A "plant for the fabrication of fuel elements" includes the equipment:

    (a) Which normally comes in direct contact with, or directly processes, or controls, the production flow of nuclear material, or

    (b) Which seals the nuclear material within the cladding.

10. The export of the whole set of items for the foregoing operations will take place only in accordance with the procedures of the Guidelines. The Government will also give consideration to application of the procedures of the Guidelines to individual items intended for any of the foregoing operations, as well as for other fuel fabrication operations such as checking the integrity of the cladding or the seal, and the finish treatment to the sealed fuel.

F. *Isotope separation plant equipment*

(Item 2.5.1 of the trigger list)

11. "Equipment, other than analytical instruments, especially designed or prepared for the separation of isotopes of uranium" includes each of the major items of equipment especially designed or prepared for the separation process. Such items include:
– gaseous diffusion barriers,
– gaseous diffuser housings,
– gas centrifuge assemblies, corrosion-resistant to UF_6,
– jet nozzle separation units,
– vortex separation units,
– large UF_6 corrosion-resistant axial or centrifugal compressors,
– special compressor seals for such compressors.

ANNEX B

Criteria for levels of physical protection

1. The purpose of physical protection of nuclear materials is to prevent unauthorized use and handling of these materials. Paragraph 3(a) of the Guidelines document calls for agreement among suppliers on the levels of protection to be ensured in relation to the type of materials, and equipment and facilities containing these materials, taking account of international recommendations.

2. Paragraph 3(b) of the Guidelines document states that implementation of measures of physical protection in the recipient country is the responsibility of the Government of that country. However, the levels of physical protection on which these measures have to be based should be the subject of an agreement between supplier and recipient. In this context these requirements should apply to all States.

3. The document INFCIRC/225 of the International Atomic Energy Agency entitled "The Physical Protection of Nuclear Material" and similar documents which from time to time are prepared by international groups of experts and updated as appropriate to account for changes in the state of the art and state of knowledge with regard to physical protection of nuclear material are a useful basis for guiding recipient States in designing a system of physical protection measures and procedures.

4. The categorization of nuclear material presented in the attached table or as it may be updated from time to

Table: Categorization of nuclear material

Material	Form	Category I	Category II	Category III
1. Plutonium[a]	Unirradiated[b]	2 kg or more	Less than 2 kg but more than 500 g	500 g or less[c]
2. Uranium-235	Unirradiated[b] – uranium enriched to 20% ^{235}U or more – uranium enriched to 10% ^{235}U but less than 20% – uranium enriched above natural, but less than 10% ^{235}U [d]	5 kg or more – 	Less than 5 kg but more than 1 kg 10 kg or more 	1 kg or less[c] Less than 10 kg[c] 10 kg or more
3. Uranium-233	Unirradiated[b]	2 kg or more	Less than 2 kg but more than 500 g	500 g or less[c]
4. Irradiated fuel			Depleted or natural uranium, thorium or low enriched fuel (less than 10% fissile content)[e,f]	

[a] As identified in the trigger list.
[b] Material not irradiated in a reactor or material irradiated in a reactor but with a radiation level equal to or less than 100 rads/hour at one metre unshielded.
[c] Less than a radiologically significant quantity should be exempted.
[d] Natural uranium, depleted uranium and thorium and quantities of uranium enriched to less than 10% not falling in Category III should be protected in accordance with prudent management practice.
[e] Although this level of protection is recommended, it would be open to States, upon evaluation of the specific circumstances, to assign a different category of physical protection.
[f] Other fuel which by virtue of its original fissile material content is classified as Category I or II before irradiation may be reduced one category level while the radiation level from the fuel exceeds 100 rads/hour at one metre unshielded.

---

time by mutual agreement of suppliers shall serve as the agreed basis for designating specific levels of physical protection in relation to the type of materials, and equipment and facilities containing these materials, pursuant to paragraph 3(a) and 3(b) of the Guidelines document.

5. The agreed levels of physical protection to be ensured by the competent national authorities in the use, storage and transportation of the materials listed in the attached table shall as a minimum include protection characteristics as follows:

CATEGORY III

Use and Storage within an area to which access is controlled.

Transportation under special precautions including prior arrangements among sender, recipient and carrier, and prior agreement between entities subject to the jurisdiction and regulation of supplier and recipient States, respectively, in case of international transport specifying time, place and procedures for transferring transport responsibility.

CATEGORY II

Use and Storage within a protected area to which access is controlled, i.e. an area under constant surveillance by guards or electronic devices, surrounded by a physical barrier with a limited number of points of entry under appropriate control, or any area with an equivalent level of physical protection.

Transportation under special precautions including prior arrangements among sender, recipient and carrier, and prior agreement between entities subject to the jurisdiction and regulation of supplier and recipient States, respectively, in case of international transport, specifying time, place and procedures for transferring transport responsibility.

CATEGORY I

Materials in this Category shall be protected with highly reliable systems against unauthorized use as follows:

Use and Storage within a highly protected area, i.e. a protected area as defined for Category II above, to which, in addition, access is restricted to persons whose trustworthiness has been determined, and which is under surveillance by guards who are in close communication with appropriate response forces. Specific measures taken in this context should have as their objective the detection and prevention of any assault, unauthorized access or unauthorized removal of material.

Transportation under special precautions as identified above for transportation of Category II and III materials and, in addition, under constant surveillance by escorts and under conditions which assure close communication with appropriate response forces.

6. Suppliers should request identification by recipients of those agencies or authorities having responsibility for ensuring that levels of protection are adequately met and having responsibility for internally co-ordinating response/recovery operations in the event of unauthorized use or handling of protected materials. Suppliers and recipients should also designate points of contact within their national authorities to co-operate on matters of out-of-country transportation and other matters of mutual concern.

Source: IAEA document INFCIRC/254.

The following states are members of the Nuclear Supplier Group, the so-called London Club: Belgium, Canada, Czechoslovakia, France, German Democratic Republic, Federal Republic of Germany, Italy, Japan, Netherlands, Poland, Sweden, Switzerland, UK, USA, USSR.

3. Status of the implementation of multilateral arms control agreements, as of 31 December 1977

I. *The 1925 Geneva Protocol for the prohibition of the use in war of asphyxiating, poisonous and other gases, and of bacteriological methods of warfare*

Note

Some states, former non-self-governing territories, acceded to the Geneva Protocol without referring to the obligations previously undertaken on their behalf by the colonial power. In these cases, the date of notification by the government of France, the depositary government, is indicated as the date of entry into force of the accession for the states concerned, in accordance with paragraph 2 of the operative part of the Protocol.

Other states, former non-self-governing territories, officially informed the government of France that they consider themselves bound by the Geneva Protocol by virtue of its ratification by the power formerly responsible for their administration. In such cases of continuity of obligations under the Geneva Protocol, the date of receipt of the state's notification by the French government is indicated.

Although the total number of ratifications, accessions and successions to the Geneva Protocol is 100, account should be taken of the facts that Estonia, Latvia and Lithuania, which signed and ratified the Protocol, no longer have independent status; that both the Federal Republic of Germany and the German Democratic Republic are bound by ratification on behalf of Germany; and that both the People's Republic of China and Taiwan are bound by accession on behalf of China.

The total number of parties to the Geneva Protocol, as of 31 December 1977, is 99.

Implementation of multilateral agreements

A. Ratifications*

Country	Deposit of ratification	Country	Deposit of ratification
Austria	9 May 1928	Japan	21 May 1970
Belgium	4 Dec 1928[1]	Latvia	3 Jun 1931
Brazil	28 Aug 1970	Lithuania	15 Jun 1933
British Empire	9 Apr 1930[2]	Luxembourg	1 Sep 1936
Bulgaria	7 Mar 1934[3]	Netherlands	31 Oct 1930[12]
Canada	6 May 1930[4]	Norway	27 Jul 1932
Chile	2 Jul 1935[5]	Poland	4 Feb 1929
Czechoslovakia	16 Aug 1938[6]	Portugal	1 Jul 1930[13]
Denmark	5 May 1930	Romania	23 Aug 1929[14]
Egypt	6 Dec 1928	Spain	22 Aug 1929[15]
Estonia	28 Aug 1931[7]	Sweden	25 Apr 1930
Ethiopia	20 Sep 1935[8]	Switzerland	12 Jul 1932
Finland	26 Jun 1929	Thailand	6 Jun 1931
France	10 May 1926[9]	Turkey	5 Oct 1929
Germany	25 Apr 1929[10]	USA	10 Apr 1975[16]
Greece	30 May 1931	Uruguay	12 Apr 1977
India	9 Apr 1930[11]	Venezuela	8 Feb 1928
Italy	3 Apr 1928	Yugoslavia	12 Apr 1929[17]

B. Accessions and successions

Country	Notification	Country	Notification
Argentina	12 May 1969	Kuwait	15 Dec 1971[30]
Australia	24 May 1930[18]	Lebanon	17 Apr 1969
Barbados	16 Jul 1976[19]	Lesotho	10 Mar 1972[31]
Central African Republic	31 Jul 1970	Liberia	17 Jun 1927
China	24 Aug 1929[20]	Libya	29 Dec 1971[32]
Cuba	24 Jun 1966	Madagascar	2 Aug 1967
Cyprus	29 Nov 1966[21]	Malawi	14 Sep 1970
Dominican Republic	8 Dec 1970	Malaysia	10 Dec 1970
Ecuador	16 Sept 1970	Maldives	27 Dec 1966[33]
Fiji	21 Mar 1973[22]	Malta	9 Oct 1970[34]
Gambia	5 Nov 1966[23]	Mauritius	23 Dec 1970[35]
Ghana	3 May 1967	Mexico	28 May 1932
Holy See	18 Oct 1966	Monaco	6 Jan 1967
Hungary	11 Oct 1952	Mongolia	6 Dec 1968[36]
Iceland	2 Nov 1967	Morocco	13 Oct 1970
Indonesia	21 Jan 1971[24]	Nepal	9 May 1969
Iran	5 Nov 1929	New Zealand	24 May 1930[37]
Iraq	8 Sep 1931[25]	Niger	5 Apr 1967[38]
Ireland	29 Aug 1930[26]	Nigeria	15 Oct 1968[39]
Israel	20 Feb 1969[27]	Pakistan	15 Apr 1960[40]
Ivory Coast	27 Jul 1970	Panama	4 Dec 1970
Jamaica	28 Jul 1970[28]	Paraguay	22 Oct 1933[41]
Jordan	17 Mar 1977[29]	Philippines	8 Jun 1973
Kenya	6 Jul 1970	Qatar	18 Oct 1976

---

* El Salvador and Nicaragua signed the Geneva Protocol but have not ratified it.

Country	Notification	Country	Notification
Rwanda	11 May 1964[42]	Togo	5 Apr 1971
Saudi Arabia	27 Jan 1971	Tonga	28 Jul 1971
Senegal	29 Jul 1977	Trinidad and Tobago	24 Nov 1970[45]
Sierra Leone	20 Mar 1967	Tunisia	12 Jul 1967
South Africa	24 May 1930[43]	Uganda	24 May 1965
Sri Lanka	20 Jan 1954	Upper Volta	3 Mar 1971
Syria	17 Dec 1968[44]	USSR	15 Apr 1928[46]
Tanzania (United Republic of)	22 Apr 1963	Yemen (Arab Republic)	17 Mar 1971

---

[1] (1) The said Protocol is only binding on the Belgian government as regards States which have signed or ratified it or which may accede to it. (2) The said Protocol shall *ipso facto* cease to be binding on the Belgian government in regard to any enemy State whose armed forces or whose allies fail to respect the prohibitions laid down in the Protocol.

[2] The British Plenipotentiary declared when signing: "My signature does not bind India or any British Dominion which is a separate Member of the League of Nations and does not separately sign or adhere to the Protocol".
(1) The said Protocol is only binding on His Britannic Majesty as regards those Powers and States which have both signed and ratified the Protocol or have finally acceded thereto. (2) The said Protocol shall cease to be binding on His Britannic Majesty towards any Power at enmity with Him whose armed forces, or the armed forces of whose allies, fail to respect the prohibitions laid down in the Protocol.

[3] The said Protocol is only binding on the Bulgarian government as regards States which have signed or ratified it or which may accede to it. The said Protocol shall *ipso facto* cease to be binding on the Bulgarian government in regard to any enemy State whose armed forces or whose allies fail to respect the prohibitions laid down in the Protocol.

[4] (1) The said Protocol is only binding on His Britannic Majesty as regards those States which have both signed and ratified it, or have finally acceded thereto. (2) The said Protocol shall cease to be binding on His Britannic Majesty towards any State at enmity with Him whose armed forces, or whose allies *de jure* or in fact fail to respect the prohibitions laid down in the Protocol.

[5] (1) The said Protocol is only binding on the Chilean government as regards States which have signed and ratified it or which may definitely accede to it. (2) The said Protocol shall *ipso facto* cease to be binding on the Chilean government in regard to any enemy State whose armed forces, or whose allies, fail to respect the prohibitions which are the object of this Protocol.

[6] The Czechoslovak Republic shall *ipso facto* cease to be bound by this Protocol towards any State whose armed forces, or the armed forces of whose allies, fail to respect the prohibitions laid down in the Protocol.

[7] (1) The said Protocol is only binding on the Estonian government as regards States which have signed or ratified it or which may accede to it. (2) The said Protocol shall *ipso facto* cease to be binding on the Estonian government in regard to any enemy State whose armed forces or whose allies fail to respect the prohibitions laid down in the Protocol.

[8] The document deposited by Ethiopia, a signer of the Protocol, is registered as an accession. The date given is therefore the date of notification by the French government.

[9] (1) The said Protocol is only binding on the government of the French Republic as regards States which have signed or ratified it or which may accede to it. (2) The said Protocol shall *ipso facto* cease to be binding on the government of the French Republic in regard to any enemy State whose armed forces or whose allies fail to respect the prohibitions laid down in the Protocol.

[10] The Protocol is now binding on both the German Democratic Republic and the Federal Republic of Germany.

[11] (1) The said Protocol is only binding on His Britannic Majesty as regards those States which have both signed and ratified it, or have finally acceded thereto. (2) The said Protocol shall cease to be binding on His Britannic Majesty towards any Power at enmity with Him whose armed forces, or the armed forces of whose allies, fail to respect the prohibitions laid down in the Protocol.

[12] Including the Netherlands Indies, Surinam and Curaçao. On 25 November 1975 Surinam became a sovereign state.

As regards the use in war of asphyxiating, poisonous or other gases, and of all analogous liquids, materials or devices, this Protocol shall *ipso facto* cease to be binding on the Royal Netherlands government with regard to any enemy State whose armed forces or whose allies fail to respect the prohibitions laid down in the Protocol.

[13] (1) The said Protocol is only binding on the government of the Portuguese Republic as regards States which have signed and ratified it or which may accede to it. (2) The said Protocol shall *ipso facto* cease to be binding on the government of the Portuguese Republic in regard to any enemy State whose armed forces or whose allies fail to respect the prohibitions which are the object of this Protocol.

[14] (1) The said Protocol only binds the Romanian government in relation to States which have signed and ratified or which have definitely acceded to the Protocol. (2) The said Protocol shall cease to be binding on the Romanian government in regard to all enemy States whose armed forces or whose allies *de jure* or in fact do not respect the restrictions which are the object of this Protocol.

[15] Declares as binding *ipso facto*, without special agreement with respect to any other Member or State accept-

ing and observing the same obligation, that is to say, on condition of reciprocity, the Protocol for the Prohibition of the Use in War of Asphyxiating, Poisonous and other Gases and of Bacteriological Methods of Warfare, signed at Geneva on 17 June 1925.

[16] The Protocol shall cease to be binding on the government of the United States with respect to the use in war of asphyxiating, poisonous or other gases, and of all analogous liquids, materials, or devices, in regard to an enemy State if such State or any of its allies fails to respect the prohibitions laid down in the Protocol.

[17] The said Protocol shall cease to be binding on the government of the Serbs, Croats and Slovenes in regard to any enemy State whose armed forces or whose allies fail to respect the prohibitions which are the object of this Protocol.

[18] Subject to the reservations that His Majesty is bound by the said Protocol only towards those Powers and States which have both signed and ratified the Protocol or have acceded thereto, and that His Majesty shall cease to be bound by the Protocol towards any Power at enmity with Him whose armed forces, or the armed forces of whose allies, do not respect the Protocol.

[19] In a note of 22 June 1976, addressed to the French government, the government of Barbados declared that it considered the Protocol to be in force in respect of Barbados in virtue of its extension to Barbados by the United Kingdom. It further declared that the reservation made on 9 April 1930 on behalf of the British Empire was withdrawn.

[20] On 13 July 1952, the People's Republic of China issued a statement recognizing as binding upon it the accession to the Protocol in the name of China. The People's Republic of China considers itself bound by the Protocol on condition of reciprocity on the part of all the other contracting and acceding powers.

[21] In a note of 21 November 1966, Cyprus declared that it was bound by the Protocol which had been made applicable to it by the British Empire.

[22] In a declaration of succession of 26 January 1973 addressed to the depositary government, the government of Fiji confirmed that the provisions of the Protocol were applicable to it by virtue of the ratification by the United Kingdom. The Protocol is only binding on Fiji as regards States which have both signed and ratified it and which will have finally acceded thereto. The Protocol shall cease to be binding on Fiji in regard to any enemy State whose armed forces or the armed forces of whose allies fail to respect the prohibitions which are the object of the Protocol.

[23] In a declaration of 11 October 1966, Gambia confirmed its participation in the Protocol which had been made applicable to it by the British Empire.

[24] In an official declaration of 13 January 1971 addressed to the French government, the government of Indonesia reaffirmed its acceptance of the Geneva Protocol which had been ratified on its behalf by the Netherlands on 31 October 1930, and stated that it remained signatory to that Protocol.

[25] On condition that the Iraq government shall be bound by the provisions of the Protocol only towards those States which have both signed and ratified it or have acceded thereto, and that it shall not be bound by the Protocol towards any State at enmity with Iraq whose armed forces, or the forces of whose allies, do not respect the provisions of the Protocol.

[26] The government of the Irish Free State does not intend to assume, by this accession, any obligation except towards the States having signed and ratified this Protocol or which shall have finally acceded thereto, and should the armed forces or the allies of an enemy State fail to respect the said Protocol, the government of the Irish Free State would cease to be bound by the said Protocol in regard to such State. In a note of 7 February 1972, received by the depositary government on 10 February 1972, the government of Ireland declared that it had decided to withdraw the above reservations made at the time of accession to the Protocol.

[27] The said Protocol is only binding on the State of Israel as regards States which have signed and ratified or acceded to it. The said Protocol shall cease *ipso facto* to be binding on the State of Israel as regards any enemy State whose armed forces, or the armed forces of whose allies, or the regular or irregular forces, or groups or individuals operating from its territory, fail to respect the prohibitions which are the object of this Protocol.

[28] Jamaica declared to the depositary government that it considered itself bound by the provisions of the Protocol on the basis of the ratification by the British Empire in 1930.

[29] The accession by Jordan to the Protocol does not in any way imply recognition of Israel, and does not oblige Jordan to conclude with Israel any arrangement under the Protocol. Jordan undertakes to respect the obligations contained in the Protocol with regard to States which have undertaken similar commitments. It is not bound by the Protocol as regards States whose armed forces, regular or irregular, do not respect the provisions of the Protocol.

[30] The accession of the State of Kuwait to this Protocol does not in any way imply recognition of Israel or the establishment of relations with the latter on the basis of the present Protocol. In case of breach of the prohibition mentioned in this Protocol by any of the Parties, the State of Kuwait will not be bound, with regard to the Party committing the breach, to apply the provisions of this Protocol. In a note of 25 January 1972, addressed to the depositary government, Israel objected to the above reservations.

[31] By a note of 10 February 1972 addressed to the depositary government, Lesotho confirmed that the provisions of the Protocol were applicable to it by virtue of the ratification by the British Empire on 9 April 1930.

[32] The accession to the Protocol does not imply recognition or the establishment of any relations with Israel. The present Protocol is binding on the Libyan Arab Republic only as regards States which are effectively bound by it and will cease to be binding on the Libyan Arab Republic as regards States whose armed forces, or the armed forces of whose allies, fail to respect the prohibitions which are the object of this Protocol. In a note of 25 January 1972 addressed to the depositary government, Israel objected to the above reservations.

[33] In a declaration of 19 December 1966, Maldives confirmed its adherence to the Protocol.

[34] By a notification of 25 September 1970, the government of Malta informed the French government that it considered itself bound by the Geneva Protocol as from 21 September 1964, the provisions of the Protocol having been extended to Malta by the government of the United Kingdom, prior to the former's accession to independence.

[35] By a notification of 27 November 1970, the govern-

[35] ment of Mauritius informed the French government that it considered itself bound by the Geneva Protocol as from 12 March 1968, the date of its accession to independence.

[36] In the case of violation of this prohibition by any State in relation to the People's Republic of Mongolia or its allies, the government of the People's Republic of Mongolia shall not consider itself bound by the obligations of the Protocol towards that State.

[37] Same reservations as Australia. (See footnote 18.)

[38] In a letter of 18 March 1967, Niger declared that it was bound by the adherence of France to the Protocol.

[39] The Protocol is only binding on Nigeria as regards States which are effectively bound by it and shall cease to be binding on Nigeria as regards States whose forces or whose allies' armed forces fail to respect the prohibitions which are the object of the Protocol.

[40] By a note of 13 April 1960, Pakistan informed the depositary government that it was a party to the Protocol by virtue of Paragraph 4 of the Annex to the Indian Independence Act of 1947.

[41] This is the date of receipt of the instrument of accession. The date of the notification by the French government "for the purpose of regularization" is 13 January 1969.

[42] In a declaration of 21 March 1964, Rwanda recognized that it was bound by the Protocol which had been made applicable to it by Belgium.

[43] Same reservations as Australia. (See footnote 18.)

[44] The accession by the Syrian Arab Republic to this Protocol and the ratification of the Protocol by its government does not in any case imply recognition of Israel or lead to the establishment of relations with the latter concerning the provisions laid down in this Protocol.

[45] By a note of 9 October 1970, the government of Trinidad and Tobago notified the French government that it considered itself bound by the Protocol, the provisions of which had been made applicable to Trinidad and Tobago by the British Empire prior to the former's accession to independence.

[46] (1) The said Protocol only binds the government of the Union of Soviet Socialist Republics in relation to the States which have signed and ratified or which have definitely acceded to the Protocol. (2) The said Protocol shall cease to be binding on the government of the Union of Soviet Socialist Republics in regard to any enemy State whose armed forces or whose allies *de jure* or in fact do not respect the prohibitions which are the object of this Protocol.

On 2 March 1970, the Byelorussian Soviet Socialist Republic stated that "it recognizes itself to be a Party" to the Geneva Protocol of 1925 (United Nations document A/8052, Annex III).

II. Major post-World War II agreements

Total number of parties

Antarctic Treaty	19
Partial Test Ban Treaty	108
Outer Space Treaty	77
Treaty of Tlatelolco	22
Non-Proliferation Treaty	103
Sea-Bed Treaty	65
BW Convention	76
ENMOD Convention (not yet in force)	44 signatories

Note

1. Key to abbreviations used in the table:
    S: signature
    R: deposit of instruments of ratification, accession or succession

Place of signature and/or deposit of the instrument of ratification, accession or succession:
    L: London
    M: Moscow
    W: Washington

Under the Antarctic Treaty, the only depositary is the US government; under the Treaty of Tlatelolco, the Mexican government; and under the ENMOD Convention, the UN Secretary-General.

For the Treaty of Tlatelolco:
    P.I: Additional Protocol I
    P.II: Additional Protocol II

For the Treaty of Tlatelolco and the NPT:
    S.A.: Safeguards agreement in force with the International Atomic Energy Agency (IAEA)

2. The footnotes are listed at the end of the table and are grouped separately under the heading for each agreement.

Implementation of multilateral agreements

Antarctic Treaty	Partial Test Ban Treaty	Outer Space Treaty	Treaty of Tlatelolco
Afghanistan	S: 8 Aug 1963 LW 9 Aug 1963 M R: 12 Mar 1964 L 13 Mar 1964 W 23 Mar 1964 M	S: 27 Jan 1967 W 30 Jan 1967 M	
Algeria	S: 14 Aug 1963 LW 19 Aug 1963 M		
Argentina S: 1 Dec 1959 R: 23 Jun 1961	S: 8 Aug 1963 W 9 Aug 1963 LM	S: 27 Jan 1967 W 18 Apr 1967 M R: 26 Mar 1969 MW	S:[1] 27 Sep 1967
Australia S: 1 Dec 1959 R: 23 Jun 1961	S: 8 Aug 1963 LMW R: 12 Nov 1963 LMW	S: 27 Jan 1967 W R: 10 Oct 1967 LMW	
Austria	S: 11 Sep 1963 MW 12 Sep 1963 L R: 17 Jul 1964 LMW	S: 20 Feb 1967 LMW R: 26 Feb 1968 LMW	
Bahamas	R:[1] 16 Jul 1976 M 13 Aug 1976 W	R:[1] 11 Aug 1976 L 13 Aug 1976 W 30 Aug 1976 M	S: 29 Nov 1976 R:[2] 26 Apr 1977
Barbados		R: 12 Sep 1968 W	S: 18 Oct 1968 R:[2] 25 Apr 1969
Belgium S: 1 Dec 1959 R: 26 Jul 1960	S: 8 Aug 1963 LMW R: 1 Mar 1966 LMW	S: 27 Jan 1967 LM 2 Feb 1967 W R: 30 Mar 1973 W 31 Mar 1973 LM	

Major post-World War II agreements

Non-Proliferation Treaty	Sea-Bed Treaty	BW Convention	ENMOD Convention	

S: 1 Jul 1968 LMW
R: 4 Feb 1970 W
    5 Feb 1970 M
    5 Mar 1970 L
S.A.: 20 Feb 1978
	S: 11 Feb 1971 LMW
	R: 22 Apr 1971 M
	    23 Apr 1971 L
	    21 May 1971 W
		S: 10 Apr 1972 LMW
		R: 26 Mar 1975 L
				Afghanistan

				Algeria

	S:[1] 3 Sep 1971 LMW	S: 1 Aug 1972 M
		    3 Aug 1972 L
		    7 Aug 1972 W
				Argentina

S:[1] 27 Feb 1970 LMW R: 23 Jan 1973 LMW S.A.: 10 Jul 1974	S: 11 Feb 1971 LMW R: 23 Jan 1973 LMW	S: 10 Apr 1972 LMW R: 5 Oct 1977 LMW		**Australia**
S: 1 Jul 1968 LMW R: 27 Jun 1969 LMW S.A.: 23 Jul 1972	S: 11 Feb 1971 LMW R: 10 Aug 1972 LMW	S: 10 Apr 1972 LMW R:[1] 10 Aug 1973 LMW		**Austria**

R:[2] 11 Aug 1976 L
    13 Aug 1976 W
    30 Aug 1976 M
				Bahamas

S: 1 Jul 1968 W		S: 16 Feb 1973 W R: 16 Feb 1973 W		**Barbados**
S: 20 Aug 1968 LMW R: 2 May 1975 LW 4 May 1975 M S.A.: 21 Feb 1977	S: 11 Feb 1971 LMW R: 20 Nov 1972 LMW	S: 10 Apr 1972 LMW	S: 18 May 1977	**Belgium**

153

Implementation of multilateral agreements

Antarctic Treaty	Partial Test Ban Treaty	Outer Space Treaty	Treaty of Tlatelolco

Benin	S:[2] 27 Aug 1963 W
	          3 Sep 1963 L
	          9 Oct 1963 M
	R: 15 Dec 1964 W
	     23 Dec 1964 M
	     22 Apr 1965 L		

Bolivia	S: 8 Aug 1963 W
	     21 Aug 1963 L
	     20 Sep 1963 M
	R: 4 Aug 1965 MW
	     25 Jan 1966 L
		S: 27 Jan 1967 W	S: 14 Feb 1967
			R:[3] 18 Feb 1969

Botswana	R:[1] 5 Jan 1968 M
	      14 Feb 1968 L
	       4 Mar 1968 W
		S: 27 Jan 1967 W	

Brazil
R: 16 May 1975
	S: 8 Aug 1963 LW
	      9 Aug 1963 M
	R: 15 Dec 1964 M
	    15 Jan 1965 W
	     4 Mar 1965 L
		S: 30 Jan 1967 M
		     2 Feb 1967 LW
		R:[2] 5 Mar 1969 LMW
			S:[3] 9 May 1967
			R:[4] 29 Jan 1968

Bulgaria	S: 8 Aug 1963 LMW
	R: 13 Nov 1963 W
	    21 Nov 1963 M
	     2 Dec 1963 L
		S: 27 Jan 1967 LMW
		R: 28 Mar 1967 M
		    11 Apr 1967 W
		    19 Apr 1967 L	

Burma	S: 14 Aug 1963 LMW R: 15 Nov 1963 LMW	S: 22 May 1967 LMW R: 18 Mar 1970 LMW	
Burundi	S: 4 Oct 1963 W	S: 27 Jan 1967 W	
Byelorussia	S: 8 Oct 1963 M R:[3] 16 Dec 1963 M	S:[3] 10 Feb 1967 M R: 31 Oct 1967 M	

154

Major post-World War II agreements

Non-Proliferation Treaty	Sea-Bed Treaty	BW Convention	ENMOD Convention	
				Benin
S: 1 Jul 1968 W R: 31 Oct 1972 W	S: 18 Mar 1971 W	S: 10 Apr 1972 W R: 25 Apr 1975 W	S: 10 Jun 1977	
				Bolivia
S: 1 Jul 1968 W R: 26 May 1970 W	S: 11 Feb 1971 LMW	S: 10 Apr 1972 W R: 30 Oct 1975 W	S: 18 May 1977	
				Botswana
S: 1 Jul 1968 W R: 28 Apr 1969 L	S: 11 Feb 1971 W R: 10 Nov 1972 W	S: 10 Apr 1972 W		
				Brazil
	S:[a] 3 Sep 1971 LMW	S: 10 Apr 1972 LMW R: 27 Feb 1973 LMW	S: 9 Nov 1977	
				Bulgaria

S: 1 Jul 1968 LMW
R: 5 Sep 1969 W
    18 Sep 1969 M
    3 Nov 1969 L
S.A.: 29 Feb 1972
	S: 11 Feb 1971 LMW
	R: 16 Apr 1971 M
	    7 May 1971 W
	    26 May 1971 L
		S: 10 Apr 1972 LMW
		R: 2 Aug 1972 L
		    13 Sep 1972 W
		    19 Sep 1972 M
			S: 18 May 1977	

				Burma
	S: 11 Feb 1971 LMW	S: 10 Apr 1972 LMW		
				Burundi
R: 19 Mar 1971 M	S: 11 Feb 1971 MW	S: 10 Apr 1972 MW		
				Byelorussia
	S: 3 Mar 1971 M R: 14 Sep 1971 M	S: 10 Apr 1972 M R: 26 Mar 1975 MW	S: 18 May 1977	

Implementation of multilateral agreements

Antarctic Treaty	Partial Test Ban Treaty	Outer Space Treaty	Treaty of Tlatelolco
Cambodia: see Democratic Kampuchea			
Cameroon: see United Republic of Cameroon			
Canada	S: 8 Aug 1963 LMW R: 28 Jan 1964 LMW	S: 27 Jan 1967 LMW R: 10 Oct 1967 LMW	
Cape Verde			
Central African Empire	R: 22 Dec 1964 W 24 Aug 1965 L 25 Sep 1965 M	S: 27 Jan 1967 W	
Chad	S: 26 Aug 1963 W R: 1 Mar 1965 W		
Chile S: 1 Dec 1959 R: 23 Jun 1961	S: 8 Aug 1963 W 9 Aug 1963 LM R: 6 Oct 1965 L	S: 27 Jan 1967 W 3 Feb 1967 L 20 Feb 1967 M	S: 14 Feb 1967 R:[5] 9 Oct 1974
China			P.II:[6] S: 21 Aug 1973 R: 12 Jun 1974

156

Major post-World War II agreements

Non-Proliferation Treaty	Sea-Bed Treaty	BW Convention	ENMOD Convention	
				Cambodia
				Cameroon
S: 23 Jul 1968 LW 29 Jul 1968 M R: 8 Jan 1969 LMW S.A.: 21 Feb 1972	S: 11 Feb 1971 LMW R:³ 17 May 1972 LMW	S: 10 Apr 1972 LMW R: 18 Sep 1972 LMW	S: 18 May 1977	**Canada**
		R: 20 Oct 1977 M		**Cape Verde**
R: 25 Oct 1970 W	S: 11 Feb 1971 W	S: 10 Apr 1972 W		**Central African Empire**
S: 1 Jul 1968 LM R: 10 Mar 1971 W 11 Mar 1971 M 23 Mar 1971 L				**Chad**
		S: 10 Apr 1972 LMW		**Chile**
				China

157

Implementation of multilateral agreements

	Antarctic Treaty	Partial Test Ban Treaty	Outer Space Treaty	Treaty of Tlatelolco
Colombia		S: 16 Aug 1963 MW 20 Aug 1963 L	S: 27 Jan 1967 W	S: 14 Feb 1967 R:[a] 4 Aug 1972
Costa Rica		S: 9 Aug 1963 L 13 Aug 1963 W 23 Aug 1963 M R: 10 Jul 1967 W		S: 14 Feb 1967 R:[a] 25 Aug 1969
Cuba			R:[4] 3 Jun 1977 M	
Cyprus		S: 8 Aug 1963 LMW R: 15 Apr 1965 L 21 Apr 1965 M 7 May 1965 W	S: 27 Jan 1967 W 15 Feb 1967 M 16 Feb 1967 L R: 5 Jul 1972 LW 20 Sep 1972 M	
Czechoslovakia	R: 14 Jun 1962	S: 8 Aug 1963 LMW R: 14 Oct 1963 LM 17 Oct 1963 W	S: 27 Jan 1967 LMW R: 11 May 1967 L 18 May 1967 M 22 May 1967 W	

Dahomey: see Benin

Democratic Kampuchea (Cambodia)

Democratic Yemen

Major post-World War II agreements

Non-Proliferation Treaty	Sea-Bed Treaty	BW Convention	ENMOD Convention	
				Colombia
S: 1 Jul 1968 W	S: 11 Feb 1971 W	S: 10 Apr 1972 W		
				Costa Rica
S: 1 Jul 1968 W R: 3 Mar 1970 W	S: 11 Feb 1971 W	S: 10 Apr 1972 W R: 17 Dec 1973 W		
				Cuba
	R:[4] 3 Jun 1977 M	S: 12 Apr 1972 M R: 21 Apr 1976 M	S: 23 Sep 1977	
				Cyprus

S: 1 Jul 1968 LMW
R: 10 Feb 1970 M
    16 Feb 1970 W
    5 Mar 1970 L
S.A.: 26 Jan 1973
	S: 11 Feb 1971 LMW
	R: 17 Nov 1971 LM
	    30 Dec 1971 W
		S: 10 Apr 1972 LW
		    14 Apr 1972 M
		R: 6 Nov 1973 L
		    13 Nov 1973 W
		    21 Nov 1973 M
			S: 7 Oct 1977	

				Czechoslovakia
S: 1 Jul 1968 LMW R: 22 Jul 1969 LMW S.A.: 3 Mar 1972	S: 11 Feb 1971 LMW R: 11 Jan 1972 LMW	S: 10 Apr 1972 LMW R: 30 Apr 1973 LMW	S: 18 May 1977	
				Dahomey
				Democratic Kampuchea (Cambodia)
R: 2 Jun 1972 W	S: 11 Feb 1971 W	S: 10 Apr 1972 W		
				Democratic Yemen
S: 14 Nov 1968 M	S: 23 Feb 1971 M	S: 26 Apr 1972 M		

Implementation of multilateral agreements

Antarctic Treaty	Partial Test Ban Treaty	Outer Space Treaty	Treaty of Tlatelolco
Denmark R: 20 May 1965	S: 9 Aug 1963 LMW R: 15 Jan 1964 LMW	S: 27 Jan 1967 LMW R: 10 Oct 1967 LMW	
Dominican Republic	S: 16 Sep 1963 W 17 Sep 1963 L 19 Sep 1963 M R: 3 Jun 1964 M 18 Jun 1964 L 22 Jul 1964 W	S: 27 Jan 1967 W R: 21 Nov 1968 W	S: 28 Jul 1967 R:[2] 14 Jun 1968 S.A.:[14]
Ecuador	S: 27 Sep 1963 W 1 Oct 1963 LM R: 6 May 1964 W 8 May 1964 L 13 Nov 1964 M	S: 27 Jan 1967 W 16 May 1967 L 7 Jun 1967 M R: 7 Mar 1969 W	S: 14 Feb 1967 R:[2] 11 Feb 1969 S.A.:[14]
Egypt	S:[4] 8 Aug 1963 LMW R: 10 Jan 1964 LMW	S: 27 Jan 1967 MW R: 10 Oct 1967 W 23 Jan 1968 M	
El Salvador	S: 21 Aug 1963 W 22 Aug 1963 L 23 Aug 1963 M R: 3 Dec 1964 W 7 Dec 1964 L 9 Feb 1965 M	S: 27 Jan 1967 W R: 15 Jan 1969 W	S: 14 Feb 1967 R:[2] 22 Apr 1968 S.A.:[14]
Equatorial Guinea			
Ethiopia	S: 9 Aug 1963 LW 19 Sep 1963 M	S: 27 Jan 1967 LW 10 Feb 1967 M	
Fiji	R:[1] 14 Jul 1972 M 18 Jul 1972 W 14 Aug 1972 L	R:[1] 18 Jul 1972 W 14 Aug 1972 L 29 Aug 1972 M	

160

Major post-World War II agreements

Non-Proliferation Treaty	Sea-Bed Treaty	BW Convention	ENMOD Convention
			Denmark
S: 1 Jul 1968 LMW R: 3 Jan 1969 LMW S.A.: 21 Feb 1977	S: 11 Feb 1971 LMW R: 15 Jun 1971 LMW	S: 10 Apr 1972 LMW R: 1 Mar 1973 LMW	S: 18 May 1977
			Dominican Republic
S: 1 Jul 1968 W R: 24 Jul 1971 W S.A.: 11 Oct 1973	S: 11 Feb 1971 W R: 11 Feb 1972 W	S: 10 Apr 1972 W R: 23 Feb 1973 W	
			Ecuador
S: 9 Jul 1968 W R: 7 Mar 1969 W S.A.: 10 Mar 1975		S: 14 Jun 1972 W R: 12 Mar 1975 W	
			Egypt
S: 1 Jul 1968 LM		S: 10 Apr 1972 LM	
			El Salvador
S: 1 Jul 1968 W R: 11 Jul 1972 W S.A.: 22 Apr 1975		S: 10 Apr 1972 W	
			Equatorial Guinea
	S: 4 Jun 1971 W		
			Ethiopia

S: 5 Sep 1968 LMW
R: 5 Feb 1970 M
    5 Mar 1970 LW
S.A.: 2 Dec 1977
	S: 11 Feb 1971 LMW
	R: 12 Jul 1977 L
	    14 Jul 1977 MW
		S: 10 Apr 1972 LMW
		R: 26 May 1975 LM
		    26 Jun 1975 W
			S: 18 May 1977

			Fiji

R:[2] 21 Jul 1972 W
    14 Aug 1972 L
    29 Aug 1972 M
S.A.: 22 Mar 1973
		S: 22 Feb 1973 L
		R: 4 Sep 1973 W
		    1 Oct 1973 L
		    5 Oct 1973 M	

Implementation of multilateral agreements

Antarctic Treaty	Partial Test Ban Treaty	Outer Space Treaty	Treaty of Tlatelolco
Finland	S: 8 Aug 1963 LMW R: 9 Jan 1964 LMW	S: 27 Jan 1967 LMW R: 12 Jul 1967 LMW	
France S: 1 Dec 1959 R: 16 Sep 1960		S: 25 Sep 1967 LMW R: 5 Aug 1970 LMW	P.II:[7] S: 18 Jul 1973 R: 22 Mar 1974

Gabon	S: 10 Sep 1963 W
	R: 20 Feb 1964 W
	    4 Mar 1964 L
	    9 Mar 1964 M		

Gambia	R:[1] 27 Apr 1965 MW 6 May 1965 L	S: 2 Jun 1967 L	
German Democratic Republic R:[1] 19 Nov 1974	S: 8 Aug 1963 M R:[5] 30 Dec 1963 M	S: 27 Jan 1967 M R:[5] 2 Feb 1967 M	
Germany, Federal Republic of	S: 19 Aug 1963 LMW R:[6] 1 Dec 1964 LW	S: 27 Jan 1967 LMW R:[6] 10 Feb 1971 LW	

Ghana	S: 8 Aug 1963 M
	    9 Aug 1963 W
	    4 Sep 1963 L
	R: 27 Nov 1963 L
	    9 Jan 1964 W
	   31 May 1965 M
		S: 27 Jan 1967 W
		   15 Feb 1967 M
		    3 Mar 1967 L	

Greece	S: 8 Aug 1963 W 9 Aug 1963 LM R: 18 Dec 1963 LMW	S: 27 Jan 1967 W R: 19 Jan 1971 L	

Major post-World War II agreements

Non-Proliferation Treaty	Sea-Bed Treaty	BW Convention	ENMOD Convention	
S: 1 Jul 1968 LMW R: 5 Feb 1969 LMW S.A.: 9 Feb 1972	S: 11 Feb 1971 LMW R: 8 Jun 1971 LMW	S: 10 Apr 1972 LMW R: 4 Feb 1974 LMW	S: 18 May 1977	**Finland**
				France
R: 19 Feb 1974 W		S: 10 Apr 1972 L		**Gabon**
S: 4 Sep 1968 L 20 Sep 1968 W 24 Sep 1968 M R: 12 May 1975 W	S: 18 May 1971 L 21 May 1971 M 29 Oct 1971 W	S: 2 Jun 1972 M 8 Aug 1972 L 9 Nov 1972 W		**Gambia**
S: 1 Jul 1968 M R:[3] 31 Oct 1969 M S.A.: 7 Mar 1972	S: 11 Feb 1971 M R: 27 Jul 1971 M	S: 10 Apr 1972 M R: 28 Nov 1972 M	S: 18 May 1977	**German Democratic Republic**
S: 28 Nov 1969 LMW R:[4] 2 May 1975 LW S.A.: 21 Feb 1977	S: 8 Jun 1971 LMW R:[5] 18 Nov 1975 LW	S: 10 Apr 1972 LMW	S: 18 May 1977	**Germany, Federal Republic of**
S: 1 Jul 1968 MW 24 Jul 1968 L R: 4 May 1970 L 5 May 1970 W 11 May 1970 M S.A.: 17 Feb 1975	S: 11 Feb 1971 LMW R: 9 Aug 1972 W	S: 10 Apr 1972 MW R: 6 Jun 1975 L		**Ghana**
S: 1 Jul 1968 MW R: 11 Mar 1970 W S.A.: 1 Mar 1972	S: 11 Feb 1971 M 12 Feb 1971 W	S: 10 Apr 1972 L 12 Apr 1972 W 14 Apr 1972 M R: 10 Dec 1975 W		**Greece**

163

Implementation of multilateral agreements

Antarctic Treaty	Partial Test Ban Treaty	Outer Space Treaty	Treaty of Tlatelolco
Grenada			S: 29 Apr 1975 R:[2] 20 Jun 1975
Guatemala	S: 23 Sep 1963 W R:[3] 6 Jan 1964 W		S: 14 Feb 1967 R:[3] 6 Feb 1970
Guinea			
Guinea-Bissau	R: 20 Aug 1976 M	R: 20 Aug 1976 M	
Guyana		S: 3 Feb 1967 W	
Haiti	S: 9 Oct 1963 W	S: 27 Jan 1967 W	S: 14 Feb 1967 R:[3] 23 May 1969
Holy See (Vatican City)		S: 5 Apr 1967 L	
Honduras	S: 8 Aug 1963 W 15 Aug 1963 L 16 Aug 1963 M R: 2 Oct 1964 W 2 Dec 1964 L	S: 27 Jan 1967 W	S: 14 Feb 1967 R:[3] 23 Sep 1968 S.A.:[14]

Major post-World War II agreements

Non-Proliferation Treaty	Sea-Bed Treaty	BW Convention	ENMOD Convention
			Grenada
R:[a] 2 Sep 1975 L 3 Dec 1975 W			
			Guatemala
S: 26 Jul 1968 W R: 22 Sep 1970 W	S: 11 Feb 1971 W	S: 9 May 1972 W R: 19 Sep 1973 W	
			Guinea
	S: 11 Feb 1971 MW		
			Guinea-Bissau
R: 20 Aug 1976 M	R: 20 Aug 1976 M	R: 20 Aug 1976 M	
			Guyana
		S: 3 Jan 1973 W	
			Haiti
S: 1 Jul 1968 W R: 2 Jun 1970 W		S: 10 Apr 1972 W	
			Holy See (Vatican City)
R:[5] 25 Feb 1971 LMW S.A.: 1 Aug 1972			S: 27 May 1977
			Honduras
S: 1 Jul 1968 W R: 16 May 1973 W S.A.: 18 Apr 1975	S: 11 Feb 1971 W	S: 10 Apr 1972 W	

165

Implementation of multilateral agreements

Antarctic Treaty	Partial Test Ban Treaty	Outer Space Treaty	Treaty of Tlatelolco
Hungary			

	S: 8 Aug 1963 LMW
	R: 21 Oct 1963 L
	  22 Oct 1963 W
	  23 Oct 1963 M
		S: 27 Jan 1967 LMW
		R: 26 Jun 1967 LMW	

Iceland			
	S: 12 Aug 1963 LMW R: 29 Apr 1964 LMW	S: 27 Jan 1967 LMW R: 5 Feb 1968 LMW	
India			

	S: 8 Aug 1963 LMW
	R: 10 Oct 1963 L
	  14 Oct 1963 M
	  18 Oct 1963 W
		S: 3 Mar 1967 LMW	

Indonesia			

	S: 23 Aug 1963 LMW
	R: 20 Jan 1964 M
	  27 Jan 1964 W
	  8 May 1964 L
		S: 27 Jan 1967 W
		  30 Jan 1967 M
		  14 Feb 1967 L	

Iran			
	S: 8 Aug 1963 LMW R: 5 May 1964 LMW	S: 27 Jan 1967 L	
Iraq			

	S: 13 Aug 1963 LMW
	R: 30 Nov 1964 L
	  1 Dec 1964 W
	  3 Dec 1964 M
		S: 27 Feb 1967 LW
		  9 Mar 1967 M
		R: 4 Dec 1968 M
		  23 Sep 1969 L	

Ireland			

	S: 8 Aug 1963 LW
	  9 Aug 1963 M
	R: 18 Dec 1963 LW
	  20 Dec 1963 M
		S: 27 Jan 1967 LW
		R: 17 Jul 1968 W
		  19 Jul 1968 L	

Israel			

	S: 8 Aug 1963 LMW
	R: 15 Jan 1964 LW
	  28 Jan 1964 M
		S: 27 Jan 1967 LMW
		R: 18 Feb 1977 W
		  1 Mar 1977 L
		  4 Apr 1977 M	

Major post-World War II agreements

Non-Proliferation Treaty	Sea-Bed Treaty	BW Convention	ENMOD Convention	
				Hungary
S: 1 Jul 1968 LMW R: 27 May 1969 LMW S.A.: 30 Mar 1972	S: 11 Feb 1971 LMW R: 13 Aug 1971 LMW	S: 10 Apr 1972 LMW R: 27 Dec 1972 LMW	S: 18 May 1977	
				Iceland
S: 1 Jul 1968 LMW R: 18 Jul 1969 LMW S.A.: 16 Oct 1974	S: 11 Feb 1971 LMW R: 30 May 1972 LMW	S: 10 Apr 1972 LMW R: 15 Feb 1973 LMW	S: 18 May 1977	
				India
	R:[6] 20 Jul 1973 LMW	S:[2] 15 Jan 1973 LMW R:[2] 15 Jul 1974 LMW	S: 15 Dec 1977	
				Indonesia
S:[6] 2 Mar 1970 LMW		S: 20 Jun 1972 MW 21 Jun 1972 L		
				Iran
S: 1 Jul 1968 LMW R: 2 Feb 1970 W 10 Feb 1970 M 5 Mar 1970 L S.A.: 15 May 1974	S: 11 Feb 1971 LMW R: 26 Aug 1971 LW 6 Sep 1972 M	S: 10 Apr 1972 MW 16 Nov 1972 L R: 22 Aug 1973 LW 27 Aug 1973 M	S: 18 May 1977	
				Iraq
S: 1 Jul 1968 M R: 29 Oct 1969 M S.A.: 29 Feb 1972	S: 22 Feb 1971 M R:[4] 13 Sep 1972 M	S: 11 May 1972 M	S: 15 Aug 1977	
				Ireland
S: 1 Jul 1968 MW 4 Jul 1968 L R 1 Jul 1968 W 2 Jul 1968 M 4 Jul 1968 L S.A.: 21 Feb 1977	S: 11 Feb 1971 LW R: 19 Aug 1971 LW	S:[3] 10 Apr 1972 LW R: 27 Oct 1972 LW	S: 18 May 1977	
				Israel

167

Implementation of multilateral agreements

Antarctic Treaty	Partial Test Ban Treaty	Outer Space Treaty	Treaty of Tlatelolco
Italy	S: 8 Aug 1963 LMW R: 10 Dec 1964 LMW	S: 27 Jan 1967 LMW R: 4 May 1972 LMW	
Ivory Coast	S: 5 Sep 1963 W R: 5 Feb 1965 W		
Jamaica	S: 13 Aug 1963 LMW	S: 29 Jun 1967 LMW R: 6 Aug 1970 W 10 Aug 1970 L 21 Aug 1970 M	S: 26 Oct 1967 R:[2] 26 Jun 1969
Japan S: 1 Dec 1959 R: 4 Aug 1960	S: 14 Aug 1963 LMW R: 15 Jun 1964 LMW	S: 27 Jan 1967 LMW R: 10 Oct 1967 LMW	
Jordan	S: 12 Aug 1963 LW 19 Aug 1963 M R: 29 May 1964 L 7 Jul 1964 M 10 Jul 1964 W	S: 2 Feb 1967 W	
Kampuchea: see Democratic Kampuchea			
Kenya	R: 10 Jun 1965 L 11 Jun 1965 W 30 Jun 1965 M		
Korea, South	S: 30 Aug 1963 LW R:[2] 24 Jul 1964 LW	S: 27 Jan 1967 W R:[4] 13 Oct 1967 W	

Major post-World War II agreements

Non-Proliferation Treaty	Sea-Bed Treaty	BW Convention	ENMOD Convention	
				Italy
S: 28 Jan 1969 LMW R:[7] 2 May 1975 LW 4 May 1975 M S.A.: 21 Feb 1977	S:[7] 11 Feb 1971 LMW R:[7] 3 Sep 1974 LMW	S: 10 Apr 1972 LMW R: 30 May 1975 LMW	S: 18 May 1977	
				Ivory Coast
S: 1 Jul 1968 W R: 6 Mar 1973 W	R: 14 Jan 1972 W	S: 23 May 1972 W		
				Jamaica
S: 14 Apr 1969 LMW R: 5 Mar 1970 LMW	S: 11 Oct 1971 LW 14 Oct 1971 M	R: 13 Aug 1975 L		
				Japan
S: 3 Feb 1970 LMW R:[8] 8 Jun 1976 LMW S.A.: 2 Dec 1977	S: 11 Feb 1971 LMW R: 21 Jun 1971 LMW	S: 10 Apr 1972 LMW		
				Jordan
S: 10 Jul 1968 W R: 11 Feb 1970 W S.A.: 21 Feb 1978	S: 11 Feb 1971 LMW R: 17 Aug 1971 W 30 Aug 1971 M 1 Nov 1971 L	S: 10 Apr 1972 W 17 Apr 1972 L 24 Apr 1972 M R: 30 May 1975 M 2 Jun 1975 W 27 Jun 1975 L		
				Kampuchea
				Kenya
S: 1 Jul 1968 W R: 11 Jun 1970 M		R: 7 Jan 1976 L		
				Korea, South
S:[9] 1 Jul 1968 W R:[10] 23 Apr 1975 W S.A.: 14 Nov 1975	S:[4] 11 Feb 1971 LW	S:[4] 10 Apr 1972 LW		

169

Implementation of multilateral agreements

Antarctic Treaty	Partial Test Ban Treaty	Outer Space Treaty	Treaty of Tlatelolco
Kuwait	S:[7] 20 Aug 1963 LMW R: 20 May 1965 W 21 May 1965 L 17 Jun 1965 M	R:[7] 7 Jun 1972 W 20 Jun 1972 L 4 Jul 1972 M	
Lao People's Democratic Republic	S: 12 Aug 1963 LMW R: 10 Feb 1965 L 12 Feb 1965 W 7 Apr 1965 M	S: 27 Jan 1967 W 30 Jan 1967 L 2 Feb 1967 M R: 27 Nov 1972 M 29 Nov 1972 W 15 Jan 1973 L	
Lebanon	S: 12 Aug 1963 W 13 Aug 1963 LM R: 14 May 1965 W 20 May 1965 L 4 Jun 1965 M	S: 23 Feb 1967 LMW R: 31 Mar 1969 LM 30 Jun 1969 W	
Lesotho		S: 27 Jan 1967 W	
Liberia	S: 8 Aug 1963 W 16 Aug 1963 L 27 Aug 1963 M R: 19 May 1964 W 22 May 1964 L 16 Jun 1964 M		
Libya	S: 9 Aug 1963 L 16 Aug 1963 MW R: 15 Jul 1968 L	R: 3 Jul 1968 W	
Luxembourg	S: 13 Aug 1963 L 3 Sep 1963 W 13 Sep 1963 M R: 10 Feb 1965 LMW	S: 27 Jan 1967 MW 31 Jan 1967 L	
Madagascar	S: 23 Sep 1963 W R: 15 Mar 1965 W	R:[8] 22 Aug 1968 W	

170

Major post-World War II agreements

Non-Proliferation Treaty	Sea-Bed Treaty	BW Convention	ENMOD Convention
			Kuwait
S: 15 Aug 1968 MW 22 Aug 1968 L		S: 14 Apr 1972 MW 27 Apr 1972 L R:[5] 18 Jul 1972 W 26 Jul 1972 L 1 Aug 1972 M	
			Lao People's Democratic Republic
S: 1 Jul 1968 LMW R: 20 Feb 1970 M 5 Mar 1970 LW	S: 11 Feb 1971 LW 15 Feb 1971 M R: 19 Oct 1971 L 22 Oct 1971 M 3 Nov 1971 W	S: 10 Apr 1972 LMW R: 20 Mar 1973 M 22 Mar 1973 W 25 Apr 1973 L	
			Lebanon
S: 1 Jul 1968 LMW R: 15 Jul 1970 LM 20 Nov 1970 W S.A.: 5 Mar 1973	S: 11 Feb 1971 LMW	S: 10 Apr 1972 LW 21 Apr 1972 M R: 26 Mar 1975 L 2 Apr 1975 M 13 Jun 1975 W	
			Lesotho
S: 9 Jul 1968 W R: 20 May 1970 W S.A.: 12 Jun 1973	S: 8 Sep 1971 W R: 3 Apr 1973 W	S: 10 Apr 1972 W R: 6 Sep 1977 L	
			Liberia
S: 1 Jul 1968 W R: 5 Mar 1970 W	S: 11 Feb 1971 W	S: 10 Apr 1972 W 14 Apr 1972 L	S: 18 May 1977
			Libya
S: 18 Jul 1968 L 19 Jul 1968 W 23 Jul 1968 M R: 26 May 1975 LMW			
			Luxembourg
S: 14 Aug 1968 LMW R: 2 May 1975 LW 4 May 1975 M S.A.: 21 Feb 1977	S: 11 Feb 1971 LMW	S: 10 Apr 1972 LM 12 Apr 1972 W R: 23 Mar 1976 LMW	S: 18 May 1977
			Madagascar
S: 22 Aug 1968 W R: 8 Oct 1970 W S.A.: 14 Jun 1973	S: 14 Sep 1971 W	S: 13 Oct 1972 L	

Implementation of multilateral agreements

Antarctic Treaty	Partial Test Ban Treaty	Outer Space Treaty	Treaty of Tlatelolco
Malawi	R:[1] 26 Nov 1964 MW 7 Jan 1965 L		
Malaysia	S: 8 Aug 1963 W 12 Aug 1963 L 21 Aug 1963 M R: 15 Jul 1964 M 16 Jul 1964 LW	S: 20 Feb 1967 W 21 Feb 1967 L 3 May 1967 M	
Maldives			
Mali	S: 23 Aug 1963 LMW	R: 11 Jun 1968 M	
Malta	R:[1] 25 Nov 1964 MW 1 Dec 1964 L		
Mauritania	S: 13 Sep 1963 W 17 Sep 1963 L 8 Oct 1963 M R: 6 Apr 1964 W 15 Apr 1964 L 28 Apr 1964 M		
Mauritius	R:[1] 30 Apr 1969 MW 12 May 1969 L	R:[1] 16 Apr 1969 W 21 Apr 1969 L 13 May 1969 M	
Mexico	S: 8 Aug 1963 LMW R: 27 Dec 1963 LMW	S: 27 Jan 1967 LMW R: 31 Jan 1968 LMW	S:[8] 14 Feb 1967 R:[3] 20 Sep 1967 S.A.: 6 Sep 1968

Major post-World War II agreements

Non-Proliferation Treaty	Sea-Bed Treaty	BW Convention	ENMOD Convention	
				Malawi
		S: 10 Apr 1972 W		
				Malaysia
S: 1 Jul 1968 LMW R: 5 Mar 1970 LMW S.A.: 29 Feb 1972	S: 20 May 1971 LMW R: 21 Jun 1972 LMW	S: 10 Apr 1972 LMW		
				Maldives
S: 11 Sep 1968 W R: 7 Apr 1970 W S.A.: 2 Oct 1977				
				Mali

S: 14 Jul 1969 W
    15 Jul 1969 M
R: 10 Feb 1970 M
    5 Mar 1970 W
	S: 11 Feb 1971 W
	    15 Feb 1971 M
		S: 10 Apr 1972 W		

				Malta
S: 17 Apr 1969 W R: 6 Feb 1970 W	S: 11 Feb 1971 LW R: 4 May 1971 W	S: 11 Sep 1972 L R: 7 Apr 1975 L		
				Mauritania
				Mauritius

S: 1 Jul 1968 W
R: 8 Apr 1969 W
    14 Apr 1969 L
    25 Apr 1969 M
S.A.: 31 Jan 1973
	S: 11 Feb 1971 W
	R: 23 Apr 1971 W
	    3 May 1971 L
	    18 May 1971 M
		S: 10 Apr 1972 W
		R: 7 Aug 1972 W
		    11 Jan 1973 L
		    15 Jan 1973 M		

				Mexico
S:[11] 26 Jul 1968 LMW R: 21 Jan 1969 LMW S.A.: 14 Sep 1973		S:[6] 10 Apr 1972 LMW R: 8 Apr 1974 LMW		

Implementation of multilateral agreements

Antarctic Treaty	Partial Test Ban Treaty	Outer Space Treaty	Treaty of Tlatelolco
Mongolia	S: 8 Aug 1963 LM R: 1 Nov 1963 M 7 Nov 1963 L	S: 27 Jan 1967 M R: 10 Oct 1967 M	

Morocco	S: 27 Aug 1963 MW
	   30 Aug 1963 L
	R: 1 Feb 1966 L
	   18 Feb 1966 M
	   21 Feb 1966 W
		R: 21 Dec 1967 LM
		   22 Dec 1967 W	

Nepal	S: 26 Aug 1963 LM
	   30 Aug 1963 W
	R: 7 Oct 1964 LMW
		S: 3 Feb 1967 MW
		   6 Feb 1967 L
		R: 10 Oct 1967 L
		   16 Oct 1967 M
		   22 Nov 1967 W	

Netherlands R: 30 Mar 1967	S: 9 Aug 1963 LMW R: 14 Sep 1964 LMW	S: 10 Feb 1967 LMW R: 10 Oct 1969 LMW	P.I:[9] S: 15 Mar 1968 R: 26 Jul 1971
New Zealand S: 1 Dec 1959 R: 1 Nov 1960	S: 8 Aug 1963 LMW R: 10 Oct 1963 LW 16 Oct 1963 M	S: 27 Jan 1967 LMW R: 31 May 1968 LMW	

Nicaragua	S: 13 Aug 1963 LW
	   16 Aug 1963 M
	R: 26 Jan 1965 L
	   26 Feb 1965 MW
		S: 27 Jan 1967 W
		   13 Feb 1967 L
			S: 15 Feb 1967
			R:[2,10] 14 Oct 1968
			S.A.:[14]

Niger	S: 24 Sep 1963 LW
	R: 3 Jul 1964 M
	   6 Jul 1964 L
	   9 Jul 1964 W
		S: 1 Feb 1967 W
		R: 17 Apr 1967 L
		   3 May 1967 W	

Nigeria	S: 30 Aug 1963 M
	   2 Sep 1963 L
	   4 Sep 1963 W
	R: 17 Feb 1967 L
	   25 Feb 1967 M
	   28 Feb 1967 W
		R: 14 Nov 1967 L	

Major post-World War II agreements

Non-Proliferation Treaty	Sea-Bed Treaty	BW Convention	ENMOD Convention
			Mongolia

S: 1 Jul 1968   M
R: 14 May 1969   M
S.A.: 5 Sep 1972
	S: 11 Feb 1971 LM
	R: 8 Oct 1971 M
	    15 Nov 1971 L
		S: 10 Apr 1972 LMW
		R: 5 Sep 1972 W
		    14 Sep 1972 L
		    20 Oct 1972 M
			S: 18 May 1977

			Morocco

S: 1 Jul 1968   LMW
R: 27 Nov 1970   M
    30 Nov 1970   L
    16 Dec 1970   W
S.A.: 18 Feb 1975
	S: 11 Feb 1971 MW
	    18 Feb 1971 L
	R: 26 Jul 1971 L
	     5 Aug 1971 W
	    18 Jan 1972 M
		S: 2 May 1972 L
		     3 May 1972 W
		     5 Jun 1972 M
			S: 18 May 1977

			Nepal

S: 1 Jul 1968   LMW
R: 5 Jan 1970   W
     9 Jan 1970   M
     3 Feb 1970   L
S.A.: 22 Jun 1972
	S: 11 Feb 1971 MW
	    24 Feb 1971 L
	R: 6 Jul 1971 L
	    29 Jul 1971 M
	     9 Aug 1971 W
		S: 10 Apr 1972 LMW	

			Netherlands
S: 20 Aug 1968 LMW R: 2 May 1975 LMW S.A.: 21 Feb 1977	S: 11 Feb 1971 LMW R: 14 Jan 1976 LMW	S: 10 Apr 1972 LMW	S: 18 May 1977
			New Zealand

S: 1 Jul 1968   LMW
R: 10 Sep 1969   LMW
S.A.: 29 Feb 1972
	S: 11 Feb 1971 LMW
	R: 24 Feb 1972 LMW
		S: 10 Apr 1972 LMW
		R: 13 Dec 1972 W
		    18 Dec 1972 L
		    10 Jan 1973 M	

			Nicaragua
S: 1 Jul 1968 LW R: 6 Mar 1973 W S.A.: 29 Dec 1976	S: 11 Feb 1971 W R: 7 Feb 1973 W	S: 10 Apr 1972 LW R: 7 Aug 1975 W	S: 11 Aug 1977
			Niger
	S: 11 Feb 1971 W R: 9 Aug 1971 W	S: 21 Apr 1972 W R: 23 Jun 1972 W	
			Nigeria

S: 1 Jul 1968   LMW
R: 27 Sep 1968   L
     7 Oct 1968   W
    14 Oct 1968   M
		S: 3 Jul 1972 M
		    10 Jul 1972 L
		     6 Dec 1972 W
		R: 3 Jul 1973 W
		     9 Jul 1973 L
		    20 Jul 1973 M	

175

Implementation of multilateral agreements

Antarctic Treaty	Partial Test Ban Treaty	Outer Space Treaty	Treaty of Tlatelolco
Norway S: 1 Dec 1959 R: 24 Aug 1960	S: 9 Aug 1963 LMW R: 21 Nov 1963 LMW	S: 3 Feb 1967 LMW R: 1 Jul 1969 LMW	
Pakistan	S: 14 Aug 1963 LMW	S: 12 Sep 1967 LMW R: 8 Apr 1968 LMW	
Panama	S: 20 Sep 1963 W R: 24 Feb 1966 W	S: 27 Jan 1967 W	S: 14 Feb 1967 R:[a] 11 Jun 1971
Paraguay	S: 15 Aug 1963 LW 21 Aug 1963 M		S: 26 Apr 1967 R:[a] 19 Mar 1969

Peru	S: 23 Aug 1963 LMW
	R: 20 Jul 1964 W
	   4 Aug 1964 L
	   21 Aug 1964 M
		S: 30 Jun 1967 W	S: 14 Feb 1967
			R:[a] 4 Mar 1969

Philippines	S: 8 Aug 1963 LW
	   14 Aug 1963 M
	R:[a] 10 Nov 1965 L
	   15 Nov 1965 W
	   8 Feb 1966 M
		S: 27 Jan 1967 LW
		   29 Apr 1967 M	

Poland R: 8 Jun 1961	S: 8 Aug 1963 LMW R: 14 Oct 1963 LMW	S: 27 Jan 1967 LMW R: 30 Jan 1968 LMW	
Portugal	S: 9 Oct 1963 LW		

Major post-World War II agreements

Non-Proliferation Treaty	Sea-Bed Treaty	BW Convention	ENMOD Convention	
				Norway
S: 1 Jul 1968 LMW R: 5 Feb 1969 LMW S.A.: 1 Mar 1972	S: 11 Feb 1971 LMW R: 28 Jun 1971 LM 29 Jun 1971 W	S: 10 Apr 1972 LMW R: 1 Aug 1973 LW 23 Aug 1973 M	S: 18 May 1977	
				Pakistan
		S: 10 Apr 1972 LMW R: 25 Sep 1974 M 3 Oct 1974 LW		
				Panama
S: 1 Jul 1968 W R: 13 Jan 1977 W	S: 11 Feb 1971 W R: 20 Mar 1974 W	S: 2 May 1972 W R: 20 Mar 1974 W		
				Paraguay
S: 1 Jul 1968 W R: 4 Feb 1970 W 5 Mar 1970 L	S: 23 Feb 1971 W	R: 9 Jun 1976 W		
				Peru
S: 1 Jul 1968 W R: 3 Mar 1970 W		S: 10 Apr 1972 LMW		
				Philippines
S: 1 Jul 1968 W 18 Jul 1968 M R: 5 Oct 1972 W 16 Oct 1972 L 20 Oct 1972 M S.A.: 16 Oct 1974		S: 10 Apr 1972 LW 21 Jun 1972 M R: 21 May 1973 W		
				Poland
S: 1 Jul 1968 LMW R: 12 Jun 1969 LMW S.A.: 11 Oct 1972	S: 11 Feb 1971 LMW R: 15 Nov 1971 LMW	S: 10 Apr 1972 LMW R: 25 Jan 1973 LMW	S: 18 May 1977	
				Portugal
R: 15 Dec 1977 LM	R: 24 Jun 1975 LMW	S: 29 Jun 1972 W R: 15 May 1975 LMW	S: 18 May 1977	

Implementation of multilateral agreements

Antarctic Treaty	Partial Test Ban Treaty	Outer Space Treaty	Treaty of Tlatelolco

Qatar

Romania
R:[a] 15 Sep 1971 | S: 8 Aug 1963 LMW
R: 12 Dec 1963 LMW | S: 27 Jan 1967 LMW
R: 9 Apr 1968 LMW |

Rwanda
| | S: 19 Sep 1963 W
R: 22 Oct 1963 L
    16 Dec 1963 M
    27 Dec 1963 W | S: 27 Jan 1967 W | |

Samoa
| | S: 5 Sep 1963 L
    6 Sep 1963 MW
R: 15 Jan 1965 W
    19 Jan 1965 L
    8 Feb 1965 M | | |

San Marino
| | S: 17 Sep 1963 W
    20 Sep 1963 L
    24 Sep 1963 M
R: 3 Jul 1964 L
    9 Jul 1964 W
    27 Nov 1964 M | S: 21 Apr 1967 W
    24 Apr 1967 L
    6 Jun 1967 M
R: 29 Oct 1968 W
    21 Nov 1968 M
    3 Feb 1969 L | |

Saudi Arabia
| | | R: 17 Dec 1976 W | |

Senegal
| | S: 20 Sep 1963 W
    23 Sep 1963 L
    9 Oct 1963 M
R: 6 May 1964 L
    12 May 1964 M
    2 Jun 1964 W | | |

Seychelles

Major post-World War II agreements

Non-Proliferation Treaty	Sea-Bed Treaty	BW Convention	ENMOD Convention	
				Qatar
	R: 12 Nov 1974 L	S: 14 Nov 1972 L R: 17 Apr 1975 L		
				Romania
S: 1 Jul 1968 LMW R: 4 Feb 1970 LMW S.A.: 27 Oct 1972	S: 11 Feb 1971 LMW R:[8] 10 Jul 1972 LMW	S: 10 Apr 1972 LMW	S: 18 May 1977	
				Rwanda
R: 20 May 1975 LMW	S: 11 Feb 1971 W R: 20 May 1975 LMW	S: 10 Apr 1972 MW R: 20 May 1975 LMW		
				Samoa
R: 17 Mar 1975 M 18 Mar 1975 W 26 Mar 1975 L				
				San Marino
S:[9] 1 Jul 1968 W 29 Jul 1968 L 21 Nov 1968 M R: 10 Aug 1970 L 20 Aug 1970 M 31 Aug 1970 W		S: 12 Sep 1972 W 30 Jan 1973 M 21 Mar 1973 L R: 11 Mar 1975 L 17 Mar 1975 W 27 Mar 1975 M		
				Saudi Arabia
	S: 7 Jan 1972 W R: 23 Jun 1972 W	S: 12 Apr 1972 W R: 24 May 1972 W		
				Senegal
S: 1 Jul 1968 MW 26 Jul 1968 L R: 17 Dec 1970 M 22 Dec 1970 W 15 Jan 1971 L	S: 17 Mar 1971 W	S: 10 Apr 1972 W R: 26 Mar 1975 W		
				Seychelles
	R: 29 Jun 1976 W			

Implementation of multilateral agreements

Antarctic Treaty	Partial Test Ban Treaty	Outer Space Treaty	Treaty of Tlatelolco
Sierra Leone			
	S: 4 Sep 1963 L	S: 27 Jan 1967 LM	
	9 Sep 1963 M	16 May 1967 W	
	11 Sep 1963 W	R: 13 Jul 1967 M	
	R: 21 Feb 1964 L	14 Jul 1967 W	
	4 Mar 1964 W	25 Oct 1967 L	
	29 Apr 1964 M		
Singapore			
	R:[1] 12 Jul 1968 MW	R: 10 Sep 1976 LMW	
	23 Jul 1968 L		
Somalia			
	S: 19 Aug 1963 MW	S: 2 Feb 1967 W	
South Africa			
S: 1 Dec 1959	R: 10 Oct 1963 LW	S: 1 Mar 1967 W	
R: 21 Jun 1960	22 Nov 1963 M	R: 30 Sep 1968 W	
		8 Oct 1968 L	
Spain			
	S: 13 Aug 1963 W	R: 27 Nov 1968 L	
	14 Aug 1963 L	7 Dec 1968 W	
	R: 17 Dec 1964 LW		
Sri Lanka			
	S: 22 Aug 1963 LW	S: 10 Mar 1967 L	
	23 Aug 1963 M		
	R: 5 Feb 1964 W		
	12 Feb 1964 M		
	13 Feb 1964 L		
Sudan			
	S: 9 Aug 1963 LMW		
	R: 4 Mar 1966 LW		
	28 Mar 1966 M		
Surinam			
			S: 13 Feb 1976
			R:[2] 10 Jun 1977

180

Major post-World War II agreements

Non-Proliferation Treaty	Sea-Bed Treaty	BW Convention	ENMOD Convention	
R: 26 Feb 1975 LMW	S: 11 Feb 1971 L 12 Feb 1971 M 24 Feb 1971 W	S: 7 Nov 1972 W 24 Nov 1972 L R: 29 Jun 1976 LMW		**Sierra Leone**
S: 5 Feb 1970 LMW R: 10 Mar 1976 LMW S.A.: 18 Oct 1977	S: 5 May 1971 LMW R: 10 Sep 1976 LMW	S: 19 Jun 1972 LMW R: 2 Dec 1975 LMW		**Singapore**
S: 1 Jul 1968 LMW R: 5 Mar 1970 L 12 Nov 1970 W		S: 3 Jul 1972 M		**Somalia**
	S: 11 Feb 1971 W R: 14 Nov 1973 W 26 Nov 1973 L	S: 10 Apr 1972 W R: 3 Nov 1975 W		**South Africa**
		S: 10 Apr 1972 LW	S: 18 May 1977	**Spain**
S: 1 Jul 1968 LMW		S: 10 Apr 1972 LMW	S: 8 Jun 1977	**Sri Lanka**
S: 24 Dec 1968 M R: 31 Oct 1973 W 22 Nov 1973 M 10 Dec 1973 L S.A.: 7 Jan 1977	S: 11 Feb 1971 L 12 Feb 1971 M			**Sudan**
R:[2] 30 Jun 1976 W S.A.: 5 Jun 1975				**Surinam**

181

Implementation of multilateral agreements

Antarctic Treaty	Partial Test Ban Treaty	Outer Space Treaty	Treaty of Tlatelolco

Swaziland
  R: 29 May 1969 LW
     3 Jun 1969 M

Sweden
  S: 12 Aug 1963 LMW   S: 27 Jan 1967 LMW
  R: 9 Dec 1963 LMW   R: 11 Oct 1967 LMW

Switzerland
  S: 26 Aug 1963 LMW   S: 27 Jan 1967 LW
  R: 16 Jan 1964 LMW   30 Jan 1967 M
                        R: 18 Dec 1969 LMW

Syria
  S: 13 Aug 1963 LMW   R:[9] 14 Nov 1968 M
  R: 1 Jun 1964 LMW

Taiwan
  S: 23 Aug 1963 W   S: 27 Jan 1967 W
  R: 18 May 1964 W   R: 24 Jul 1970 W

Tanzania: see United Republic of Tanzania

Thailand
  S: 8 Aug 1963 LMW   S: 27 Jan 1967 LMW
  R: 15 Nov 1963 L   R: 5 Sep 1968 L
     21 Nov 1963 M   9 Sep 1968 M
     29 Nov 1963 W   10 Sep 1968 W

Togo
  S: 18 Sep 1963 W   S: 27 Jan 1967 W
  R: 7 Dec 1964 W

Major post-World War II agreements

Non-Proliferation Treaty	Sea-Bed Treaty	BW Convention	ENMOD Convention	
				Swaziland

S: 24 Jun 1969 L
R: 11 Dec 1969 L
  16 Dec 1969 W
  12 Jan 1970 M
S.A.: 28 Jul 1975
	S: 11 Feb 1971 W
	R: 9 Aug 1971 W			

				Sweden
S: 19 Aug 1968 LMW R: 9 Jan 1970 LMW S.A.: 14 Apr 1975	S: 11 Feb 1971 LMW R: 28 Apr 1972 LMW	S: 27 Feb 1975 LMW R: 5 Feb 1976 LMW		
				Switzerland
S: 27 Nov 1969 LMW R:[12] 9 Mar 1977 LMW	S: 11 Feb 1971 LMW R: 4 May 1976 LMW	S: 10 Apr 1972 LMW R:[7] 4 May 1976 LMW		
				Syria
S: 1 Jul 1968 M R:[9] 24 Sep 1969 M		S: 14 Apr 1972 M	S: 4 Aug 1977	
				Taiwan
S: 1 Jul 1968 W R: 27 Jan 1970 W	S: 11 Feb 1971 W R: 22 Feb 1972 W	S: 10 Apr 1972 W R:[8] 9 Feb 1973 W		
				Tanzania
				Thailand
R: 7 Dec 1972 L S.A.: 16 May 1974		S: 17 Jan 1973 W R: 28 May 1975 W		
				Togo
S: 1 Jul 1968 W R: 26 Feb 1970 W	S: 2 Apr 1971 W R: 28 Jun 1971 W	S: 10 Apr 1972 W		

Implementation of multilateral agreements

Antarctic Treaty	Partial Test Ban Treaty	Outer Space Treaty	Treaty of Tlatelolco
Tonga	R:[1] 22 Jun 1971 M 7 Jul 1971 W	R:[1] 22 Jun 1971 L 7 Jul 1971 W 24 Aug 1971 M	
Trinidad and Tobago	S: 12 Aug 1963 LW 13 Aug 1963 M R: 14 Jul 1964 W 16 Jul 1964 L 6 Aug 1964 M	S: 24 Jul 1967 L 17 Aug 1967 M 28 Sep 1967 W	S: 27 Jun 1967 R:[2] 3 Dec 1970
Tunisia	S: 8 Aug 1963 W 12 Aug 1963 L 13 Aug 1963 M R: 26 May 1965 LM 3 Jun 1965 W	S: 27 Jan 1967 LW 15 Feb 1967 M R: 28 Mar 1968 L 4 Apr 1968 M 17 Apr 1968 W	
Turkey	S: 9 Aug 1963 LMW R: 8 Jul 1965 LMW	S: 27 Jan 1967 LMW R: 27 Mar 1968 LMW	
Uganda	S: 29 Aug 1963 LW R: 24 Mar 1964 L 2 Apr 1964 W	R: 24 Apr 1968 W	
Ukraine	S: 8 Oct 1963 M R:[3] 30 Dec 1963 M	S:[3] 10 Feb 1967 M R: 31 Oct 1967 M	
Union of Soviet Socialist Republics S: 1 Dec 1959 R: 2 Nov 1960	S: 5 Aug 1963 M R: 10 Oct 1963 LMW	S: 27 Jan 1967 LMW R: 10 Oct 1967 LMW	
United Arab Emirates			

Major post-World War II agreements

Non-Proliferation Treaty	Sea-Bed Treaty	BW Convention	ENMOD Convention	
R:[2] 7 Jul 1971 L 15 Jul 1971 W 24 Aug 1971 M		R: 28 Sep 1976 L		Tonga
S: 20 Aug 1968 W 22 Aug 1968 L				Trinidad and Tobago
S: 1 Jul 1968 LMW R: 26 Feb 1970 LMW	S: 11 Feb 1971 LMW R: 22 Oct 1971 M 28 Oct 1971 L 29 Oct 1971 W	S: 10 Apr 1972 LMW R: 18 May 1973 W 30 May 1973 M 6 Jun 1973 L		Tunisia
S: 28 Jan 1969 LMW	S: 25 Feb 1971 LMW R: 19 Oct 1972 W 25 Oct 1972 L 30 Oct 1972 M	S: 10 Apr 1972 LMW R: 25 Oct 1974 M 4 Nov 1974 L 5 Nov 1974 W	S:[1] 18 May 1977	Turkey
			S: 18 May 1977	Uganda
	S: 3 Mar 1971 M R: 3 Sep 1971 M	S: 10 Apr 1972 M R: 26 Mar 1975 M	S: 18 May 1977	Ukraine
S: 1 Jul 1968 LMW R: 5 Mar 1970 LMW	S: 11 Feb 1971 LMW R: 18 May 1972 LMW	S: 10 Apr 1972 LMW R: 26 Mar 1975 LMW	S: 18 May 1977	Union of Soviet Socialist Republics
		S: 28 Sep 1972 L		United Arab Emirates

185

Implementation of multilateral agreements

Antarctic Treaty	Partial Test Ban Treaty	Outer Space Treaty	Treaty of Tlatelolco
United Kingdom S: 1 Dec 1959 R: 31 May 1960	S: 5 Aug 1963 M R:[8] 10 Oct 1963 LMW	S: 27 Jan 1967 LMW R:[10] 10 Oct 1967 LMW	P.I:[11] S: 20 Dec 1967 R: 11 Dec 1969 P.II:[11] S: 20 Dec 1967 R: 11 Dec 1969
United Republic of Cameroon	S:[2] 27 Aug 1963 W 6 Sep 1963 L	S: 27 Jan 1967 W	
United Republic of Tanzania	S: 16 Sep 1963 L 18 Sep 1963 W 20 Sep 1963 M R: 6 Feb 1964 L		
United States S: 1 Dec 1959 R: 18 Aug 1960	S: 5 Aug 1963 M R: 10 Oct 1963 LMW	S: 27 Jan 1967 LMW R: 10 Oct 1967 LMW	P.I: S: 26 May 1977 P.II:[12] S: 1 Apr 1968 R: 12 May 1971
Upper Volta	S: 30 Aug 1963 W	S: 3 Mar 1967 W R: 18 Jun 1968 W	
Uruguay	S: 12 Aug 1963 W 27 Sep 1963 LM R: 25 Feb 1969 L	S: 27 Jan 1967 W 30 Jan 1967 M R: 31 Aug 1970 W	S: 14 Feb 1967 R:[2] 20 Aug 1968 S.A.:[14]
Venezuela	S: 16 Aug 1963 MW 20 Aug 1963 L R: 22 Feb 1965 M 3 Mar 1965 L 29 Mar 1965 W	S: 27 Jan 1967 W R: 3 Mar 1970 W	S: 14 Feb 1967 R:[2,13] 23 Mar 1970
Viet Nam*			

Major post-World War II agreements

Non-Proliferation Treaty	Sea-Bed Treaty	BW Convention	ENMOD Convention	
				United Kingdom
S: 1 Jul 1968 LMW R:[13] 27 Nov 1968 LW 29 Nov 1968 M S.A.:[14] 6 Sep 1976	S: 11 Feb 1971 LMW R:[9] 18 May 1972 LMW	S: 10 Apr 1972 LMW R:[9] 26 Mar 1975 LMW	S: 18 May 1977	
				United Republic of Cameroon
S: 17 Jul 1968 W 18 Jul 1968 M R: 8 Jan 1969 W	S: 11 Nov 1971 M			
				United Republic of Tanzania
	S: 11 Feb 1971 W	S: 16 Aug 1972 L		
				United States
S: 1 Jul 1968 LMW R: 5 Mar 1970 LMW S.A:[15]	S: 11 Feb 1971 LMW R: 18 May 1972 LMW	S: 10 Apr 1972 LMW R: 26 Mar 1975 LMW	S: 18 May 1977	
				Upper Volta
S: 25 Nov 1968 W 11 Aug 1969 M R: 3 Mar 1970 W				
				Uruguay
S: 1 July 1968 W R: 31 Aug 1970 W S.A.: 17 Sep 1976	S: 11 Feb 1971 W			
				Venezuela
S: 1 Jul 1968 W R: 25 Sep 1975 L 26 Sep 1975 W 3 Oct 1975 M		S: 10 Apr 1972 W		
				Viet Nam*

Antarctic Treaty	Partial Test Ban Treaty	Outer Space Treaty	Treaty of Tlateloco
Yemen**	S: 13 Aug 1963 M 6 Sep 1963 W		
Yugoslavia	S: 8 Aug 1963 LMW R: 15 Jan 1964 L 31 Jan 1964 M 3 Apr 1964 W	S: 27 Jan 1967 LMW	
Zaire	S: 9 Aug 1963 LW 12 Aug 1963 M R: 28 Oct 1965 W	S: 27 Jan 1967 W 29 Apr 1967 M 4 May 1967 L	
Zambia	R:[1] 11 Jan 1965 MW 8 Feb 1965 L	R: 20 Aug 1973 W 21 Aug 1973 M 28 Aug 1973 L	

* South Viet Nam signed the Partial Test Ban Treaty (on 1 October 1963), the Outer Space Treaty (on 27 January 1967), the Non-Proliferation Treaty (on 1 July 1968), the Sea-Bed Treaty (on 11 February 1971) and the BW Convention (on 10 April 1972); it ratified the Non-Proliferation Treaty (on 10 September 1971) and concluded a safeguards agreement with the IAEA under that Treaty (on 9 January 1974). On 30 April 1975, the Republic of South Viet Nam ceased to exist as a separated political entity. As from 2 July 1976, North and South Viet Nam constitute a single state under the official name of the Socialist Republic of Viet Nam. The government of the unified state may decide whether it will adhere to international commitments undertaken by the former administration.

** Yemen refers to the Yemen Arab Republic (Northern Yemen). For the People's Democratic Republic of Yemen (Southern Yemen), see Democratic Yemen.

The Antarctic Treaty
[1] The German Democratic Republic stated that in its view Article XIII, paragraph 1 of the Antarctic Treaty was inconsistent with the principle that all states whose policies are guided by the purposes and principles of the United Nations Charter have a right to become parties to treaties which affect the interests of all states.

[2] Romania stated that the provisions of Article XIII, paragraph 1 of the Antarctic Treaty were not in accordance with the principle according to which multilateral treaties whose object and purposes concern the international community, as a whole, should be open for universal participation.

The Partial Test Ban Treaty
[1] Notification of succession.
[2] With a statement that this does not imply the recognition of any territory or régime not recognized by this state.
[3] The United States considers that Byelorussia and Ukraine are already covered by the signature and ratification by the USSR.
[4] Egypt stated that its ratification of the Treaty does not mean or imply any recognition of Israel or any treaty relations with Israel.
[5] The United States did not accept the notification of signature and deposit of ratification of the Treaty in Moscow by the German Democratic Republic, which it then did not recognize as a state. On 4 September 1974, the two countries established diplomatic relations with each other.
[6] The Federal Republic of Germany stated that the Treaty applies also to *Land* Berlin.
[7] Kuwait stated that its signature and ratification of the

Major post-World War II agreements

Non-Proliferation Treaty	Sea-Bed Treaty	BW Convention	ENMOD Convention	
				Yemen**
S: 23 Sep 1968 M	S: 23 Feb 1971 M	S: 10 Apr 1972 W 17 Apr 1972 M 10 May 1972 L	S: 18 May 1977 R: 20 Jul 1977	
				Yugoslavia
S: 10 Jul 1968 LMW R:[16] 4 Mar 1970 W 5 Mar 1970 LM S.A.: 28 Dec 1973	S: 2 Mar 1971 LMW R:[10] 25 Oct 1973 LMW	S: 10 Apr 1972 LMW R: 25 Oct 1973 LMW		
				Zaire
S: 22 Jul 1968 W 26 Jul 1968 M 17 Sep 1968 L R: 4 Aug 1970 W S.A.: 9 Nov 1972		S: 10 Apr 1972 MW R: 16 Sep 1975 L 28 Jan 1977 W		
				Zambia
	R: 9 Oct 1972 L 1 Nov 1972 W 2 Nov 1972 M			

Treaty does not in any way imply its recognition of Israel, nor does it oblige it to apply the provisions of the Treaty in respect of the said country.

[8] The UK stated its view that if a régime is not recognized as the government of a state, neither signature nor the deposit of any instrument by it nor notification of any of those acts will bring about recognition of that régime by any other state.

The Outer Space Treaty

[1] Notification of succession.

[2] The Brazilian government interprets Article X of the Treaty as a specific recognition that the granting of tracking facilities by the parties to the Treaty shall be subject to agreement between the states concerned.

[3] The United States considers that Byelorussia and Ukraine are already covered by the signature and ratification of the USSR.

[4] With a statement that this does not imply the recognition of any territory or régime not recognized by this state.

[5] The USA stated that this did not imply recognition of the German Democratic Republic. On 4 September 1974, the two countries established diplomatic relations with each other.

[6] The Federal Republic of Germany stated that the Treaty applies also to *Land* Berlin.

[7] Kuwait acceded to the Treaty with the understanding that this does not in any way imply its recognition of Israel and does not oblige it to apply the provisions of the Treaty in respect of the said country.

[8] Madagascar acceded to the Treaty with the understanding that under Article X of the Treaty the state shall retain its freedom of decision with respect to the possible installation of foreign observation bases in its territory and shall continue to possess the right to fix, in each case, the conditions for such installation.

[9] Syria acceded to the Treaty with the understanding that this should not mean in any way the recognition of Israel, nor should it lead to any relationship with Israel that could arise from the Treaty.

[10] On depositing its instrument of ratification, the United Kingdom declared that the Treaty will not be applicable in regard to Southern Rhodesia unless and until the United Kingdom informs the other depositary governments that it is in a position to ensure that the obligations imposed by the Treaty in respect of that territory can be fully implemented.

The Treaty of Tlatelolco

[1] Argentina stated that it understands Article 18 as recognizing the right of parties to carry out, by their own means or in association with third parties, explosions of

nuclear devices for peaceful purposes, including explosions which involve devices similar to those used in nuclear weapons.

[2] The Treaty is in force for this country due to a declaration, annexed to the instrument of ratification in accordance with Article 28, paragraph 2, which waived the requirements specified in paragraph 1 of that Article: namely, that all states in the region deposit the instruments of ratification; that Additional Protocol I and Additional Protocol II be signed and ratified by those states to which they apply; and that agreements on safeguards be concluded with the IAEA. Colombia made this declaration subsequent to the deposit of ratification (on 6 September 1972), as did Nicaragua (on 24 October 1968) and Trinidad and Tobago (on 27 June 1975).

[3] On signing the Treaty, Brazil stated that, according to its interpretation, Article 18 of the Treaty gives the signatories the right to carry out, by their own means or in association with third parties, nuclear explosions for peaceful purposes, including explosions which involve devices similar to those used in nuclear weapons.

[4] Brazil stated that it did not waive the requirements laid down in Article 28 of the Treaty. The Treaty is therefore not yet in force for Brazil. In ratifying the Treaty, Brazil reiterated its interpretation of Article 18, which it made upon signing.

[5] Chile has not waived the requirements laid down in Article 28 of the Treaty. The Treaty is therefore not yet in force for Chile.

[6] On signing Protocol II, China stated, *inter alia:* "China will never use or threaten to use nuclear weapons against non-nuclear Latin American countries and the Latin American nuclear-weapon-free zone; nor will China test, manufacture, produce, stockpile, install or deploy nuclear weapons in these countries or in this zone, or send her means of transportation and delivery carrying nuclear weapons to cross the territory, territorial sea or airspace of Latin American countries. It is necessary to point out that the signing of Additional Protocol II to the Treaty for the Prohibition of Nuclear Weapons in Latin America by the Chinese Government does not imply any change whatsoever in China's principled stand on the disarmament and nuclear weapons issue and, in particular, does not affect the Chinese Government's consistent stand against the treaty on non-proliferation of nuclear weapons and the partial nuclear test ban treaty..."

"The Chinese Government holds that, in order that Latin America may truly become a nuclear-weapon-free zone, all nuclear countries, and particularly the superpowers, which possess huge numbers of nuclear weapons, must first of all undertake earnestly not to use or threaten to use nuclear weapons against the Latin American countries and the Latin American nuclear-weapon-free zone, and they must be asked to undertake to observe and implement the following: (1) dismantling of all foreign military bases in Latin America and refraining from establishing any new foreign military bases there; (2) prohibition of the passage of any means of transportation and delivery carrying nuclear weapons through Latin American territory, territorial sea or air space."

[7] On signing Protocol II, France stated that it interprets the undertaking contained in Article 3 of the Protocol to mean that it presents no obstacle to the full exercise of the right of self-defence enshrined in Article 51 of the United Nations Charter; it takes note of the interpretation of the Treaty given by the Preparatory Commission and reproduced in the Final Act, according to which the Treaty does not apply to transit, the granting or denying of which lies within the exclusive competence of each state party in accordance with the pertinent principles and rules of international law; it considers that the application of the legislation referred to in Article 3 of the Treaty relates to legislation which is consistent with international law. The provisions of Articles 1 and 2 of the Protocol apply to the text of the Treaty of Tlatelolco as it stands at the time when the Protocol is signed by France. Consequently, no amendment to the Treaty that might come into force under the provision of Article 29 thereof would be binding on the government of France without the latter's express consent. If this declaration of interpretation is contested in part or in whole by one or more contracting parties to the Treaty or to Protocol II, these instruments would be null and void as far as relations between the French Republic and the contesting state or states are concerned. On depositing its instrument of ratification of Protocol II, France stated that it did so subject to the statement made on signing the Protocol. On 15 April 1974, France made a supplementary statement to the effect that it was prepared to consider its obligations under Protocol II as applying not only to the signatories of the Treaty, but also to the territories for which the statute of denuclearization was in force in conformity with Article 1 of Protocol I.

[8] In signing the Treaty, Mexico said that if technological progress makes it possible to differentiate between nuclear weapons and nuclear devices for peaceful purposes, it will be necessary to amend the relevant provisions of the Treaty, according to the procedure established therein.

[9] The Netherlands stated that Protocol I shall not be interpreted as prejudicing the position of the Netherlands as regards its recognition or non-recognition of the rights of or claims to sovereignty of the parties to the Treaty, or of the grounds on which such claims are made. With respect to nuclear explosions for peaceful purposes on the territory of Surinam and the Netherlands Antilles, no other rules apply than those operative for the parties to the Treaty. Upon Surinam's accession to independence on 25 November 1975, the obligations of the Netherlands under the Protocol apply only to the Netherlands Antilles.

[10] Nicaragua stated that it reserved the right to use nuclear energy for peaceful purposes such as the removal of earth for the construction of canals, irrigation works, power plants, and so on, as well as to allow the transit of atomic material through its territory.

[11] When signing and ratifying Additional Protocol I and Additional Protocol II, the United Kingdom made the following declarations of understanding:

In connection with Article 3 of the Treaty, defining the term "territory" as including the territorial sea, airspace and any other space over which the state exercises sovereignty in accordance with "its own legislation", the UK does not regard its signing or ratification of the Additional Protocols as implying recognition of any legislation which does not, in its view, comply with the relevant rules of international law.

The Treaty does not permit the parties to carry out explosions of nuclear devices for peaceful purposes unless and until advances in technology have made possible the development of devices for such explosions which are not capable of being used for weapon purposes.

The signing and ratification by the UK could not be regarded as affecting in any way the legal status of any territory for the international relations of which the UK is responsible, lying within the limits of the geographical zone established by the Treaty.

Should a party to the Treaty carry out any act of aggression with the support of a nuclear weapon state, the UK would be free to reconsider the extent to which it could be regarded as committed by the provisions of Additional Protocol II.

In addition, the UK declared that its undertaking under Article 3 of Additional Protocol II not to use or threaten to use nuclear weapons against the parties to the Treaty extends also to territories in respect of which the undertaking under Article 1 of Additional Protocol I becomes effective.

[12] The United States signed and ratified Additional Protocol II with the following declarations of understanding:

In connection with Article 3 of the Treaty, defining the term "territory" as including the territorial sea, airspace and any other space over which the state exercises sovereignty in accordance with "its own legislation", the US ratification of the Protocol could not be regarded as implying recognition of any legislation which did not, in its view, comply with the relevant rules of international law.

Each of the parties retains exclusive power and legal competence, unaffected by the terms of the Treaty, to grant or deny non-parties transit and transport privileges.

As regards the undertaking not to use or threaten to use nuclear weapons against the parties, the United States would consider that an armed attack by a party, in which it was assisted by a nuclear weapon state, would be incompatible with the party's obligations under Article 1 of the Treaty.

The definition contained in Article 5 of the Treaty is understood as encompassing all nuclear explosive devices; Articles 1 and 5 of the Treaty restrict accordingly the activities of the parties under paragraph 1 of Article 18.

Article 18, paragraph 4 permits, and US adherence to Protocol II will not prevent, collaboration by the USA with the parties to the Treaty for the purpose of carrying out explosions of nuclear devices for peaceful purposes in a manner consistent with a policy of not contributing to the proliferation of nuclear weapon capabilities.

The United States will act with respect to such territories of Protocol I adherents, as are within the geographical area defined in Article 4, paragraph 2 of the Treaty, in the same manner as Protocol II requires it to act with respect to the territories of the parties.

[13] Venezuela stated that in view of the existing controversy between Venezuela on the one hand and the United Kingdom and Guyana on the other, Article 25, paragraph 2 of the Treaty should apply to Guyana. This paragraph provides that no political entity should be admitted, part or all of whose territory is the subject of a dispute or claim between an extra-continental country and one or more Latin American states, so long as the dispute has not been settled by peaceful means.

[14] Safeguards under the NPT cover the Treaty of Tlatelolco.

The Non-Proliferation Treaty

[1] On signing the Treaty, Australia stated, *inter alia*, that it regarded it as essential that the Treaty should not affect security commitments under existing treaties of mutual security.

[2] Notification of succession.

[3] On 25 November 1969, the United States notified its non-acceptance of notification of signature and ratification by the German Democratic Republic which it then did not recognize as a state. On 4 September 1974, the two countries established diplomatic relations with each other.

[4] On depositing the instrument of ratification, the Federal Republic of Germany reiterated the declaration made at the time of signing: it reaffirmed its expectation that the nuclear weapon states would intensify their efforts in accordance with the undertakings under Article VI of the Treaty, as well as its understanding that the security of FR Germany continued to be ensured by NATO; it stated that no provision of the Treaty may be interpreted in such a way as to hamper further development of European unification; that research, development and use of nuclear energy for peaceful purposes, as well as international and multinational co-operation in this field, must not be prejudiced by the Treaty; that the application of the Treaty, including the implementation of safeguards, must not lead to discrimination of the nuclear industry of FR Germany in international competition; and that it attached vital importance to the undertaking given by the United States and the United Kingdom concerning the application of safeguards to their peaceful nuclear facilities, hoping that other nuclear weapon states would assume similar obligations.

In a separate note, FR Germany declared that the Treaty will also apply to Berlin (West) without affecting Allied rights and responsibilities, including those relating to demilitarization. In notes of 24 July, 19 August, and 25 November 1975, respectively, addressed to the US Department of State, Czechoslovakia, the USSR and the German Democratic Republic stated that this declaration by FR Germany had no legal effect.

[5] On acceding to the Treaty, the Holy See stated, *inter alia,* that the Treaty will attain in full the objectives of security and peace and justify the limitations to which the states party to the Treaty submit, only if it is fully executed in every clause and with all its implications. This concerns not only the obligations to be applied immediately but also those which envisage a process of ulterior commitments. Among the latter, the Holy See considers it suitable to point out the following:

(*a*) The adoption of appropriate measures to ensure, on a basis of equality, that all non-nuclear weapon states party to the Treaty will have available to them the benefits deriving from peaceful applications of nuclear technology.

(*b*) The pursuit of negotiations in good faith on effective measures relating to cessation of the nuclear arms race at an early date and to nuclear disarmament, and on a treaty on general and complete disarmament under strict and effective international control.

[6] On signing the Treaty, Indonesia stated, *inter alia,* that the government of Indonesia attaches great importance to the declarations of the USA, the UK and the USSR affirming their intention to provide immediate assistance to any non-nuclear weapon state party to the Treaty that is a victim of an act of aggression in which nuclear weapons are used.

Of utmost importance, however, is not the action *after* a nuclear attack has been committed but the guarantees to prevent such an attack. The Indonesian government trusts that the nuclear weapon states will study further this question of effective measures to ensure the security of the non-nuclear weapon states. Its decision to sign the Treaty is not to be taken in any way as a decision to ratify the Treaty. The ratification will be considered after matters of national security, which are of deep concern to the government and people of Indonesia, have been clarified to their satisfaction.

[7] Italy stated that in its belief nothing in the Treaty was an obstacle to the unification of the countries of Western Europe; it noted full compatibility of the Treaty with the existing security agreements; it noted further that when technological progress would allow the development of peaceful explosive devices different from nuclear weapons, the prohibition relating to their manufacture and use shall no longer apply; it interpreted the provisions of Article IX, paragraph 3 of the Treaty, concerning the definition of a militarily nuclear state, in the sense that it referred exclusively to the five countries which had manufactured and exploded a nuclear weapon or other nuclear explosive device prior to 1 January 1967, and stressed that under no circumstance would a claim of pertaining to such category be recognized by the Italian government to any other state.

[8] On depositing the instruments of ratification, Japan expressed the hope that France and China would accede to the Treaty; it urged a reduction of nuclear armaments and a comprehensive ban on nuclear testing; appealed to all states to refrain from the threat or use of force involving either nuclear or non-nuclear weapons; expressed the view that peaceful nuclear activities in non-nuclear weapon states party to the Treaty should not be hampered and that Japan should not be discriminated against in favour of other parties in any aspect of such activities. It also urged all nuclear weapon states to accept IAEA safeguards on their peaceful nuclear activities.

[9] A statement was made containing a disclaimer regarding the recognition of states party to the Treaty.

[10] On depositing the instrument of ratification, the Republic of Korea took note of the fact that the depositary governments of the three nuclear weapon states had made declarations in June 1968 to take immediate and effective measures to safeguard any non-nuclear weapon state which is a victim of an act or an object of a threat of aggression in which nuclear weapons are used. It recalled that the UN Security Council adopted a resolution to the same effect on 19 June 1968.

[11] On signing the Treaty, Mexico stated, *inter alia*, that none of the provisions of the Treaty shall be interpreted as affecting in any way whatsoever the rights and obligations of Mexico as a state party to the Treaty for the Prohibition of Nuclear Weapons in Latin America (Treaty of Tlatelolco).

It is the understanding of Mexico that at the present time any nuclear explosive device is capable of being used as a nuclear weapon and that there is no indication that in the near future it will be possible to manufacture nuclear explosive devices that are not potentially nuclear weapons. However, if technological advances modify this situation, it will be necessary to amend the relevant provisions of the Treaty in accordance with the procedure established therein.

[12] On depositing the instrument of ratification, Switzerland stated that activities not prohibited under Articles I and II of the Treaty include, in particular, the whole field of energy production and related operations, research and technology concerning future generations of nuclear reactors based on fission or fusion, as well as production of isotopes. Switzerland defines the term "source or special fissionable material" in Article III of the Treaty as being in accordance with Article XX of the IAEA Statute, and a modification of this interpretation requires Switzerland's formal consent; it will accept only such interpretations and definitions of the terms "equipment or material especially designed or prepared for the processing, use or production of special fissionable material", as mentioned in Article III of the Treaty, that it will expressly approve; and it understands that the application of the Treaty, especially of the control measures, will not lead to discrimination of Swiss industry in international competition.

[13] The United Kingdom recalled its view that if a régime is not recognized as the government of a state, neither signature nor the deposit of any instrument by it, nor notification of any of those acts, will bring about recognition of that régime by any other state. The provisions of the Treaty shall not apply with regard to Southern Rhodesia unless and until the government of the United Kingdom informs the other depositary governments that it is in a position to ensure that the obligations imposed by the Treaty in respect of that territory can be fully implemented. Cameroon stated that it was unable to accept the reservation concerning Southern Rhodesia. Also Mongolia stated that the obligations assumed by the United Kingdom under the Non-Proliferation Treaty should apply equally to Southern Rhodesia. In a note addressed to the British Embassy in Moscow, the Soviet government expressed the view that the United Kingdom carries the entire responsibility for Southern Rhodesia until the people of that territory acquire genuine independence, and that this fully applies to the Non-Proliferation Treaty.

[14] This agreement, signed between the United Kingdom, Euratom and the IAEA, provides for the submission of British non-military nuclear installations to safeguards under IAEA supervision. By 31 December 1977 it was not yet in force.

[15] This agreement, under which US civilian nuclear facilities will be placed under IAEA safeguards, was approved by the IAEA Board but not signed by 31 December 1977.

[16] In connection with the ratification of the Treaty, Yugoslavia stated, *inter alia*, that it considered a ban on the development, manufacture and use of nuclear weapons and the destruction of all stockpiles of these weapons to be indispensable for the maintenance of a stable peace and international security; it held the view that the chief responsibility for progress in this direction rested with the nuclear weapon powers, and expected these powers to undertake not to use nuclear weapons against the countries which have renounced them as well as against non-nuclear weapon states in general, and to refrain from the threat to use them. It also emphasized the significance it attached to the universality of the efforts relating to the realization of the NPT.

The Sea-Bed Treaty

[1] On signing the Treaty, Argentina stated that it interprets the references to the freedom of the high seas as in no way implying a pronouncement of judgement on the different positions relating to questions connected with international maritime law. It understands that the reference to the rights of exploration and exploitation by coastal states over their continental shelves was included solely

because those could be the rights most frequently affected by verification procedures. Argentina precludes any possibility of strengthening, through this Treaty, certain positions concerning continental shelves to the detriment of others based on different criteria.

[2] On signing the Treaty, Brazil stated that nothing in the Treaty shall be interpreted as prejudicing in any way the sovereign rights of Brazil in the area of the sea, the sea-bed and the subsoil thereof adjacent to its coasts. It is the understanding of the Brazilian government that the word "observation", as it appears in paragraph 1 of Article III of the Treaty, refers only to observation that is incidental to the normal course of navigation in accordance with international law.

[3] In depositing the instrument of ratification Canada declared: Article I, paragraph 1 cannot be interpreted as indicating that any state has a right to implant or emplace any weapons not prohibited under Article I, paragraph 1 on the sea-bed and ocean floor, and in the subsoil thereof, beyond the limits of national jurisdiction, or as constituting any limitation on the principle that this area of the sea-bed and ocean floor and the subsoil thereof shall be reserved for exclusively peaceful purposes. Articles I, II and III cannot be interpreted as indicating that any state but the coastal state has any right to implant or emplace any weapon not prohibited under Article I, paragraph 1 on the continental shelf, or the subsoil thereof, appertaining to that coastal state, beyond the outer limit of the sea-bed zone referred to in Article I and defined in Article II. Article III cannot be interpreted as indicating any restrictions or limitation upon the rights of the coastal state, consistent with its exclusive sovereign rights with respect to the continental shelf, to verify, inspect or effect the removal of any weapon, structure, installation, facility or device implanted or emplaced on the continental shelf, or the subsoil thereof, appertaining to that coastal state, beyond the outer limit of the sea-bed zone referred to in Article I and defined in Article II. On 12 April 1976, the Federal Republic of Germany stated that the declaration by Canada is not of a nature to confer on the government of this country more far-reaching rights than those to which it is entitled under current international law, and that all rights existing under current international law which are not covered by the prohibitions are left intact by the Treaty.

[4] A statement was made containing a disclaimer regarding recognition of states party to the Treaty.

[5] On ratifying the Treaty, the Federal Republic of Germany declared that the Treaty will apply to Berlin (West).

[6] On the occasion of its accession to the Treaty, the government of India stated that as a coastal state, India has, and always has had, full and exclusive sovereign rights over the continental shelf adjoining its territory and beyond its territorial waters and the subsoil thereof. It is the considered view of India that other countries cannot use its continental shelf for military purposes. There cannot, therefore, be any restriction on, or limitation of, the sovereign right of India as a coastal state to verify, inspect, remove or destroy any weapon, device, structure, installation or facility, which might be implanted or emplaced on or beneath its continental shelf by any other country, or to take such other steps as may be considered necessary to safeguard its security. The accession by the government of India to the Sea-Bed Treaty is based on this position. In response to the Indian statement, the US government expressed the view that, under existing international law, the rights of coastal states over their continental shelves are exclusive only for purposes of exploration and exploitation of natural resources, and are otherwise limited by the 1958 Convention on the Continental Shelf and other principles of international law. On 12 April 1976, the Federal Republic of Germany stated that the declaration by India is not of a nature to confer on the government of this country more far-reaching rights than those to which it is entitled under current international law, and that all rights existing under current international law which are not covered by the prohibitions are left intact by the Treaty.

[7] On signing the Treaty, Italy stated, *inter alia,* that in the case of agreements on further measures in the field of disarmament to prevent an arms race on the sea-bed and ocean floor and in their subsoil, the question of the delimitation of the area within which these measures would find application shall have to be examined and solved in each instance in accordance with the nature of the measures to be adopted. The statement was repeated at the time of ratification.

[8] Romania stated that it considered null and void the ratification of the Treaty by the Taiwan authorities.

[9] The United Kingdom recalled its view that if a régime is not recognized as the government of a state, neither signature nor the deposit of any instrument by it, nor notification of any of those acts, will bring about recognition of that régime by any other state.

[10] On 25 February 1974, the Ambassador of Yugoslavia transmitted to the US Secretary of State a note stating that in the view of the Yugoslav government, Article III, paragraph 1 of the Treaty should be interpreted in such a way that a state exercising its right under this Article shall be obliged to notify in advance the coastal state, in so far as its observations are to be carried out "within the stretch of the sea extending above the continental shelf of the said state". On 16 January 1975, the US Secretary of State presented the view of the USA concerning the Yugoslav note, as follows: "Insofar as the note is intended to be interpretative of the Treaty, the United States cannot accept it as a valid interpretation. In addition, the United States does not consider that it can have any effect on the existing law of the sea". In so far as the note was intended to be a reservation to the Treaty, the United States placed on record its formal objection to it on the grounds that it was incompatible with the object and purpose of the Treaty. The United States also drew attention to the fact that the note was submitted too late to be legally effective as a reservation. A similar exchange of notes took place between Yugoslavia and the United Kingdom. On 12 April 1976, the Federal Republic of Germany stated that the declaration by Yugoslavia is not of a nature to confer on the government of this country more far-reaching rights than those to which it is entitled under current international law, and that all rights existing under current international law which are not covered by the prohibitions are left intact by the Treaty.

The BW Convention

[1] Considering the obligations resulting from its status as a permanently neutral state, Austria declares a reservation to the effect that its co-operation within the framework of this Convention cannot exceed the limits determined by the status of permanent neutrality and membership with the United Nations.

[2] In a statement made on the occasion of the signature of the Convention, India reiterated its understanding that the objective of the Convention is to eliminate biological and toxin weapons, thereby excluding completely the possibility of their use, and that the exemption in regard to biological agents or toxins, which would be permitted for prophylactic, protective or other peaceful purposes, would not in any way create a loophole in regard to the production or retention of biological and toxin weapons. Also any assistance which might be furnished under the terms of the Convention would be of a medical or humanitarian nature and in conformity with the Charter of the United Nations. The statement was repeated at the time of the deposit of the instrument of ratification.

[3] Ireland considers that the Convention could be undermined if reservations made by the parties to the 1925 Geneva Protocol were allowed to stand, as the prohibition of possession is incompatible with the right to retaliate, and that there should be an absolute and universal prohibition of the use of the weapons in question. Ireland notified the depositary government for the Geneva Protocol of the withdrawal of its reservations to the Protocol, made at the time of accession in 1930. The withdrawal applies to chemical as well as to bacteriological (biological) and toxin agents of warfare.

[4] The Republic of Korea stated that the signing of the Convention does not in any way mean or imply the recognition of any territory or régime which has not been recognized by the Republic of Korea as a state or government.

[5] In the understanding of Kuwait, its ratification of the Convention does not in any way imply its recognition of Israel, nor does it oblige it to apply the provisions of the Convention in respect of the said country.

[6] Mexico considers that the Convention is only a first step towards an agreement prohibiting also the development, production and stockpiling of all chemical weapons, and notes the fact that the Convention contains an express commitment to continue negotiations in good faith with the aim of arriving at such an agreement.

[7] The ratification by Switzerland contains the following reservations:

1. Owing to the fact that the Convention also applies to weapons, equipment or means of delivery designed to use biological agents or toxins, the delimitation of its scope of application can cause difficulties since there are scarcely any weapons, equipment or means of delivery peculiar to such use; therefore, Switzerland reserves the right to decide for itself what auxiliary means fall within that definition.

2. By reason of the obligations resulting from its status as a perpetually neutral state, Switzerland is bound to make the general reservation that its collaboration within the framework of this Convention cannot go beyond the terms prescribed by that status. This reservation refers especially to Article VII of the Convention as well as to any similar clause that could replace or supplement that provision of the Convention (or any other arrangement).

In a note of 18 August 1976, addressed to the Swiss Ambassador, the US Secretary of State stated the following view of the US government, with regard to the first reservation: The prohibition would apply only to (a) weapons, equipment and means of delivery the design of which indicated that they could have no other use than that specified, and (b) weapons, equipment and means of delivery the design of which indicated that they were specifically intended to be capable of the use specified. The government of the United States shares the view of the government of Switzerland that there are few weapons, equipment or means of delivery peculiar to the uses referred to. It does not, however, believe that it would be appropriate, on this ground alone, for states to reserve unilaterally the right to decide which weapons, equipment or means of delivery fell within the definition. Therefore, while acknowledging the entry into force of the Convention between itself and the government of Switzerland, the United States government enters its objection to this reservation.

[8] The USSR stated that it considered the deposit of the instrument of ratification by Taiwan as an illegal act, because the government of the Chinese People's Republic is the sole representative of China.

[9] The United Kingdom recalled its view that if a régime is not recognized as the government of a state, neither signature nor the deposit of any instrument by it, nor notification of any of those acts will bring about recognition of that régime by any other state. It declared that the provisions of the Convention shall not apply in regard to Southern Rhodesia unless and until the British government informs the other depositary governments that it is in a position to ensure that the obligations imposed by the Convention in respect of that territory can be fully implemented. In a note addressed to the British Embassy in Moscow, the Soviet government expressed the view that the United Kingdom carries the entire responsibility for Southern Rhodesia until the people of that territory acquire genuine independence, and that this fully applies to the BW Convention.

The ENMOD Convention

[1] On signing the Convention, Turkey declared that the terms "widespread", "long-lasting" and "severe effects" contained in the Convention need to be more clearly defined, and that so long as this clarification was not made, Turkey would be compelled to interpret the terms in question and, consequently, reserved the right to do so as and when required. Turkey also stated its belief that the difference between "military or any other hostile purposes" and "peaceful purposes" should be more clearly defined so as to prevent subjective evaluations.

APPENDIX A

Member states of the United Nations and other states party to major arms control agreements (listed in Chapter 3)

NOTE

The names of states used here are in accordance with UN practice. The estimates for population, gross national product (GNP) and military expenditures relate to the year 1975 unless otherwise indicated, the latter two estimates being preliminary and given in prices current for that year.

Primary sources

For area, *Demographic Yearbook 1975* (United Nations, New York, 1976).
For population, *Monthly Bulletin of Statistics* (United Nations, New York, June 1977).
For gross national product, *World Bank Atlas* (World Bank, Washington, 1976).
For military expenditures, the *SIPRI Yearbooks*.

State	Year of UN admission	Area[a] km^2	Population[a] mn	Per capita GNP US $	Per capita military expenditure US $[b]
Afghanistan	1946	647 497	19.28	112	3
Albania	1955	28 748	2.48	585	62
Algeria	1962	2 381 741	16.78	732	16
Angola	1976	1 246 700	5.47[c]	678	..
Argentina	1945	2 766 889	25.38	1 569	54
Australia	1945	7 686 848	13.50	5 644	178
Austria	1955	83 849	7.52	4 723	58
Bahamas	1973	13 935	0.20	2 650	..
Bahrain	1971	622	0.26	2 423	54
Bangladesh	1974	143 998	76.82	115	1
Barbados	1966	431	0.25	1 240	4[w]
Belgium	1945	30 513	9.80	6 065	194
Benin	1960	112 622	3.11	135	2
Bhutan	1971	47 000	1.18[c]	76	..
Bolivia	1945	1 098 581	5.63	314	9
Botswana	1966	600 372	0.69	319	..
Brazil	1945	8 511 965	106.23	1 015	12
Bulgaria	1955	110 912	8.72	2 038	54/193
Burma	1948	676 552	30.34	108	4
Burundi	1962	27 834	3.76	98	2
Byelorussia	1945	207 600	9.34[d]	..[e]	..[e]
Cambodia: see Democratic Kampuchea					
Cameroon: see United Republic of Cameroon					
Canada	1945	9 976 139	22.83	6 646	135
Cape Verde	1975	4 033	0.29	483[f]	..
Central African Empire	1960	622 984	1.79[c]	229	4
Chad	1960	1 284 000	4.03	122	6
Chile	1945	756 945	10.25	785	16

UN members and other parties to major arms control agreements

State	Year of UN admission	Area[a] km²	Population[a] mn	Per capita GNP US $	Per capita military expenditure US $[b]
China	1945	9 596 961[a]	838.80[a]	341	33
Colombia	1945	1 138 914	23.54	559	5
Comoros	1975	2 171	0.31	226	..
Congo	1960	342 000	1.35	489	19
Costa Rica	1945	50 700	1.97	909	6
Cuba	1945	114 524	9.33	796	42
Cyprus	1960	9 251	0.64	1 156	34
Czechoslovakia	1945	127 869	14.80	3 719	153/215
Dahomey: see Benin					
Democratic Kampuchea (Cambodia)	1955	181 035	8.11	70[f]	8[x]
Democratic Yemen[h]	1967	332 968	1.69	243	24
Denmark	1945	43 069	5.06	6 923	182
Djibouti	1977	22 000	0.10[d]	1 800[f]	..
Dominican Republic	1945	48 734	4.70	719	12
Ecuador	1945	283 561	6.73	578	15
Egypt	1945	1 001 449	37.23	310	112
El Salvador	1945	21 041	4.01	454	7
Equatorial Guinea	1968	28 051	0.31	323	16
Ethiopia	1945	1 221 900	27.94	102	5
Fiji	1970	18 272	0.57	912	2
Finland	1955	337 009	4.71	5 096	84
France	1945	547 026	52.79	5 770	247
Gabon	1960	267 667	0.53	2 264	32
Gambia	1965	11 295	0.52	192	..
German Democratic Republic	1973	108 178	16.85	4 228	167/231
Germany, Federal Republic of	1973	248 577	61.83	6 611	247
Ghana	1957	238 537	9.87	464	9
Greece	1945	131 944	9.05	2 376	150
Grenada	1974	344	0.10	400	..
Guatemala	1945	108 889	6.08	581	7
Guinea	1958	245 957	4.42	161	5
Guinea-Bissau	1974	36 125	0.53	396[f]	..
Guyana	1966	214 969	0.79	396	13
Haiti	1945	27 750	4.58	177	2
Holy See[i] (Vatican City)	–	0[j]	0[k]	..	..
Honduras	1945	112 088	3.04	332	6
Hungary	1955	93 030	10.54	2 473	65/135
Iceland	1946	103 000	0.22	5 682	..
India	1945	3 287 590	598.10	154	5
Indonesia	1950	1 904 345	136.04	178	7
Iran	1945	1 648 000	33.02	1 478	220
Iraq	1945	434 924	11.12	1 282	169
Ireland	1955	70 283	3.13	2 415	42
Israel	1949	20 770	3.39	3 658	1 152
Italy	1955	301 225	55.81	2 941	85

UN members and other parties to major arms control agreements

State	Year of UN admission	Area[a] km²	Population[a] mn	Per capita GNP US $	Per capita military expenditure US $[b]
Ivory Coast	1960	322 463	4.89	685	9
Jamaica	1962	10 991	2.04	336	9
Japan	1956	372 313	110.56	4 479	41
Jordan	1955	97 740	2.70	459	64
Kampuchea: see Democratic Kampuchea					
Kenya	1963	582 646	13.40	216	4
Korea, South[l]	–	98 484	35.28	529	27
Kuwait	1963	17 818	1.00	11 280	914
Lao People's Democratic Republic	1955	236 800	3.30	67[f]	5
Lebanon	1945	10 400	2.87	1 146[f]	48
Lesotho	1966	30 355	1.04	202	..
Liberia	1945	111 369	1.71	368	3
Libya	1955	1 759 540	2.44	5 082	803
Luxembourg	1945	2 586	0.36	6 111	64
Madagascar	1960	587 041	8.02	216	3
Malawi	1964	118 484	5.04	151	1
Malaysia	1957	329 749	11.90	730	36
Maldives	1965	298	0.12	83[f]	..
Mali	1960	1 240 000	5.70	95	2
Malta	1964	316	0.30	1 607[m]	7[w]
Mauritania	1961	1 030 700	1.32	311	21
Mauritius	1968	2 045	0.86	593	10
Mexico	1945	1 972 547	60.15	1 183	10
Mongolia	1961	1 565 000	1.44	694	78
Morocco	1956	446 550	17.31	456	13
Mozambique	1975	783 030	9.24	308	..
Nepal	1955	140 797	12.57	111	1
Netherlands	1945	40 844	13.65	5 593	210
New Zealand	1945	268 676[n]	3.07	4 710	74
Nicaragua	1945	130 000	2.16	699	13
Niger	1960	1 267 000	4.60	130	1
Nigeria	1960	923 768	62.93	367	29
Norway	1945	324 219	4.01	6 544	228
Oman	1971	212 457	0.77	2 078	906
Pakistan	1947	803 943	70.26	140	10
Panama	1945	75 650[o]	1.67[o]	1 060	9
Papua New Guinea	1975	461 691[n]	2.76[n]	442	..
Paraguay	1945	406 752	2.65	551	9
Peru	1945	1 285 216	15.62	802	41
Philippines	1945	300 000	42.52	370	9
Poland	1945	312 677	34.02	2 909	88/150
Portugal	1955	92 082[p]	9.45[p]	1 592	82
Qatar	1971	11 000	0.20[c]	8 400	530[w]
Romania	1955	237 500	21.25	1 301	48/105
Rwanda	1962	26 338	4.20	86	2
Samoa	1976	2 842	0.15	333	..

UN members and other parties to major arms control agreements

State	Year of UN admission	Area[a] km²	Population[a] mn	Per capita GNP US $	Per capita military expenditure US $[b]
San Marino[q]	–	61	0.02	. .	. .
Sao Tome and Principe	1975	964	0.08	500[f]	. .
Saudi Arabia	1945	2 149 690	8.97	2 783	532
Senegal	1960	196 192	4.14	447	8
Seychelles	1976	280	0.06	500[f]	. .
Sierra Leone	1961	71 740	2.98[c]	198	2
Singapore	1965	581	2.25	2 507	138
Somalia	1960	637 657	3.17	101	8
South Africa	1945	1 221 037	25.50	1 315	48
Spain	1955	504 782[r]	35.60[r]	2 686	50
Sri Lanka	1955	65 610	13.99	142	2
Sudan	1956	2 505 813	15.73	287	8
Surinam	1975	163 265	0.42	1 095[f]	. .
Swaziland	1968	17 363	0.49	469	. .
Sweden	1946	449 964	8.19	7 885	286
Switzerland[s]	–	41 288	6.40	8 048	170
Syria	1945	185 180	7.35	663	97
Taiwan[t]	–	35 981[u]	16.00[c]	888	63
Tanzania: see United Republic of Tanzania					
Thailand	1946	514 000	41.87	347	10
Togo	1960	56 000	2.22	266	4
Tonga[v]	–	699	0.10	300[f]	. .
Trinidad and Tobago	1962	5 128	1.08	1 898	6
Tunisia	1956	163 610	5.61	754	12
Turkey	1945	780 576	39.18	883	56
Uganda	1962	236 036	11.55	249	8
Ukraine	1945	603 700	48.83[d]	. .[e]	. .[e]
Union of Soviet Socialist Republics	1945	22 402 200	254.39	2 618	240/468/92[u]
United Arab Emirates	1971	83 600	0.66[c]	10 409	109
United Kingdom	1945	244 046	55.96	3 841	205
United Republic of Cameroon	1960	475 442	6.40	303	8
United Republic of Tanzania	1961	945 087	15.31	163[m]	5
United States	1945	9 363 123	213.54	7 065	426
Upper Volta	1960	274 200	6.03	93	3
Uruguay	1945	177 508	3.06	1 199	31
Venezuela	1945	912 050	11.99	2 224	47
Viet Nam	1977	329 556	45.21	157	. .
Yemen[h]	1947	195 000	6.67	207	9
Yugoslavia	1945	255 804	21.35	1 482	79
Zaire	1960	2 345 409	24.90	150	6
Zambia	1964	752 614	4.98	532	18

[a] Overseas territories are not included, unless otherwise indicated.
[b] For the Warsaw Treaty Organization countries two sets of figures are given: the first based on SIPRI estimates, and the second on those of the US Arms Control and Disarmament Agency (ACDA). See also note w. For the USSR, three sets of figures are given; see note y.
[c] Source: *World Bank Atlas* (World Bank, Washington, 1976).
[d] Population data for 1974. Source: *Statistisk Årsbok för Sverige 1976* (Statistiska centralbyrån, Stockholm, 1976).
[e] Included in the data for the Union of Soviet Socialist Republics.
[f] Calculated on the basis of the gross national product estimate for 1974.
[g] Including Taiwan. See also separate entry for Taiwan.
[h] The name Democratic Yemen refers to the People's Democratic Republic of Yemen (Southern Yemen). The name Yemen refers to the Yemen Arab Republic (Northern Yemen).
[i] The Holy See, not a UN member, is party to the NPT.
[j] Area: 0.44 km².
[k] Population: 724. Source: *Demographic Yearbook 1975* (United Nations, New York 1976).
[l] South Korea (Republic of Korea), not a UN member, is party to the Partial Test Ban Treaty, the Outer Space Treaty and the NPT. North Korea (Democratic People's Republic of Korea), not a UN member either, has not joined any of the major arms control agreements listed in Chapter 3. The relevant data for North Korea are: area 220 277 km²; population 15.85 million; GNP per capita US $428; military expenditure per capita US $58.
[m] Source: *International Financial Statistics* (International Monetary Fund, Washington, September 1977).
[n] Including islands.
[o] Excluding the Canal Zone.
[p] Including the Azores and Madeira islands.
[q] San Marino, not a UN member, is party to the Partial Test Ban Treaty, the Outer Space Treaty, the NPT and the BW Convention.
[r] Including the Balearic and Canary Islands, as well as Alhucemas, Ceuta, Chafarinas, Melilla and Peñón de Vélex de la Gomera.
[s] Switzerland, not a UN member, is party to the Partial Test Ban Treaty, the Outer Space Treaty, the NPT, the Sea-Bed Treaty and the BW Convention.
[t] Taiwan (Republic of China) is party to the Partial Test Ban Treaty, the Outer Space Treaty, the NPT, the Sea-Bed Treaty and the BW Convention. Until 25 October 1971, Taiwan occupied the place of China at the United Nations. On that day, the UN General Assembly conferred the right of representation on the People's Republic of China and recognized the representatives of its government as the only legitimate representatives of China to the United Nations.
[u] Source: *The Statesman's Year-Book, 1976–1977* (Macmillan, London, 1976).
[v] Tonga, not a UN member, is party to the Partial Test Ban Treaty, the Outer Space Treaty, the NPT and the BW Convention.
[w] Calculated on the basis of estimates given in *World Military Expenditures and Arms Transfers 1966–1975* (US Arms Control and Disarmament Agency, Washington, 1976).
[x] Calculated on the basis of estimates for 1974.
[y] Third figure calculated on the basis of data published in *Narodnoye Hoziaistvo SSR v 1975g* (Statistika, Moscow, 1976), and using the official rate of exchange.

APPENDIX B

Major UN General Assembly arms control resolutions adopted in the Disarmament Decade of the 1970s, and the voting record

NOTE

This list includes resolutions concerning exclusively arms control and disarmament matters, as well as certain other resolutions making reference to arms control. In the latter case, the negative votes or abstentions do not necessarily reflect the positions of states towards the arms control paragraphs of the relevant resolutions.

Only the essential parts of each resolution are given here. The text has been abridged, but the wording is close to that of the resolution.

The resolutions are grouped according to subject, irrespective of the agenda items under which they were discussed.

In the case of non-recorded votes, the voting results may be incomplete.

The formulae "adopted without vote", "adopted without objection", or "adopted by consensus", used instead of a formal vote, are usually understood to denote broad agreement as regards the general lines of the resolution; delegations have sometimes made explanatory statements recording their views or reservations on certain provisions of the adopted text.

The names of states listed under the voting results are in accordance with UN usage at the time of the adoption of any given resolution.

Subject, number, date of adoption, and contents of the resolution	Voting results

Disarmament Decade

2602 E (XXIV)
16 December 1969
Declares the 1970s a Disarmament Decade. Calls on governments to intensify their efforts for effective measures relating to the cessation of the nuclear arms race at an early date and to nuclear disarmament and the elimination of other weapons of mass destruction, and for a treaty on general and complete disarmament under strict and effective international control.

In favour 104
Against 0
Abstentions 13: Bulgaria, Byelorussia, Cuba, Czechoslovakia, El Salvador, France, Hungary, Malawi, Mongolia, Poland, Syria, Ukraine, USSR
Absent or not participating in the vote: Albania, Barbados, Botswana, Cambodia, Dominican Republic,[a] Equatorial Guinea, Gambia, Guinea, Zambia

31/68
10 December 1976
Deplores the meagre achievements of the Disarmament Decade in terms of truly effective disarmament and arms limitation agreements, and the detrimental effects on world peace and economy of the continuing unproductive and wasteful arms race, particularly the nuclear arms race. Calls again upon all states, as well as the organs concerned with disarmament issues, to place at the centre of their preoccupations the adoption of effective measures for the cessation of the arms race, especially in the nuclear field, and for the reduction of military expenditures, and to make sustained efforts with a view to achieving progress towards general and complete disarmament. Calls upon member states and the Secretary-General to intensify their efforts in support of the link between dis-

Adopted without vote

armament and development, so as to promote disarmament negotiations and to ensure that the human and material resources freed by disarmament are used to promote economic and social development, particularly in the developing countries.

Urges the CCD to adopt a comprehensive programme dealing with all aspects of the problem of the cessation of the arms race and general and complete disarmament under strict and effective international control, and calls upon non-governmental organizations and international institutions and organizations to further the goals of the Disarmament Decade.

32/80
12 December 1977

Calls upon member states and the Secretary-General to intensify their efforts in support of the link between disarmament and development envisaged in the General Assembly resolution on the Disarmament Decade, so as to promote disarmament negotiations and to ensure that the human and material resources freed by disarmament are used to promote economic and social development, particularly in the developing countries. Urges that the unparalleled technical possibilities now available to mankind should be exploited for the purposes of combating poverty, ignorance, disease and hunger throughout the world.

In favour 130
Against 0
Abstentions 1: Sierra Leone[a]
Absent or not participating in the vote: Albania, Angola, Central African Empire, China, Comoros, Democratic Kampuchea, Djibouti, Equatorial Guinea, Grenada, Guinea, Madagascar,[a] Malawi, Mauritius,[a] Samoa, Saudi Arabia, Seychelles, Somalia, South Africa

Strategic arms limitation

2661 A (XXV)
7 December 1970

Urges the governments of the nuclear weapon powers to bring about an immediate halt in the nuclear arms race and to cease all testing as well as deployment of offensive and defensive nuclear weapon systems.

In favour 102
Against 0
Abstentions 14: Australia, Austria, Belgium, China, Finland, France, Greece, Haiti, Italy, Luxembourg, Netherlands, Turkey, UK, USA
Absent or not participating in the vote: Albania, Barbados, Botswana, Burundi, Costa Rica, Equatorial Guinea, Guinea, Honduras, Malawi, Maldives, Trinidad and Tobago

31/189 A
21 December 1976

Regrets the absence of positive results in the bilateral negotiations between the governments of the USSR and the USA on the limitation of their strategic nuclear weapon systems. Expresses concern for the very high ceilings on nuclear arms set for themselves by both states, for the total absence of qualitative limitations of such arms, for the protracted timetable contemplated for the negotiation of further limitations and possible reductions of the nuclear arsenals, and for the situation thus created. Urges anew the USSR and the USA to broaden the scope and accelerate the pace of their strategic nuclear arms limitation talks, and stresses once again the necessity and urgency of reaching agreement on important qualitative limitations and substantial reductions of their strategic nuclear weapon systems as a positive step towards nuclear disarmament.

In favour 107
Against 10: Bulgaria, Byelorussia, Czechoslovakia, German Democratic Republic, Hungary, Mongolia, Poland, Ukraine, USA, USSR
Abstentions 11: Belgium, France, Federal Republic of Germany, Greece, Israel, Italy, Lao People's Democratic Republic, Luxembourg, Malawi, Turkey, UK
Absent or not participating in the vote: Albania, Angola, Benin, Cape Verde, China, Comoros, Congo, Cuba, Democratic Kampuchea, El Salvador, Gambia, Haiti, Honduras, Liberia, Mozambique, Samoa, Seychelles, Somalia, South Africa

Subject, number, date of adoption, and contents of the resolution	Voting results
32/87 G 12 December 1977 Regretting the absence of definitive results in the US-Soviet negotiations on the limitation of strategic nuclear weapon systems, notes with satisfaction the statements made on 4 October 1977 by the President of the USA, and on 2 November 1977 by the President of the Supreme Soviet of the USSR. Stresses the necessity and urgency for the USSR and the USA to strive to implement as soon as possible these statements and reiterates with special emphasis the invitation to the governments of both countries to keep the General Assembly informed in good time of the results of their negotiations.	*In favour* 134 *Against* 2: Albania, China *Abstentions* 0 *Absent or not participating in the vote:* Angola, Comoros, Democratic Kampuchea, Djibouti, Equatorial Guinea, Grenada, Madagascar,[a] Malawi, Samoa, Saudi Arabia, Seychelles, South Africa, Viet Nam

Nuclear weapon tests

2828 A (XXVI) 16 December 1971 Reiterates solemnly and most emphatically the condemnation of all nuclear weapon tests and urges the governments of nuclear weapon states to bring to a halt all nuclear weapon tests at the earliest possible date.	*In favour* 74 *Against* 2: Albania, China *Abstentions* 36: Algeria, Australia, Belgium, Bulgaria, Byelorussia, Canada,[a] Central African Republic, Congo, Cuba, Czechoslovakia, Democratic Yemen, Finland, France, Greece, Guinea, Hungary, Italy, Japan, Khmer Republic, Luxembourg, Madagascar, Mongolia, Netherlands, Pakistan, Philippines, Poland, Portugal, Romania, South Africa, Spain, Thailand, Turkey, Ukraine, UK, USA, USSR *Absent or not participating in the vote:* Barbados, Bolivia, Botswana, Gabon, Gambia, Haiti,[a] Iraq,[b] Malawi, Maldives, Mauritania, Mauritius, Nicaragua, Niger, Oman, Panama, Sierra Leone, Sudan, Swaziland, Syria, United Arab Emirates
3078 A (XXVIII) 6 December 1973 Reiterates its conviction that, whatever the differences on the question of verification, there is no valid reason for delaying the conclusion of a comprehensive test ban of the nature contemplated in the preamble to the Treaty banning nuclear weapon tests in the atmosphere, in outer space and under water; once again urges the governments of nuclear weapon states to bring all nuclear weapon tests to a halt without delay, either through a permanent agreement or through unilateral or agreed moratoria.	*In favour* 89 *Against* 5: Albania, China, France, Gabon, Portugal *Abstentions* 33: Afghanistan, Algeria, Belgium, Bulgaria, Burundi, Byelorussia, Central African Republic, Cuba, Czechoslovakia, Democratic Yemen, German Democratic Republic, Federal Republic of Germany, Greece, Haiti, Hungary, Iraq, Italy, Japan, Luxembourg, Malawi, Mongolia, Netherlands, Poland, Romania, Rwanda, Saudi Arabia, South Africa, Syrian Arab Republic, Turkey, Ukraine, UK, USA, USSR *Absent or not participating in the vote:* Ecuador, El Salvador, Equatorial Guinea, Gambia, Guyana, Maldives, Mauritius, Paraguay
3154 A (XXVIII) 14 December 1973 Noting with concern that there has been additional radioactive fall-out resulting in additions to the total doses of ionizing radiation, deplores environmental pollution by ionizing radiation from the testing of nuclear weapons.	*In favour* 86 *Against* 0 *Abstentions* 28: Belgium, Central African Republic, Chad, Democratic Yemen, Denmark, Equatorial Guinea, France, Gabon, Federal Republic of Germany, Ghana,[a] Greece, Ireland, Italy, Luxembourg, Morocco, Netherlands, Nicaragua, Pakistan, Portugal, Qatar, Romania, Saudi Arabia, Senegal, South Africa, Spain, Tunisia, UK, USA *Absent or not participating in the vote:* Albania, Bahamas, Bahrain, Botswana, China, Dominican Republic,

Subject, number, date of adoption, and contents of the resolution	Voting results
	Egypt, El Salvador, Gambia, Iraq, Jamaica, Kuwait, Lebanon, Maldives, Mauritius, Niger, Nigeria,[a] Sierra Leone, Swaziland, Syrian Arab Republic, Trinidad and Tobago[a]
3226 (XXIX) 12 November 1974 Notes with concern that there has been further radioactive contamination from nuclear weapon tests since the UN Scientific Committee on the Effects of Atomic Radiation submitted its last report.	Adopted without objection
3466 (XXX) 11 December 1975 Deplores the continued lack of progress towards a comprehensive test ban agreement; calls upon all nuclear weapon states to bring to a halt all nuclear weapon tests through an agreed suspension subject to review after a specified period, as an interim step towards the conclusion of a formal and comprehensive test ban agreement. Emphasizes the particular responsibility of the nuclear weapon states which are party to international agreements in which they have declared their intention to achieve at the earliest possible date the cessation of the nuclear arms race. Calls upon all states not yet parties to the Treaty banning nuclear weapon tests in the atmosphere, in outer space and under water to adhere to it forthwith; and urges the CCD to give the highest priority to the conclusion of a comprehensive test ban agreement.	*In favour* 106 *Against* 2: Albania, China *Abstentions* 24: Algeria, Belgium, Bulgaria, Burundi, Byelorussia, Cuba, Czechoslovakia, France, German Democratic Republic, Federal Republic of Germany, Greece, Hungary, Italy, Luxembourg, Madagascar, Mauritania, Mongolia, Morocco, Mozambique, Poland, Ukraine, UK, USA, USSR *Absent or not participating in the vote:* Bahamas, Cambodia, Cape Verde, Central African Republic, Ecuador, Gambia, Guinea-Bissau, Maldives, Sao Tome and Principe, South Africa, Surinam, Yemen
32/78 12 December 1977 Reiterates its grave concern that in spite of the repeated resolutions of the General Assembly related to nuclear weapon testing in all environments, adopted by very large majorities, such testing has continued unabated during the past year; notes with satisfaction that negotiations have begun among three nuclear weapon states with a view to drafting an agreement on the subject of this resolution; and declares that the conclusion of such an agreement and its opening for signature would be the best possible augury for the success of the General Assembly special session devoted to disarmament. Urges the three nuclear weapon states to expedite their negotiations with a view to bringing them to a positive conclusion as soon as possible, and to transmit the results for full consideration by the CCD.	*In favour* 126 *Against* 2: Albania, China *Abstentions* 1: France *Absent or not participating in the vote:* Angola, Burma,[a] Central African Empire, Comoros, Democratic Kampuchea, Djibouti, Equatorial Guinea, Grenada, Guinea, Lao People's Democratic Republic, Madagascar,[a] Malawi, Mauritania, Mauritius,[a] Samoa, Saudi Arabia, Seychelles, Somalia, South Africa, Viet Nam

Non-proliferation of nuclear weapons

31/75 10 December 1976 Referring to the Final Declaration of the first Review	*In favour* 115 *Against* 2: Albania, China *Abstentions* 19: Algeria, Argentina, Bhutan, Bolivia,

Subject, number, date of adoption, and contents of the resolution	Voting results
Conference of the parties to the NPT, urgently calls for determined efforts by all nuclear weapon states: (a) to bring about the cessation of the nuclear arms race; (b) to undertake effective measures in the direction of nuclear disarmament; and (c) to find an early solution to the difficulties in reaching agreement to discontinue all test explosions of nuclear weapons for all time as a step towards the realization of these objectives; and emphasizes the particular responsibility of the two major nuclear weapon states in this regard. Stresses the urgency of international co-operative efforts in appropriate forums to prevent the further proliferation of nuclear weapons or other nuclear explosive devices; recognizes that states accepting effective non-proliferation restraints have a right to full access to the peaceful uses of nuclear energy, and underlines the importance of all efforts to increase the availability of energy, particularly for the needs of the developing countries of the world; and requests the International Atomic Energy Agency to accord high priority to its programme of work in these areas.	Brazil, Burma, Chile, Comoros, Cuba, France, India, Mauritania, Mozambique, Nigeria,[c] Pakistan, Portugal, Spain, Uganda, United Republic of Tanzania *Absent or not participating in the vote:* Angola, Cape Verde, Democratic Kampuchea, Guinea, Haiti, Honduras, Sao Tome and Principe, Seychelles, South Africa, Zambia
32/49 8 December 1977 Notes with appreciation the contribution of the International Atomic Energy Agency in facilitating the elaboration of a convention on the physical protection of nuclear materials and urges prompt completion of the work on this convention. Also notes with appreciation the Agency study on regional nuclear fuel cycle centres, the intention of the Agency to continue its research in this field, especially with regard to economic and non-proliferation implications, and the decision of the IAEA Board of Governors to keep the matter of peaceful nuclear explosions under review, seeking the services of the *Ad Hoc* Advisory Group on nuclear explosions for peaceful purposes, as required.	Adopted by consensus
32/87 F 12 December 1977 Emphasizes the particular responsibility of those nuclear weapon states that have already accepted international obligations, namely, in Article VI of the NPT, with respect to the cessation of the nuclear arms race and the discontinuance of nuclear weapon tests, and notes as encouraging the recent efforts under way towards these ends; urges states that as yet have not adhered to the NPT to do so at an early date or, at a minimum, to accept other arrangements involving the application of safeguards to their complete nuclear fuel cycle that would provide satisfactory assurances to the international community against the dangers of proliferation while guaranteeing to the states concerned unhindered and non-discriminatory access to the peaceful benefits of nuclear energy. Emphasizes the importance of common efforts to study satisfactory arrangements for an adequate supply of nuclear fuels and other materials and facilities neces-	*In favour* 111 *Against* 2: Albania, China *Abstentions* 16: Algeria, Benin, Bhutan, Burma, Colombia, France, Guyana, Israel, Kuwait, Mauritania, Pakistan, Peru, Spain, Uganda, United Republic of Tanzania, Zambia *Absent or not participating in the vote:* Angola, Argentina, Barbados, Botswana, Brazil, Chile, Comoros, Cuba, Democratic Kampuchea, Djibouti, Equatorial Guinea, Grenada, India, Madagascar,[a] Malawi, Samoa, Saudi Arabia, Seychelles, South Africa, Viet Nam

sary for the efficient implementation and operation of national nuclear power programmes without jeopardizing the respective fuel cycle policies or international co-operation agreements and contracts for the peaceful uses of nuclear energy, provided that agreed safeguard measures are applied. Solemnly affirms the following principles: (*a*) states should not convert civil nuclear materials or facilities to the production of nuclear weapons; and (*b*) all states have the right, in accordance with the principle of sovereign equality, to develop their programmes for the peaceful use of nuclear technology for economic and social development in conformity with their priorities, interests and needs, and should have, without discrimination, access to, and be free to acquire, technology and materials for the peaceful use of nuclear energy under effective and non-discriminatory safeguards against the proliferation of nuclear weapons.

Expresses its strong support for the efforts of the International Atomic Energy Agency to increase the effectiveness of its safeguards system in order to ensure that the peaceful uses of nuclear energy will not lead to the proliferation of nuclear weapons or other nuclear explosive devices. Recognizes the need adequately to ensure the physical protection of nuclear materials, facilities and transport, and requests the International Atomic Energy Agency to continue the consideration of reaching an international agreement for such protection. Expresses its support for the continuation of the studies by the International Atomic Energy Agency on the question of multinational fuel cycle centres and an international régime for plutonium management.

Outer space

31/8
8 November 1976

Invites states which have not yet become parties to the Treaty on principles governing the activities of states in the exploration and use of outer space, including the Moon and other celestial bodies, the Agreement on the rescue of astronauts, the return of astronauts and the return of objects launched into outer space; the Convention on international liability for damage caused by space objects; and the Convention on registration of objects launched into outer space, to give early consideration to ratifying or acceding to those international agreements.

Adopted unanimously

32/195
20 December 1977

Requests the Secretary-General to undertake research analysing the experience gained in the application of the Treaty on principles governing the activities of states in the exploration and use of outer space, including the Moon and other celestial bodies, over the past 10 years and showing its importance for the development of international co-operation in the practical application of space

Adopted by consensus

Subject, number, date of adoption, and contents of the resolution	Voting results

technology. Recommends that the Committee on the peaceful uses of outer space should consider measures to encourage the largest possible number of states to participate in the Treaty.

Sea-bed

2660 (XXV)
7 December 1970
Commends the Treaty on the prohibition of the emplacement of nuclear weapons and other weapons of mass destruction on the sea-bed and the ocean floor and in the subsoil thereof (the text of which is annexed to the resolution); and requests the depositary governments to open the Treaty for signature and ratification.

In favour 104
Against 2: El Salvador, Peru
Abstentions 2: Ecuador, France
Absent or not participating in the vote: Albania, Barbados, Botswana, Burundi, Congo, Costa Rica, Democratic Yemen, Dominican Republic, Equatorial Guinea, Guinea, Haiti, Honduras, Malawi, Maldives, Nicaragua, Somalia, Sudan, Swaziland, Trinidad and Tobago

2749 (XXV)
17 December 1970
(Declaration of the principles governing the sea-bed)
Declares that the sea-bed and ocean floor, and the subsoil thereof, beyond the limits of national jurisdiction, shall be reserved exclusively for peaceful purposes, without prejudice to any measures which have been or may be agreed upon in the context of international negotiations undertaken in the field of disarmament and which may be applicable to a broader area. One or more international agreements shall be concluded as soon as possible in order to implement effectively this principle and to constitute a step towards the exclusion of the sea-bed, the ocean floor and the subsoil thereof from the arms race.

In favour 108
Against 0
Abstentions 14

32/87 A
12 December 1977
Welcomes the positive assessment by the Review Conference of the effectiveness of the Treaty on the prohibition of the emplacement of nuclear weapons and other weapons of mass destruction on the sea-bed and the ocean floor and in the subsoil thereof since its entry into force, and invites all states that have not yet done so, particularly those possessing nuclear weapons or any other types of weapons of mass destruction, to ratify or accede to the Treaty as a significant contribution to international confidence. Affirms its strong interest in avoiding an arms race in nuclear weapons or any other types of weapons of mass destruction on the sea-bed, the ocean floor or the subsoil thereof; requests the CCD—in consultation with the states parties to the Treaty and taking into account the proposals made during the Review Conference and any relevant technological developments—to proceed promptly with the consideration of further measures in the field of disarmament for the prevention of an

Adopted without vote

Subject, number, date of adoption, and contents of the resolution	Voting results

arms race in that environment; and calls upon all states to refrain from any action which might lead to the extension of the arms race to the sea-bed and the ocean floor.

Nuclear weapon-free zone in Africa

3261 E (XXIX)
9 December 1974
Reaffirms its call upon all states to consider and respect the continent of Africa as a nuclear-free zone; reiterates its call upon all states to respect and abide by the declaration of the Assembly of Heads of state and government of the Organization of African Unity on the denuclearization of Africa; and reiterates further its call upon all states to refrain from testing, manufacturing, deploying, transporting, storing, using or threatening to use nuclear weapons on the African continent.

In favour 131
Against 0
Abstentions 0
Absent or not participating in the vote: Albania, Gabon, Malawi, Maldives, Saudi Arabia, South Africa, Swaziland

31/69
10 December 1976
Reaffirms its call to consider and respect Africa, including the continental African states, Madagascar and other islands surrounding Africa, as a nuclear weapon-free zone, and appeals to all states not to deliver to South Africa or place at its disposal any equipment or fissionable material or technology that will enable it to acquire a nuclear weapon capability.

Adopted without vote

32/81
12 December 1977
Condemns any attempt by South Africa to introduce nuclear weapons into the continent of Africa and demands that South Africa refrain forthwith from conducting any nuclear explosion on the continent of Africa or elsewhere. Urgently requests the Security Council to take appropriate effective steps to prevent South Africa from developing and acquiring nuclear weapons, thereby endangering international peace and security, and appeals to all states to refrain from such co-operation with South Africa in the nuclear field as will enable the racist régime to acquire nuclear weapons, and to dissuade corporations, institutions and individuals within their jurisdiction from any such co-operation.

In favour 131
Against 0
Abstentions 0
Absent or not participating in the vote: Albania, Angola, Argentina, Central African Empire, Comoros, Democratic Kampuchea, Djibouti, Equatorial Guinea, Grenada, Guinea, Madagascar,[a] Malawi, Mauritius,[a] Paraguay, Samoa, Saudi Arabia, Seychelles, South Africa

Nuclear weapon-free zone in the Middle East

3263 (XXIX)
9 December 1974
Commends the idea of the establishment of a nuclear weapon-free zone in the region of the Middle East; considers that, in order to advance the idea of a nuclear weapon-free zone in the region of the Middle East, it is

In favour 128
Against 0
Abstentions 2: Burma, Israel
Absent or not participating in the vote: Albania, Gabon, Iraq, Libya, Malawi, Maldives, Saudi Arabia, South Africa

Subject, number, date of adoption, and contents of the resolution	Voting results

indispensable that all parties concerned in the area proclaim solemnly and immediately their intention to refrain, on a reciprocal basis, from producing, testing, obtaining, acquiring or in any other way possessing nuclear weapons; calls upon the parties concerned in the area to accede to the Non-Proliferation Treaty; and expresses the hope that all states and, in particular, the nuclear weapon states, will lend their full co-operation for the effective realization of the aims of this resolution.

31/71
10 December 1976
Expresses the need for further action to generate momentum towards realization of the establishment of a nuclear weapon-free zone in the Middle East, and urges all parties directly concerned to adhere to the NPT as a means of promoting this objective.

In favour 130
Against 0
Abstentions 1: Israel
Absent or not participating in the vote: Albania, Angola, Benin, Burma, Cape Verde, Democratic Kampuchea, Guatemala, Guinea, Haiti, Honduras, Libya, Nicaragua, Sao Tome and Principe, Seychelles, South Africa

32/82
12 December 1977
Reiterates its recommendation that, pending the establishment of a nuclear weapon-free zone under an effective system of safeguards, the states concerned should: (a) proclaim solemnly and immediately their intention to refrain, on a reciprocal basis, from producing, acquiring or in any other way possessing nuclear weapons and nuclear explosive devices and from permitting the stationing of nuclear weapons in their territory or the territory under their control by any third party; (b) refrain, on a reciprocal basis, from any other action that would facilitate the acquisition, testing or use of such weapons or would in any other way be detrimental to the objective of the establishment of a nuclear weapon-free zone in the region under an effective system of safeguards; and (c) agree to place all their nuclear activities under International Atomic Energy Agency safeguards. Reaffirms its recommendation to the nuclear weapon states to refrain from any action contrary to the purpose of the present resolution and the objective of establishing, in the region of the Middle East, a nuclear weapon-free zone under an effective system of safeguards and to extend their co-operation to the states of the region in their efforts to promote this objective.

In favour 131
Against 0
Abstentions 1: Israel
Absent or not participating in the vote: Albania, Angola, Central African Empire, Comoros, Democratic Kampuchea, Djibouti, Equatorial Guinea, Grenada, Guinea, Libya, Madagascar,[a] Malawi, Mauritius,[a] Samoa, Saudi Arabia, Seychelles, South Africa

Nuclear weapon-free zone in South Asia

3265 B (XXIX)
9 December 1974
Having considered the question of the establishment of a nuclear weapon-free zone in South Asia without prejudice to the extension of the zone to include such other regions of Asia as may be practicable, takes note of the affirmation by the states of the region not to acquire or manufacture nuclear weapons and to devote their nuclear pro-

In favour 96
Against 2: Bhutan, India
Abstentions 36: Bahamas, Bangladesh, Barbados, Bulgaria, Burma, Byelorussia, Chad, Cuba, Cyprus, Czechoslovakia, Denmark, Fiji, France, Gambia, German Democratic Republic, Greece, Grenada, Cuyana, Hungary, Israel, Malawi, Malaysia, Mauritius, Mongolia, Norway, Poland, Portugal, Sweden, Thailand, Ukraine, United

Subject, number, date of adoption, and contents of the resolution	Voting results

grammes exclusively to the economic and social advancement of their peoples. Endorses, in principle, the concept of a nuclear weapon-free zone in South Asia; invites the states of the South Asian region and such other neighbouring non-nuclear weapon states as may be interested, to initiate, without delay, necessary consultations with a view to establishing a nuclear weapon-free zone and urges them, in the interim, to refrain from any action contrary to the achievement of these objectives. Expresses the hope that all states, in particular the nuclear weapon states, will lend their full co-operation for the effective realization of the aims of the resolution.

Republic of Tanzania, UK, USA, USSR, Yugoslavia, Zambia
Absent or not participating in the vote: Albania, Equatorial Guinea, Maldives, South Africa

32/83
12 December 1977

Reaffirms its endorsement, in principle, of the concept of a nuclear weapon-free zone in South Asia; urges once again the states of South Asia, and such other neighbouring non-nuclear weapon states as may be interested, to continue to make all possible efforts to establish a nuclear weapon-free zone in South Asia and to refrain, in the meantime, from any action contrary to this objective; and calls upon those nuclear weapon states which have not done so to respond positively to this proposal and to extend the necessary co-operation in the efforts to establish a nuclear weapon-free zone in South Asia.

In favour 105
Against 0
Abstentions 28: Argentina, Australia, Austria, Bhutan, Bulgaria, Burma, Byelorussia, Congo, Cuba, Cyprus, Czechoslovakia, Denmark, France, German Democratic Republic, Greece, Hungary, India, Indonesia, Israel, Lao People's Democratic Republic, Mongolia, Norway, Poland, Singapore, Sweden, Ukraine, USSR, Yugoslavia
Absent or not participating in the vote: Albania, Angola, Comoros, Democratic Kampuchea, Djibouti, Equatorial Guinea, Grenada, Guinea, Madagascar,[a] Malawi, Samoa, Saudi Arabia, Senegal, Seychelles, South Africa, Viet Nam

Nuclear weapon-free zone in the South Pacific

3477 (XXX)
11 December 1975

Endorses the idea of the establishment of a nuclear weapon-free zone in the South Pacific; invites the countries concerned to carry forward consultations about ways and means of realizing this objective; expresses the hope that all states, in particular the nuclear weapon states, will co-operate fully in achieving the objectives of this resolution.

In favour 110
Against 0
Abstentions 20: Belgium, Bulgaria, Byelorussia, Congo, Cuba, Czechoslovakia, Egypt, France, German Democratic Republic, Federal Republic of Germany, Greece, Hungary, Italy, Luxembourg, Mongolia, Poland, Ukraine, UK, USA, USSR
Absent or not participating in the vote: Albania, Bahamas, Cambodia, Cape Verde, Central African Republic, Comoros, Gambia, Guinea-Bissau, Libya, Maldives, Sao Tome and Principe, South Africa, Surinam, Yemen

Nuclear weapon-free zone in Latin America

32/76
12 December 1977

Recalling that the United Kingdom and the Netherlands became parties to Additional Protocol I of the Treaty of Tlatelolco in 1969 and 1971, respectively, notes that the Protocol was signed on 26 May 1977 by the President of the USA and that the government of that country has decided to take the necessary steps for its ratification. Again urges France to sign and ratify the Protocol.

In favour 113
Against 0
Abstentions 14: Argentina, Bulgaria, Byelorussia, Cuba, France, German Democratic Republic, Greece, Guyana, Hungary, Mongolia, Poland, Uganda, Ukraine, USSR
Absent or not participating in the vote: Albania, Angola, Central African Empire, Comoros, Congo, Cyprus,[a] Czechoslovakia, Democratic Kampuchea, Djibouti, Equatorial Guinea, Grenada, Guinea, Lesotho, Madagascar,[a] Malawi, Mauritius,[a] Samoa, Saudi Arabia, Seychelles, Somalia, South Africa, Viet Nam

Subject, number, date of adoption, and contents of the resolution	Voting results

32/79
12 December 1977

Recalling that the UK, the USA, France and China are already parties to Additional Protocol II of the Treaty of Tlatelolco, again urges the USSR to sign and ratify the Protocol.

In favour 118
Against 0
Abstentions 13: Bulgaria, Byelorussia, Congo, Cuba, Czechoslovakia, German Democratic Republic, Guyana, Hungary, Mongolia, Poland, Uganda, Ukraine, USSR
Absent or not participating in the vote: Albania, Angola, Central African Empire, Comoros, Democratic Kampuchea, Djibouti, Equatorial Guinea, Grenada, Guinea, Madagascar,[a] Malawi, Mauritius,[a] Samoa, Saudi Arabia, Seychelles, Somalia, South Africa, Viet Nam

Definition of a nuclear weapon-free zone and obligations of nuclear powers

3472 B (XXX)
11 December 1975

Solemnly adopts the following declaration:
A "nuclear weapon-free zone" shall, as a general rule, be deemed to be any zone, recognized as such by the United Nations General Assembly, which any group of states, in the free exercise of their sovereignty, has established by virtue of a treaty or convention whereby: (*a*) the statute of total absence of nuclear weapons to which the zone shall be subject, including the procedure for the delimitation of the zone, is defined; and (*b*) an international system of verification and control is established to guarantee compliance with the obligations deriving from that statute.
In every case of a nuclear weapon-free zone that has been recognized as such by the General Assembly, all nuclear weapon states shall undertake or reaffirm, in a solemn international instrument having full legally binding force, such as a treaty, a convention or a protocol, the following obligations: (*a*) to respect in all its parts the statute of total absence of nuclear weapons defined in the treaty or convention which serves as the constitutive instrument of the zone; (*b*) to refrain from contributing in any way to the performance in the territories forming part of the zone of acts which involve a violation of the aforesaid treaty or convention; and (*c*) to refrain from using or threatening to use nuclear weapons against the states included in the zone.
The above definitions in no way impair the resolutions which the General Assembly has adopted or may adopt with regard to specific cases of nuclear weapon-free zones nor the rights emanating for the member states from such resolutions.

In favour 82
Against 10: Belgium, Denmark, France, Federal Republic of Germany, Ireland, Italy, Luxembourg, Netherlands, UK, USA
Abstentions 36: Australia, Bhutan, Bulgaria, Byelorussia, Canada, Colombia, Cuba, Czechoslovakia, Egypt, German Democratic Republic, Greece, Hungary, Iceland, India, Indonesia, Iraq, Israel, Japan, Kuwait, Laos, Liberia, Malawi, Mongolia, Mozambique, New Zealand, Norway, Poland, Portugal, Singapore, Spain, Sweden, Turkey, Ukraine, United Arab Emirates, United Republic of Tanzania, USSR
Absent or not participating in the vote: Albania, Bahamas, Cambodia, Cape Verde, Central African Republic, Democratic Yemen, Ecuador, Gambia, Guinea-Bissau, Libya, Maldives, Malta, Sao Tome and Principe, South Africa, Surinam, Yemen

Indian Ocean as a zone of peace

2832 (XXVI)
16 December 1971

Solemnly declares that the Indian Ocean, within limits to be determined, together with the airspace above and the ocean floor subjacent thereto, is hereby designated for all time as a zone of peace.
Calls upon the great powers to enter into immediate

In favour 61[d]
Against 0
Abstentions 55: Argentina, Australia, Austria, Belgium, Bolivia, Brazil, Bulgaria, Byelorussia, Canada, Central African Republic, Chile, Cuba, Czechoslovakia, Dahomey, Democratic Yemen, Denmark, Dominican Republic, Fiji, Finland, France, Greece, Guatemala, Haiti, Hon-

Subject, number, date of adoption, and contents of the resolution	Voting results

consultations with the littoral states of the Indian Ocean with a view to: (*a*) halting the further escalation and expansion of their military presence in the Indian Ocean; and (*b*) eliminating from the Indian Ocean all bases, military installations, logistical supply facilities, the disposition of nuclear weapons and weapons of mass destruction and any manifestation of great power military presence in the Indian Ocean conceived in the context of great power rivalry.

Calls upon the littoral and hinterland states of the Indian Ocean, the permanent members of the Security Council and other major maritime users of the Indian Ocean, in pursuit of the objective of establishing a system of universal collective security without military alliances and strengthening international security through regional and other co-operation, to enter into consultations with a view to the implementation of this declaration and such action as may be necessary to ensure that: (*a*) warships and military aircraft may not use the Indian Ocean for any threat or use of force against the sovereignty, territorial integrity and independence of any littoral or hinterland state of the Indian Ocean in contravention of the purposes and principles of the UN Charter; (*b*) subject to the foregoing and to the norms and principles of international law, the right to free and unimpeded use of the zone by the vessels of all nations is unaffected; and (*c*) appropriate arrangements are made to give effect to any international agreement that may ultimately be reached for the maintenance of the Indian Ocean as a zone of peace.

duras, Hungary, Ireland, Israel, Italy, Ivory Coast, Jamaica, Lesotho, Luxembourg, Madagascar, Mongolia, Netherlands, New Zealand, Norway, Peru, Philippines, Poland, Portugal, Rwanda, Senegal, Singapore, South Africa, Spain, Thailand, Turkey, Ukraine, UK, USA, USSR, Upper Volta, Venezuela, Zaire
Absent or not participating in the vote: Albania, Bahrain, Barbados, Botswana, Ecuador, Gabon, Gambia, Iraq,[a] Malawi, Maldives, Mauritius, Niger, Oman, Paraguay, Sierra Leone, United Arab Emirates

2992 (XXVII)
15 December 1972
Calls upon the littoral and hinterland states of the Indian Ocean, the permanent members of the Security Council and other major maritime users of the Indian Ocean to support the concept that the Indian Ocean should be a zone of peace. Decides to establish an *ad hoc* committee to study the implications of the proposal, with special reference to the practical measures that may be taken in furtherance of the objectives of the resolution, having due regard to the security interests of the littoral and hinterland states of the Indian Ocean and the interests of any other state consistent with the purposes and principles of the UN Charter.

In favour 95
Against 0
Abstentions 33: Argentina, Austria, Belgium, Bulgaria, Byelorussia, Canada, Cuba, Czechoslovakia, Denmark, Finland, France, Greece, Guatemala, Honduras, Hungary, Ireland, Israel, Italy, Luxembourg, Mongolia, Netherlands, Norway, Oman, Poland, Portugal, South Africa, Sweden, Thailand,[a] Turkey, Ukraine, UK, USA, USSR
Absent or not participating in the vote: Albania, Democratic Yemen, Dominican Republic, Rwanda[a]

3259 A (XXIX)
9 December 1974
Urges the littoral and hinterland states of the Indian Ocean, the permanent members of the Security Council and other major maritime users of the Indian Ocean to give tangible support to the establishment and preservation of the Indian Ocean as a zone of peace; calls upon the great powers to refrain from increasing and strengthening their military presence in the region of the Indian Ocean as an essential first step towards the relaxation of tension and the promotion of peace and security in the

In favour 103
Against 0
Abstentions 26: Austria, Belgium, Bulgaria, Byelorussia, Canada, Cuba, Czechoslovakia, Denmark, France, German Democratic Republic, Federal Republic of Germany, Greece, Hungary, Ireland, Israel, Italy, Luxembourg, Mongolia, Netherlands, Norway, Poland, Turkey, Ukraine, UK, USA, USSR
Absent or not participating in the vote: Bhutan, Chad, Gabon, Guinea-Bissau, Maldives, Mali, Saudi Arabia, South Africa, Swaziland

Subject, number, date of adoption, and contents of the resolution	Voting results

area; requests the littoral and hinterland states of the Indian Ocean to enter, as soon as possible, into consultations with a view to convening a conference on the Indian Ocean; and invites all states, especially the great powers, to co-operate in a practical manner with the *Ad Hoc* Committee on the Indian Ocean in the discharge of its functions.

3468 (XXX)
11 December 1975

Notes that, as a result of consultations, an agreement in principle on the convening of a conference on the Indian Ocean has emerged, and requests the littoral and hinterland states of the Indian Ocean to continue their consultations to this end.

In favour 106
Against 0
Abstentions 25: Austria, Belgium, Bulgaria, Byelorussia, Canada, Cuba, Czechoslovakia, Denmark, France, German Democratic Republic, Federal Republic of Germany, Greece, Hungary, Ireland, Israel, Italy, Luxembourg, Mongolia, Netherlands, Norway, Poland, Ukraine, UK, USA, USSR
Absent or not participating in the vote: Albania, Bahamas, Cambodia, Cape Verde, Central African Republic, Ecuador, Gambia, Guinea-Bissau, Maldives, Sao Tome and Principe, South Africa, Surinam, Yemen

31/88
14 December 1976

Deeply concerned that there has been an escalation of the military presence of the great powers conceived in the context of great power rivalry in the Indian Ocean, and believing therefore that the implementation of the purposes and objectives of the Declaration of the Indian Ocean as a zone of peace, contained in Resolution 2832 (XXVI) of 16 December 1971, has acquired a new urgency, requests the *Ad Hoc* Committee on the Indian Ocean and the littoral and hinterland states of the Indian Ocean to continue their consultations with a view to formulating a programme of action leading to the convening of a conference on the Indian Ocean.

In favour 106
Against 0
Abstentions 27: Austria, Belgium, Bulgaria, Byelorussia, Canada, Cuba, Czechoslovakia, Denmark, France, German Democratic Republic, Federal Republic of Germany, Hungary, Ireland, Israel, Italy, Luxembourg, Mongolia, Netherlands, Norway, Pakistan, Poland, Sweden, Turkey, Ukraine, UK, USA, USSR
Absent or not participating in the vote: Albania, Angola, Benin, Cape Verde, Congo, Democratic Kampuchea, Equatorial Guinea, Grenada, Guinea-Bissau, Haiti, Lebanon, Seychelles, South Africa

32/86
12 December 1977

Renews its invitation to the great powers and other major maritime users of the Indian Ocean to enter with the least possible delay into consultations with the littoral and hinterland states of the Indian Ocean in pursuance of Resolution 3468 (XXX). Decides that, as the next step towards the convening of a conference on the Indian Ocean, a meeting of the littoral and hinterland states of the Indian Ocean be convened in New York at a suitable date. Other states not falling within this category, but which have participated or have expressed their willingness to participate in the work of the *Ad Hoc* Committee, could attend the meeting.

In favour 123
Against 0
Abstentions 13: Belgium, Canada, Denmark, France, Federal Republic of Germany, Ireland, Israel, Italy, Luxembourg, Netherlands, Norway, UK, USA
Absent or not participating in the vote: Albania, Angola, Comoros, Democratic Kampuchea, Djibouti, Equatorial Guinea, Grenada, Madagascar,[a] Malawi, Samoa, Saudi Arabia, Seychelles, South Africa

Security of non-nuclear weapon states

3261 G (XXIX)
9 December 1974

Believing it necessary to consider ways to strengthen

Adopted without vote

Subject, number, date of adoption, and contents of the resolution	Voting results

assurances against nuclear attack or threat and thus give greater confidence to the non-nuclear weapon states, declares firm support for the independence, territorial integrity and sovereignty of non-nuclear weapon states; and recommends to member states to consider in all appropriate forums the question of strengthening the security of non-nuclear weapon states.

31/189 C
21 December 1976
Requests the nuclear weapon states, as a first step towards a complete ban on the use or threat of use of nuclear weapons, to consider undertaking, without prejudice to their obligations arising from treaties establishing nuclear weapon-free zones, not to use or threaten to use nuclear weapons against non-nuclear weapon states not parties to the nuclear security arrangements of some nuclear weapon powers.

In favour 95
Against 0
Abstentions 33: Algeria, Argentina, Australia, Austria, Belgium, Bhutan, Bulgaria, Byelorussia, Canada, Czechoslovakia, Denmark, France, German Democratic Republic, Federal Republic of Germany, Greece, Hungary, Iceland, India, Iraq, Ireland, Italy, Japan, Luxembourg, Mongolia, New Zealand, Norway, Poland, Sweden, Ukraine, UK, USA, USSR, Yugoslavia
Absent or not participating in the vote: Albania, Angola, Benin, Cape Verde, Comoros, Congo, Cuba, Democratic Kampuchea, Democratic Yemen, El Salvador, Gambia, Haiti, Honduras, Liberia, Mozambique, Samoa, Seychelles, Somalia, South Africa

32/87 B
12 December 1977
Recalling Resolution 31/189 C of 21 December 1976, urges the nuclear weapon powers to give serious consideration to extending the undertaking proposed by that resolution and to take expeditious action in all relevant forums to strengthen the security of non-nuclear weapon states; recommends that all possible efforts be made at the special session devoted to disarmament to evolve binding and credible security assurances to non-nuclear weapon states.

In favour 95[e]
Against 0
Abstentions 38: Algeria, Argentina, Australia, Austria, Belgium, Benin, Bhutan, Bulgaria, Byelorussia, Canada, Congo, Cuba, Cyprus, Czechoslovakia, Denmark, France, German Democratic Republic, Federal Republic of Germany, Greece, Hungary, Iceland, India, Iraq, Ireland, Italy, Japan, Luxembourg, Mongolia, Norway, Oman, Poland, Sierra Leone, Sweden, Ukraine, UK, USA, USSR, Yugoslavia
Absent or not participating in the vote: Albania, Angola, Comoros, Democratic Kampuchea, Djibouti, Equatorial Guinea, Grenada, Guinea, Madagascar,[a] Malawi, Samoa, Saudi Arabia, Senegal, Seychelles, South Africa, Viet Nam

Renunciation of the use of force and prohibition of the use of nuclear weapons

2936 (XXVII)
29 November 1972
Solemnly declares the renunciation of the use or threat of force in all its forms and manifestations in international relations, in accordance with the Charter of the United Nations, and the permanent prohibition of the use of nuclear weapons. Recommends that the Security Council should take, as soon as possible, appropriate measures for the full implementation of this declaration.

In favour 73
Against 4: Albania, China, Portugal, South Africa
Abstentions 46: Argentina, Australia, Austria, Belgium, Bolivia, Botswana, Brazil, Burundi, Canada, Central African Republic, Colombia, Costa Rica, Denmark, Dominican Republic, El Salvador, France, Greece, Guatemala, Honduras, Iceland, Ireland, Israel, Italy, Ivory Coast, Japan, Luxembourg, Malawi, Mexico, Morocco, Netherlands, New Zealand, Norway, Pakistan, Paraguay, Peru, Spain, Sweden, Thailand, Togo, Tunisia, Turkey, UK, USA, Uruguay, Venezuela, Zaire
Absent or not participating in the vote: Dahomey, Ecuador, Equatorial Guinea, Gambia, Haiti, Liberia,[a] Nicaragua, Somalia,[a] Swaziland

Subject, number, date of adoption, and contents of the resolution	Voting results
32/150 19 December 1977 Decides to establish a Special Committee on enhancing the effectiveness of the principle of non-use of force in international relations, and instructs the Committee to consider proposals and suggestions submitted by any state, bearing in mind the views expressed during the debate on this item, with the goal of drafting a world treaty on the non-use of force in international relations as well as the peaceful settlement of disputes.	*In favour* 111 *Against* 4: Albania, China, UK, USA *Abstentions* 27: Australia, Austria, Belgium, Canada, Chad, Denmark, France, Federal Republic of Germany, Iceland, Ireland, Israel, Italy, Ivory Coast, Japan, Liberia, Luxembourg, Mauritania, Netherlands, New Zealand, Norway, Pakistan, Portugal, Saudi Arabia, Somalia, Spain, Sweden, Turkey *Absent or not participating in the vote:* Cape Verde, Democratic Kampuchea, Equatorial Guinea, Gambia, Grenada, Seychelles, South Africa

Chemical and biological weapons

2603 A (XXIV) 16 December 1969 Declares as contrary to the generally recognized rules of international law, as embodied in the Geneva Protocol of 17 June 1925, the use in international armed conflicts of any chemical agents of warfare—chemical substances, whether gaseous, liquid or solid; and any biological agents of warfare—living organisms, whatever their nature, or infective material derived from them.	*In favour* 80 *Against* 3: Australia, Portugal, USA *Abstentions* 36: Austria, Belgium, Bolivia, Canada, Chile, China, Denmark, El Salvador, France, Greece, Iceland, Israel, Italy, Japan, Laos, Liberia, Luxembourg, Madagascar, Malawi, Malaysia, Netherlands, New Zealand, Nicaragua, Norway, Paraguay, Philippines, Sierra Leone, Singapore, South Africa, Swaziland, Thailand, Tunisia, Turkey, UK, Uruguay, Venezuela
2826 (XXVI) 16 December 1971 Commends the Convention on the prohibition of the development, production and stockpiling of bacteriological (biological) and toxin weapons and on their destruction (the text of which is annexed to the resolution), and requests the depositary governments to open the Convention for signature and ratification at the earliest possible date.	*In favour* 110 *Against* 0 *Abstentions* 1: France *Absent or not participating in the vote:* Albania, Barbados, Bolivia, Botswana, China, El Salvador,[a] Gabon, Gambia, Haiti,[a] Iraq,[a] Lebanon, Malawi, Maldives, Mauritius, Niger, Oman, Sierra Leone, Sudan, Swaziland, Syria, United Arab Emirates
2933 (XXVII) 29 November 1972 Stresses the importance of working towards the complete realization of the objective of effective prohibition of chemical weapons and urges governments to work to that end. Reaffirms the hope for the widest possible adherence to the Convention on the prohibition of biological and toxin weapons; invites all states that have not yet done so to accede to the Protocol of 17 June 1925 and/or ratify this Protocol, and calls anew for the strict observance by all states of the principles and objectives contained therein.	*In favour* 113 *Against* 0 *Abstentions* 2: China, France *Absent or not participating in the vote:* Albania, Botswana, Dahomey, Ecuador, Equatorial Guinea, Gabon, Gambia, Guinea, Haiti, Honduras, Malawi, Morocco, Nicaragua, Sierra Leone, Somalia, Trinidad and Tobago,[a] Yemen
32/77 12 December 1977 Requests the CCD to undertake the elaboration of an agreement on effective measures for the prohibition of the development, production and stockpiling of all chemical	Adopted without vote

weapons and for their destruction, taking into account all existing proposals and future initiatives submitted for its consideration.

Environmental warfare

3264 (XXIX)
9 December 1974
Considers it necessary to adopt, through the conclusion of an appropriate international convention, effective measures to prohibit action to influence the environment and climate for military and other hostile purposes, which are incompatible with the maintenance of international security, human well-being and health, and requests the CCD to proceed as soon as possible towards achieving agreement on the text of such a convention.

In favour   126
Against   0
Abstentions   5: Chile, France, Mali, Paraguay, USA
Absent or not participating in the vote: Albania, Burundi, China, Maldives, Saudi Arabia, South Africa, Togo

31/72
10 December 1976
Refers the Convention on the prohibition of military or any other hostile use of environmental modification techniques (the text of which is annexed to this resolution) to all states for their consideration, signature and ratification. Requests the Secretary-General, as depositary of the Convention, to open it for signature and ratification, and expresses the hope for the widest possible adherence to the Convention.

In favour   96
Against   8: Albania, Ecuador, Grenada, Kenya, Kuwait, Mexico, Panama, Zambia
Abstentions   30: Argentina, Bahamas, Barbados, Burundi, Chile, Comoros, Congo, Costa Rica, Dominican Republic, Equatorial Guinea, France, Gabon, Gambia, Iraq, Ivory Coast, Jamaica, Malaysia, Mauritius, New Zealand, Pakistan, Paraguay, Peru, Rwanda, Togo, Trinidad and Tobago, Uganda, United Republic of Cameroon, United Republic of Tanzania, Venezuela, Yemen
Absent or not participating in the vote: Angola, Benin, Cape Verde, China, Democratic Kampuchea, Guatemala, Guinea, Haiti, Honduras, Sao Tome and Principe, Seychelles, South Africa

Napalm and other incendiary weapons

3255 B (XXIX)
9 December 1974
Deeply disturbed at the continuing use of napalm and other incendiary weapons, condemns the use of napalm and other incendiary weapons in armed conflicts in circumstances where it may affect human beings or may cause damage to the environment and/or natural resources. Urges all states to refrain from the production, stockpiling, proliferation and use of such weapons, pending the conclusion of agreements on the prohibition of these weapons, and invites all governments, the International Committee of the Red Cross, the specialized agencies and the other international organizations concerned to transmit to the Secretary-General all information about the use of napalm and other incendiary weapons in armed conflicts.

In favour   98
Against   0
Abstentions   27: Australia, Austria, Belgium, Bulgaria, Byelorussia, Canada, Czechoslovakia, Denmark, France, German Democratic Republic, Federal Republic of Germany, Greece,[a] Hungary, Ireland, Israel, Italy, Japan, Luxembourg, Mongolia, Netherlands, Norway, Poland, Turkey, Ukraine, UK, USA, USSR
Absent or not participating in the vote: Bhutan, Chad, Gabon, Grenada, Guinea,[a] Guinea-Bissau, Jamaica, Lesotho, Maldives, Mali, Saudi Arabia, South Africa, Swaziland

New weapons of mass destruction

3479 (XXX)
11 December 1975
Takes note of the draft agreement on the prohibition of

In favour   112
Against   1: Albania
Abstentions   15: Belgium, Denmark, France, Federal Re-

Subject, number, date of adoption, and contents of the resolution	Voting results

the development and manufacture of new types of weapons of mass destruction and of new systems of such weapons, submitted to the General Assembly by the USSR, as well as the points of view and suggestions put forward during the discussion of this question, and requests the CCD to proceed as soon as possible, with the assistance of qualified governmental experts, to work out the text of such an agreement.

public of Germany, Ireland, Israel, Italy, Luxembourg, Malawi, Mauritania, Morocco, Netherlands, Uganda, UK, USA
Absent or not participating in the vote: Bahamas, Cambodia, Cape Verde, Central African Republic, China, Comoros, El Salvador, Gambia, Guinea-Bissau, Maldives, Mozambique, Sao Tome and Principe, South Africa, Surinam, Trinidad and Tobago, Yemen

32/84 A
12 December 1977
Requests the CCD to continue negotiations aimed at working out the text of an agreement on the prohibition of the development and manufacture of new types of weapons of mass destruction and new systems of such weapons, and, when necessary, specific agreements on this subject; and urges all states to refrain from any action which would impede international talks aimed at working out an agreement or agreements to prevent the use of scientific and technological progress for the development of new types of weapons of mass destruction and new systems of such weapons.

In favour 110
Against 1: Albania
Abstentions 25: Australia, Austria, Belgium, Canada, Denmark, France, Federal Republic of Germany, Greece, Iceland, Ireland, Israel, Italy, Ivory Coast, Japan, Luxembourg, Mauritania, Netherlands, New Zealand, Norway, Portugal, Spain, Sweden, Turkey, UK, USA
Absent or not participating in the vote: Angola, China, Comoros, Democratic Kampuchea, Djibouti, Equatorial Guinea, Grenada, Madagascar,[a] Malawi, Samoa, Saudi Arabia, Seychelles, South Africa

32/84 B
12 December 1977
Urges states to refrain from developing new weapons of mass destruction based on new scientific principles; calls upon states to apply scientific discoveries for the benefit of mankind; reaffirms the definition of weapons of mass destruction contained in the resolution of the UN Commission for Conventional Armaments of 12 August 1948, which defined weapons of mass destruction as atomic explosive weapons, radioactive material weapons, lethal chemical and biological weapons and any weapons developed in the future which have characteristics comparable in destructive effect to those of the atomic bomb or other weapons mentioned above. Welcomes the active continuation of negotiations relating to the prohibition and limitation of identified weapons of mass destruction, and requests the CCD, while taking into account its existing priorities, to keep under review the question of the development of new weapons of mass destruction based on new scientific principles, and to consider the desirability of formulating agreements on the prohibition of any specific new weapons which may be identified.

In favour 102
Against 1: Albania
Abstentions 28: Austria, Barbados, Benin, Botswana, Bulgaria, Burundi, Byelorussia, Cuba, Czechoslovakia, Egypt, German Democratic Republic, Ghana, Guyana, Hungary, Jamaica, Kenya, Mali, Mauritania, Mongolia, Nigeria, Poland, Sierra Leone, Tunisia, Uganda, Ukraine, USSR, United Republic of Tanzania, Upper Volta
Absent or not participating in the vote: Angola, Brazil, China, Comoros, Democratic Kampuchea, Djibouti, Equatorial Guinea, Grenada, Lao People's Democratic Republic, Madagascar,[b] Malawi, Samoa, Saudi Arabia, Senegal, Seychelles, South Africa, Trinidad and Tobago, Viet Nam

Human rights in armed conflicts

2677 (XXV)
9 December 1970
Calls upon all parties to any armed conflict to observe the rules laid down in the Hague Conventions of 1899 and 1907, the Geneva Protocol of 1925, the Geneva Conventions of 1949 and other humanitarian rules applicable in armed conflicts, and invites those states which have not yet done so to adhere to those conventions.

In favour 111
Against 0
Abstentions 4

Subject, number, date of adoption, and contents of the resolution	Voting results

32/44
8 December 1977

Welcomes the successful conclusion of the Diplomatic Conference on the reaffirmation and development of international humanitarian law applicable in armed conflicts which has resulted in two Protocols additional to the Geneva Conventions of 12 August 1949, adopted by the Diplomatic Conference on 8 June 1977, namely, Protocol I relating to the protection of victims of international armed conflicts and Protocol II relating to the protection of victims of non-international armed conflicts. Notes the recommendation, approved by the Diplomatic Conference, that a special conference be called on the issue of the prohibition or restriction of the use for humanitarian reasons of specific conventional weapons. Urges states to consider without delay the matter of signing and ratifying or acceding to the two Protocols additional to the Geneva Conventions of 1949, and calls upon all states to take effective steps for the dissemination of humanitarian rules applicable in armed conflicts.

Adopted by consensus

32/152
19 December 1977

Decides to convene in 1979 a United Nations conference with a view to reaching agreements on prohibitions or restrictions on the use of specific conventional weapons, including those which may be deemed to be excessively injurious or have indiscriminate effects, taking into account humanitarian and military considerations, and on the question of a system of periodic review of this matter and for consideration of further proposals. Decides to convene a UN preparatory conference for the conference referred to above and requests the Secretary-General to transmit invitations to all states and parties invited to attend the Diplomatic Conference on the reaffirmation and development of international humanitarian law applicable in armed conflicts.

In favour 115
Against 0
Abstentions 21: Belgium, Bulgaria, Byelorussia, Canada, Cuba, Czechoslovakia, France, German Democratic Republic, Federal Republic of Germany, Hungary, Israel, Italy, Japan, Luxembourg, Mongolia, Poland, Turkey, Ukraine, UK, USA, USSR
Absent or not participating in the vote: Albania, Burma,[a] Cape Verde, China, Democratic Kampuchea, Djibouti, Gambia, Grenada, Guinea, Lao People's Democratic Republic, Seychelles, South Africa, Viet Nam

Reduction of military budgets

3093 A (XXVIII)
7 December 1973

Recommends that all states permanent members of the Security Council should reduce their military budgets by 10 per cent from the 1973 level during the next financial year; appeals to the aforementioned states to allot 10 per cent of the funds released as a result of the reduction in military budgets for the provision of assistance to developing countries so as to permit the execution in those countries of the most urgent economic and social projects; expresses the desire that other states, particularly those with a major economic and military potential, should also take steps to reduce their military budgets and allot part of the funds thus released for the provision of assistance to developing countries.

In favour 83
Against 2: Albania, China
Abstentions 38: Australia, Austria, Bahamas, Belgium, Brazil, Canada, Congo, Denmark, France, Federal Republic of Germany, Greece, Guinea, Guyana, Iceland, Ireland, Israel, Italy, Ivory Coast, Jamaica, Japan, Luxembourg, Malawi, Mauritania, Netherlands, New Zealand, Norway, Pakistan, Portugal, South Africa, Sweden, Thailand, Trinidad and Tobago, Turkey, UK, United Republic of Tanzania, USA, Zambia
Absent or not participating in the vote: Bolivia, Burundi, Equatorial Guinea, Gambia, Maldives, Mauritius,[a] Morocco, Paraguay, Sierra Leone, Somalia, Upper Volta, Zaire[a]

UN General Assembly arms control resolutions

Subject, number, date of adoption, and contents of the resolution	Voting results
3463 (XXX) 11 December 1975 Appeals to all states, in particular the permanent members of the Security Council, as well as any other state with comparable military expenditures, to strive to reach agreed reductions of their military budgets. Urges the two states with the highest levels of military expenditure in absolute terms, pending such agreement, to carry out reductions of their military budgets.	*In favour* 108 *Against* 2: Albania, China *Abstentions* 21: Belgium, Bulgaria, Byelorussia, Canada, Cuba, Czechoslovakia, France, German Democratic Republic, Federal Republic of Germany, Hungary, Italy, Luxembourg, Mauritania, Mongolia, Netherlands, Poland, Uganda, Ukraine, UK, USA, USSR *Absent or not participating in the vote:* Bahamas, Cambodia, Cape Verde, Central African Republic, Ecuador, Gambia, Guinea-Bissau, Guyana, Maldives, Sao Tome and Principe, South Africa, Surinam, Yemen
31/87 14 December 1976 Recalling that the General Assembly requested the Secretary-General to prepare, with the assistance of a group of qualified experts, a report containing an analysis and examination in concrete terms of issues regarding a system of international measurement, reporting and comparisons of military expenditures, and noting with appreciation the report submitted in response to that request, invites all states to communicate to the Secretary-General their comments with regard to matters covered in the report and in particular: (*a*) their views and suggestions on the proposed standardized reporting instrument contained in the report; (*b*) any information they may wish to convey on their military expenditure accounting practices, including a description of methods currently in use; and (*c*) suggestions and recommendations concerning possible practical approaches for the further development and operation of a standardized reporting system.	*In favour* 120 *Against* 2: Albania, China *Abstentions* 11: Bulgaria, Byelorussia, Cuba, Czechoslovakia, German Democratic Republic, Hungary, Mongolia, Poland, Uganda, Ukraine, USSR *Absent or not participating in the vote:* Angola, Benin, Cape Verde, Congo, Democratic Kampuchea, Equatorial Guinea, Grenada, Guinea-Bissau, Haiti, Lebanon, Oman, Seychelles, South Africa
32/85 12 December 1977 Recognizing the value of the availability of a satisfactory instrument for standardized reporting on the military expenditures of member states, particularly of the states permanent members of the Security Council, as well as any other state with comparable military expenditures, requests the Secretary-General to ascertain those states which would be prepared to participate in a pilot test of the proposed reporting instrument and to report on this to the General Assembly at its special session devoted to disarmament.	*In favour* 120 *Against* 2: Albania, China *Abstentions* 13: Bulgaria, Byelorussia, Cuba, Czechoslovakia, German Democratic Republic, Hungary, Mauritania, Mongolia, Poland, Swaziland, Uganda, Ukraine, USSR *Absent or not participating in the vote:* Angola, Comoros, Democratic Kampuchea, Djibouti, Equatorial Guinea, Grenada, Lao People's Democratic Republic, Madagascar,[a] Malawi, Samoa, Saudi Arabia, Seychelles, South Africa, Viet Nam

Disarmament and development

3176 (XXVIII) 17 December 1973 (First biennial overall review and appraisal of progress in the implementation of the international development strategy for the second UN Development Decade) States that the resources that may be released as a result of effective measures of actual disarmament should be used for the promotion of the economic and social de-	Adopted without vote

Subject, number, date of adoption, and contents of the resolution	Voting results

velopment of all nations. The release of resources resulting from those measures should increase the capacity of developed countries to provide support to developing countries in their efforts towards accelerating their economic and social progress.

3281 (XXIX)
12 December 1974
(Charter of economic rights and duties of states)
Adopts and proclaims a charter of economic rights and duties of states, which in Article 15 provides that all states have the duty to promote the achievement of general and complete disarmament under effective international control and to utilize the resources freed by effective disarmament measures for the economic and social development of countries, allocating a substantial portion of such resources as additional means for the development needs of developing countries.

In favour 120
Against 6: Belgium, Denmark, Federal Republic of Germany, Luxembourg, UK, USA
Abstentions 10: Austria, Canada, France, Ireland, Israel, Italy, Japan, Netherlands, Norway, Spain
Absent or not participating in the vote: Maldives, South Africa

3470 (XXX)
11 December 1975
Deplores the wastage of resources in expenditures on armaments, particularly nuclear armaments; calls upon member states and the Secretary-General to intensify their efforts in support of the link between disarmament and development, so as to promote disarmament negotiations and to ensure that the human and material resources freed by disarmament are used to promote economic and social development, particularly in the developing countries.

Adopted without vote

32/88 A
12 December 1977
Endorses the recommendation by the Preparatory Committee for the General Assembly special session devoted to disarmament that the General Assembly should initiate a study on the relationship between disarmament and development, the terms of reference of the study to be determined by the Assembly itself at its special session.

Adopted without vote

Disarmament and international security

32/154
19 December 1977
(Resolution on the implementation of the Declaration on the strengthening of international security)
Urges effective measures to put an end to the arms race and to promote disarmament, particularly nuclear disarmament, the creation of zones of peace and co-operation, the withdrawal of foreign military bases and the achievement of tangible progress towards general and

In favour 118
Against 2: Israel, USA
Abstentions 19: Australia, Austria, Belgium, Canada, Denmark, France, Federal Republic of Germany, Iceland, Ireland, Italy, Japan, Luxembourg, Netherlands, New Zealand, Norway, Portugal, Sweden, Turkey, UK
Absent or not participating in the vote: Albania, Cape Verde, China, Democratic Kampuchea, Djibouti, Gambia, Grenada, Paraguay, Seychelles, South Africa

Subject, number, date of adoption, and contents of the resolution	Voting results

complete disarmament under effective international control and the strengthening of the role of the United Nations in this regard. Expresses the hope that further positive results will be achieved at the meeting of representatives of states participating in the Conference on Security and Co-operation in Europe, concerning the full implementation of the Final Act of the Conference, which will be conducive also to the strengthening of world security, bearing in mind the close interrelation of the security of Europe to the security of the Mediterranean, the Middle East and all other regions of the world. Supports the conversion of the Mediterranean into a zone of peace and co-operation in the interests of peace and security.

Disarmament and détente

32/155
19 December 1977
(Declaration on the deepening and consolidation of international détente)

Convinced that progress in arms control and disarmament negotiations and the elimination of the threat of war are of great importance for the continued relaxation of tension and for further development of friendly relations among states, declares the determination to consider taking new and meaningful steps aimed at achieving the objective of a cessation of the arms race, in particular the nuclear arms race, and realization of disarmament measures, especially nuclear disarmament, with the ultimate objective of general and complete disarmament under strict and effective international control.

Adopted by consensus

Regional disarmament

32/87 D
12 December 1977
Invites all states to inform the Secretary-General of their views and suggestions concerning the regional aspects of disarmament, including measures designed to increase confidence and stability as well as means of promoting disarmament on a regional basis. Decides to consider the desirability of requesting the Secretary-General to prepare, with the collaboration of a special group of qualified governmental experts, a comprehensive study of all the regional aspects of disarmament, bearing in mind, *inter alia*, the decisions and recommendations of the special session devoted to disarmament.

In favour 91
Against 0
Abstentions 40: Algeria, Argentina, Bahamas, Bahrain, Benin, Bhutan, Brazil, Cape Verde, Congo, Cuba, Democratic Yemen, Egypt, India, Indonesia, Iraq, Jamaica, Jordan, Kuwait, Lebanon, Malaysia, Mauritania, Morocco, Mozambique, Nigeria, Oman, Peru, Philippines, Qatar, Sao Tome and Principe, Sri Lanka, Sudan, Syria, Thailand, Trinidad and Tobago, Tunisia,[a] United Arab Emirates, United Republic of Tanzania, Upper Volta, Yemen, Yugoslavia
Absent or not participating in the vote: Albania, Angola, China, Comoros, Democratic Kampuchea, Djibouti, Equatorial Guinea, Ethiopia, Grenada, Lao People's Democratic Republic, Libya, Madagascar,[b] Malawi, Samoa, Saudi Arabia, Seychelles, South Africa, Viet Nam

General and complete disarmament

2625 (XXV)
24 October 1970
(Declaration of principles of international law concerning friendly relations and co-operation among states)

Adopted without vote

Subject, number, date of adoption, and contents of the resolution	Voting results

Proclaims as a principle of international law relating to friendly relations and co-operation among states: states shall refrain in their international relations from the threat or use of force against the territorial integrity or political independence of any state, or in any other manner inconsistent with the purposes of the United Nations.

All states shall pursue in good faith negotiations for the early conclusion of a universal treaty on general and complete disarmament under effective international control and strive to adopt appropriate measures to reduce international tensions and strengthen confidence among states.

2627 (XXV)
24 October 1970   Adopted without vote

(Declaration on the occasion of the twenty-fifth anniversary of the UN)

Welcomes the international agreements which have already been achieved in the limitation of armaments, especially nuclear arms. Looks forward to the early conclusion of further agreements of this kind and to moving forward from arms limitation to a reduction of armaments and disarmament everywhere, particularly in the nuclear field, with the participation of all nuclear weapon powers. Calls upon all governments to renew their determination to make concrete progress towards the elimination of the arms race and the achievement of the final goal—general and complete disarmament under effective international control.

UN role in disarmament

31/90
14 December 1976   Adopted without vote

Having considered the report of the *Ad Hoc* Committee on the review of the role of the United Nations in the field of disarmament, which contains agreed proposals with regard to the following subjects: (*a*) improved methods of work of the First Committee in disarmament matters; (*b*) relationship between the General Assembly and other United Nations bodies in the field of disarmament; (*c*) role of the United Nations Disarmament Commission; (*d*) role of the United Nations in providing assistance on request in multilateral and regional disarmament negotiations; (*e*) relationship between the General Assembly and the CCD; (*f*) increased use of in-depth studies of the arms race, disarmament and related matters; (*g*) improvement of existing United Nations facilities for the collection, compilation and dissemination of information on disarmament issues, in order to keep all governments, as well as world public opinion, properly informed on progress achieved in the field of disarmament; (*h*) assistance by the Secretariat, on request, to states parties to multilateral disarmament agreements in their duty to ensure the effective functioning of such agreements, including appropriate reviews; and (*i*) strengthening of the resources of the Secretariat, endorses

Subject, number, date of adoption, and contents of the resolution	Voting results
the proposals and requests the Secretary-General to implement as soon as possible the measures recommended.	

World Disarmament Conference

| 2930 (XXVII)
29 November 1972
Invites all states to exert further efforts with a view to creating adequate conditions for the convening of a World Disarmament Conference at an appropriate time. | *In favour* 105
Against 0
Abstentions 1: USA
Absent or not participating in the vote: Albania, Bolivia, Botswana, Colombia, Congo,[a] Dahomey, Equatorial Guinea, Gabon, Gambia, Ghana, Guinea, Haiti, Honduras, Malawi, Morocco, Nepal, Nicaragua, Pakistan,[a] Panama, Saudi Arabia, Sierra Leone, Sudan, Trinidad and Tobago,[a] Uganda, United Republic of Tanzania, Yemen |
| 32/89
12 December 1977
Requests the *Ad Hoc* Committee on the World Disarmament Conference to submit to the General Assembly at its special session devoted to disarmament a special report on the state of its work and deliberations. | Adopted without vote |

UN General Assembly special session on disarmament

| 31/189 B
21 December 1976
Decides to convene a General Assembly special session devoted to disarmament, to be held in New York in May/June 1978, and to establish a preparatory committee, composed of 54 member states, with the mandate of examining all relevant questions relating to the special session, including its agenda. | Adopted without vote |
| 32/88 B
12 December 1977
Endorses the report of the Preparatory Committee for the General Assembly special session devoted to disarmament and the recommendations contained therein for the special session to be held between 23 May and 28 June 1978. Requests the Preparatory Committee to continue its work in order to prepare a draft final document or documents for consideration and adoption by the General Assembly at its special session. | Adopted without vote |

[a] Later advised the Secretariat it had intended to vote in favour.

[b] Later advised the Secretariat it had intended to abstain.

[c] The vote of the delegation of Nigeria should have been recorded as being in favour.

[d] Nicaragua later advised the Secretariat it had intended to abstain.

[e] New Zealand later advised the Secretariat it had intended to abstain.

APPENDIX C

Notifications of military manoeuvres in compliance with the Final Act of the Conference on Security and Co-operation in Europe*

State giving notification	Date of notification	Duration of manoeuvre	Designation of manoeuvre	Number of troops involved	Area of manoeuvre
	1975	**1975**			
Canada	21 Aug	15–19 Sep	Grosse Rochade[1]	..	FRG
FR Germany	22 Aug	15–19 Sep	Grosse Rochade[1]	68 000	FRG: Marktredwitz–Passau–Munich–Augsburg–Nuremberg
USA	22 Aug	15–19 Sep	Grosse Rochade[1]	..	FRG
France	25 Aug	15–19 Sep	Grosse Rochade[1]	500[2]	FRG
Turkey	22 Aug	12–28 Sep	Deep Express 75[3]	~18 000	Aegean Sea and Eastern Thrace
UK	25 Aug	12–28 Sep	Deep Express 75[3]	6 000–7 000[2]	Aegean Sea and Turkish Thrace
USA	10 Sep	Early Oct–late Nov	Reforger 75[4]	10 000	FRG
FR Germany	9 Sep	14–23 Oct	Certain Trek[5]	57 000	Northwestern Bavaria
USA	10 Sep	14–23 Oct	Certain Trek[5]	57 000	Northwestern Bavaria
Canada	10 Sep	14–23 Oct	Certain Trek[5]	..	FRG
Norway	12 Sep	3–7 Oct	Batten Bolt 75[6]	8 000	Östfold area southeast of Oslo
Yugoslavia	29 Sep	21–25 Oct	Division in Action[7]	~18 000	Southwest Macedonia
Switzerland	10 Oct	10–18 Nov	..[8]	40 000	Northeast Switzerland: Schaffhouse–Winterthur–St Gall–Rhine–Schaffhouse
Netherlands	14 Oct	28 Oct–6 Nov	Pantser Sprong[9]	~10 000	FRG: Küstenkanal–Weser River–Mittellandkanal–Ems River–Dortmund–Emskanal
	1976	**1976**			
USSR	4 Jan	25 Jan–6 Feb	Kavkaz[10]	~25 000	Region of Kutaisi, Yerevan and Tbilisi
Norway	3 Feb	24 Feb–23 Mar	Atlas Express[11]	~17 000	Northern Norway
Hungary	5 Apr	6–9 Apr	..	~10 000	..
USSR	24 May	14–18 Jun	Sever[12]	~25 000	Leningrad military district: Petrozavodsk, Sestroretsk, Vyborg
FR Germany	16 Aug	6–10 Sep	Grosser Bär[13]	~50 000	Papenburg–Oldenburg–Bremen–Uelzen–Gifhorn–Hildesheim–Paderborn–Coesfeld–Rheine–Lingen–Meppen
USA	16 Aug	6–10 Sep	Grosser Bär[13]	~50 000	FRG
FR Germany	16 Aug	7–11 Sep	Gordian Shield[14]	~30 000	Hessen
USA	16 Aug	7–11 Sep	Gordian Shield[14]	~30 000	FRG
Yugoslavia	17 Aug	20–23 Sep	Golija-76[15]	24 000	Southwest Socialist Republic of Serbia
Poland	19 Aug	9–16 Sep	Tarcza-76[16]	~35 000	Bydgoszcz–Szczecin–Wroclaw
FR Germany	23 Aug	13–17 Sep	Lares Team[17]	~44 000	Bavaria and Baden-Württemberg
USA	23 Aug	13–17 Sep	Lares Team[17]	~44 000	FRG
Canada	23 Aug	13–17 Sep	Lares Team[17]	~44 000	FRG
Norway	31 Aug	20–24 Sep	Team Work[18]	13 500	North Tröndelag, Central Norway

Military manoeuvres in Europe

State giving notification	Date of notification	Duration of manoeuvre	Designation of manoeuvre	Number of troops involved	Area of manoeuvre
Sweden	2 Sep	2–6 Oct	Poseidon[19]	~12 000	Eastern Military Command and adjacent sea area
Denmark	17 Sep	11–18 Oct	Bonded Item[20, 21]	~8 000	West Jutland
FR Germany	20 Sep	17–21 Oct	Bonded Item[20, 22]	~9 000	Schleswig-Holstein: Flensburg–Förde and the Baltic coast to Eckernförde-Schleswig
USA	20 Sep	11–21 Oct	Bonded Item[20, 23]	~11 000	Denmark and FRG
UK	12 Oct	2–11 Nov	Spearpoint[24]	~18 000	Northwest Germany: Detmold, Hameln and Hildesheim
Hungary	18 Oct	18–23 Oct	. .[25]	15 000	Hungary
	1977	**1977**			
Sweden	3 Feb	5–9 Mar	VÖNN[26]	~10 000	Lower Norrland in the vicinity of Östersund
USSR	9 Mar	31 Mar–5 Apr	. .[27]	~25 000	Region of Kishinev–Odessa–Nikolayev
USA	7 Apr	1–8 May	Certain Fighter[28]	~24 000	FRG: Hessen
USSR	20 Jan	11–16 Jul	Karpaty[29]	~27 000	Western Ukraine: region of Lutsk, Lvov, Rovno
Spain	10 Aug	8–15 Oct	Great unity of army corps[30]	~8 000	Region of La Manca, province of Ciudad Real
Belgium	22 Aug	12–23 Sep	Blue Fox[31]	~24 000	FRG: Münster, Bielefeld, Hildesheim–Harzgebirge–Göttingen, Borgentreich, Soest
FR Germany	22 Aug	12–23 Sep	Blue Fox[31]	~24 000	Osnabrück–Hildesheim–Göttingen–Plettenberg–Hagen–Münster
Denmark	22 Aug	19–23 Sep	Arrow Express 77[32]	~16 000	The Zealand group of islands
FR Germany	22 Aug	12–15 Sep	Standhafte Chatten[33]	~38 000	Brilon–Kassel–Bad Hersfeld–Siegen–Plettenberg
USA	22 Aug	13–23 Sep	Carbon Edge[34]	~59 000	FRG: Southeast Bavaria and Swabia region of Southwest Baden-Württemberg
FR Germany	23 Aug	13–23 Sep	Carbon Edge[35]	~59 000	Swabia, Bavaria
Netherlands	2 Sep	24 Sep–1 Oct	Interaction[36]	12 000	FRG: Oldenburg–Bremen–Rotenburg–Visselhoevede–Walsrode–Nienburg–Vechta–Cloppenburg–Linders–Friesoythe
Turkey	13 Sep	13–14 Oct	Tayfun-77[37]	15 000	Marmara Sea–Black Sea–Black Sea Straits and the adjoining land area
Austria	4 Oct	11–19 Nov	Herbstübung 1977[38]	~12 000	Ried im Innkreis–Vöcklabruck–Attersee–Mondsee–Mattsee–Mattighofen
	1978	**1978**			
USSR	16 Jan	6–10 Feb	Berezina	~25 000	Byelorussian military district: Minsk, Orsha, Polotsk
Norway	30 Jan	1–6 Mar	Arctic Express[40]	15 300	Troms, Northern Norway

* For the text of the relevant part of the Final Act, see page 121.

[1] "Grosse Rochade" took place in the context of the "Autumn Forge" exercise series. Command level: 2nd Corps.

Participating units: FRG 10th Armoured Division, 4th "Jäger" Division, parts of 1st Airborne Division, parts of corps support and logistic forces and parts of home defence units; one US brigade, one Canadian brigade, one French reconnaissance regiment, and air support by parts of tactical air forces from some participating states. In addition, US tactical aircraft assigned to the European Theatre were to provide air support to the land forces involved as part of an air exercise designated "Cold Fire" in the Central European Region.

Absence of land forces from garrisons: 11–13 to 19–20 September 1975.

"Autumn Forge" exercise series is a co-ordinated series of regular national and multinational field training and command post exercises conducted by certain members of NATO.

[2] This is the contribution of the forces of the notifying country only.

[3] "Deep Express" took place in the context of the "Autumn Forge" exercise series (see footnote 1). Purpose of the manoeuvre: to improve the capability of NATO forces to react quickly and to improve standardization and interoperability. Command level: Allied Forces Southern Europe.

Participating units: ground force element—approximately one infantry division, one amphibious brigade and some airborne units; naval element—51 warships; air element—6 fighter-bomber squadrons.

Absence from garrisons: 10–30 September 1975.

In addition, elements of forces of USA, UK, FRG, Belgium, Netherlands and Italy took part.

UK amphibious forces and UK forces assigned to the Allied Command Europe (ACE) Mobile Force, together with maritime and air support, were involved. The UK was to contribute five warships with associated support to this manoeuvre.

[4] "Reforger"—annual exercise deployment of US forces to FRG.

After the October 1975 field manoeuvres, some of the "Reforger" units were to conduct weapon test-firing exercises in major training areas prior to returning their equipment to storage and returning to the USA.

[5] "Certain Trek"—field manoeuvre conducted within the framework of the "Reforger 75" exercise taking place in the context of the "Autumn Forge" exercise series (see footnotes 1 and 4). Type of forces: predominantly regular ground forces with tactical air support. Command level: US corps.

Participating units: 3rd US Infantry Division, two brigades of 1st US Infantry Division, one FRG tank brigade, a brigade of 2nd US Armoured Division, one Canadian mechanized brigade group, 2nd US Armoured Cavalry Regiment, elements of a French dragoon regiment, one British airborne regiment. Air support by parts of the FRG tactical air force, as well as US and Canadian forces.

Foreign observers were invited to attend.

In addition, "Straffe Zügel"—field training exercise.

Participating units: parts of an FRG armoured infantry division and one armoured reconnaissance regiment; 3rd US Armoured Cavalry Regiment and 36th US Marine Amphibious Unit.

[6] "Batten Bolt 75"—refresher training with allied co-operation. Command level: Land Command Östlandet.

Participating units: ground force element—Regimental Combat Team No. 1, one commando group (UK), one parachute company (UK), one commando company (Netherlands); naval element—minor naval support; air element—participation by Norwegian and Danish squadrons; air defence—elements of air defence forces of Rygge and Fornebu.

Absence from garrisons: 2–7 October 1975.

[7] Participating units in "Division in Action" manoeuvre: infantry division.

Absence from garrisons: 20–26 October 1975.

[8] Purpose of this Swiss manoeuvre: co-operation between different types of armed forces and between the army and the organization of civil defence, occupation and preparation of a zone of defence; defence against a simulated attack. Command level: 4th Corps.

Participating units: 7th Frontier Division (reinforced), part of 11th Mechanized Division, one combat brigade, part of the air force, logistic units, civilian authorities and organizations; 5 800 vehicles, 300 tracked vehicles, 200 horses.

Foreign observers were invited to attend.

[9] "Pantser Sprong"—national manoeuvres with troops and air support. Purpose of the exercise: operations at brigade level. Command level: 4th Division.

Participating units: 43rd Pantserbrigade, units of 41st Pantserbrigade, support and maintenance units from 1st Army Corps, staff—4th Division.

Absence from garrisons: 26–27 October to 7–8 November 1975.

[10] Purpose of the "Kavkaz" manoeuvre: co-operation of different types of forces under winter conditions. Command level: army corps.

Participating units: ground forces, including airborne detachments, as well as air force units.

Foreign observers were invited to attend.

[11] "Atlas Express"—multinational combined manoeuvre with the participation of Allied Command Europe Mobile Forces land and air components (AMF [L and A]).

Purpose of the manoeuvre: to exercise the deployment of AMF to northern Norway and alongside Norwegian forces under winter conditions. Command level: Commander Allied Forces North Norway.

Participating units: Brigade North, Regimental Combat Team No. 15, AMF (L) and, in addition, one commando group UK Royal Marines and one company Royal Netherlands Marine Commando; AMF (A) and, in addition, air force units from Norway, USA, UK, Canada, Netherlands, FRG and Italy; and minor Norwegian naval forces.

Foreign forces were to start deployment into the manoeuvre area on 2 March and return to their duty stations on 23 March 1976.

[12] Purpose of the "Sever" manoeuvre: co-operation of different types of forces.

Participating units: army and air force.

Foreign observers were invited to attend.

[13] "Grosser Bär" manoeuvre took place in the context of "Autumn Forge" exercise series (see footnote 1).

Purpose of the manoeuvre: to exercise ground forces supported by air forces. Command level: 1st Corps.

Participating units: 41st Netherlands Brigade, 103rd Netherlands Reconnaissance Battalion, one FRG corps, one US brigade, 7th UK Brigade.

Absence from garrisons: 1–14 September 1976.

Foreign observers were invited to attend.

[14] "Gordian Shield" manoeuvre took place in the context of "Autumn Forge" exercise series (see footnote 1), and included US troops transported in the "Reforger" movement (see footnote 4).

Purpose of the manoeuvre: to exercise sea and air strategic deployment and test unique capabilities of air assault division in the European environment.

Participating units: elements of 5th US Corps, 101st

US Airborne Division, 13th FRG Mechanized Infantry Brigade, and Belgian forces.

[15] Participating units in the "Golija-76" manoeuvre: one infantry division with air support and smaller units of the territorial defence.

Absence from garrisons: one to three days before the beginning of the manoeuvre—one day after the end of the manoeuvre.

Foreign observers were invited to attend.

[16] In addition to Polish troops, units from the USSR, the German Democratic Republic (GDR) and Czechoslovakia took part in the "Tarcza 76" manoeuvre. Command level: Polish Minister of National Defence.

Foreign observers were invited to attend.

[17] "Lares Team" manoeuvre took place in the context of "Autumn Forge" exercise series (see footnote 1), and included US troops transported in the "Reforger" movement (see footnote 4).

Purpose of the manoeuvre: to exercise sea and air strategic deployment and test unique capabilities of air assault division in the European environment.

Participating units: elements of 7th Corps and 101st US Airborne Division; FRG armoured brigade; elements of 4th Canadian Mechanized Brigade Group and elements of the Canadian Air Group in Europe.

Foreign observers were invited to attend.

[18] This manoeuvre was part of the larger NATO "Team Work" manoeuvre which took place from 10 to 24 September 1976.

Purpose of the manoeuvre: routine training of procedures related to NATO supporting forces. Command level: Regional Commander of South Norway.

Participating units: Regimental Combat Team No. 13 (reinforced), one US Marine amphibious brigade, one UK parachute brigade, one UK commando brigade including one company of Netherlands Marines, supported by US, UK and FRG naval air forces.

Foreign observers were invited to attend.

[19] Purpose of the "Poseidon" manoeuvre: co-ordinated training for army, navy and air force units.

[20] "Bonded Item" manoeuvre took place in the context of "Autumn Forge" exercise series (see footnote 1). It was held in two phases: one in Denmark and one in FRG (see footnotes 21, 22 and 23).

[21] Purpose of the manoeuvre: reinforcement operations at brigade level. Command level: Allied Command Baltic Approaches.

Participating units: ground, air, naval and amphibious forces. Major units—3rd Jutland Brigade and 4th US Marine Amphibious Brigade.

[22] Purpose of the manoeuvre: exercise with opposing forces, with support of air forces; reinforcement training; operations at brigade level. Command level: 6th FRG Armoured Infantry Division.

Participating units: headquarters and elements of 6th FRG Armoured Infantry Division, elements of 18th FRG Armoured Infantry Brigade, elements of territorial command Schleswig-Holstein, one US amphibious brigade.

Absence from garrisons: 16-25 October 1976.

[23] Purpose of the manoeuvre: field training with opposing forces, including reinforcement training.

Major participating units: headquarters and elements of 6th FRG Armoured Infantry Division, 18th FRG Armoured Infantry Brigade, one US amphibious brigade, Danish 3rd Jutland Brigade.

[24] "Spearpoint" manoeuvre took place in the context of "Autumn Forge" exercise series (see footnote 1).

Purpose of the manoeuvre: annual corps field training exercise.

Major participating units: 2nd UK Armoured Division, 4th UK Division, 4th US Mechanized Brigade and two Danish battalions.

Foreign observers were invited to attend.

[25] This manoeuvre took place within the framework of the annual training plans.

Participating units: formations of the Hungarian People's Army with units of the Soviet troops stationed in Hungary.

[26] VONN manoeuvre was part of the basic military training and the periodical refresher courses for conscript personnel.

Purpose of the manoeuvre: co-ordinated training of brigade and battalion functions under winter conditions. Command level: Lower Norrland Military Command.

Participating units: Army and Air Force.

Foreign observers were invited to attend.

[27] Purpose of this Soviet manoeuvre: co-operation between land and air forces.

[28] "Certain Fighter"—field training manoeuvre by troops of the US Army and Air Force.

Purpose of the manoeuvre: exercise with simulated opposing forces; ground assault forces with air cover.

Major participating units: headquarters and elements of Command and Combat Support Forces of 5th US Corps.

[29] "Karpaty"—exercise of the troops of the Cis-Carpatian Military District.

Foreign observers were invited to attend.

[30] Participating units in the "Great unity of army corps" manoeuvre: one armoured division from the land force and units from the air force.

Foreign observers were invited to attend.

[31] Purpose of the "Blue Fox" manoeuvre: field exercise of opposing forces to test and improve the co-operation procedures with NATO allies. Command level: Belgian Corps.

Participating units: 1st Belgian Division, 17th Belgian Armoured Brigade, 3rd US Mechanized Brigade, 4th Belgian Armoured Infantry Brigade, 20th FRG Armoured Brigade, Belgian Commando Regiment, 4th FRG Infantry Brigade.

[32] "Arrow Express 77"—joint mobile force field training manoeuvre.

Purpose of the manoeuvre: to exercise and train Allied Mobile Forces (AMF) northern component in its deterrent and combat roles alongside host nations' forces, according to contingency plans, to demonstrate NATO solidarity and to exercise and train UK mobile force. Command level: Commander Allied Forces Baltic Approaches.

Participating units: Danish—2 armoured infantry brigades, air bases, air squadrons; AMF—AMF northern component (land and air forces). Contingents from eight countries (Belgium, FRG, Italy, Luxembourg, UK, USA, Canada and Netherlands); UK—one brigade (reduced) air squadrons.

Foreign observers were invited to attend.

[33] "Standhafte Chatten"—combat exercise of opposing land forces with support of air forces—was conducted in the context of the "Autumn Forge" exercise series (see footnote 1).

Purpose of the manoeuvre: operations at division level; co-operation of forces under rapidly changing conditions. Command level: 3rd Corps.

Participating units: FRG 2nd "Jäger" Division, 5th Armoured Division, parts of 26th Air Brigade, parts of corps support and logistic forces, one US brigade. Air support—within the framework of the simultaneously conducted multinational manoeuvre "Cold Fire 77" (NATO air force manoeuvre).

Absence from garrisons: 5–12 to 18 September 1977.

Foreign observers were invited to attend.

[34] "Carbon Edge"—opposing forces ground manoeuvre supported by air exercise "Cold Fire"—took place in the framework of the "Autumn Forge" exercise series (see footnote 1).

Purpose of the manoeuvre: to test NATO Forces' ability to co-operate during simulated wartime conditions; examination of procedures of joint logistical support; joint communication and standardization of doctrines, procedures and equipment. Command level: Commander, Central Army Group.

Participating units: 7th US Corps, one armoured brigade of the *Bundeswehr,* one mechanized Canadian brigade and UK, Netherlands and Belgian units; air support provided by elements of the Tactical Air Forces. The number, 59 000, included troops transported to Europe in the "Reforger" movement (see footnote 4).

[35] See footnote 34.

Foreign observers were invited to attend.

[36] "Interaction"—national training manoeuvre of Netherlands troops and air forces.

Purpose of the manoeuvre: training of operations on brigade level under division control.

Participating units: headquarters of the 4th Division combat and support units of 1st Netherlands Corps, and small allied forces.

Foreign observers were invited to attend.

[37] "Tayfun-77"—national combined manoeuvre within the "Autumn Forge" exercise series (see footnote 1).

Purpose of the manoeuvre: to improve co-ordination and co-operation of forces in coastal defence and to exercise amphibious and airborne landing operations as well as defence against such types of operation. Command level: Operational Command—Army, Sea Area Command and Tactical Air Force Command.

Participating units: one infantry division, one paratrooper company, one commando company, one helicopter battalion; landing ships and craft and a number of direct support ships; fighter-bomber squadrons and transport aircraft.

Foreign observers were invited to attend.

[38] Purpose of the "Herbstübung 1977" manoeuvre: combat exercise.

Participating units: parts of 2nd Corps, parts of 1st Armoured Infantry Division and parts of the Air Force Division.

[39] Purpose of the "Berezina" manoeuvre: co-operation of different types of forces.

Participating units: army and air force.

Foreign observers were invited to attend.

[40] This multinational field exercise is part of the NATO manoeuvre "Arctic Express" which took place on 14 February–14 March 1978 in the framework of the "Express" series.

Purpose of the manoeuvre: routine exercise of NATO procedures for the deployment of forces and co-operation with national troops under winter conditions. Command level: Commander, North Norway.

Participating units: Norwegian 6th Division, Combined Regiment No. 5 and other smaller units; Allied Command Europe Mobile Forces (AMF) land and air components; UK Marine unit (battalion size) including one Netherlands Marine company; and two companies of US Marines. In addition to AMF air components, smaller Allied air units and small Norwegian naval forces are to participate.

Absence from garrisons: from 20 February until a few days after the end of the manoeuvre.

APPENDIX D

Nuclear explosions, 1945–77 (known and presumed)

I. 16 July 1945–5 August 1963 (the signing of the Partial Test Ban Treaty)

USA	USSR	UK	France	Total
293	164	23	8	**488**

II. 5 August 1963–31 December 1977

a atmospheric
u underground

Year	USA a	USA u	USSR a	USSR u	UK a	UK u	France a	France u	China a	China u	India a	India u	Total
5 Aug–31 Dec 1963	0	14	0	0	0	0	0	1					15
1964	0	28	0	6	0	1	0	3	1	0			39
1965	0	29	0	9	0	1	0	4	1	0			44
1966	0	40	0	15	0	0	5	1	3	0			64
1967	0	29	0	15	0	0	3	0	2	0			49
1968	0	39[a]	0	13	0	0	5	0	1	0			58
1969	0	28	0	15	0	0	0	0	1	1			45
1970	0	33	0	12	0	0	8	0	1	0			54
1971	0	15	0	19	0	0	5	0	1	0			40
1972	0	15	0	22	0	0	3	0	2	0			42
1973	0	11	0	14	0	0	5	0	1	0			31
1974	0	9	0	19	0	1	7	0	1	0	0	1	38
1975	0	16	0	15	0	0	0	2	0	1	0	0	34
1976	0	15	0	17	0	1	0	4	3	1	0	0	41
1977	0	12	0	16	0	0	0	6	1	0	0	0	35[b]
Total	**0**	**333**	**0**	**207**	**0**	**4**	**41**	**21**	**19**	**3**	**0**	**1**	**629**

III. 16 July 1945–31 December 1977

USA	USSR	UK	France	China	India	Total
626	371	27	70	22	1	**1 117**

[a] Five devices used simultaneously in the same test (Buggy) are counted here as one.
[b] The data for 1977 are preliminary.

Sources:
US Geological Survey;
US Energy Research and Development Administration (ERDA);
US Department of Energy;
Research Institute of the Swedish National Defence;
Press reports.

APPENDIX E

Summaries of bilateral arms control agreements, 1963–77*

US-Soviet Memorandum of understanding regarding the establishment of a direct communications link (US-Soviet "Hot Line" Agreement)

Signed at Geneva on 20 June 1963.
Entered into force on 20 June 1963.

Establishes a direct communications link between the governments of the USA and the USSR for use in time of emergency. An annex attached to the Memorandum provides for two circuits, namely a duplex wire telegraph circuit and a duplex radio telegraph circuit, as well as two terminal points with telegraph-teleprinter equipment between which communications are to be exchanged.

Statements by the USA and the USSR on the reduction of fissionable materials production

Made on 20 April 1964, simultaneously by the US President and the Soviet Prime Minister.

The US government orders a substantial reduction in the production of enriched uranium, to be carried out over a four-year period. When added to previous reductions, this will mean an overall decrease in the production of plutonium by 20 per cent, and of enriched uranium by 40 per cent.

The Soviet government decides to stop the construction of two new large atomic reactors for the production of plutonium; to reduce substantially during the next few years, the production of uranium-235 for nuclear weapons; and to allocate accordingly more fissionable materials for peaceful uses.

---

* The documents summarized in this Appendix relate to arms control in the broad sense of this term (see the discussion in the Introduction). The wording of the summaries is close to the language of the original documents.

British-Soviet Agreement on the establishment of a direct communications line (British-Soviet "Hot Line" Agreement)

Signed at London on 25 August 1967.
Entered into force on 27 October 1967.

Establishes a direct teletype communications line between the Kremlin and 10 Downing Street for contacts at government level.

Agreement on measures to improve the USA-USSR direct communications link (US-Soviet "Hot Line" Modernization Agreement)

Signed at Washington on 30 September 1971.
Entered into force on 30 September 1971.
Amended on 29 April 1975.

Establishes, for the purpose of increasing the reliability of the direct communications link set up pursuant to the Memorandum of understanding of 20 June 1963 (see above), two additional circuits between the USA and the USSR, each using a satellite communications system, and a system of terminals (more than one) in the territory of each party. Matters relating to the implementation of these improvements are set forth in an annex to the Agreement.

Agreement on measures to reduce the risk of outbreak of nuclear war between the USA and the USSR (US-Soviet Nuclear Accidents Agreement)

Signed at Washington on 30 September 1971.
Entered into force on 30 September 1971.

Provides for immediate notification in the event of an accidental, unauthorized incident involving a possible detonation of a nuclear weapon (the party whose nuclear weapon is involved should take necessary measures to render harmless or destroy such weapon); immediate notification in the event of detection by missile warning systems of unidentified objects, or in the event of signs of interference with these systems or with related communications facilities; and advance notification of planned missile launches extending beyond the national territory in the direction of the other party.

US-Soviet Agreement on the prevention of incidents on and over the high seas

Signed at Moscow on 25 May 1972.
Entered into force on 25 May 1972.

Provides for measures to assure the safety of navigation of the ships of the armed forces of the USA and the USSR on the high seas and flight of their military aircraft over the high seas, including rules of conduct for ships engaged in surveillance of other ships as well as ships engaged in launching or landing aircraft. The parties also undertake to give notification of actions on the high seas which represent a danger to navigation or to aircraft in flight, and to exchange information concerning instances of collisions, instances which result in damage, or other incidents at sea between their ships and aircraft.

US-Soviet Treaty on the limitation of anti-ballistic missile systems (SALT ABM Treaty)

Signed at Moscow on 26 May 1972.
Entered into force on 3 October 1972.

Prohibits the deployment of ABM systems for the defence of the whole territory of the USA and the USSR or of an individual region, except as expressly permitted. Permitted ABM deployments are limited to two areas in each country—one for the defence of the national capital, and the other for the defence of some intercontinental ballistic missiles (ICBMs). No more than 100 ABM launchers and 100 ABM interceptor missiles may be deployed in each ABM deployment area. ABM radars should not exceed specified numbers and are subject to qualitative restrictions. National technical means of verification will be used to provide assurance of compliance with the provisions of the Treaty.

The ABM Treaty is accompanied by agreed interpretations and unilateral statements made during the negotiations.

US-Soviet Interim Agreement on certain measures with respect to the limitation of strategic offensive arms (SALT Interim Agreement)

Signed at Moscow on 26 May 1972.
Entered into force on 3 October 1972.

Provides for a freeze for up to five years of the aggregate number of fixed land-based intercontinental ballistic missile launchers and ballistic missile launchers on modern submarines. The parties are free to choose the mix, except that conversion of land-based launchers for light ICBMs, or for ICBMs of older types, into land-based launchers for modern "heavy" ICBMs is prohibited. National technical means of verification will be used to provide assurance of compliance with the provisions of the Agreement.

A protocol which is an integral part of the Interim Agreement specifies that the USA may have not more than 710 ballistic missile launchers on submarines and 44 modern ballistic missile submarines, while the USSR may have not more than 950 ballistic missile launchers on submarines and 62 modern ballistic missile submarines. Up to those levels, additional ballistic missile launchers—in the USA over 656 launchers on nuclear-powered submarines and in the USSR over 740 launchers on nuclear-powered submarines, operational and under construction—may become operational as replacements for equal numbers of ballistic missile launchers of types deployed prior to 1964, or of ballistic missile launchers on older submarines.

The Interim Agreement is accompanied by agreed interpretations and unilateral statements made during the negotiations.

In September 1977 the USA and the USSR formally stated that, although the Interim Agreement was to expire on 3 October 1977, they intended to refrain from any actions incompatible with its provisions, or with the goals of the ongoing talks on a new agreement.

Agreement on basic principles of relations between the USA and the USSR

Signed at Moscow on 29 May 1972.

States that the USA and the USSR will proceed from the common determination that in the nuclear age there is no alternative to conducting their mutual relations on the basis of peaceful coexistence. They will do their utmost to avoid military confrontations and to prevent the outbreak of nuclear war. The prerequisite for maintaining and strengthening peaceful relations between the USA and the USSR are the recognition of the security interests of the parties based on the principle of equality and the renunciation of the use or threat of force. The parties will continue their efforts to limit armaments on a bilateral as well as on a multilateral basis. They will continue to make special efforts to limit strategic armaments. Whenever possible, they will conclude concrete agreements aimed at achieving these purposes. They regard as the ultimate objective of their efforts the achievement of general and complete disarmament and the establishment of an effective system of international security in accordance with the purposes and principles of the United Nations.

US-Soviet Memorandum of understanding regarding the establishment of a Standing Consultative Commission

Signed at Geneva on 21 December 1972.
Entered into force on 21 December 1972.

Establishes a Standing Consultative Commission to promote the objectives and implementation of the provisions of the SALT ABM Treaty and Interim Agreement, of 26 May 1972, and of the Nuclear Accidents Agreement of 30 September 1971. Each government shall be represented by a commissioner and a deputy commissioner, assisted by such staff as it deems necessary. The Commission is to hold at least two sessions per year.

Protocol to the US-Soviet agreement on the prevention of incidents on and over the high seas (see above)

Signed at Washington on 22 May 1973.
Entered into force on 22 May 1973.

Provides that ships and aircraft of the parties shall not make simulated attacks by aiming guns, missile launchers, torpedo tubes and other weapons at non-military ships of the other party, nor launch nor drop any objects near non-military ships of the other party in such a manner as to be hazardous to these ships or to constitute a hazard to navigation.

Protocol with regulations regarding the US-Soviet Standing Consultative Commission

Signed at Geneva on 30 May 1973.
Entered into force on 30 May 1973.

Establishes regulations governing procedures and other relevant matters of the Standing Consultative Commission pursuant to the provisions of the US-Soviet Memorandum of understanding of 21 December 1972 (see above).

US-Soviet Agreement on basic principles of negotiations on the further limitation of strategic offensive arms

Signed at Washington on 21 June 1973.

Provides that the two powers will continue negotiations in order to work out a permanent agreement on more complete measures for the limitation of strategic offensive arms, as well as their subsequent reduction. Both powers will be guided by the recognition of each other's equal security interests and by the recognition that efforts to obtain unilateral advantage, directly or indirectly, would be inconsistent with the strengthening of peaceful relations between the USA and the USSR. The limitations placed on strategic offensive weapons could apply both to their quantitative aspects as well as to their qualitative improvement. Limitations on strategic offensive arms must be subject to adequate verification by national technical means. The modernization and replacement of strategic offensive arms would be permitted under conditions formulated in the agreements to be concluded. Pending a permanent agreement, both sides are prepared to reach agreements on separate measures to supplement the SALT Interim Agreement of 26 May 1972. Each power will continue to take necessary organizational and technical measures for preventing accidental or unauthorized use of nuclear weapons under its control in accordance with the Nuclear Accidents Agreement of 30 September 1971.

US-Soviet Agreement on the prevention of nuclear war

Signed at Washington on 22 June 1973.
Entered into force on 22 June 1973.

Provides that the parties will act in such a manner as to exclude the outbreak of nuclear war between them and between either of the parties and other countries. Each party will refrain from the threat or use of force against the other party, against the allies of the other party and against other countries in circumstances which may endanger international peace and security. If at any time relations between the parties or between either party and other countries appear to involve the risk of a nuclear conflict, or if relations between countries not parties to this Agreement appear to involve the risk of nuclear war between the USSR and the USA or between either party and other countries, the Soviet Union and the United States, acting in accordance with the provisions of this Agreement, shall immediately enter into urgent consultations with each other and make every effort to avert this risk.

Protocol to the US-Soviet treaty on the limitation of anti-ballistic missile systems

Signed at Moscow on 3 July 1974.
Entered into force on 25 May 1976.

Provides that each party shall be limited to a single area for deployment of anti-ballistic missile systems or their components instead of two such areas as allowed by the SALT ABM Treaty (see above). Each party will have the right to dismantle or destroy its ABM system and the components thereof in the area where they were deployed at the time of signing the Protocol and to deploy an ABM system or its components in the alternative area permitted by the ABM Treaty, provided that, prior to initiation of construction, notification is given during the year beginning on 3 October 1977, and ending on 2 October 1978, or during any year which commences at five-year intervals thereafter, those being the years for periodic review of the ABM Treaty. This right may be exercised only once. The deployment of an ABM system within the area selected shall remain limited by the levels and other requirements established by the ABM Treaty.

US-Soviet Treaty on the limitation of underground nuclear weapon tests (Threshold Test Ban Treaty—TTBT)

Signed at Moscow on 3 July 1974.
Not in force by 31 December 1977.

Prohibits from 31 March 1976 the carrying out of any underground nuclear weapon test having a yield exceeding 150 kilotons. Each party undertakes to limit the number of its underground nuclear weapon tests to a minimum. The provisions of the Treaty do not extend to underground nuclear explosions for peaceful purposes which are to be governed by a separate agreement. National technical means of verification will be used to provide assurance of compliance and a protocol to the Treaty specifies the data that have to be exchanged between the parties to ensure such verification.

Since by 31 March 1976, the agreed cut-off date for explosions above the established threshold, the Treaty was not yet in force, the parties stated that they would observe the limitation during the entire pre-ratification period.

Joint US-Soviet Statement on the question of further limitations of strategic offensive arms

Signed in the area of Vladivostok on 24 November 1974.

States that a new US-Soviet agreement on the limitation of strategic offensive arms will incorporate the relevant provisions of the SALT Interim Agreement of 26 May 1972 and will cover the period from October 1977 through 31 December 1985. Based on the principle of equality and equal security, it will include the following limitations: both powers will be entitled to have a certain agreed aggregate number of strategic delivery vehicles and to have a certain agreed aggregate number of intercontinental ballistic missiles (ICBMs) and submarine-launched ballistic missiles (SLBMs) equipped with multiple independently targetable warheads. The Agreement will include a provision for further negotiations beginning no later than 1980–81 on the question of further limitations and possible reductions of strategic arms after 1985.

Joint British-Soviet Declaration on the non-proliferation of nuclear weapons

Signed at Moscow on 17 February 1975.

Emphasizes the importance and necessity of urgent efforts to prevent the spread of nuclear weapons. The two powers agree that further measures could be undertaken to provide nuclear materials, equipment and information for peaceful uses in non-nuclear weapon states. However, such measures should be under effective safeguards by the IAEA and should not in any way contribute to the spread of nuclear weapons. They express the hope that all suppliers of nuclear material and equipment will observe the safeguards applied by the IAEA to meet article III of the Non-Proliferation Treaty. Until the conclusion of an international agreement for the discontinuance of all test explosions of nuclear weapons for all time, both powers will work for agreements limiting the number of underground nuclear weapon tests to a minimum. The UK and the USSR share a common concern that nuclear materials should be carefully protected at all times.

US-Soviet Treaty on underground nuclear explosions for peaceful purposes (Peaceful Nuclear Explosions Treaty—PNET)

Signed at Moscow and Washington on 28 May 1976.
Not in force by 31 December 1977.

Prohibits the carrying out of any individual underground nuclear explosion for peaceful purposes, having a yield exceeding 150 kilotons, or any group explosion (consisting of two or more individual explosions) with an aggregate yield exceeding 1 500 kilotons. The Treaty governs all nuclear explosions carried out outside the weapon test sites after 31 March 1976. The question of carrying out individual explosions with a yield exceeding 150 kilotons will be considered at an appropriate time to be agreed. In addition to the use of national technical means of verification, the Treaty provides for an exchange of information and, in certain specified cases, access to sites of explosions. A protocol to the Treaty sets forth operational arrangements for ensuring that no weapon-related benefits precluded by the TTBT are derived from peaceful nuclear explosions. The PNET may not be terminated while the TTBT remains in force.

French-Soviet Agreement on the prevention of the accidental or unauthorized use of nuclear weapons (French-Soviet Nuclear Accidents Agreement)

Concluded through an exchange of letters on 16 July 1976 between the foreign ministers of France and the USSR.
Entered into force on 16 July 1976.

Provides that the parties will maintain and, possibly, improve their organizational and technical arrangements to prevent the accidental or unauthorized use of nuclear weapons under their control. They will notify each other immediately of any accidental occurrence or any other unexplained incident that could lead to the explosion of one of their nuclear weapons and could be construed as likely to have harmful effects on the other party. In the event of an unexplained nuclear incident, each party will act in such a manner as to avoid the possibility of its actions being misinterpreted by the other party. For transmission of urgent information, primary use will be made of the direct communications link between the Elysée Palace and the Kremlin. (The link has been established following an accord of 9 November 1966 between France and the USSR.)

French-Soviet Declaration on the non-proliferation of nuclear weapons

Signed at Rambouillet on 22 June 1977.

Reaffirms the common will to spare no effort in seeking to prevent the proliferation of nuclear weapons. The two powers are prepared to contribute to the improvement of IAEA controls over the observance of the commitments assumed in the field of non-proliferation. For their part, they will make sure, each insofar as it is concerned, that their co-operation with third countries in the field of nuclear industry affords all the necessary safeguards to prevent proliferation. In applying their policy of exporting nuclear materials, equipment and technology, the two parties will abide by their international commitments in this field and be guided by the aims of non-proliferation of nuclear weapons. They are prepared to strengthen the appropriate provisions and guarantees relating to equipment, materials and technology, and will continue to contribute to the co-ordination of the general principles relating to nuclear exports. France and the USSR favour the drafting of an international convention on the physical protection of nuclear materials.

British-Soviet Agreement on the prevention of an accidental outbreak of nuclear war (British-Soviet Nuclear Accidents Agreement)

Signed at Moscow on 10 October 1977.
Entered into force on 10 October 1977.

Provides that the parties will maintain and, whenever necessary, improve their organizational and technical arrangements for guarding against the accidental or unauthorized use of nuclear weapons under their control. They will notify each other immediately of any accident or other unexplained or unauthorized incident which could result in the explosion of one of their nuclear weapons or could otherwise create the risk of the outbreak of nuclear war, and the party whose nuclear weapon is involved will immediately take the necessary measures to render harmless or destroy such a weapon without causing damage. Each party will act in such a manner as to reduce the possibilities of its action being misinterpreted. For transmission of, or requests for, urgent information, the parties will use the direct communications link between their governments.